DATE DUE

FEB 18 '89			
MAR 13 '89			
JUN 2 '94			

The Library Store   #47-0103

The construction of reality

The construction of reality

MICHAEL A. ARBIB *and* MARY B. HESSE

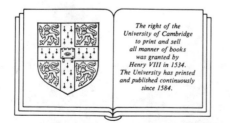

The right of the
University of Cambridge
to print and sell
all manner of books
was granted by
Henry VIII in 1534.
The University has printed
and published continuously
since 1584.

CAMBRIDGE UNIVERSITY PRESS

Cambridge
London   New York   New Rochelle
Melbourne   Sydney

Published by the Press Syndicate of the University of Cambridge
The Pitt Building, Trumpington Street, Cambridge CB2 1RP
32 East 57th Street, New York, NY 10022, USA
10 Stamford Road, Oakleigh, Melbourne 3166, Australia

First published 1986

Printed in the United States of America

Library of Congress Cataloging-in-Publication Data
Arbib, Michael A.
The construction of reality.
Includes index.
1. Knowledge, Theory of.   2. Religion.
I. Hesse, Mary B.   II. Title.
BD161.A62   1986   120   86-6832

British Library Cataloguing in Publication Data
Arbib, Michael A.
The construction of reality.
1. Reality   2. Perception
I. Title   II. Hesse, Mary B.
153.7   BD331

ISBN 0 521 32689 3

To the Memory of

May Brodbeck
Richard Reiss
and
Bernate Unger

*whose friendship and constructive
criticism will be sorely missed*

Contents

Preface

The Construction of Reality develops an integrated perspective on human knowledge, extending ideas from cognitive science and philosophy of science to address fundamental questions concerning human action in the world and whether the space–time world exhausts all there is of reality. We seek to reconcile a theory of the individual's construction of reality through a network of schemas or mental representations with an account of the social construction of language, science, ideology, and religion. Along the way, we take account of much current research and debate in philosophy, linguistics, artificial intelligence, brain theory, cognitive science, evolutionary biology, social anthropology, history of religions, theology, and biblical and literary criticism. However, the reader will find no breathless pastiche here but a cumulative marshalling of evidence for a coherent and integrated view of the individual and social dimensions of human knowledge. We hope that it will stimulate the reader to find that within this integrated perspective there remains much scope for lively debate, particularly in our discussion of free will and of the reality of God.

For many people, even in today's secular world, God is the fundamental reality that gives meaning to human existence; for others, God does not exist, and whatever meaning human existence holds is to be found in society and in the more intimate groupings of family and friends. Even among people who believe in God, not all find value in natural theology, the study of the natural world for signs of God's existence and His plan; they prefer systematic theology, the study of God and His plan as revealed in sacred writings and institutions and in individual religious experience. This lack of consensus would seem to be compounded by the wide difference in religious and professional affiliations of the two people invited to share the Gifford Lectures in Natural Theology at the University of Edinburgh in November 1983. Michael Arbib is an atheist (but not without a sense of wonder) whose research includes artificial intelligence, brain theory, and cognitive science. Mary Hesse is an Anglican (but not uncritical of the pronouncements of her Church) whose research includes the history and philosophy of science. Our tasks since June of 1981 – when we first met, summoned from our mutual ignorance of each other by the invitation from Edinburgh's Gifford Committee – have been to build these differences into a thesis and antithesis and to define a new synthesis that meets Lord Gifford's brief in a manner appropriate to the century that has passed since he wrote it.

The common core in *The Construction of Reality* is given by the theory of knowledge in all its aspects. Arbib has sought to develop a theory of schemas to explain how the individual brain – of animal, human being, or robot – represents the world around it. In contrast to this individualistic emphasis, Hesse has taken a more social and holistic view in her attempt to understand the interactions of pragmatic criteria and social consensus in the development of physical theories. One clear challenge for synthesis, then, is to understand better how individuals can become members of, and can in turn change, a community or society. The other challenge, posed by the charge of the Gifford Lectures, is to raise our sights from the epistemology of visually guided behavior or physical science to that most pretentious, yet compelling, of subjects – our knowledge of ultimate reality. Can this knowledge only be given by the sciences? Is it to be found in the teachings of some religion? Or can it, at best, be approximated in a network of shifting metaphors that connects the most abstract of concepts, scientific and religious, with the realities of everyday life? We argue for the last viewpoint, only to discover that it does not preclude the others. We seek to construct a philosophical framework in which the discussion of honest differences can continue with new clarity.

Schema theory probes the interrelations between and the mechanisms of perception, action, and memory, relating these to intelligence, language, and culture. Evolution has structured our brains so they are able to provide the basic schemas for manipulating in and locomoting about our world, with senses to monitor our interactions and motivational systems to evaluate the outcomes. Schemas lay the basis for the consideration of actions to be taken to ensure certain outcomes in interaction with our environment and other people. The schemas "represent reality" to the extent that any departure of outcome from prediction remains within tolerable bounds. "Reality" can often be assimilated to pre-existing schemas, yet, as Piaget has explored, it will often in its turn dictate the accommodation of schemas and the development of new schemas to adapt to new circumstances of a wider range of interactions.

The challenge is to build on a theory of schemas that represent immediate experience (it hurts to kick a stone or to cause embarrassment) in order to understand the construction of social reality and what it tells us about knowledge of the sciences and of God. Much of the construction of reality is guided by convention. An individual's development is shaped by previous structuring obtained by society – as in the "rules" of language and social intercourse. Within this context, we can then analyze the need to find order – be it in the scientist's search for unifying principles or in society's search for the good life or the quest for God. To the extent that the formation of these unifying schemas is a social process, we may understand the diversity of the gods or pantheons of different societies or the differing emphases of scientific knowledge and research in different communities and at different times. The scientist would insist that the differences of knowledge reflect the imperfection of varying approximations to a common reality. The theist (but not the atheist) might assert that the same is true of different religions. One of our tasks, then, must be to compare different views of how religious beliefs may be formed, seeking to sharpen methodological tools for analyzing how history-driven or reality-driven a schema might be – always conscious that the reality with which we poor humans strive to compare the schema is itself a schema, albeit at a more abstract or higher level.

Some readers of *The Construction of Reality* in draft form have expressed curiosity as to the provenance of the project and the views we each brought to it, wishing to gauge how far our opinions have converged and to get a fuller sense of the dialogue that was at work. A full response would burden this preface unduly, but the following few remarks may be helpful. At the start of our collaboration, Arbib had given much thought to the construction of reality in terms of a schema theory addressing mechanisms for perception, action, and language embodied within the individual. He had also pondered the implications of this schema theory for philosophy of mind but was little informed about issues in theology or philosophy of religion. By contrast, Hesse had explored the history of physics and the structure of scientific inference. Moreover, she had extended her concern with the social construction of knowledge to anthropology and hermeneutics, delivering the Stanton Lectures in philosophy of religion at Cambridge University in 1978, 1979, and 1980. Both of us, however, shared an initial scientific training, which meant for Hesse as well as for Arbib a preference for monistic theories of mind and brain. Arbib interprets this preference in terms of a physical naturalism: there is nothing that we want to explain about the mind/brain that is not in the spatiotemporal world. Hesse interprets it in a unified view of the human person, brain, mind, and soul, in a single creation, all parts of which exist in appropriate creaturely relations to the Creator.

From the start, we agreed to write a coherent book that could also serve as the basis for the lectures, rather than preparing two separate sets of lectures, or having one of us prepare a set of lectures to which the other would reply. Hesse taught Arbib to temper a tendency to reduce all knowledge to brain mechanisms with a fuller understanding of the multiple levels, from neural to social, at which knowledge has a quasi-independent existence. She also helped him come to understand the importance of anthropology, and of the questions asked by theologians even though he remained resistant to their answers. Arbib taught Hesse much about artificial intelligence, brain theory, and cognitive science and convinced her of the importance of both Sigmund Freud and Jonathan Edwards in exploring the hermeneutic dialogue between science and religion.

We then worked hard to extend schema theory to embrace social constructs as well as individual mental representations. We achieved so much convergence that is came as a great joy to discover that we differed on the nature of free will! The outcome of our debate on this topic is in Chapter 5, where the voluntarist is Hesse and the decisionist is Arbib. We had many probing discussions about religious belief in the course of our collaboration and refined our own beliefs in the process. Hesse's world view informs the Chapter 11 presentation of the Bible as a Great Schema embodying a reality transcending space and time; Arbib's world view informs the secular schemas of Chapter 12. But even with these differences, the authors have collaborated on every chapter of this book, and the reader should not seek too clean a separation of our contributions. For example, Arbib introduced Hesse to Northrop Frye's *The Great Code,* thus stimulating her to view the Bible as being, rather, "the Great Schema"; Hesse provided the analysis of E. O. Wilson's sociobiology for Chapter 12. Nonetheless, we have agreed that final editorial authority for a given chapter should rest with the author whose lectures dealt more fully with the topics of that chapter. In this way, Hesse has sign-off responsibility for Chapters 1, 5, 8, 9, 10 and 11, and Arbib has the last word in Chapters 2, 3, 4, 6, 7, and 12.

We express our thanks to our friends in Edinburgh and to the Gifford Committee for the invitation that made this collaboration possible; to the Institute for Advanced Study in the Humanities at the University of Massachusetts at Amherst, which was host to a Faculty Seminar in the Fall of 1983 in which we tried out many of our developing ideas; to the National Science Foundation for partial support of our study of language; and to our friends, colleagues, and students. Arbib thanks the University of Massachusetts for the freedom afforded by a Faculty Fellowship Award in 1981; Bernate Unger for her detailed critique of an earlier draft, with its stress on the person; and Richard Noland and Mason Lowance for valuable discussions of Freud and Edwards, respectively. We thank Gwyn Mitchell, Louise Till, Rae Ann Weymouth, Barbara Nestingen, and Darlene Freedman for their help with version after version of electronic typescript.

Michael A. Arbib
Mary B. Hesse

1   Posing the problem

1.1 Lord Gifford's brief

"I wish the lecturers to treat their subject as a strictly natural science, the greatest of all possible sciences, indeed, in one sense, the only science, that of Infinite Being, without reference to or reliance upon any supposed special exceptional or so-called miraculous revelation. I wish it considered just as astronomy or chemistry is."

This is Lord Gifford's statement in the deed of foundation of his lectures in 1885. Much water has flowed under the bridge since then, and we can no longer take for granted either the character of "natural science" or of "revelation" in the sense in which these concepts were understood in Gifford's time. We therefore make no excuse (and believe it to be within the spirit of his foundation) that this book concentrates on the problem of what it is to be a "science," and what kind of continuity, if any, exists between the knowledge of "nature," of "persons," or of "society," and the possibility of knowledge of God.

We speak of "knowledge," but our difficulty today in addressing Lord Gifford's brief is that the theory of knowledge (epistemology) has come to mean almost exclusively the methodology of the natural sciences and, more recently and belatedly, the social sciences, to the exclusion of any possibility of knowing extraspatiotemporal reality, if such can be said to exist. Our culture leads us to believe in a natural space–time reality that is explored and increasingly discovered to us in natural science. For us unreflective empiricists, this is the paradigm of reality against which all other claims to objectivity have to be measured. We also believe in the existence of other persons with whom we join in groups and societies and who create a kind of man-made reality of social rules, roles, norms, and institutions. These are also space–time entities, available for study as are the objects of natural science. Among these entities are the objective facts of religion: the creeds, rituals, churches, hierarchies, sacred places. They form a humanly created reality like other social phenomena. In this case, however, their adherents generally claim more –

1

they claim that there is a reality outside space and time, that we can know this reality, albeit imperfectly, and that it is not discovered by our various scientific methods. Our culture typically does not have room for any taken-for-granted reality of this kind. If it is believed at all, it will either be an optional extra to the reality in which we all live, or it will have to be integrated with our other beliefs as a result of a much deeper critique of space–time reality and of natural knowledge.

Crudely stated, this is the epistemological problem posed by our naturalist and scientific culture. Note that our culture makes "reality" dependent on methodology; reality is intrinsically "verificationist" in that it assumes that what is in space–time is all there is, because that is what we appear to have direct access to, and it is reinforced in everyday interactions and in the success of science.

Our title, *The Construction of Reality*, is intended to challenge this positivist or "verificationist" view at its foundations. It draws attention to a different tradition, in which "reality" is held to be humanly "constructed" and not "given." This tradition seems to be the antithesis of our everyday conception on which science builds. Indeed it is, and we shall not adopt it in an extreme idealist form. To sharpen up the issues in a preliminary way, let us look in diagrammatic form at the positivist theory of knowledge, with application to natural and to social science, and compare this theory with the possibility of religious knowledge.

Figure 1.1 shows a "thinking head." To the left is the two-way interaction with an external spatiotemporal reality (s–t), which results in a model of that reality in the head. We shall develop a theory of how a mental model can be seen as consisting of a network of entities called schemas. The model of spatio–temporal reality is not "projected on to nothing," but is constrained by physical feedback, a process that runs from the child's acquisition of mental schemas to the scientist's testing and verification of theories. Of course, as we see in detail in Chapter 3, Figure 1.1 is oversimplified. The child's learning depends on the sensory and motor capabilities of the whole body and on his interactions with family and other people, as well as his sensing the physical environment. Learning also involves the social phenomena of language and its feedback cycles.

We use the term *construction* for the building of schemas in the head whether or not they are projected out on the external world. We refer to coherent sets of such schemas as "cognitive systems," thus using the word *cognitive* in the sense adopted by social anthropologists, rather than in the narrow sense of the positivists' "knowledge." In our analysis of space–time reality, we do not speak of pure projection of our models on a mere blank; that is, we reject both the idealism of "pure projection" and the naïve realism that sees nature as merely impressing our minds via the senses. Thus, arrows point both ways between space–time and the schemas in the head. In a sense,

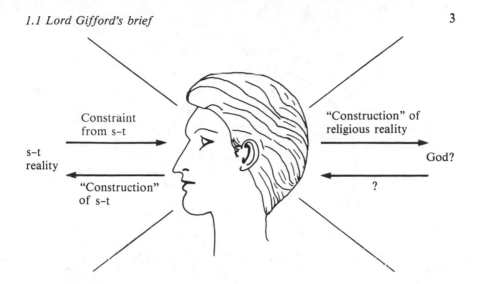

Figure 1.1. A thinking head

s–t and the head are inside each other. A model of s–t is in the head, and the head is part of s–t. The scientist may hope to develop laws to explain s–t, including in particular how these interactions enable the brain to build its schemas. This is explained in cognitive science, which recognizes a process of feedback correction and learning, as a result of which the models are not entirely arbitrary. We can, for example, develop Euclidean geometry and then raise the ontological question of whether the external s–t reality conforms to Euclidean geometry. We construct the natural world in our science, but s–t constrains these constructions by feedback.

Returning to Figure 1.1, the arrow on the right from head to God represents the construction of religious reality, for which there are no doubt sometimes "models in the head." The fact that people have religious beliefs can be included as part of what is to be explained about s–t reality, and some sociologists have adopted evolutionary or functional theories of this fact. But is there a return arrow for a feedback constraint on this construction? Freud, for example, would claim that our God schema is a modification of the father concept, with no external reality to which it answers. But most believers in theistic religion want to say there is a God reality that is not just constructed within the head but is out there, not contained within s–t. Certainly, there are myths and fables embodying people's constructs of God, so if there is a God reality, it has to impinge on the s–t world – it has to impinge on our physiology. The naturalist would simply offer a story of why it is useful to society to invent myths about God, without requiring a God "out there" that these myths are about.

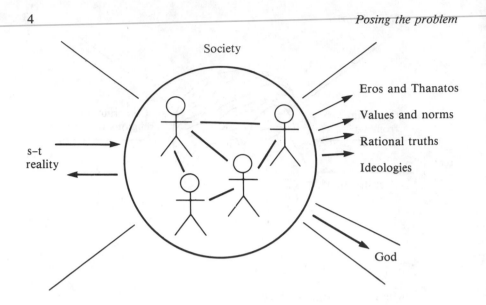

Figure 1.2. The collective social model

Reference to such "social schemas" reminds us that the representation in Figure 1.1 is too individualistic; we must consider not just the individual with models in the head and the external reality to which they may or may not answer, but also the fact that the individual is an interacting member of a society with its own "constructed" realities. Figure 1.2 represents the collective model as constituted by all these interactions, that is, by socially accepted concepts that include taken-for-granted scientific theories of the s–t world and also the values, norms, myths, and religions that make up the network of social life. From the naturalist point of view, the same question arises about the "objectivity" of values and norms that arose already about God; namely, is there an external reality against which they can be tested and corrected, or are they purely the internal constructs of societies?

Marx, Durkheim, and Weber all discussed a social reality within space–time, but constructed when groups transcend the capabilities of the isolated individual. Indeed, the notion of the isolated individual itself is a social legacy from the Enlightenment and ultimately from the Protestant notion of each individual soul's having unique value before God and direct access to him. Marx and Durkheim came in different ways to postulate social realities, such as the class struggle, or symbolic systems *sui generis,* which emerge from the behavior of large groups of people and their institutions and which could not have been predicted from individual or small-group behavior alone. Thus, Durkheim claimed there are "social facts" as well as "natural facts" and "individual facts." Durkheim also claimed that "society is God." In a social theory parallel to Freud's individual theory of father projection, he concluded that individuals project their idea of society beyond space–time to construct God and religious symbolisms:

[Religion] is a system of ideas by means of which individuals represent to themselves the society of which they are members, and the obscure but intimate relations which they have with it. Such is its primordial role; and though metaphorical and symbolic, this representation is not unfaithful. (Durkheim 1915, p. 225, translation in Lukes 1973, p. 461)

We might try to capture the ontological question suggested by Figures 1.1 and 1.2 by asking, "Is God more like gravitation or like embarrassment?" Gravitation is a reality that constrains our schemas of the physical world by the well-understood processes of testing and experimental feedback. Theories of gravitation give us at least part of the truth about it. Embarrassment, on the other hand, may be seen as a social artifact, arising when the person finds she has broken the social rules and is isolated from her group; this depends on the society's having a set of rules that are easily broken. One could conceive of a society in which there is no such thing as embarrassment, because of the support people give to those who display their imperfect mastery of the social rules. In any case, the conditions for embarrassment depend on social conventions. Gravitation exists independently of human activity and is known by human beings in terms of its testable interaction with them. Embarrassment is based on how we perceive certain kinds of human situations and would not exist independently of this perception.

There is a sense in which the religious believer would hold that God is more like gravitation than embarrassment. The same sense will be true for the holder of any ideology with respect to the reality of the concepts that underlie the ideology, such as the class struggle for Marxists, or the soul for Eccles. We have distinguished Reality "out there" (capital *R*) from the stories or models people have about what they take reality to be (which we call their constructed "reality," with a lower-case *r*). To claim that God is like gravitation is to say there is some kind of constraint and feedback on our knowledge of him, which in this case is from beyond space–time. On the other hand, "naturalism" is the thesis that there is only space–time Reality and that this Reality is sufficiently understandable in terms of scientific methods.

To say that God is like embarrassment, on the other hand, is to say that religion is a purely social construct. If God is understood as an unconscious projection of the father figure, or as society itself in its role as the source of corporate authority, constraint, and desire, then the problem of his empirical existence is solved, though at the price of the falsity of most of what most believers of all faiths have believed about him. Such psychological and social accounts of the origin and function of religion are widely taken to have fatally undermined any pretensions of religion to be an independent source of knowledge. We may in fact conjecture that Marx, Durkheim, and Freud on religion are now much more potent sources of science–religion conflict than Galileo, Newton, and Darwin ever were.

Before challenging this naturalist interpretation of Figures 1.1 and 1.2, we examine in more detail what is represented on their left-hand sides. It is crucial to any conclusions about "Reality" and "realities" that we understand the claim to have knowledge of the spatiotemporal and to describe it more adequately than is done in crude empiricism and naïve realism. This examination has two parts. We first look at the way philosophy of science itself has moved away from crude empiricism and brought into question the realist interpretation even of natural science. Second, we shall introduce schema theory as a general science of the cognitive, basing it on studies of everyday perception, action, and learning. We find these studies also support the view that knowledge is essentially constructive.

1.2 Empiricism undermined

We have described constructive feedback procedures as the basis of our knowledge of s–t reality. This basis provides a demarcation of scientific knowledge that is common to the scientific positivists, to Popper's use of falsifiability, and to Peirce's and Habermas's views of natural scientific method as a convergent limiting process. Science is what survives experimentation and test; the results of experiments may feed back to change the theory; and sometimes, as with Kuhn's (1962) paradigm change, to suggest revolutionary changes in natural cosmology. During the past four centuries, however, we have learned that scientific theories do not provide final, true, and objective knowledge of the world. The Aristotelian worldview was displaced by the Newtonian, which has in turn been displaced by the modern physics of relativity and quantum mechanics. Yet, it may seem paradoxical that with our increasing understanding of the mutability of scientific theory goes an increased confidence in the predictions we make on the basis of scientific theory. We can explain the motion of the planet Mercury better and better in terms of successive theories that are radically different from one another: earth-centered epicycles (Ptolemy), sun-centered epicycles (Copernicus), an ellipse with one focus at the sun (Kepler), a body moving according to the inverse square law (Newton), or in terms of relativity theory (Einstein).

In 1906 Duhem first clearly pointed out that a multiplicity of theoretical models may all fit a given set of data relatively well yet presuppose different ontologies (Duhem 1954). Each theory may use a different vocabulary of concepts to represent what it takes to be the fundamental entities and properties that exist in nature. The data underdetermine the theoretical ontology, and there seems no reason in principle to suppose that a final theory corresponding with what "there really is" in the world will ever be realized. How, then, can we reconcile this view of "no final theory" with the progressive success of our knowledge about the world since the sixteenth and seventeenth centuries?

There is certainly instrumental progress in science in that the pragmatic possibilities of predicting and controlling empirical events have vastly increased. When a new theory replaces the ontology of an old theory, it may also change the set of phenomena we choose to consider important. But for those phenomena addressed by both theories, the observation language of the new theory must be able to represent the observations made within the old theory, and the new theory must explain the phenomena so represented. In particular, a successful new theory should help us understand where the old theory succeeded even while replacing the ontology of the old explanation. A given theory lets us develop an observation language (based in part on the scientific instruments made possible by that theory), which enables us confidently to specify the nature of experiments and the results to be obtained under specific conditions. This procedure not only enables us to express the success of the theory but also to represent the discrepancies that provide the "error signals" for what Peirce characterized as the self-corrective feedback procedure of experimental science.

We adopt the *pragmatic criterion* (see Hesse, 1980, Introduction) of predictive success by means of such a feedback procedure. The pragmatic criterion is therefore the criterion of "truth" or "acceptability" that operates specifically in natural science. Though pragmatic success may be said in some sense to be a criterion for anything deserving the name *knowledge,* we shall see that it does not operate in so direct a way, if at all, for social and religious cognitive systems. The pragmatic criterion as just defined may therefore be regarded as the demarcating criterion for what we mean by natural science – the criterion according to which we *construct* the scientifically "objective" natural world.

Such construction is constrained by the pragmatic criterion, and we do not take it to imply a radically nonrealist view of science. In this interpretation, we differ from some recent sociologists of science who, in the swing away from empiricism, have rejected even this minimal attempt to demarcate natural science from other cognitive systems. In a new form of social idealism, they have suggested that in complex developments of theory, feedback from the world is altogether excluded, so that science becomes a socially generated imaginative schema like other social myths (see, for example, the "strong programme" of Bloor 1976; and also Barnes 1974, 1977; Collins & Pinch 1982; Collins 1985). It seems, however, that this extreme conclusion has resulted in part from exclusive concern with either "fringe" sciences like parapsychology, or with theories that have taken off far from their original empirical bases and that depend on highly elaborate and artificial instrumentation, such as current research in fundamental physics. However that may be, it is rare to find a sociologist who does not recognize some natural constraints on scientific knowledge. As Barry Barnes puts it, even in a nonliterate hunting culture, the hunters know they must throw the spear to the front of the running lion. Natural knowledge that is continuous with animal-type predictive skills and habits still forms the basis of science, at least up to the point at which science becomes indistinguishable from pure mathematics or pure science fiction.

What the sociologists of science are recognizing, however, is that this formulation of the pragmatic criterion is a minimal characterization of science, and that only on this narrow basis can science be demarcated from other types of cognitive systems. The pragmatic criterion exhausts the content of the feedback arrow from space–time Reality to the "model-in-the-head," and yet it is strong enough to prevent the model's being purely an intersubjective representation of social realities. But there is a strong arrow in the "constructive" direction, too, and only recently have we come to understand how many characteristics of science previously thought to be "objective" ("read off" the real world) are, after all, products of construction, albeit constrained by the pragmatic criterion. Here are a few of these characteristics.

1. Science is in a literal sense constructive of new facts. It has no fixed body of facts passively awaiting explanation, for successful theories allow the construction of new instruments – electron microscopes and deep space probes – and the exploration of phenomena that were beyond description – the behavior of transistors, recombinant DNA, and elementary particles, for example. This is a key point in the progressive nature of science – not only are there more elegant or accurate analyses of phenomena already known, but there is also extension of the range of phenomena that exist to be described and explained.

2. The facts themselves are *theory laden*. There is no representation of facts without the observation language, and no observation language is just "given" as theory-free. Hence, there is a pressure toward relativism. How can we ascribe perennial truth value to statements of fact, given that these statements presuppose theories that come and go? The answer is that we cannot ascribe perennial truth value; but we do generally have an observation language rich enough to express observations not assimilable to current theory. Moreover, we also have the ability to recognize experiences that are not well described in the observation language. We can thus talk of feedback even though our language may not be able to formulate the range of such feedback. Observation language and even perception are theory laden, yet they are rich enough to contain feedback that contradicts the theory. We have, as it were, a spiraling set of nested feedback systems, as advances in theory respond to feedback and in turn enrich the observation language to make new corrections possible. Ptolemy used observations to correct the description of the epicycles for planetary motion, but it took a higher level of feedback to question the concept of epicycles themselves. It took an even

higher level to perform what Galileo (1953, p. 328) called the "violence upon the senses" involved in recognizing that what looked and felt like the movement of the sun round a stable earth is to be described as the motion of the earth. At each stage, concepts about space and time previously taken for granted as almost tautologies come to be seen as representing choices within a larger framework in which feedback correction is possible.

3. There is a different sense in which theory is richer than data and is therefore empirically underdetermined by data. Logically speaking, theories are not deducible from data, and many theories may fit the same data reasonably well. Duhem argued that any particular hypothesis is always embedded in a more general theory, all of which has to be tested as a whole against experience. Any given hypothesis may always be saved from falsification by modifying surrounding hypotheses or by modifying the interpretation they put on the data. Thus, no theory can claim unique and permanent validity, since over the long term it may not only be falsified by new experience but also one or more of its rivals may come to look better or be in greater conformity with prevailing fashion. How, then, does scientific theory, when accepted, give such an appearance of stability and consensus that it was taken by Descartes and his successors as the very paradigm of progressive knowledge?

At any given time, several factors explain this apparent stability. First, the underlying pragmatic criterion ensures that where prediction and experimental control in local domains have been successful in the past, any theory must incorporate at least these predictions. Second, the logically possible multiplicity of theories relative to given data is reduced by the operation of criteria of simplicity, economy, and elegance. These criteria may even temporarily be preferred to the criteria of empirical fit; for example, Copernicus's heliocentric theory had at first little to recommend it as a more accurate representation of data than Ptolemy's theory, but it was mathematically simpler and more elegant and implied fewer unexplained coincidences in the relation between planetary motions. Third, "local" modifications of hypotheses may not succeed in saving large-scale theories because their implications may extend far beyond the phenomena that prompted the change. For example, creationists try to reject Darwin's theory because their way of life is grounded in a reading of the Bible inconsistent with an evolutionary account. They therefore try to amend auxiliary hypotheses to make creationism consistent with the data. But current evolutionary theory is embedded in a whole web of observations related to other sciences – to modern physics (carbon–14 dating of fossils) and molecular biology (the mechanisms of the gene), as well as to agricultural applications of genetics. The creationists cannot explain these phenomena, but the reality of their religious beliefs may be such that it is easier for them to sever the links in the causal network that binds such observations to evolutionary theory than either to accept evolution or construct an alternative theory. It is logically possible to sever these links, but this violates other currently accepted methodological criteria of simplicity and the unity of science.

4. The upshot of these arguments is to question any strong version of scientific realism. By a "strong version" is meant the view that takes acceptable scientific theory to be the true or approximately true description of unobservable as well as observable entities, and regards its pragmatic success as sufficient to guarantee this, in spite of underdetermination and the theory-ladenness of observation. This strong realism often goes along with a naturalist epistemology according to which acceptable scientific theory is not only the best but also the only type of knowledge we can get.

There is certainly a sense in which we accept our current science as representing the "real" every time we rely on the inventions of modern technology. But this sense of "reality" commits us to no more than acceptance of theory as a local instrument for successful prediction, yielding approximate truth in local domains. It does not imply universality or perennial truth for theories that extrapolate far from the data, much less the exclusive knowledge claims for science that often accompany such a full-blooded realism.

To undermine positivism and realism in these ways is to raise an opposite objection, namely, that we are in danger of making scientific theory merely relative to historical circumstances. (For recent discussions of relativism, see Hollis and Lukes 1982.) Scientific relativists, like the sociologists of science mentioned earlier, regard theories as internally connected propositional systems, or "language games," which are worldviews to be given as much or as little significance as any other mythical cosmology. "Truth" is defined as coherence with the theoretical systems, and "knowledge" becomes socially institutionalized belief. Ironically, the "queen of the cognitive systems," theoretical science, comes to be seen as just one of the mythologies, though no doubt better worked out as a logical system and more useful for empirical prediction and control.

Such a statement of relativism can be taken two ways. It may be a *reductio ad absurdum* of the critique of scientific realism and empiricism, requiring rehabilitation of the queen of cognitive systems to her methodological palace. Or, it may be taken as an invitation to raise the status of the other "mythologies" by a more careful investigation of their methodological and cognitive credentials. We attempt this second response here. We seek to avoid a relativism in which "anything goes" by examining the various kinds of criteria of acceptability that apply to different kinds of constructed models and myths.

Scientific theories, then, have some characteristics of ideological or social myths; they also have many of their social functions. We have only to think of crucial episodes in the debates between science and religion to see that this is so. The Copernican system may or may not have originally been intended as a realistic description of the cosmos, but it was certainly perceived

universe of Aristotelian geocentric
and the Holy Office over the new
eligious consequences of displacing
e among the factors weighing against
ts on theory cannot be neglected in
s in the historical debate, or even in
lar case, the issues were not clear-cut
tic" religion because Galileo himself
om the available data to arrive at the
not only the formal simplicity and
thrown into the scales, but also the
entific conservatism, as against new
of social and religious as well as of

at cognitive science has implications
problem, and for our understanding
its still somewhat limited pragmatic
eople need the special relationship of
meaning to what it is to be human.
bly still feel the need for "something
– to make us human, beyond the bio-
n, and the historical richness of inter-
c and social milieu in which we each
accept the biological basis of our hu-
manity will, in general, find themselves uncomfortable that, as a result, we
are to be seen as machines. Yet, in a century or so, people may find this
view as strange as most of us now find the rejection of the heliocentric or
the evolutionary theories. Just as, for most of us, being at the center of the
universe and being God's special creation on the sixth day, are not part of
what defines being human, so it may come to seem quaint that anything
more than the complexity of our biological constitution and our social interactions is required to define us as human – a definition as malleable as human
culture itself.

Thus, we expect to find scientific theories being influenced by, and in turn
influencing, surrounding cultural and social thought. This is increasingly being
demonstrated by social studies in the history of science. We no longer have
to think of the contribution of science to the stock of social ideas as a one-
way process; much less are we bound to accept this contribution because of
some peculiar certainty that resides in scientific theory. Rather, the influence
is mutual; and in our revised view of science, space is left for regarding scientific theory as one way in which a culture exhibits its general view of the
world and of people, in other words, as one among the many sets of social
schemas.

1.3 Cognitive science and schema theory

This section looks more closely at an example of science as a challenge to humanist "mythology" – the question of mind/brain reductionism. This introduces the more extended discussion in Chapters 2 to 5. We should note that the relevance of the cognitive sciences to our general science/religion problem lies at two levels:

1. The cognitive sciences are themselves empirical studies of epistemology – of how animals and human beings acquire knowledge and what kind of knowledge it is. This means that these sciences give us potential frameworks for knowledge schemas of more complex kinds, which lie at the far end of a spectrum from simple learning processes through scientific knowledge to social and religious "knowledge" systems. It also means that cognitive science is essentially self-reflective; that is, it must subject its own methodology to its own critique. In the course of doing this, cognitive science has broken with the notion of "scientific method" as purely empiricist and positivist. For example, we look at the contributions of Piaget (Chapter 3) and Freud (Chapter 6) to the understanding of the cognitive, and also find parallels within cognitive science for the theory of interpretation, or hermeneutics.
2. The cognitive sciences also raise the particular problem of reduction of the human to the natural and therefore contribute to the modern science/religion problem in a way that challenges belief in the essential uniqueness of "persons" among natural objects.

Two positions may be taken with respect to reductionism. One might say that an information processing view, driven in part by studies of artificial intelligence, can contribute to, but not even potentially exhaust, our understanding of what it is to be human. In the same way, some brain scientists (for example, Eccles) hold the Cartesian view that no matter how much we come to understand the brain we cannot explain all of human nature, and that the mind and the will are separate entities that somehow communicate with the brain's left hemisphere to influence our behavior. But we do not yet have any evidence of the limits on what mechanism or brain can achieve, and thus need not argue for a separate, nonmaterial soul or mind to complete our humanity. However, this lack of evidence does not mean that all our talk of humanity must be reduced to talk of neurons or transistors. A major challenge for this book is to present a modified reductionism compatible with (or complementary to) the social and cultural sciences. Certainly, someone with a certain type of religious conviction or under the sway of Cartesian dualism may note that there are many aspects of human experience that we cannot now trace down to mechanisms within the brain, and may thus speak persuasively of the hypothesis of dualism – and yet contribute to our better understanding of what it is that brain mechanisms, or computer programs, can indeed achieve. On the other hand, cognitive scientists can point to our continuing successes in increasing the sophistication of computers and in exploring brain mechanisms, and argue that there is no reason to doubt that this progress will continue.

To place the claims of cognitive science in perspective, consider the theory of evolution. We now have enough evidence to understand how natural selection can yield more and more complex organisms. There is a real sense, then, in which a person is an animal. But when we say this, we do not assert that a person is the same as any other animal. In particular, a person is not the same as an amoeba; and if we did not have the evolutionary record – fragmentary though it still is – we would be hard put to accept the story that the forces of nature could yield the transition from an amoeba-like creature to a human being without the intervention of explicit design. But the cognitive scientist now has no need to postulate that at some time a creator suddenly attached a mind to the brain, as Descartes had to say in distinguishing the human soul from the body and from beast machines.

Within cognitive science much progress has been made in the study of vision, control of movement, memory, and some aspects of language processing and problem solving. Less has been achieved in the study of motivation, personality, and emotion. We thus broaden the scope of cognitive science to a perspective wider than that accepted by most of its practitioners today (who may be expert in artificial intelligence, or brain theory, or cognitive science, but rarely in all three) to include a concern for social and emotional issues. In particular, it is useful to study Freud's work and to consider its roots in nineteenth-century neurology, the appeal of his mature theory and case studies to humanists and literary scholars, and the extent to which psychoanalysis justifies his critique of religion. It is easy to dismiss Freud's work as nonscientific from a narrow positivist view of science. One task here is to understand how cognitive science must grow if it is to address the fundamental questions of human personality that occupied Freud, whether or not we accept his answers.

We see "schema theory" as being at the heart of cognitive science, though our own development of schema theory by no means offers a view that has gained the consensus of cognitive scientists. For us, a "schema" is a "unit of representation" of a person's world. Schema theory is an attempt at an information-processing theory of the mind. It is a materialist theory in that it seeks to show that all human mental phenomena reduce to (complex) patterns of schema activation and that schemas are instantiated as dynamic processes in the brain. The theory of schemas has two different aspects: synchronic and diachronic. The synchronic aspect concerns what happens at a particular time – each individual mind contains a collection of schemas that constitute the person's knowledge, or long-term memory. While awake, the person is engaged in a continuing action/perception cycle. At any time, a particular assemblage of certain schemas constitutes the individual's representation of current situation and goals. During perception, this representation and plan are updated. The individual acts on this basis, is afforded new stimulation, the schema assemblage is updated, and the cycle continues. This theory is a far cry from stimulus-response theory; what we do is in terms of the schemas available to us, subtle processes acting on rather subtle representations.

We rely, in part, on Piaget for the diachronic aspect, the mechanisms whereby the individual's "stock" of schemas changes over time. Piaget does not give us a full theory, and we do not accept his theory of "stages," but he does give some idea of how schemas could arise and change over time, by a process of reflective abstraction. In many instances, a new situation can be assimilated to (made sense in terms of) available schemas; but other situations require one to go beyond what one already knows, forming new schemas by a process Piaget calls accommodation. It is no mere coincidence that the title of one of Piaget's books (1954) is *The Construction of Reality in the Child*.

We best understand the early sensory-motor schemas, such as grasping or recognizing objects, which are highly constrained by the physics of the world. Because of these common physical constraints, we expect there to be a moderate amount of commonality in what children can be expected to know, at least in the early stages. There are only so many ways to approach a glass if you want to get a drink of water. But our expectation is that other schemas that constitute how the child represents or constructs reality depend more on the child's individual experience and on the social milieu in which he or she lives. This perspective gives us some understanding of both the commonality and the individuality in a person's knowledge.

The construction of schemas for natural spatiotemporal reality follows constraints akin to those of the pragmatic criterion of the sciences, as the schemas evolve on the basis of interaction with the reality we posit outside – not a Reality we can fully know, but a reality we can at least postulate and approximate. But the child's reality is constituted by social as well as natural feedback, immediately in life within the family and later as the child acquires schemas peculiar to that particular society. Interactions that in one social milieu may lead to pleasurable consequences may lead to ostracism in another.

The developing child, and the adult deciding how to behave, find social structures appearing as an external reality that is in part determinative of behavior. How do we see such a reality arising out of the coherence of the schemas within the heads of the members of that society? Because people act according to certain schemas, the growing child internalizes schemas and we can talk of intersubjectivity. If, in developing a social critique, we consider how society might change, we note that even though "the schemas are just in our heads," the fact that many people think a certain way makes it difficult for the individual to "step out of line" and change the social structure.

We need a multilevel description of the human being. Schema theory, as it develops, is to provide an ever more appropriate mental vocabulary, while neural processes provide the mechanism for schema storage and dynamics. This is both more and less than reductionism. In some sense, everything in human behavior or society is mediated by neural firing and other physico-chemical processes. And yet, there is no useful sense in which our analysis of human beings can be conducted exclusively at that level. We have many different levels of description, including neural, mental, and social, and we find ways of illuminating any particular level of discourse by placing it within a higher level context and by seeking lower level mechanisms. In this way, we see how to think coherently of the neural and the social levels as placing constraints on the schema level of analysis without claiming that any level is the one true level at which we should conduct all discussion.

The knowledge of words and how to use them is culturally conditioned to an extent that basic grasping and object–concept schemas are not. But note that as people build up their representation of the world, although it is shaped to some extent by their social milieu, as in the choice of words, for example, it is also built on the schemas acquired through their own idio-syncratic experience, shaped in no small part by the basic and individual emo-tionality arising from the genetically based structure of the brain.

In analyzing language, we again encounter the mixture of commonality and individuality. We need to understand how it is that we have a core of meaning that can be reasonably agreed on, while there is no firm boundary that demarcates a completely "literal" meaning from all others. Language is to be seen not as a self-contained system but rather as a way of giving us an imperfect representation of the schema assemblages each of us has, which, in turn, are our own personal constructions on the basis of feedback from the world and other persons. Schemas are richer than words; and so although a sentence may have a relatively fixed meaning, we can often go indefinitely further, both in articulating the knowledge implicit in our schemas and in exploring the network of associations between schemas.

In Chapters 7 and 8 we shall build on schema theory to establish a theory of language general enough to handle language use in everyday contexts, in science, and in religion. We argue that no strict dichotomy exists between literal or scientific language on the one hand and metaphorical language on the other. We do not use "metaphor" as a pejorative term. Rather, whenever we use language, there is a richness of association that goes beyond any restricted notion of what we might call "literal" meaning. Certainly, when we say "Pass the salt," we would be hard-pressed to take this in any but a single, obvious sense; but we wish to see the literal sense as the limit of a continuum of metaphor rather than as a sharply distinct form of meaning from which metaphor is to be defined as a deviation. In particular, we sug-gest that much of our understanding of language rests on our being within a holistic symbol system, encoded in the schemas in our heads, many of which have been assimilated unconsciously. Our use of language rests not on precise definitions but on the (not necessarily conscious) use of schemas that have resulted from rich, complex, and by no means unambiguous interaction with a physical and social reality.

In our social applications of schema theory, we seek to reconcile the holistic position that approaches knowledge and belief "from the top down" (from a holistic net of social symbolism), and the individualist position that seeks to analyze knowledge "from-the-bottom-up" approach of mental schemas. This dichotomy is more apparent than real, for a study of the development of mental schemas must also involve a top–down analysis of the holistic net that constitutes a social reality, whether it be custom, language, or religion. The schemas in the head themselves form a network that represents the social holistic network. The question remains of how the individual acquires representations, and how the development of individual conceptions can come to alter social schemas. One basic question in approaching "the construction of reality" is, "What can schema theory contribute to an epistemology that can analyze the interaction of individual and society in the construction of the individual's view of reality?"

1.4 The claims of natural theology

We have moved from the positivist critique of religion, through the revolutions of modern philosophy of science, to the consideration of cognitive science as a potential basis for a new epistemology, and schema theory as a new framework for cognitive systems. We now return to religion. Where Karl Barth was troubled by the challenge of the Gifford lectures (Barth 1938) because he saw no need for nature in the understanding of God, we find a situation in which there appears to be no need for God in the understanding of nature. Nevertheless, in accepting the challenge of the lectures, we may agree that whether or not God is part of an external reality, he is certainly part of a social reality; and as we come to understand how human individuals assimilate the reality of their society, so we may come to understand how they do or do not come to assimilate the religious beliefs of that society. In concluding this first chapter, we relate this possibility to some more usual approaches to natural theology.

   The effect of the scientific revolution was to dissociate knowledge of nature from knowledge of persons and society – the "objective," outer, natural, and behavioral world from "subjective" inner experience and moral and aesthetic judgments. In this dualism, "rationality" was generally regarded as an "objective" feature of the world, providing *a priori* knowledge to complement the empirical knowledge due to science. Religion was increasingly pushed out from concern with the scientific world, and the positivist attack on metaphysics therefore undermined the foundation of natural theology. It seemed that only two options remained for religion:

1. To accept relegation to the inner subjective world that did not admit objective rational discussion, along with matters of taste and aesthetics, and perhaps along with a subjective view of morality. Such acceptance would, however, be to abandon Gifford's brief altogether; we reject its implication that there is no possibility of rational discussion of religion, or, for that matter, of aesthetics and morality.
2. To rehabilitate metaphysics and "reason," and to try to reconstruct religion on a foundation of objective rationality. This is what Gifford's brief ex-

plicitly calls for, and it is the task undertaken by most modern philosophers of religion.

We do not want to reject the spirit of option (2), but our view is that the possibilities under this heading have been put in a different light by the recent changes in interpretation of natural science, by the potentialities of cognitive science for a new epistemology, and by greater attention to the social dimensions of both science and religion. From these three developments, we try to derive a new rational approach to religion.

In the light of our understanding of natural science, it is no longer possible to see the task of natural theology as reading off relevant facts about the universe from scientific theories, nor by using the methods of natural science. The claims of scientific theory are indeed most vulnerable just where they have traditionally been taken to conflict most strongly with religion. For example, cosmological theories about the beginning and end of the universe are distant extrapolations from the evidence, and they contain a high proportion of theoretical construction of unobservable entities and processes. Just because they are the stuff of which myths are made, they are most subject to changes of scientific and ideological fashion. The same applies to wide extrapolations of evolution theory: there may be a core of agreement about the process of biological evolution, but this agreement has no uncontroversial entailments for the evolution of human beings in society, much less for the view that natural evolution is coincident with spiritual evolution, or that God is evolving, or anything of that kind.

In cases like this, it is not that two literal stories clash and exclude each other, but rather that there are two sorts of metaphorical story with different criteria of acceptability and put forward for different purposes. The scientific stories may be, and often have been, inspirations for myths and ideologies, but in themselves they are neutral to religion: they may be used for the expression of either religious or atheist belief. For example, at some periods in the history of science, it has been held that atomist theory of matter is atheistic because it reduces reality to mechanical matter in motion. At other times, it has been held that atomism conforms better to a theist view because it safeguards the transcendence of God and rids the world of semidivine spirits, fates, and magical powers. On the other hand, the contrary theory of space as filled by dynamic force or active "ether" has on different occasions been held as a powerful metaphor for the omnipresence of God or as a heretical idolization of space and time. However, religion and atheism take what metaphors they can from science and try to gain prestige in doing so. In this way, science often expresses important ideological conflicts, but not serious logical conflicts, because no final truths are found in scientific theories of this generality. The importance of a theory of metaphor for understanding such ideological uses of language is considered in Chapter 8.

A different, more "rationalist," tradition in natural theology is still powerful. This tradition seeks to derive the existence and nature of God not from the details of natural science but from general metaphysical arguments about the origin, causation, and character of the cosmos and from such rational concepts as "perfection," "being," and "infinity." It is questionable whether such arguments have ever had much impact on the faith of the ordinary believer or the thoughtful secularist. Indeed, it is probable that the understanding of religion and secularism in our day demands more fundamental analysis than this; analysis drawn from epistemology, psychology, and sociology rather than metaphysics. In any case, we do not offer direct arguments to refute this kind of natural theology, but we try to put it in historical perspective in relation to the science/religion debates referred to in this chapter.

Traditional Christian theology saw its task as setting forth doctrines of God based on natural reason and revelation. Enlightenment rationality subjected many of the arguments from natural reason to critical scrutiny; the result was to undermine proofs for the existence of God, the concept of human freedom, and the idea of provident interventions of God in the world, including the concept of miracle. Thus, the "rational" basis of Christianity declined, but apart from Deist and Unitarian deviations, all this cast little doubt on orthodox belief derived from revelation, until nineteenth-century studies of Biblical origins. Then, the new historical sciences began to undermine belief in the historical accuracy and literal inspiration of the Scriptures. Other cultures, including the Hebrew and the Greek, began to appear increasingly "foreign." Hermeneutics was born as the theory of Biblical interpretation, and an uncomplicated view of the "Jesus of history" became impossible to maintain. Theology began to talk increasingly of human existence and its problems. For example, Schleiermacher's *On Religion: Speeches to Its Cultured Despisers* (1958) set the tone of theological liberalism, offering rapprochment with the modern enlightenment world.

Theological traditions since then have diverged along a continuum between the extremes of literal fundamentalism, holding on by faith against all reason, and liberal humanism, with some defections and plenty of agnostic agonizing. The most substantial twentieth-century representatives of contrasted positions on this continuum are Barth and Bultmann. In the aftermath of World War I, Barth sought a return from discredited rationalism to the revelation of the Christ-event as the basis of faith. He was the most dramatic exponent of neo-orthodoxy, the power of which derived from the surrounding social crisis. Barth retained dogma by making a sharp dichotomy between the "vertical" God-given dimension of faith on the one hand, and the "horizontal" concerns of humanity, which include all of reason, science, and culture on the other – all regarded by Barth as worthless except as illuminated by divine grace. Barth and his followers argued that the radical transcendence of God has been sacrificed by the appeal to modernity. They claimed that rationalism followed in isolation leads to idolatry and insisted that the claims of scripture are ultimately extrarational. However, although the starting point is not the individual but the Bible, Barth did not insist on literal interpretations, and he steered a course that avoided collision with such secular theorists as Marx and Freud. Reinhold Niebuhr, indeed, in *The Nature and Destiny of Man* (1941), offered a view of humanity closely influenced by both Marx and Freud.

Since World War II, the claim of extrarational truth for Scripture has conflicted with the modern temper, and modern theology has become very pluralistic, though still within the liberal agenda. The Barthian tradition generally neglected the hermeneutical problem of interpreting traditional expressions of doctrine in terms that were intelligible (let alone acceptable) in a climate of science and analytic philosophy. Bultmann, to whom we return in Chapter 11, attempted to come to terms with the limitations apparently imposed by modern science. His demythologization of the New Testament was an attempt to exclude "objectionable" transcendental interpretations of such Biblical concepts as God's intervention in the world; the global saving act identified with Christ's death; and the concepts of sin, judgment, heaven and hell; and even of the existence of God. In place of such interpretations, Bultmann adopted a Heideggerian philosophy, in which religious experience is interpreted in existential terms as the subjective Christ-event occurring in the here and now.

Bultmannian theology is in danger of becoming more and more religiously vacuous. It is no accident that for many theologians today the primary concern is with social and political problems, as in so-called "liberation theology" (see, for example, Gutierrez 1973), which originated in the special social circumstances of Latin America. There has been a general loss of nerve with respect to the "logic of the divine" and the possibility of giving any sort of philosophical grounding to faith. In the less metaphysical and more empiricist tradition of English-speaking philosophy, however, there has been a tendency to analyze religious belief by borrowing models from contemporary philosophy of science (usually a decade or so behind). We can detect several phases of this development.

1. Parallel with the interpretation of science as largely positivist, inductivist, and antitheoretical, we have antidogmatic interpretations of religion depending on the appeal to direct religious experience. This is exemplified in the "death of God" and "man for others" interpretations of Jesus of the 1960s. Also, Bultmann's demythologizing must be said, though at a much more serious level, to be influenced by this type of positivism.

2. Next, the interpretation of science became hypothetico-deductive; with Carnap (1966), Hempel (1965), and Popper (1959), theory assumed more importance as falsifiable hypothesis or conjecture. In parallel, the "hypothesis of God" is said to be justifiable if it is related to testable experience in a coherent fashion. This type of apologetics is to be found in Van Buren (1972), John Hick (1974), and Mitchell (1973).

3. The rehabilitation of scientific theory led to recognition of the importance of scientific models and of metaphoric language in science. This revived in-

terest in Thomist discussions of metaphor, analogy, and religious language
and initiated a more sophisticated analysis of how religious expressions get
their meaning and justification.
4. The Kuhnian revolution in philosophy of science picked up Wittgenstein's
    (1953) theme of "language games": scientific theories were seen as internally
    consistent paradigms or world views, whose meaning, interpretation of
    evidence and criteria of acceptability are internal, with only indirect rela-
    tion to hard data. This relativist tendency was reinforced by studies of symbol
    systems in social anthropology, in which religions are analyzed as internally
    coherent "symbolic games," and led to similar interpretations of Christian
    religion by Wittgensteinian philosophers.
5. More recently, there has been a flight from relativism back into scientific
    realism. This is beginning to be paralleled by a similarly "realist" and
    "literalist" view of religious doctrine – a development that may perhaps yield
    some philosophical foundations for currently lively, but generally nonintel-
    lectualist, schools of fundamentalism.

Our program in this book is in the tradition of these attempts to build
a theory of religion on science and empiricism, if not in content at least in
methodology. In what follows, we incorporate elements from most of these
parallel theories of science and religion, particularly the third and fourth.
We effectively try to explore a sixth entry, which will identify a general schema
theory based on cognitive science as its interpretation of scientific and religious
knowledge. It follows from this that criteria for religious belief, and, for
that matter, belief in any secular ideology, will be holistic in operation and
closely intertwined with its own society and history. Two characteristics of
such religious systems should be emphasized.

First, these systems share with other social belief systems and with scientific paradigms the characteristic of inertia. This partially accounts for the
apparent and scientifically unattractive inflexibility of religious beliefs in face
of changing experience. The history of theology may seem like a constant
struggle to maintain orthodox dogma by authoritarian fiat against "heresies"
that deviate from tradition. But a closer look at the history of theology and
of the Church in fact reveals radical changes and "reformations" over the
generations. "Orthodoxy" and "heresy" interact in a dialectical way to produce new "orthodoxy," which is seen as an advance on previous understanding. There can and should also be dialogue between doctrine and changing
secular experience, including science itself. This dialogue often results in
changing theological interpretations, as exemplified by the ultimate response
to such challenges as the Copernican world system and Darwinian evolution.
There are also changing religious interpretations throughout history of such
social issues as slavery, race, democracy, and war.

Such social critique provides a kind of falsifiability that philosophers of
science can recognize as an extension of the pragmatic criterion. It is true,
however, that reformations and reformulations often take the form of appeal back to the "sacred books" or the sacred authority. In some sense, this
is inevitable because religious systems are holistic and symbolic and need to

define themselves in terms of their tradition. This is also true of many central social institutions, and even where these institutions are admittedly imperfect, their disruption in war or revolution usually reduces rather than enhances social and intellectual well being and the quality of life. Thus, the history of the Church and of theology as social institutions will be expected to exhibit continual tension between tradition and the adaptation to experience. There is, however, no authority or text whose interpretation is fixed by revelation or philosophical foundations once and for all. The concept of "revelation" never was a simple given for theology. As Locke pointed out in 1690 (Locke 1947, Bk IV, Ch XVIII), there always has to be rational debate about what event, person, or process is to be taken as revelatory and which not. Individual claims to certainty that "God has spoken to me" are rarely taken at face value in the history of religion, if only because different individuals' certainties are often in conflict.

On the other hand, to abandon totally the traditional sources of a religion would result in loss of identity, and, worse, to such an accommodation to the spirit of the age that no dialectical progress is possible. A contemporary ideology needs to be subject to criticism from the historic past and from the wide-ranging view of the nature of human beings and the world that religion provides. Without this possibility, contemporary dogma becomes authoritarian in its turn. Whether one accepts the God hypothesis or not, one can still appreciate its critical function, and one can seek to understand faith in terms of its interactions with other parts of experience, whether these be relations of coherence or conflict.

We have stressed the holistic character of religious belief systems; this means that the individual claims of a religion must not be judged bit by bit. Nor can an individual meaningfully construct a religion from his or her eclectic fancies. The individualist view that "everyone is the creator and judge of their own religion" is a distorted legacy of Protestant individualism in which everyone has the right of access to God, not necessarily mediated through the Church. Subsequent western secular liberalism has exaggerated this into the view that everyone is autonomous with respect to his or her belief and has neglected the social domain and the importance of history and cultural transformation. For this point of view, the Marx–Durkheim–Weber development is salutary. Marx and Durkheim both, although in different ways, question "autonomy" in face of ineradicable social constraints.

Holism is also important in considering the justification of beliefs themselves. There is no question of asking, "Is it true?" about isolated doctrines, such as the existence of God or the credentials of Mohammed. There is no question of eclectically picking and choosing bits of approved doctrine out of different religions from widely different cultural contexts. This does not, of course, exclude the possibility of dialogue between secularists and believers, or between believers in different religions. Taking account of each others' contexts, they can extract lessons from another network of belief in testing and refining their own. In this respect, interaction between religious systems resembles the interaction between general scientific theories or paradigms. Religious systems do, however, differ in the range of criteria relevant to their justification. These criteria are concerned with internal coherence and correspondence with human experience, and "experience" will include not just that of the individual, and not just the empirical basis of natural science, but also personal, emotional, social, and moral dimensions that are outside the "objective" experience recognized by the pragmatic criterion. For example, Enlightenment secularism has held that the problem of human life would be solved if people were better educated and became more rational. The Judaeo–Christian tradition, on the other hand, sees the fundamental problem of human life as its need to be saved supernaturally from endemic evil. Hypotheses such as the existence of God and the seriousness of the problem of evil are to be tested by their coherence with whatever there is, historically, personally, socially, and morally. They are tested partly by the natural world, partly by the theory-laden social world, and partly by interpreted personal experience. Of course, there is circularity here, but so, as we have learned, is there in natural science as well. Against this whole background, a judgment can be made as to which view, for example, of the problem of evil, is more consonant with human experience.

We do not attempt here to develop arguments for and against particular doctrines or particular religions but only to address the sociological question, "Why have human beings developed God-schemas?" and the epistemological question, "Do such schemas make any sense, and how would we go about testing them?"

The following table summarizes in a preliminary way the relations as we see them between methods of justifying scientific theory and religious systems.

Science	*Religion*
a. Evidence is from the observable natural world, assumed objective and value-free.	Evidence is primarily from the world of history, society, persons, values, and emotions, though also from the natural world, giving natural theology a place, but not the primary place.
b. Criteria of truth: primarily pragmatic success and internal coherence; secondarily aesthetics and conformity with social and cultural context.	Criteria of truth: coherence of a variety of factors drawn from personal, social, and historical life; these factors have different weights with different people and in different societies.

c. The criterion of pragmatic success often makes possible consensus on theoretical truth,
relative to the specific purposes
of science.

No similar criterion, hence consensus unlikely in conditions of
free enquiry.

Chapters 2 and 3 give an account of the relevant parts of schema theory. This provides the basis for a number of challenges to the study of religion. Chapters 4 and 5 consider whether the reductionism implicit in schema theory excludes a humanist concept of persons and how it affects our conception of free will. Chapters 6 and 10 move to the psychological and social constructions of religion as analyzed respectively by Freud and Durkheim and ask whether these constructions can be ontologically significant. Chapter 7 examines how these considerations of language and social critique foster new developments in our schema theory.

Chapter 8 introduces the more specifically social approach to religion by showing how a metaphoric theory of language evolves both from cognitive science and from modern philosophy of science and language. This chapter is concerned with some of the most far-reaching debates in modern analytic philosophy; we do not claim in one chapter to address them in any sort of detail. Instead of recapitulating all the arguments found elsewhere against standard positions, we thought it best to present an alternative view, hoping that the reader will be prepared to consider it sympathetically and judge it according to the new insights on science and language it may contain. Chapter 9 moves the methodological discussion explicitly away from natural science and considers how cognitive justification takes place in hermeneutics and critique of ideology. Chapters 10 and 11 explicitly recognize the character of religion as a holistic symbol system, using irreducibly metaphorical language, and discuss some examples of the justification of religious schemas. Finally, Chapter 12 considers the upshot of all this from a secular point of view, by looking at the possible grounds of ethics and the question of how to be "human in a secular age."

2 The intelligence of the artificial

This chapter examines artificial intelligence (AI) – the dimension of cognitive science that focuses on programming computers to exhibit aspects of intelligence, without necessary regard for the constraints of human behavior (cognitive psychology) or of brain function (brain theory). We suggest that the achievements of AI to date are limited, but we deny that these are limitations in principle. Nonetheless, we argue that much of what is human about intelligence depends on our being embodied within human bodies and being members of human societies.

In this chapter, we distinguish formal systems in which words are related only to other words within a closed system from systems in which symbols are linked to action "in the world." We then argue that Gödel's incompleteness theorem does not prove that machines cannot be intelligent, but rather that an intelligent machine must learn, and that some element of inconsistency is an inescapable facet of intelligence, whether in human being or machine. In the next chapter, we see the view of *The Construction of Reality* Piaget offers in his study of assimilation and accommodation in the child. We then build on Piaget's insights and work in brain theory and artificial intelligence to outline a schema theory that provides our bridge from cognitive science to epistemology. But, in the spirit of our investigation, we find in later chapters that schema theory not only shapes our approach to natural theology but is also shaped by it in turn as we seek to extend it to analyze the construction of the realities of person, society, . . . and God?

2.1 Intentionality

For many philosophers, the concept of intentionality replaces traditional theology as backing for the uniqueness of people. As a result, many philosophers have an interest in rejecting any notion that intentionality or intelligence could be attributed to computers. In this section, we try to refute these arguments on scientific and philosophical grounds. In so far as we succeed, of course, we reopen the question of the extent to which human beings are unique and to what extent most human attributes are shared by animals and will be shared by machines.

24

When artificial intelligence became defined as a separate branch of endeavor in the late 1950s, there were many naïvely optimistic predictions as to how much human intelligence would not only be explained in principle but would actually be simulated on a computer within a mere ten years or so. Such naïve optimism led to a counterreaction as actual progress, interesting though it might have been, fell far short. Perhaps the most trenchant critic of that early optimism was Hubert Dreyfus, who wrote the book *What Computers Can't Do* (1972); we argue, however, that many of Dreyfus's arguments demonstrate "What Computers Can't Do Yet." The claim is *not* that computers as currently programmed are intelligent in a human way, but that such computers exhibit aspects of intelligence and that the end to progress is not in sight.

One of the most telling analogies that Dreyfus made was that AI is in the position of a man climbing a tree and claiming he was on his way to the moon: he argued that AI is unable, in principle, to give us the intellectual equivalent of the moon. Unfortunately, Dreyfus's arguments seem to turn on observing that certain things are very difficult or complicated. Then, rather than saying that because of this it may take a long time to bridge the gap, Dreyfus asserts that there is no way of closing the gap at all. To see the problems with this argument, recall the anecdote of Galileo's dropping weights from the leaning tower of Pisa to disprove the Aristotelian notion that the heavier the object, the faster it would fall. It would be an equally compelling caricature to that offered by Dreyfus to say that Galileo was dropping weights from the tower of Pisa to help us to get to the moon. But, in giving us a better understanding of the laws of motion, Galileo helped us understand the dynamic laws that hold the moon in orbit around the Earth and that would govern the path of a spaceship. Of course, we know now that it took 300 years to go from Galileo's understanding of the motion to the actual implementation.

Artificial intelligence has not yet achieved the intellectual clarity of the Galilean or Newtonian revolution, nor have we proved it can. But the study of artificial intelligence should not be seen as a closed system. It is not limited to the study of heuristic search or backtracking or ATN's or any of the particular technicalities that dominate its study today. Rather, it is the beginning of a conscious attempt to understand how complex symbol systems, including numerical systems, can interact with one another so information can be processed, stored, updated, and modified in diverse ways. However, while we disagree with Dreyfus as to whether a computer could be intelligent, we agree that much of *human* intelligence depends on having a human body and belonging to a human society. We return to this notion of the *essentially embodied self* in Section 2.3. First, we look at an essay by John Searle to see why intelligence per se may not be limited to an embodied self.

Searle (1980) chose the work of Roger Schank (see, e.g., Schank & Abelson 1977) as the focus for his critique of "strong AI" – the claim that AI programs really could exhibit understanding or intelligence, rather than simply simulate aspects of behaviors we construe as intelligent when performed by a human being (weak AI). Schank programmed a computer with "scripts" embodying general knowledge about some limited domain of experience. The program enabled the computer to answer questions about stories related to this domain, even when the story did not contain the explicit answer to the given question – using the script to "fill in the gaps." Searle's critique that such a program "really" understands appears convincing at first sight. He imagines that Schank's "script," "story," and "questions" are not given in suitably coded form to a computer that manipulates them by a control program to provide "answers" but are instead given in Chinese to a person who understands only English and who follows instructions (analogous to the computer's control program) to produce Chinese characters that are to count as the answer. Searle tries to convince us that the Anglophone's symbol manipulations are completely analogous to those performed by Schank's computer; and that just as the person does not understand the meaning of the questions or answers, so the computer does not "understand" them either.

Searle argues that his "Chinese box" example shows that not the slightest reason has been given to suppose that Schank's program is even "part of the story" of understanding. He claims that "as long as the program is defined in terms of computational operations on purely formally defined elements, what the example suggests is that these elements by themselves have no interesting connection with understanding." Searle has been injudicious in his choice of words, for he has allowed a critique of strong AI to become a critique of weak AI or even of cognitive psychology in general. For example, this argument could be used to support a claim that Chomsky's transformational grammar (see Lyons 1977, for an overview) is not even part of a theory of language since, for example, an English speaker could carry out formal parsing operations according to a transformational grammar for Chinese without understanding the Chinese language. Even though we do not share Chomsky's emphasis on syntactic competence, it still seems clear that this adaptation of Searle's "Chinese box" example does not invalidate the claim of Chomsky's work to be part of the theory of language. In the same way, we might argue that, by giving a theory of how general knowledge might be organized so use of it can fill lacunae in a story, Schank does provide "part of the story" of understanding. In any case, whether it does is an empirical issue for psychologists to address and cannot be simply dismissed out of hand on general philosophical grounds. In the next section, we begin to explore some dimensions of understanding that Schank's approach excludes.

The requirements of a science of intentionality

Searle claims that the formal manipulation of symbols is not the essence or interesting part of "understanding." His arguments, if taken literally, seem to rule out any hope for a neuropsychology of cognitive capacities. He states that "Whatever formal principles you put into the computer they will not be *sufficient* for understanding since a human will be able to follow the formal principles without understanding anything" (our italics). But one might just as well conclude that "People do not understand by virtue of the function of their brains" on the basis that "Whatever neural networks you simulate on a computer they will not be sufficient for understanding since a human being will be able to follow the formal principles without understanding anything." What, then, are the extra features one requires for a sufficient theory of understanding? Searle does not ask for any nonmaterial mind or soul; indeed, he adopts a wholly physicalist view of the mind. He accepts without discussion positions that have been at the center of the debate within the philosophy of mind: "We are able to think because we have brains," and even "A digital computer could think since we are the instantiations of any number of computer programs [whatever that means!] and we can think."

Searle's view is indeed that *only* a machine could think or exhibit intentional behavior and that thinking can only be done by special kinds of machines, namely, "brains, and machines that had the same causal powers as brains." However, his subsequent analysis weakens rather than strengthens these physicalist positions because it tends to show that *no* machine could think. His approach is dogmatic; he does not begin to provide criteria for telling of a given machine if it thinks, nor does he define what it means for two machines to have the "same causal powers" as each other. A plausible definition would say that two machines have the same causal powers as each other if they exhibit the same input–output behavior – and, in that case, a computer with video input and motor output should, in principle, be able to exhibit intelligent behavior even if its internal workings are little related to the cell–circuit–synapse level of neural analysis. In this connection, there seems no force in Searle's argument that AI has had little to tell us about thinking since it is about programs and not machines – for a program is a way of representing machines. It is like saying that Newton's *Principia* has had little to tell us about motion since it is about conic sections, and conic sections do not move.

Searle seems to think that the realization of a program for thinking must be in a certain kind of hardware. He asserts that "Intentionality is a biological phenomenon and it is as likely to be as dependent on the specific biochemistry of its origins as lactation, photosynthesis or any other biological phenomenon." He dismisses what he calls "a deep and abiding dualism" – the supposition that "mind . . . is a matter of formal processes in the way that milk and sugar are not." That is, it is not the formal complexity of its program that distinguishes a cognitive from a noncognitive machine, but the structure of its biochemistry. Searle forgets that milk can also be characterized "intentionally" as "a white fluid expressed from the body of a female mammal for the nutrition of her offspring." Here, the radical scientific step is to say that there would be a biochemical synthesis that produces a substance to which the word "milk" applies. Involved here are two descriptions, one in nonbiochemical language, and one in biochemical terms. They are equivalent in that they both describe "milk." Not every concept admits an equivalence. For example, there is no interesting sense in which the concept of "chair" is dependent on specific biochemistry, yet chairs are best characterized in terms of "sitting," which is both an "intentional" and "biological" phenomenon.

To assess Searle's claims fully, then, we need a nonbiochemical definition of intentionality and an analysis of what in the definition seems to invite biochemical redefinition. Searle defines "intentionality as that feature of certain mental states by which they are directed at or about objects and states of affairs in the world. Thus, beliefs, desires, and intentions are intentional states; undirected forms of anxiety and depression are not." Thus, it seems, intentions are to be characterized in a high-level descriptive vocabulary far removed from the level of neural circuitry or its chemical substrate. It can thus be argued that the language of AI may be better suited for exhibiting the true nature of intentionality than the language of biochemistry. This does not deny that biochemical details will play a major part in unraveling the neural instantiation of intentionality – we know that food and drugs and health can drastically alter our mental state. Nonetheless, it still seems that the question, "Must an intentional system be biochemical?" is an empirical question we expect to be answered in the negative; it is not a philosophical question that can now be answered in the affirmative. Is Searle's assertion that "No program by itself [without a brain-like instantiation] is sufficient for intentionality" any better supported than the long-since discredited claim that "no inanimate chemical synthesis by itself is sufficient to produce an organic substance"?

Sometimes, a simulation is the real thing

Presumably, "weak" AI, cognitive psychology, and certain approaches to brain theory seek to design programs that *simulate* the mental while remaining agnostic as to whether such programs *exhibit* the mental. We incline to the view that programs can in principle exhibit the mental – but not yet to a great degree. Here, we want simply to weaken Searle's claim that a program cannot exhibit the mental. To do this, we must disentangle a model or simulation from what it models. Certainly, a simulation should not in general be elided with what it represents – one cannot drink the output of a computer printing out a symbolic simulation of the biochemical synthesis of milk. But we must not fall into the trap of falsely inferring that a simulation of an X system can never itself be an X system.

Clearly, a set of differential equations can model motion but not exhibit motion. Yet, machines can be built that can move of themselves. In other words, a simulation *may* or *may not* exhibit the property it is designed to simulate. Searle claims to be showing that we cannot design programs that *exhibit* thought, yet his arguments time and again can be read as equally strongly in support of the claim that we cannot *model* thought at all – and this realization that he has gone too far makes the force of the original argument suspect.

In Section 4.1 we analyze Sperry's view (an example of what Searle calls a "modified dualism") that what is specifically mental about the mind has no intrinsic connection with the actual properties of the brain. Certainly, some computer programs do exhibit (not just simulate) stereopsis, and stereopsis is part of visual perception, which is itself a component of human understanding. We thus assert that a program (when run on a machine, of course) can exhibit certain aspects of understanding and that no good arguments have yet been given that limit the extent of such understanding; but we in no way deny that the exact style of understanding exhibited by human brains may depend on the biochemistry and other evolutionary characteristics of the circuitry.

The evolution of complexity

A familiar paradox goes as follows: "The number 0 is small. If n is a small number, then so, too, is $n + 1$. Therefore, all numbers are small." A dualist might give a similar argument against intelligence for any living creature, thus inferring that mind must be *added* to matter: "An amoeba obviously cannot think. If an n-celled creature cannot think, adding a single cell will make no difference. Then certainly no multicellular creature can think unless some nonmaterial mind is added to the biological substrate." Searle, in fact, accepts that multicellular creatures can think by virtue of their biological properties. He does not see that there is anything to be explained here. But a neuroscientist might ask how to characterize thought in such a way that one could tell of an organism whether it thinks – evolution undoubtedly produced thinking organisms from those that do not think. If the debates of biologists over a definition of "life" are any guide, neuroscience will not converge on any hard-and-fast rule for telling if a given neural net (in the biological, rather than simulation, sense) can "support thought." Rather, the cellular basis of more and more "aspects" of thought will become understood. Now, let us try to recast Searle's argument in the same way. "It seems impossible to believe that a program such as Schank's itself exhibits (simulates) understanding if we can carry out the operation of the program as a symbol-manipulation task without ourselves understanding what the symbols represent and thus what the task is. Adding a few lines of code (or a video input; or a motor output; or . . .) cannot give intelligence to an unintelligent system. Therefore, we cannot hope to program a computer to exhibit understanding."

Our point here is not to claim that Schank's program "understands." Rather, it is to say that even if we accept Searle's contention that it does not understand, we should not accept the broader case against "strong AI" that Searle builds from the initial "Chinese box" example. The overly bold claims of many workers in AI and Searle's wholesale indiscriminate rejection of all such claims now *and in the future* both stem from a lack of evolutionary perspective. That current AI systems exhibit *limited* aspects of mental activity does not justify the claim that they already exhibit "understanding" in anything like the full range of nuances the word carries in everyday use or in philosophical analysis. But neither do the limitations of current programs justify Searle's claim that an unbridgeable gap exists between programs that can be written for computers and the functioning of brains.

2.2 Gödel's incompleteness theorem

In this section we weaken another attack on the claims for the potential of AI by showing that the use of Gödel's incompleteness theorem for a proof of "nonintelligence" of mechanisms is based on an inadequate concept of mechanism. Basically, we see that a machine that merely proves theorems is not adequate even as a caricature of the human mind in action, but that other types of machines are more mindlike in their operation.

Descartes based his epistemology on "clear and distinct ideas," making clarity a virtue in itself. But the concepts with which we "get a handle on" reality are, in most cases, inherently ill-defined at the edges. Again, the model of decision making we get from mathematics and formal logic is based on the notion of proceeding from unequivocal facts (axioms) by rigorous argument (applying rules of inference) to obtain statements whose truth is unarguable, being inherited from the axioms. However, mathematicians work with concepts abstracted from reality (e.g., the line of no thickness), and may take decades to establish a particular theorem. By contrast, human beings must usually make time-limited decisions, working with incomplete and often inconsistent information.

Note that we are *not* denying the utility of logic, only the universality of that logic. Consider the argument that "If A or B is true but A is false, then B is true." There are many situations in which this logic works: Given that "I leave my sunglasses in the kitchen or the bedroom" and that "I've checked the kitchen, and they're not there," we may conclude, "They are in the bedroom." The practical conclusion is to search in the bedroom. If I cannot find the sunglasses there, I do not abandon the utility of logic (though, in the history of mathematics, there may be *changes* in logic, as in the adoption, but only by a few mathematicians, of intuitionistic logic). Rather, I doubt my premises. Perhaps I didn't look carefully enough in the kitchen or the bedroom. But if a new search fails, I had better try to reconstruct the scene when I last wore my sunglasses to hypothesize some place other than kitchen or bedroom where I left my sunglasses on the last occasion. Finding them may not change my heuristic of "kitchen or bedroom," though memory of this specific event may ease the search next time my sunglasses are misplaced. The point is that this overall process of successful search uses processes, like analogy and visual reasoning, that are not part of a closed chain of logical inference from a given set of axioms.

Science has discovered that there are experimental situations in which a few laws, coupled with logic, can yield predictions of uncanny accuracy. Engineering has shown that even outside the laboratory are cases in which these scientific laws can yield practical estimates of how something will perform. The whole problem of quality control is to learn about, and then find ways to limit, situations that can cause the product to differ from the theoretically prescribed set of alternatives. A good maintenance manual attempts to catalog and provide the remedy for departures from the norm. But, as anyone who owns a car knows, this list does not address all that can go wrong. Incidentally, note that when we say "all that can go wrong," we are already bringing the terminology of norms and values into the quasi-scientific discourse of engineering. The machine has prescribed ways of performing: if it does not conform, it has "gone wrong," and we take steps to modify it back to conformity. If we cannot repair it, we throw it away. These are interesting points to bear in mind when considering the implications of comparing people to machines.

But to return to the story of the missing sunglasses: The conclusion is not to deny the importance of reason. In fact, the reaction described to the unexpected absence of the sunglasses from their usual place was a rational one – as distinct from, say, an outburst of rage at "those damned sunglasses" for deliberately hiding. Rational behavior is not to be seen as identical with a process that accepts a few statements as incontrovertibly true and then institutes a purely deductive procedure to find the answer to what is at hand. Rather, we continually work with a partial understanding of a situation, perhaps only a partial idea of our goals, and use whatever is at our disposal (not necessarily consciously) to determine how to act – be it rational argument, some well-rehearsed routines (schemas) for dealing with the situation, or unconscious "hunches." In many cases, our expectations are confirmed and we go smoothly about our task. In other cases, we are forced to explore until we hit on the solution, or we may change our mind; or we may continue until exasperation or fatigue closes off the enterprise.

With these considerations in mind, we can re-examine an argument, based on mathematical logic, that some philosophers (e.g., Lucas 1961) claim demonstrates that machines cannot be intelligent. We shall come to see things in a rather different light.

Gödel's incompleteness theorem (Gödel 1931) states that any adequate consistent mathematical logic is incomplete: if the logic is *adequate* to express a full range of arithmetical statements and *consistent* in that it does not allow the deduction of any contradictions, then it is *incomplete* in that there are true statements about arithmetic that can be neither proved nor disproved using the axioms and rules of that logic. (For more accessible proofs of Gödel's theorem, see Nagel and Newman 1958 or Arbib 1964.) A human being does not behave like a machine, embodying a mathematical logic, enouncing just those statements that can be obtained by applying given rules of inference to a given set of axioms. However, neither are machines limited to finding results in this way, and so Gödel's incompleteness theorem does not imply the answer "No" to the questions, "Is a person a machine?" or "Could a machine be intelligent?" Let us examine this further by considering a machine which, though still restricted, unrealistically, to analyzing well-formed formulas in a logical language, is now required, given such a formula, to print out "yes" or "no" within limited time to the question of whether the formula is a theorem, given certain axioms and rules of inference.

Gödel's theorem implies that a machine that *only gives correct answers* must fail to answer certain questions – it will be incomplete. But, as the real world does to a human being, we have imposed a time limit, within which the machine must deliver an answer "yes" or "no." In the human world, not to act is itself a decision. By forcing the machine always to reach a decision, we have in effect changed the rules of inference, for example, by adding to the rules a running confidence level evaluator and having the machine choose that answer, "yes" or "no," that is more highly evaluated when the time is up, unless a complete proof has already yielded the answer. The new "logic" embodied in this machine is now complete – every question must receive an answer – so Gödel's theorem tells us that the logic must be inconsistent. In other words, time pressures guarantee that mistakes will be made. This is hardly a result that separates person from machine!

Next, let us modify our machine somewhat further to give us insight into learning machines. When mathematicians have proved a theorem, they thenceforth treat it as if it were an axiom, that is, as a truth from which other truths may be derived. Imagine that our machine is similarly equipped to add to its "data base" statements it has evaluated to be true. Imagine, also, that its evaluations may have effects on the external world, such as the execution of an action whose appropriateness is asserted by the statement just "verified." In some cases, no adverse consequences will follow, and so the assertion of the correctness of the action will appear to be confirmed. But if there are adverse consequences, the statement should be removed from the data base. But is this enough? Is it only the time constraint that led to the incorrect evaluation or the consequence of false statements having entered the data base earlier? If the latter, and if many statements were invoked in the "proof" of the assertion just rejected, how are we to "assign blame" to weed the data base? These considerations, all in the context of formal statements that are unequivocally true or false, point up some difficulties that must be faced by people – or machines – in forming their own "construction of reality."

Human beings do not live by rigorous arguments, but rather make decisions that seem plausible, living within a net of "elastic" entailments and continual interaction with their environment. Particular situations may force us to question specific entailments and change accordingly, but there is no guarantee that this will be for the better. As an example of the dilemmas posed by nonformal systems, consider these beliefs when faced with the staggering news that "Ron is a murderer.": "I must do everything possible to protect someone I love"; "I must tell the police of anyone I know to be a murderer"; and "I love Ron." Does this entail that I should or should not report Ron to the police? or that I should stop loving Ron? or that protecting a murderer exceeds the bounds of the possible? Faced with this agonizing situation, I may have to change my concepts of "love" and "possibility"; or accept my inconsistency; or repress some knowledge to protect other cherished beliefs, banishing the thought that Ron is a murderer, or the memory of the events that led me to that conclusion, from consciousness. This simple analysis forces us to consider both the inherent plasticity of meaning, taken up in our discussion of "Language as Metaphor" in Chapter 7, as well as the Freudian themes to which we turn in Chapter 6.

We have seen that our decisions will, almost inevitably, be inconsistent taken as a whole. Certain relatively coherent and well-rehearsed domains will, of course, be "almost" free from contradictions. (We can avoid much inconsistency by regimenting our lives to the point at which we seldom face decisions of any great moment, so that "real-time decision making" poses no restriction. The meek shall inherit the consistency.) Given more time, we can seek more data, consider more alternatives, and thus extend the network of consistency (where we now use consistency in the sense of avoiding situations in which we seem to have compelling grounds both for and against a given course of action). Mathematics is the limiting case in which time restrictions are removed. But even here, in the actual work of the mathematician, mistakes can be made, with subtleties omitted from a proof or intuitions overriding a fatal flaw in a logical argument.

Our everyday beliefs do not differ from mathematics only in the time constraints that attend their formation or application, nor in the fuzziness (limitation of consensus as to applicability) that attends them. Perhaps even more important is that a belief is not possessed of a simple binary indicator, "true" or "false." Rather (and this is reflected in the notion of activation level in the schema theory of the next chapter), a belief may be more or less strongly held, and this "degree of belief" will vary with the circumstance. "Thou shalt not kill" holds strongly in the form "Thou shalt not kill human beings" for most of us unless we are in a situation of war or self-defense, but it does not prevent the carnivorous from ignoring the call of vegetarianism. There have been attempts to develop logics of belief in which each assertion is assigned a "degree of rational belief," the odds an omniscient gambler would take against an ingenious opponent with exactly the same information. However, just as Gödel's theorem blocks us from correctly evaluating the truth of all statements in a formal system, so it is that we, in finite time, cannot come up with exact degrees of rational belief. Still, theories of learning and of evolution can address ways that may (but cannot always) improve the odds of success or survival.

Our analysis of human belief systems in later chapters take us even further from the domain of mathematical logic, for such systems do not consist of a set of simple declarative sentences. For one thing, we now argue that human sensibility is essentially embodied. For another, to deal with agonizing questions rationally (by no means the only option), a person has to have more than a grab bag of disconnected beliefs but a (reasonably well) articulated system in which apparent clashes on one level may be resolved at a higher level.

In all this, we see cognitive science not as reducing human beings to the level of current AI programs but rather as open-ended, expanding in response to critiques of the limitations of our current understanding of mind and person.

2.3 From semantic nets to embodied selves

The concurrent emergence of computer technology and cognitive science requires an immense effort of philosophical imagination if they are not to lead to yet another massive tragedy in human experience. It is here that humanity's self-understanding will be forged for the coming age. Our new technology allows us to make massive changes in workplace, social structure, and self-image. With what do we structure this endless array of choices? AI is still struggling with problems in search, language understanding, and vision, and so its practitioners cannot program into their computers a full measure of what real human beings might be (even if that is possible, *pace* Dreyfus). But human self-understanding is so plastic that it is not impossible that people might view themselves as AI must currently model them – and *then* what would we have lost?

For example, emotion is not just an appendage to the brain composed of a few simple elements such as love and compassion (good) and hate (bad). In confronting the work of Freud (Chapter 6), we try to counteract the naïve view that the computational aspects of the brain are in principle separable from the emotional ones. It is precisely this separation we want to deny – think of the passion that even the most cerebral scientists bring to the life of the mind, the interweaving of mind and feeling. We repeatedly confront cognitive science with the human sciences and with "person–reality" to chart the challenges to extending cognitive science to do justice to our humanity, rather than reducing our humanity to simple semantic nets.

Our defense of the *potential* of AI does not mean that we hold that the *current* methodology of AI or cognitive science is adequate as an epistemology on which to base our approach to theology. In this section, we turn to a more critical view of artificial intelligence, focusing on the distinction between "experiential knowledge" and its "symbolic encoding."

To relate the contributions of AI to our broader quest, we must emphasize not the program but the *person*. People interact with other people, in their idiosyncratic, deviant, imaginative, and social aspects. Society is thus in some sense an artifact – a secondary creation out of certain commonalities in some of these interactions. However, we do see society as coming to constitute a reality, even though constituted in this way (Chapter 7 and following chapters). To understand the quality of life (to have meaningful ethical schemas), we have to take seriously the question of what it means to be human, which means that we cannot treat people as mere data-processing machines. When Shylock affirms his humanity, he says:

Hath not a Jew eyes? Hath not a Jew hands, organs, dimensions, senses, affections, passions? fed with the same food, hurt with the same weapons, subject to the same diseases, healed by the same means, warmed and cooled by the same winter and summer, as a Christian is? If you prick us, do we not bleed? if you tickle us, do we not laugh? If you poison us, do we not die? And if you wrong us, shall we not revenge? (Shakespeare, *The Merchant of Venice*, Act 3, Scene 1)

This is the person–reality in which our construction of reality is rooted. It is his *experience* that makes Shylock human. He shares much of this with animals, but is distinguished by his conscious knowledge of much of this experience.

By two, a child has a personality, which means that information will be screened, modified, sometimes rejected, to fit in with the information she already has. Different information will be differently processed. For example, if you tell her "That's not a cow, it's a horse," she will probably have no trouble revising schemas for the horse picture. If she has already got set in her head that she herself (a big part, after all, of the universe she is modelling) is a dirty, wretched, worthless object, you will not find there is much data from reality that will change her mind about this statement. In between, there are thousands of degrees of modification, rejection, and acceptance of world information that change the data received by the person – that is the schema the child makes it. The child has intentions and does not swallow whole whatever society tells her. The symbol system is embodied in individual schemas as well as for social artifacts.

People carry in their heads what appears to them to be a total model of the universe because what they have no information about they fill in from their world modelling. Starting from their current picture of the world, when confronted with something new they "tell a story" to fit the new data. In some cases, then, most of this new schema assemblage is imaginary, peculiar to each individual, and to the world view already in place. What we already know provides the "equipment" through which we incorporate new data. One has not only experiences of the outside world (and long before she learns to talk, the child may be extraordinarily and irreversibly sensitive to signals from the world around her) but she inhabits a body that is in a constant state of experience from within as well as without.

This highly personal network has a coherence; it is this coherence we call the self. A self seems to be something that develops in a sentient being, able to reflect on personal experience. Our selves are not equally coherent any more than we are equally sensitive to experience or adept at reflecting on it, but everyone is conscious of being and having a self. Let us contrast our everyday concepts of persons and selves with AI approaches to representing knowledge.

Consider, first, our use of the dictionary. If we encounter an unfamiliar word, we can look in the dictionary to find out what it means. But in what sense? Understanding the definition requires knowledge of how the structures of sentences can bear meaning and also that we be familiar with the words that comprise it. If we are not familiar with those words, we must look them up in turn. If this process continues, words already looked up may recur in later definitions, but our search usually stops within a few definitions, when we have seen enough words with which we are already familiar to give us a workable understanding of the word that started it all; workable, that is, in allowing us to continue with our reading or conversation with a sufficient approximation to the local meaning so as not to overly distort our global progress.

The dictionary, then, is a closed device. We can only escape from this net of words if we have acquired knowledge that is not in the dictionary – if finally seeing the word *cat,* we can think of cats we have seen; or seeing the word *run,* we can remember what it is like to run or to watch someone else running. It is a great achievement of the dictionary makers to encapsulate so much of what we can do with words within the pages of their books; yet no dictionary will ever, by words alone, enable a person without any knowledge of the language for which the dictionary was written to pick up the dictionary and from it learn the word meanings of that language. Only because we have certain pointers out into the world of experience is the dictionary worthwhile.

The analog of the dictionary in artificial intelligence is the semantic net or some other form of data base or knowledge representation (see, e.g., Bobrow & Collins 1975). In one form of such a network, the nodes correspond to words in the dictionary, and the edges provide linkages between those nodes such that starting from any node we may come to understand the place of that node whether it is in the long-term body of knowledge, such as is represented in a dictionary, or purely contextual knowledge corresponding to the current sentence in a book or conversation or the "scripts" discussed in Section 2.1. Such a network has certain advantages over the dictionary because it is explicitly coded in a form that allows it to be stored within a computer. A sophisticated AI program could be designed to keep track of the word senses a specific user had already comprehended, and then, when the user looks for the definition of a new word, the program would automatically configure a definition based on the known words. This program would exhibit considerable "skill" and "intelligence" not simply in tracing through a tree of definitions but also in then editing the definitions to use only the vocabulary with which the user starts, rather than requiring the user to assimilate the definitions of all the words along the way.

The work of artificial intelligence on the construction of semantic nets and the programs to use them is still at an early stage. Currently, a semantic net may contain just a few hundred nodes. We may say that most of the understanding is still in the brain of the human being who interacts with this machine, even though some people would concede a measure of intelligence to a system if it could assemble the answers to questions in a satisfactory way.

Yet, despite its partial intelligence, an AI question-answering system does not know what a book or table is when it responds to the question "Where is the book?" with the answer "The book is on the table." As we have suggested in the face of Searle's critique (Section 2.1), we begin to close the gap if we use machine vision, programming a computer to take a television image and determine whether the picture is that of a table or of a book. Yet, we might insist that pattern recognition does not constitute understanding, and that you do not really understand the concept of a book unless you know how to pick it up, scan a page, and on the basis of scanning that page extract the information printed there. Notice a certain paradox here: we have written our argument in words, and these sentences could have been generated by a computer equipped with a sufficiently rich semantic network. Nonetheless, we argue that the ability to generate strings of words from an associative network does not constitute understanding unless that network is firmly based in some form of experience, and that we feel cheated if we are told that the experience is that of the programmer rather than that of the machine itself. We are not quite out of the woods of paradox yet, though – a virtue of language is that we can teach our children about lions and war without their ever having to experience them directly; this ability to live vicariously is one of the greatest powers, sometimes for good, sometimes for evil, that language has for us.

In summary, it does seem that our full concept of understanding requires a rich pattern of interaction with the world rather than the hermetically closed loops of the dictionary or the semantic network. Our aim, in the next two chapters, is to build a schema theory that applies AI techniques to analyze the knowledge of an organism which is *embodied* (and recall Vesey's *The Embodied Mind* 1965) and whose existence is defined within a cycle of continual action and perception. We say much more of the social dimension in later chapters. In any case, the notion of *essentially embodied subject* aspires to break the dualisms of mind/body, mind/brain, subject/object, materialism/idealism, self/other, and fact/value. It holds these dualisms to be untenable.

Dreyfus seems to endorse some form of this Heideggerian view of the essentially embodied subject. It is not contingent that the mind or soul is in the body. It is not an immaterial substance that could be detached from the body without change. It is bound up with the character of our embodiment. The fact that we can walk and run and can perceive the world through a variety of senses is crucial to the form that perception assumes. The percept has built into it an understanding of other viewpoints and experiences. This understanding allows us to constitute objects in terms of the available repertoire of our sensory–motor interactions. Our schemas depend on the particular nature of our embodiment. Certainly, our Piagetian analysis (Section 3.1) sees sensori–motor schemas as providing a crucial substrate – though by no means a complete determinant – for later cognitive development. We need some biological basis for our knowledge, yes, but we build on that by mental processes, conditioned by a highly evolved social structure, so that the final shape of our knowledge and behavior may have relatively little genetic determination. Because of such processes of abstraction, studies of "pure" AI may still be relevant to cognitive science. Playing chess or proving mathematical theorems both require real intelligence, but that intelligence is of a symbol-manipulating kind, and therefore a system that manipulates symbols should be able to partake of intelligence, even if it has no body in a human sense. Moreover, we do not take the argument for embodiment as a claim against the potential contributions of AI, for we see robotics as an increasingly central area of AI (cf. Arbib, Overton, & Lawton 1984; and Iberall & Lyons 1984). Our point is not to belittle current AI but rather to chart patterns of change, for change it must to contribute fully to a cognitive science capable of yielding deep insights into the human condition.

Concepts certainly depend on one's repertoire of behavior. If A works with fabrics, he may have a subtlety of color use terms denied to B; or if A is a keen gardener, he may use words B does not have or uses differently. Yet B can speak enough of flowers and shapes and colors for A to explain his terminology, which B may then come to learn or, maintaining his indifference to gardening, may continue to ignore. In some cases, the differences may be so great, yet so tied up with what is important to both parties, that they can lead to the breakup of a friendship; or, proving its efficacy, the new concept can establish itself and lead to a major conceptual restructuring. But (recall our discussion of observation language in Chapter 1), there must be enough in common for the participants to recognize both the differences and their importance. Our conceptual disagreements with someone from another culture have little effect, emotional or conceptual, if we cannot communicate even at the level of action. Even if one does not come to accomodate these new schemas, we may become more self-conscious of our own beliefs and how they are supported.

Our bodily structure, for example, leads us to regard up and front as superior (note the word!) to down and back and thus lays the basis for our use of metaphors. We argue in Chapter 7 that metaphors are crucial for language. The nature of our embodiment helps us create the metaphors through which we organize multiple experiences (cf. von Uexkull 1921, on the "worlds" of different animals; and our own studies [Arbib 1982b] of frog brains that make essential use of the animal's ethological repertoire). The fact that essentially embodied selves are born, mature in dependent relations, and die gives us a temporal experience that leads us to view ourselves in terms of a past and a future. We each build a notion of self from the notion of being the same person today as yesterday. Our capacity for purposeful action lays the basis for the relation between thought and action and gives a certain practical character to our thought. Human thought is not purely abstract, but is a mode of praxis. There is no pure cognition because we are essentially embodied. Our thought enters into, and helps constitute, our actions, emotions, and desires. To come to terms with the thinking subject is to come to terms with the actions and practices its thoughts are implicated in.

The theory of the embodied subject claims to transcend mind/body dualism, but its proponents have not coherently articulated this unity. Talk of human beings as responsible agents does not articulate well with the concepts of natural science; we confront this problem in our discussion of free will and responsibility in Chapter 5. Hegel tried to close the gap between cause and effect and human agents arguing rationally with each other by a philosophy of nature that is quite coherent but that we can no longer accept because of its essential teleology. Most attempts since have sought a reduction to one mode or the other. The challenge to schema theory, then, is to develop a single set of categories to articulate our experience of ourselves as essentially embodied subjects, the physical preconditions for forming our beliefs and appraising those beliefs. How do we reconcile our understanding of mechanism with the categories of self? We swim in a sea of preconceptions, only part of which we may come to make explicit.

In later sections, we address some of these issues in a schema-theoretic analysis of Freudian theory. To begin to *approximate* what is involved, one might imagine the construction of "The Jane Austen Semantic Net." If we can take the work of hundreds of commentators and distill the nuances they have perceived in Austen's plotting of our human foibles and sensibilities, we might begin to say we have a more formal appreciation of some of these complex human emotions. And yet no matter how expert the computer equipped with such a semantic net might become in the hermeneutics of generating its own fine variations on themes suggested by paragraphs of a book, we will still not say it understands what love or hate is without the body's tingling. Perhaps in the same way we should say we really do not understand some of the subtleties of electronic computation because we do not have the bodies of computers!

When humanists analyze literature, they can appeal to shared meanings rather than having to appeal to explicit formal representations of the kind to which artificial intelligence aspires; and in so doing, they may appeal to meanings not shared after all, so that each reader of the original book as well as each reader of the critique comes away with a somewhat different meaning (as we see in our later discussion of the metaphorical character of language in Chapter 7). For one reader, love may have been a blissful experience; for another, a bitter one. And so, when humanists use emotive words to appeal to the knowledge of the human listener, they may evoke a far richer spectrum than they could get from any semantic network we can imagine being programmed in this century. On the other hand, however, the humanists may not have the precision of reference to which they aspire because of the diversity of experiences they evoke. For example, the swastika has long been a powerful religious symbol. To someone who has not seen it before, it might simply be a cross with bent arms. When Rudyard Kipling published a uniform edition of his works in the 1920s, he used the swastika as a symbol of good luck on the covers. Yet, for most of us today, this simple geometric design cannot be seen without a flood of associations with the human capacity for evil.

Again, one can certainly code music in terms of the notes of the score, and a computer programmed with a suitable semantic net could retrieve the name of the song or anything else that might appear in a musical encyclopedia. But when we listen to that music, it may evoke many memories that have little to do with the sequence of notes. It may be that the sound of one particular instrument evokes a performance by a gifted player of a completely different work, leading us to remember our life in a distant town of many years ago. Or, it might be that the rhythm evokes a certain memory of moving on the dance floor with someone we have not thought of for a long time. Even though each of these different aspects could be coded into a semantic network, it is implausible to expect a semantic network to be constructed containing all the knowledge of any one person rather than a sampling of the type of knowledge that such a person might have. Yet, we cannot divorce the subtlety of the human condition from this richness not only of associations that can be coded at the symbolic level, but also of recollections tying back to our experiences in the real world.

We suspect that relatively little of these "knowledge structures" will be fully formalized in the near future and that the performance of individuals will depend on idiosyncracies that will be formalizable in principle but not, *a priori,* in practice. After the fact, we may reconstruct that a particularly novel approach to solving a problem depended on a chance remark overheard in a hotel bar in Copenhagen twenty years before; but the chances of such an item's being included beforehand in a workable model of an individual's

"Long-Term Memory" are negligible. However, this argument against complete representation does not diminish the importance of seeking an adequate formalism for the representation of knowledge and of developing computational models of how knowledge is used in planning. Linguists increasingly appreciate the need for an articulated model of the dictionary or lexicon for linguistic theory; the work of AI linguists on knowledge structures may be viewed as the development of an articulated model of the encyclopedia. The thrust of the schema theory we develop in the next chapter is to link these structures with "being in the world." In no case is completeness the criterion for progress.

3   Schema theory

Our task now is to develop a theory of human knowledge that makes contact with the AI concepts and the notion of the embodied subject of the previous chapter. We call this approach *schema theory,* and have already outlined its features in Section 1.3. We provide our view of the current shape of schema theory as a scientific discipline within cognitive science and also point to ways the theory must develop if we are to use it in addressing such issues as freedom, the person in society, and the possibilities of religious knowledge. We stress that schema theory is not a closed subject, nor is there any consensus as to what constitutes its current status. Even the notion of a "schema" as "intermediate functional entity" in cognitive processes is not fully delimited but will evolve with developments in cognitive science.

Our approach to schema theory denies language the primary role in cognition. True, with language "in place," we seek to understand its substrates, both within the human brain and in the social nexus. But when we take an evolutionary or developmental view, language is no longer primary. Even though as adults we are immersed in language, we seek to burst the bounds of language to construct a richer epistemology. Schema theory seeks to mediate between the billionsfold complexity of neurons and the thousandsfold complexity of words. We have to probe downwards to constrain schemas by brain-theoretic analysis of their neural instantiation and probe upward to constrain schemas by hypothesizing how they can mediate the individual's participation in the "holistic net" that constitutes the social reality of custom, language, and religion.

Schemas may represent objects, but many schemas may be better characterized as representing actions (such as, in the infant, grasping and suckling), with perceptual schemas serving to supply the parameters that afford the action. Moreover, just as one program may serve as a unit in the construction of a larger program, so may schemas be built from other schemas. Thus, schemas may be complex enough to represent persons (cf. Freud's notion of identification) or social situations or contexts (cf. Goffman's 1974 *Frame Analysis*). A schema may represent a skill, or it may represent an episode (crystallizing into what we call a schema assemblage) that can provide a reference point for future thought and action.

The next three sections accomplish the following: Section 3.1 analyzes Peirce's notion of a *habit* and Piaget's notion of a *scheme* (which we translate from the French as "schema") to show that our notion of a schema has roots in both philosophy and psychology. Section 3.2 then suggests how schemas may be used in modeling perception and control of movement in human, animal, and robot. These sections provide background for the schema-based models of language use and acquisition in Section 7.3. Our task in Section 3.3 is then to turn from schemas as components of cognitive science models to the schema as a driving concept in our philosophical analysis of the construction of reality, showing the consonance between a schema-based individual epistemology and the view of scientific knowledge advanced in Section 1.2. In some sense, then, only section 3.2 is about schema theory itself – Section 3.1 samples its precursors, and Section 3.3 initiates the discussions of its philosophical implications. The reader who wishes to evaluate the extent to which schema-based studies have begun to cohere into a genuine theory may turn to Arbib, Conklin, and Hill (1986) to see schema theory used in modeling language performance or to the forthcoming second edition of Arbib's *The Metaphorical Brain,* which thoroughly analyzes the use of schemas in modeling brain mechanisms of perception and action. In Chapter 4, we turn to the relationship of schema theory to neural mechanisms, thus introducing our Chapter 6 discussion of Freud as someone who "merged the horizons" of neurology and myth in extending our view of the human mind.

3.1 From Peirce to Piaget on learning and evolution

Our use of the word "schema" can be traced back to Head and Holmes (1911), who introduced the notion of the "body schema" into neurology. People with a parietal lobe lesion may ignore half of their body – not feeling pain in it, not even dressing it, since they do not see or feel it as part of the body (their own!) they are dressing. Conversely, an amputee may still have a phantom limb and speak of feeling the movements of the missing limb. This representation in the brain, this body schema, constructs these people's reality, making them extraordinarily resistant to discordant sensory data about the state of their bodies. This occurrence militates against a purely empiricist view of knowledge. Instead of thinking of ideas as impressions of sense data, we visualize an active and selective process of schema formation that in some sense constructs reality as much as it embodies it.

Bartlett, who had been a student of Head, transferred the idea of schema from neurology to experimental psychology. In his study of *Remembering* (Bartlett 1932), he noted that people do not passively remember stories ver-

batim but rather actively code them in terms of their schemas and then re-
count the stories by retranslating their schema assemblages into words.

Perhaps the most influential user of the word *schema* has been Piaget,
who, in Beth and Piaget (1966, p. 235), defines the *schema of an action* as
the structure of "the generalisable characteristics of this action, that is, those
which allow the repetition of the same action or its application to a new
content."

He offers a constructivist theory of knowledge (see, e.g., Piaget 1954, 1971).
The child builds up a basic repertoire of schemas (e.g., for grasping) through
his or her sensorimotor interactions with the world. These develop through
various stages until the child has schemas for abstract thought that are no
longer rooted in the sensorimotor particularities. (Early translations of Piaget
into English use the term *schema;* more recently, at Piaget's urging, the term
scheme for Piaget's French term *scheme* is used. Here, we use *schema* since
our aim is to assimilate Piaget's concepts, not to highlight differences between
various approaches to schema theory.)

The notion of schema is also related to Peirce's notion of a "habit," with
its connections between the individual and the social. Peirce held that there
is a strong analogy between the evolution of species and the evolution of
science. He used the term *habit* in a sense sufficiently general to cover the
hereditary action patterns of the individuals of a species; learned habits of
individuals; and the concepts, rules, methods, and procedures of social institutions. In science, the habits are the procedures and methods of inquiry
as well as the accepted theories. Burks (1980) observes that Peirce intended
his notion of habit to cover *any set of operative rules embodied in a system*.
It has the two characteristics essential to the construction of complex components by an evolutionary process – stability and adaptability. Thus,
Peircean habits are appropriate building blocks in a natural hierarchy.
Generalizations, laws, and theories established at one level become the background assumptions for those tested at the next level. For example, in conducting an experiment, scientists rely on the laws governing the apparatus.
Within the Peircean perspective, we can see that our concepts have developed
in a manner similar to the way our genetic programs have evolved. Concepts
and rules have been modified, compounded with other concepts and rules,
tested for their utility in helping us adjust to the environment, with the most
useful ones being retained at each stage. This modification, compounding
and testing is done at successive levels of the hierarchy, beginning with
common-sense concepts and generalizations, moving to scientific concepts
and causal laws, and on up to the concepts and theories of highly advanced
science.

Clearly, Peirce's notion of "habit" is designed to address the same task
as "schemas." The various authors have emphasized different aspects of the
problem, and their approaches are not always consistent. Nonetheless, each
author has much to offer to what we see as the evolving study of schema

theory. Both Peirce and Piaget emphasize the problems of evolution, learning, and induction – that is, of schema change in general. The specification of mechanisms of induction in any detail will provide a major meeting ground for cognitive science, philosophy of science, and the social sciences. For such a specification, we require both an account of learning machines themselves and a theory of the means of communication that enable a community to attain consensus as to a set of instances of a concept by a process of mutual verification.

As Burks (1979) notes, this learning-machine view provides a new translation of the rationalist–empiricist controversy (of renewed topicality with the debate between Piaget, as neo-empiricist, and Chomsky, as rationalist, reported in Piattelli-Palmarini 1980):

Let us call the basic structure of the central nervous system together with any program stored in it initially 'man's innate structure-program complex,' and let us assume some substantial correspondence between the operations of the human mind and the neural mechanisms of the central nervous system. . . . The rationalist would hold that certain specific innate concepts (e.g., space–time, cause and effect), rules (e.g., for grammar and inference), or principles (e.g., the uniformity of nature) exist in man's innate structure-program complex. The empiricist would hold that man's innate structure-program complex does not contain any such specific concepts, rules, or principles, but only a very general learning program.

Piaget adopts a constructivist view of mental development, with his schemas being the constructions that mediate and explain that development. He views himself as what might be called a "dynamic Kantian," where the categories are no longer *a priori* but change over time. Categories are constructed through the individual's experience; but yet – following Lorenz – Piaget sees that these constructions may to some extent be species-specific (cf. our discussion of embodiment-dependence in Section 2.3). The processes that underlie these constructions are innate. In the same vein, many of the constraints on linguistic structure that Chomsky views to be innate would be seen by Piaget to be capable of "constructive" explanation.

It must be stressed that Piaget's theory is, for the most part, informal, based on generalizations culled at the verbal level from accounts of children's mental development. Thus, the concepts that follow are not part of that cognitive science expressible in AI-like programs, but rather provide a preformal set of concepts from which such modeling may proceed. (We return to this issue in our study of language learning in Section 7.3.)

Piaget distinguishes four main stages of cognitive development: the sensory-motor, the pre-operational, the concrete operational, and the hypothetico-deductive or formal operational. He warns in (Beth and Piaget 1966, p. 246), that it would be a mistake to see the first two stages as proceeding purely by the coordination of actions that ignore all mechanisms of form. Even at these stages, schemas (which he sees as formal mechanisms – in the sense of mechanisms expressing certain general forms, not as formally defined mechanisms) are capable of assimilating new content, of conferring meaning on it by virtue of the schematic implications themselves, and entail kinds of practical implications that direct behavior.

Below, we discuss the process of reflective abstraction, which increasingly abstracts (yet does not separate) form from immediate sensorimotor content. For Piaget, however, the process of adaptation in cognitive development is composed of the inextricably intertwined processes of assimilation and accommodation: *assimilation* is the process whereby the data of the world are assimilated to currently available schemas, forming (in our terminology) a schema assemblage that is not merely a passive representation but an active process leading to activity and exploration within a structure of anticipations. To the extent that the structure of anticipations proves dissonant with consequent experience, there is grist for *accommodation*. Accommodation is the process whereby the individual's repertoire of schemas changes over time to reflect better other aspects of the world beyond those assimilable to current schemas. These processes can be conscious and linguistic, but need not be, and must be understood apart from language and consciousness.

Note that the processes of assimilation and accommodation include the conduct of science according to the pragmatic criterion. The scientist describes a situation in terms of an available observation language, applies theory to determine a course of action to achieve some stated criterion, and then compares the outcome with that criterion. If the outcome is satisfactory, no changes are required. But if there is a discrepancy, the cause must be located, be it in the observation language, the technique of observation, the underlying theory, the methods of applying theory to infer a course for action, or the actual execution of the action. We see what AI workers call the "assignment of credit problem" (Samuel 1959): when things go wrong in a complex process, to which components (or to which pattern of interaction between the components) must we assign the blame, and what changes are then appropriate? (Recall the related discussion for the "neo-Gödelian" learning machine of Section 2.2.)

For the scientist or the adult going about well-defined tasks, there may be explicit goal criteria. However, evolution is an example of adaptation for which we cannot say that the "actors," (here, species) have explicit criteria, such as "evolving into another species." Rather, the interaction of reproductive opportunities, phenotypic expression of genetic changes, and even happenstances of environmental regularity allow new species to stabilize – in the same "undirected" way we see neural pattern recognizers emerging "without a teacher." Similarly, much of our behavior is to be seen as "crystallizing" within a diverse flux of happenstance and evaluation – aesthetic, sensual, moral, personal, social, religious – rather than under a pragmatic criterion restricted to achieving an alteration of the state of the external world (describable in the available observation language). In social situations, the social rules themselves create the social data.

The child starts with schemas for basic homeostatic mechanisms, including breathing, eating, digesting and excreting, as well as certain basic sensorimotor schemas, such as suckling and grasping, and basic coordination of eye and hand movements. Note that objects are secondary to these primary schemas, and that schemas for (or employing) object permanence come later (cf. Freud on primary narcissism). Through assimilation and accommodation, a complex *schema network* arises that can mediate first the child's, and then the adult's reality. Processes change a *set* of *interdependent* schemas, so that each schema finds meaning only in relation to others. For example, a house is defined in terms of parts, such as a roof, yet a roof may be recognized because it is part of a house recognized on the basis of other criteria – all criteria enrich and are defined by the others (and may change when a formal linguistic system allows explicit [partial] definition).

How does a child come to know the world, both physical and social? This knowing involves both physical interactions and the child's presence within a social milieu. It may be a mistake for us to label some interactions as social and others as physical and expect these distinctions to be at all meaningful for the child. "Mother" is defined in terms of affective and nutritional relationships long before there is a concept of objects, let alone an object with distinguishing characteristics that let it be called "Mother." Our scholarly attempts to parcel knowledge into different categories may be a relatively late intellectualizing operation on a network of schemas in which many categorizations in fact "bleed" into each other. Moreover, Trevarthen (1982) argues that the human brain has systems that integrate interpersonal and practical areas together from the first few months after birth.

As we have mentioned, Piaget traces the child's cognitive development through a sequence of stages. Piaget describes the process of reflective abstraction whereby these successive stages are obtained in the following words (Beth & Piaget 1966, p. 242):

Expressed schematically, the process [of reflective abstraction] which characterizes [the transition from concrete to hypothetico-deductive operations] is, in effect, reduced to this:

a. In order to build a more abstract and general structure from a more concrete and particular structure, it is first of all necessary to abstract certain operational relationships from the antecedent structure, so as to generalize them in the later one;

b. But both this abstraction and generalization presuppose that the relationships thus abstracted should be *"reflected"* (in the true sense) on a new plane of thought . . . ;

c. Now this *"reflection"* consists of new operations related to the antecedent operations whilst continuing them. So it is these new operations, necessary for the abstraction of the antecedent relationships, which form the novelty of the derived system whilst abstraction from the antecedent operations guarantees continuity between the two systems.

d. These new operations permit systems, which up till now were separated, to be combined in new wholes.

Clearly, this view of cognitive development has much in common with the Peircean views introduced above. Here, we must note two problems with Piaget's formulation. First, as mentioned, it represents Piaget's reflections on his data, rather than being a predictive theory tested against specific experiments. Since many of Piaget's conclusions are based on informal observations of child behavior, much work has been done on psychological testing of his theory under more rigorous conditions. (Forman 1982 presents an excellent sample of such work, with an insightful epilogue by the editor.) The second problem with Piaget's formulation, and a problem more central to our concerns, is that it reads too much as if the dynamics of reflective abstraction must lead to a coherent network of schemas that will allow all children (at least within a given culture) to construct a common reality. We stress that this is not so, both because of the innate individuality of children and because of the inevitable inconsistency (cf. Section 2.2) of complex cognitive structures.

It is also necessary to treat the objectivity of schemas with some caution. Consider the schema of object permanence. We may notice a regularity in overt behavior – the child comes to seek objects where they have just been hidden. But, in fact, how are we to know that this is just *one* schema rather than a collection? Is it really a schema or an observable property shared by many schemas? The child learns to look for an object placed under a blanket, but not to look for an apple that has been eaten. When using adult talk, we must be careful about how we characterize what schemas the child has acquired. At an early stage, the child will not look for an object once it has been hidden; at an intermediate stage, if the child has learned to retrieve an object repeatedly hidden at A, and the object is then hidden at B, the child will still go to A to retrieve the object! At this stage, one might say the child has developed a schema for retrieval of that object, but far removed from the concept of a spatial framework that we asssociate with the adult notion of object permanence as including continuity of spatial movement.

We may see "object permanence" as an acquired strategy (set of strategies) for the child's behavior, but it is not to be seen at this level as itself an object of knowledge. One may say that the young child "knows how," but does not "know that." This statement raises the crucial question of how we move from the level of sensory–motor schemas to the level of schemas that can be said to be "knowledge." To talk about object permanence, we must have the notion of an object; to have the concept of an object, we must have the notion of object permanence, or otherwise we cannot posit an underlying thread binding together different sensory experiences. Just as we express doubt as to whether in fact one could regard object permanence as a single schema, so it must be noted that the notion of an object need not come "in full blush." One may start with the notion of a dog or a doll or a glass being treated as an enduring object without being explicitly known to be an enduring object. When sufficient examples of this kind are available, the child can learn the word *object* by a process of reflective abstraction from these examples.

This account exemplifies the twofold movement of diversification or differentiation (constructing distinct schemas for "dog," "doll," "glass," etc.) and unification (assimilating these schemas to the schema for "object" or "object permanence"). As Piaget stresses (Beth & Piaget 1966, p. 243), "neither the diversification nor the unification can develop on the same plane of construction as the initial systems, which must each be diversified and unified in relation to the other." The point here is that once the concept of "object" is available, the concepts of "dog," " doll," and "glass" are thereby enriched and changed. The schemas from which the schema for object was reflectively abstracted are themselves reconstructed using the new schemas and operations now available and thus cohere into a new, more abstract, system "situated on another plane of construction and constitut[ing] psychologically a new form of thought, subordinating and integrating the lower form, but sometimes contradicting the initial intuitions." As Piaget sums this up,

"The picture furnished by natural thought is not that of a simple duality between, on the one hand, a content directly attained through intuition, and on the other, forms provided by language or hypothetico-deductive thought alone etc.: it is that of a continuous hierarchy such that the cognitive structures of a certain level always take on *simultaneously* the role of forms in relation to the structures of lower levels (which are also forms), and the role of content in relation to the structures of higher levels." (Beth & Piaget 1966, p. 243)

Within this perspective, we see processes and needs independent of any particular culture or society as the motor for the child's construction (acquisition) of language and also see (perhaps to a greater extent than Piaget would admit, cf. Arbib, to appear) social and cultural factors, including education, as playing a critical role in shaping the development of language, beliefs, and behavior in the child.

Returning to a Peircean theme, an analogy with the theory of evolution is again appropriate. It is almost impossible for evolutionary theorists to predict *a priori* the emergence of new species. However, given fossil or other evidence for the emergence of such a species, it is often possible for the evolutionist to give a causal account of the factors that appear to favor one species over others, given the available data on the ecological niche and other factors. In the case of the development of the young child, we can hope to give a "universal" account of the early development of sensorimotor schemas because the physical environment to which children react is similar in most cases. However, when we consider the development of social schemas, we may expect the environment and the experience of the individual to differ drastically. A causal theory might hope to explain how, given the currently available schemas and particular experiential factors, new schemas may develop. What structures we can come to understand by reflection will be causally determined not only by the nature of the initial structures on which we reflect (determined by the evolution of the human brain, perhaps), but also – in a microexplanation at any time – by the structures currently in place and the nature of the experiential environment.

Anticipating our discussion of cooperative phenomena in Section 4.1, we here posit that the changes in neural circuitry with experience cohere in such a way that we can aggregate them to speak of changes both in schemas and in the mechanisms of assimilation and accommodation. These changes affect each other. Whole assemblages of schemas come to mediate assimilation, and these assemblages reflect the history and plans of the organism, yielding a densely interconnected network of schemas, teasable apart only at some cost. Though processes of schema change may certainly affect only a few schemas at any time, such changes may "cohere" to yield a mental "phase transition" into a pattern of holistic organization. There is change yet continuity, with many schemas held in common yet changed because they can never again be used in the old context. Phenomena that appear to fall under this general rubric include stage changes in the sense of Piaget; paradigm shifts in science in the sense of Kuhn (1962) (so that paradigms correspond to Piagetian stages); religious conversion (cf. William James [1902] on "The Varieties of Religious Experience"); and dramatic personality changes (including Freudian transference).

As was implicit when we noted that schemas may be built or abstracted from sets of other schemas, we now see that such a holistic structure – be it a paradigm, an ideology, or a religious symbol system – will itself constitute a schema at a higher level. Such a great schema can certainly be analyzed in terms of its constituent schemas, but these constituents attain their full meaning only in terms of the overall network of the schema that encompasses them. In this sense we use the phrase *the Great Schema* in Chapter 11 when we present the Bible of Christianity as a holistic network and ask whether it does point to a reality beyond space and time.

3.2 Schemas within the action/perception cycle

There is no fixed formal definition of a schema. Nonetheless, through a body of research in brain theory, robotics, and computational linguistics runs as a connecting thread a concept of schema that, if not a constant, at least comprises instances with a marked "family resemblance." This family resemblance lends the papers a certain cohesion and justifies the use of the phrase *schema theory* to encourage the emergence of a unifying theory from the many studies now available.

The slide-box metaphor (Arbib & Didday 1971; Arbib 1972) described perceptual representations as made up of "slides," each representing different "domains of interaction" and each tagged with information relevant both to perception and action. To avoid overly literal misinterpretation of the term *slide,* the term *schema* was later adopted for this unit of representation. Where frames (Minsky 1975), scripts (Schank and Abelson 1977), and schemas in the sense of Piaget represented an overall context of a class of situations, these schemas were to be seen as units from which complex representations were to be structured. Perceptual structures were seen to be assemblages of perceptual schemas that could be used in the planning of, and which could provide crucial parameters for, action. The representation directing motor control was a distributed structure, a coordinated control program, for the interleaved serial and/or concurrent activation of motor schemas. Schemas were seen as providing a level of representation intermediate between a high-level functional representation (as given, e.g., by a typical AI program) and the detailed implementation in patterns of spatiotemporal activity in neural nets (Arbib 1981a). This is further discussed in Chapter 4.

The two main areas for development of the theory of perceptual structure and distributed motor control have been the study of visuomotor coordination in frog and toad and the study of the integration of vision and touch in the control of (human and robot) hand movements. For the former area, Lara, Arbib, and Cromarty (1982) introduced a basic neural network, the tectal column, to explain data on facilitation of prey acquisition; and Cervantes, Lara, and Arbib (1985) showed how an array of such columns could, in interaction with pretectum, implement basic schemas for pattern recognition in frog and toad. Two alternative approaches to modeling detour behavior (a toad detouring around a barrier to approach its prey) in terms of interacting schemas have been offered by Arbib and House (1986) and Lara et al. (1984). In each case, separate schemas provide depth maps for prey and barriers (and, in the latter model, for gaps between barriers); and these maps must interact to generate an approriate pattern of activation for motor schemas for sidestepping, orienting, and snapping.

Turning to hand movement, Arbib, Iberall, and Lyons (1985) developed a coordinated control program of interacting schemas for control of the three "virtual fingers" engaged in the task of picking up a coffee mug and also discussed the neural implementation of such schemas. Hanson et al. (1985) have shown how processes of visual interpretation in a machine vision system can be carried out through a network of interacting schemas. We argue that this model has much to tell us about the style of human perceptual processes. Arbib and Caplan (1979) adapted schema theory in suggesting how language might be rooted in evolutionarily more primitive sensorimotor processes and sketched a neurological theory of language in terms of the cooperative computation of a network of schemas. A portion of this theory was explicitly developed by Gigley (1983). Other schema-theoretic models of language were provided for scene description (Conklin, Ehrlich, and McDonald 1983) and language acquisition (Hill 1983; see also Section 7.3).

With this general perspective in place, we devote the rest of the section to an informal introduction to the portion of schema theory developed in attempts to model processes of perception and of control of movement in human, animal, and robot. We thus initiate a theory of the *embodied self,* rooting human knowledge in the body's interaction with the world. We glimpsed some of these notions briefly in Section 1.3 and use them in later chapters to undergird our schema-based theory of social interactions underlying language, science, and religion. In the present section, we analyze visuomotor coordination in terms of the interaction of schemas, viewed as concurrently active processes that serve as building blocks for both representations and programs. We stress that our explicit analysis of schemas does not imply that human beings have conscious access to all, or even most, of the schemas that direct their behavior. Chapters 4 and 6 offer explicit accounts of the exceptional role of consciousness in both schema-theoretic and Freudian terms.

The control of locomotion may be specified at varying levels of refinement: the goal of the motion, the path to be traversed in reaching the goal, the actual pattern of footfalls in the case of a legged animal, and the detailed pattern of muscle activation required for each footfall. It is well known that the fine details of activation will be modified on the basis of sensory feedback, but we stress that even the path plan will be continually modified as locomotion proceeds. For example, locomotion will afford new viewpoints that will reveal shortcuts or unexpected obstacles that must be considered in modifying the projected path. We thus speak of the *action/perception cycle* (Neisser 1976; Arbib 1981a) – the system perceives as the basis of action; each action affords new data for perception.

We owe to the Russian school founded by Bernstein the general strategy that views the control of movement in terms of selecting and coordinating from a relatively short list of synergies or modes of activity, which we shall call *motor schemas.* (Whiting 1984, reprints Bernstein's classic papers together with recent commentary.) The parameters required by each schema must then be specified to tune the movement (e.g., a motor schema for locomoting will, given a path plan as input, yield the first step along that path as output; or a motor schema will direct a hand to grasp an object, given its position as input). The problem of motor control is thus one of sequencing and coordinating such motor schemas, rather than of directly controlling the vast number of degrees of freedom offered by the independent activity of all the muscles.

Similarly, the raw pattern of retinal stimulation cannot guide behavior directly. Rather, it must be interpreted in terms of objects and other "domains of interaction" in the environment. We use the phrase *perceptual schema* for the process whereby the system determines whether a given "domain of interaction" is present in the environment. The state of activation of the schema will then determine the credibility of the hypothesis that what the schema represents is indeed present; other schema parameters will represent further properties, such as size, location, and motion relative to the behaving system.

We may view the *schema assemblage* – the structure of perceptual schemas that relates the organism to its environment – as a spatial structure with temporal characteristics (e.g., representing the motion of objects relative to the animal). We shortly discuss the possible nature of "coordinated control programs" that can coordinate the activation of motor schemas. Such programs serve to control the temporal unfolding of movement but have spatial characteristics since interaction with objects will usually depend on their position in the environment.

Perceptual schemas will not be driven directly by retinal activity but rather by the output of segmentation processes that provide an intermediate representation in terms of regions or segments (usually corresponding to the surfaces of objects) separated from one another by edges and characterized internally by continuities in hue, texture, depth, and velocity. As locomotion proceeds and as objects move in the environment, most of these regions will change gradually, and the segmentation processes must be equipped with a dynamic memory that allows the intermediate representation to be continually updated to provide current input for the perceptual schemas, so the schema assemblage representing the environment will be kept up to date.

Cognitive science demands not just representation, but also processes whereby the representations can be used. Could we write a program, or wire up a neural net, that can acquire and use schemas? In fact, we have such mechanisms for a number of tasks, though by no means for anything yet approaching the full range of human thought and mental development. For example, machine vision now offers programs to process a photo to segment it into regions distinguished by cues of texture, depth, color, movement, or separated by boundaries across which discontinuities can be found. We thus see cooperative computation between region growers and boundary followers. But this process is imperfect. The image of an object may, because of shadows, be segmented into several regions; the images of two objects of similar color may be lumped into a single region. Further processing by a machine vision system invokes high-level knowledge (such as recognizing a roof by connecting edges to form a near parallelogram beneath a blue region, at the top of the image, that can be interpreted as sky). Such an analysis may require holding multiple hypotheses with different confidence ratings (schemas with different activity levels) until some hypotheses are rejected and others reach a sufficiently high rating to cohere into an overall interpretation of the image (Hanson et al. 1985; Arbib 1985). High-level hypotheses may also call for finer low-level analysis of portions of the image that may confirm or disconfirm the hypothesis. Perception is then seen to be a process of *cooperative computation* – resulting from the concurrent operation of many processes, both high level and low level, to instantiate various hypotheses, each with its current confidence level and support structure. For example, a roof hypothesis can be supported by the analysis of tile texture within the region, by the detection of windows below the region, or by a house hypothesis for an encompassing region. Our schema-theoretic model of the mind thus involves both highly parallel low-level processes and high-level concurrent schema activation.

We explore some dimensions of the notion of a schema assemblage in Figure 3.1 (Arbib 1981b). Suppose that whenever we seek a duck there is a characteristic pattern of neural activity in the brain, which we refer to as "activation of the duck schema," and suppose that we may also speak of a "rabbit schema." When we are confronted with the duck–rabbit of Figure 3.1(a), we may see it either as a duck with its bill pointing to the right, or as a rabbit with its ears pointing to the right; but we cannot see it as both simultaneously. This pair of possible percepts might suggest that the schemas for duck and rabbit are neural assemblies with mutually inhibitory interconnections as indicated in Figure 3.1(b). However, we are capable of perceiving a duck and a rabbit side by side within the scene, so that it seems more appropriate to suggest, as in Figure 3.1(c), that the inhibition between the duck schema and rabbit schema that would seem to underlie our perception of the duck–rabbit is not so much "wired in" as it is based on the restriction of low-level features to activate only one of several schemas. In other words, we postulate that to the extent that a higher level schema is activated are the features that contributed to that activation made unavailable to other schemas. Finally, it must be noted that we are able to see a scene with several ducks in it. Thus, we can no longer think of a single localized schema for each familiar object in our environment; we might rather imagine that the appropriate pattern of activity can be reproduced (instantiated) to an extent compatible with the number of occurrences of an object of the given type within the current visual scene, as in Figure 3.1(d); we might further imagine that each instantiation is tuned with appropriate parameters to represent the particularities of the particular instance of the object so represented.

Programs for action

We stress that a schema is both a process and a representation. The formation and updating of the internal representation, a schema assemblage, are viewed as a distributed process, involving the concurrent activity of all those schema instantiations that receive appropriately patterned input. The resultant environmental representation interacts with the processes representing the system's goal structures to generate the plan of action – exemplified by the projected path in the case of locomotion – that can provide the coordinated control program of the various motor schemas that directly control behavior. Coming on unexpected obstacles can alter the elaboration of higher-level structures – the animal continually makes, executes, and updates its plans as it moves. We emphasize that the current assemblage of active schemas may contain hundreds of schema instantiations, and the entire stock of knowledge of an individual may reside in a vast network of hundreds of thousands of constituent schemas. To get some idea of the size of this "long-term" memory, just imagine the number of entries in a "personal encyclopedia" of the kind envisaged in Section 2.3, then enlarge it from the verbal

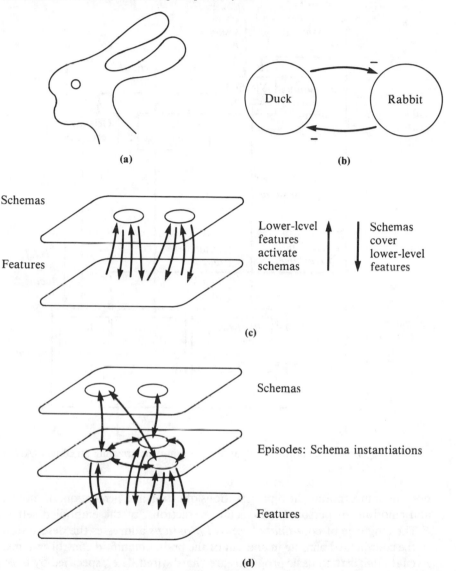

Figure 3.1. From schemas to schema assemblages. The duck–rabbit (a) suggests that mutual inhibition between the schemas (internal representations)
of duck and rabbit are mutually inhibitory (b). However, the fact that we
can see a scene containing both a duck and a rabbit suggests that this inhibition is not wired in, but rather is mediated by the competition for low-
level features (c). Finally, our ability to see a scene with several ducks, say,
argues that perception does not so much activate a set of particular schemas
as it activates a schema assemblage consisting of instantiations of schemas
(d). (Arbib 1981a)

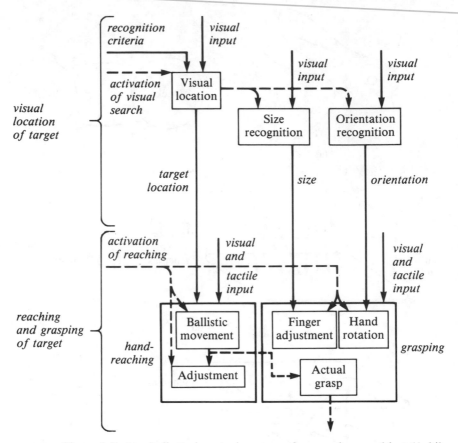

Figure 3.2. A coordinated control program for grasping an object (Arbib 1981b)

domain to incorporate the representations of action and perception, of motive and emotion, of personal and social interactions, of the embodied self.

The language of *coordinated control programs* addresses the description of the coordinated phasing in and out of the brain's manifold control systems. Even though certain basic programs are "hard wired," i.e., specified by fixed circuitry in the brain, most programs are generated as the result of an explicit planning process. Following Arbib (1981a), we exemplify this for a person's grasping an object, motivated by the data of Jeannerod and Biguer (1982). The spoken instructions given to the subject drive the planning process that leads to the creation of the appropriate plan of action – which we here hypothesize to take the form of the coordinated control program shown in the lower half of Figure 3.2, involving the interwoven activation of motor schemas for reaching and grasping. In Figure 3.2, each box corresponds to the activation of some subsystem. Several subsystems may be active at the same time, but not all systems need be concurrently active. In addition to its own internal changes, the activity of a particular subsystem may serve both to pass messages as indicated by the solid lines to other activated subsystems and also to change the activation level of other systems, as indicated by the dashed lines. In the particular diagram shown here, we have only indicated system activation, but we can just as well have deactivation.

Activation of the program is posited to initiate simultaneously a ballistic movement toward the target and a preshaping of the hand during which the fingers are adjusted to the size of the object and the hand is rotated to the appropriate orientation. When the hand is near the object, feedback adjusts the position of the hand; completion of this adjustment activates the actual grasping of the hand about the object (cf. Arbib, Iberall and Lyons 1985).

The perceptual schemas hypothesized in the upper half of Figure 3.2 need not be regarded as a separate part of the program. Rather, they provide the algorithms required to identify parameters of the object to be grasped and to pass their values to the motor schemas. This analysis of visual input locates the target object within the subject's "reaching space," and extracts the size and orientation of the target object and feeds them to the control surface of the grasping schema. When the actual grasping movement is triggered, it shapes the hand on the basis of a subtle spatial pattern of tactile feedback.

What is particularly interesting about the hypothetical program shown here is that the activation of the "actual grasp" subschema of the motor schema for grasping is not internally activated by completion of finger adjustment or hand rotation; rather it is separately activated when adjustment of the hand-reaching schema signals the appropriate positioning of the hand. Even though Figure 3.2 is certainly hypothetical, it does begin to give us a language in which we can talk about the coordination and control of multiple activations of different motor schemas and thus begin to analyze complex feats of motor coordination in terms of units (schemas) whose implementation we can explore in terms of neural circuitry.

The social dimension

Schemas are not to be seen as isolated monads. They are, rather, entities that interact with one another to model a complex situation, to mediate the organism's learning, and to determine the organism's course of action. Moreover, these processes are interdigitated, so that the action–perception cycle is also a learning cycle, as experience is matched against the structure of anticipations generated within the schema assemblage. The schemas of any individual themselves form a holistic network that represents the social network. How does the individual acquire personal representation of the social network, and how does the development of individual schemas come to alter the social network? In particular, how is it that as a person assimilates the reality of society, he or she assimilates certain (e.g., religious) beliefs and not others? Clearly, the process of learning involves testing schemas acquired through diverse experiences against new experiences. This testing may result in a move to conformity, to a questioning of authority, or to explicit conceptual conflict and even neurosis. Since a schema acquires its meaning through its interaction with other schemas, there are great complexities here: our analysis must proceed cautiously because we have rational access only to parts of the network, and plausible changes of one schema may have unforeseen implications when the schema is involved in new combinations with other schemas. In the same way, mathematicians know changes in one axiom of a theory can drastically change the properties of apparently separate concepts, as reflected in the theorems of the modified theory.

We all seem to have common schemas for getting up when we fall down but different schemas for discussing ideas. We may see a progression from innate sensorimotor schemas to sensorimotor schemas well determined (at least at the external level of description) by the needs of interacting with objects using a normal human body to schemas shaped by social convention yielding, for example, the divergence of languages and consequent lack of "total" translatability. There is no reason that schemas developed in one culture should be fully translatable into patterns of schemas in another language. Even for persons raised in the same society, the differences in genetic constitution and individual experience provide "individuality" and "personality" as is constituted by a distinctive network of schemas for each person.

3.3 Schemas and reality

Previous sections suggested that cognitive science, in the broad sense that includes artificial intelligence and brain theory, implies a new theory of the mind and a new theory of knowledge. We must therefore expect that cognitive science will have a profound effect on how we think about reality, whether this be based on individual experience, or on our scientific and social constructions and religious images of the world. The cognitive science idiom of "construction" and "schemas," is, however, unfamiliar in epistemology and philosophy of science and religion. We therefore need in later chapters to relate the consequences of cognitive science to more familiar discussions of science, society, and religion.

Our schema-theoretic view of "knowledge" and "world construction" goes beyond the objectified world of natural science as constrained by the pragmatic criterion. New criteria for the cognitive are suggested, for example, in evolution theory, including sociobiology, and in psychoanalytic theory and therapy. In all such sciences, large n–body problems are involved, and there is strong interaction between the subject matter (e.g., the psychiatric patient) and the methods and norms of the investigator (e.g., the therapist).

In these circumstances, the methodology of the pragmatic criterion becomes progressively less applicable with decreasing possibilities of free experimentation, objective test, and elimination of the investigator's theoretical and value-laden standpoint. Thus, even if "pure" objective knowledge is possible "in principle" in the long run, it is not sufficient for decision making and action in the short run in which we all live. Such sciences therefore require methodologies that supplement the pragmatic criterion of prediction, test, and corrective feedback.

New cognitive methods in the human sciences and new scientific descriptions of cognitive systems do, in fact, come together in a unique way in cognitive science, which is "self-reflective" in the sense that it is potentially part of its own subject matter of cognitive systems in general. Cognitive science concerns how schemas of linguistic meaning and scientific theory develop in human organisms in interaction with each other and with their environment. We can draw another parallel here with biological evolution. As new species evolve, they change the available ecological niches through the web of their relationships with extant species; it is only with respect to the resultant that we can speak of their "adaptation" to their dynamic environments. Just as there is no single solution to the problem of "adaptation" in evolution, so there is no single "correspondence" of cognitive schemas to the world. "The world" (specifically, of course, the social world) is altered in the interaction of a schema with itself and with the schemas of other individuals. As will be particularly the case when we enter the social realm, schemas are holistic evaluative projections of a multitude of interacting individuals, which reach varying degrees of stability as a result of their mutual interaction.

Seen in this light, schema theory (in the extended sense, including the social, of this volume) makes an advance on the traditional naturalist ontology in recognizing that "reality" as constructed in mental schemas comes in a variety of modes. We are dealing not just with the physical object ontology of *things,* but also with mental states, social constructions, and perhaps gods. In its own terms, schema theory may be neutral about the objectivity of "construction" in all these realms, but it inevitably has an air of subjectivism when applied beyond the naturalistic domain.

Let us begin by considering the common core of the standard philosophical accounts of knowledge, reality, and mental constructions. According to this common core, knowledge is justified true belief about the real. Empiricists and rationalists differ as to whether the mind contributes a structure in terms of which the real is known. More important than this distinction for our present purposes, however, is the question of whether "the real" is identified with the spatiotemporal world, with the possible addition of logical and mathematical "truths," or whether there is "reality" and hence "truth" other than the spatiotemporal or the logical. (Since our primary concern here is not with logic, we do not consider further the question of whether the real includes the logical and mathematical but will speak only of the possibility of a nonspatiotemporal reality that is also nonlogical).

We call the view that there is only spatiotemporal reality *naturalism*. This view is more liberal than early positivism, since it is in the first place an ontological, not an epistemological, view; that is, it does not exclude the possible existence of unobserved or even unobservable space–time entities and events. Unobserved entities and events may become known in scientific theories that postulate them as theoretical terms and that are utlimately justified by the pragmatic criterion of successful empirical prediction and test (Chapter 1). Consequently, naturalism embraces theoretical science as the most adequate form of knowledge. Conversely, because theoretical science has in fact had notable success in providing knowledge according to its own criteria of success, naturalists feel no need to recognize such other forms of knowledge as the religious where criteria of success are unclear and where, even if they can be stated, there is no obvious consensus about their satisfaction. It should be added to avoid misunderstanding that we do not use the word *naturalism* to exclude *social* knowledge, which we discuss later (Chapters 8 and 9) but merely to represent the view that reality is spatiotemporal and space–time contains all sorts of things, from stars and atoms to human beings, societies, religions, and languages. All these things, according to naturalism, can and should be studied by the methodology of natural science, whose products alone deserve to be called objective knowledge.

Now, to return to schemas. Naturalism will accept cognitive science as a proper form of science that has discovered something about how the human mind sets up various representations of its world. If these representations, or schemas, correspond to knowledge in the naturalists' sense, that is, are justified true beliefs about the space–time ontology, there is no problem – cognitive science has merely but usefully shown us what the mechanism of knowledge gathering is. No talk about a new theory of knowledge or the mind is appropriate. But naturalists will notice at once that when we talk about schemas, we are not just talking about the rationalists' categories plus empirical knowledge, or about justified theories of the natural world, but also about other kinds of mental representation that the naturalist would not want to call knowledge. These other kinds of mental representations include false but useful models of the natural world; ideal types of human behavior and social order that may never be realized; and all kinds of fictional or mythical utopias, heavens and hells, and domains of the beautiful, the true, and the good. All such schemas may be seen as observable ways in which human beings "cope" (Rorty 1979, p. 269) with their natural and social environment, irrespective of their "truth." Theories of mental schemas do not depend on the type of distinctions made in naturalism, and they suggest that the concept of "cognition" be extended beyond naturalism, reinforcing, for example, the hermeneutic approaches to knowledge we discuss in Chapter 9. In this sense, cognitive science justifies speaking of a "new" theory of mind and knowledge.

The cognitive dimension of schema theory, as sketched so far in this chapter, is strong scientifically, but the symbolic, moral, and evaluative aspects are weak. Our discussion of Freud in Chapter 6 is one of our first attempts to address this deficit. Later, especially in Chapters 10 and 11, we attempt to link schema theory (expressed in purely rational terms) to religious symbolism and moral concerns. Schema theory is to explain and structure our behavior, and so we must relate it to religious myth, bodies of doctrine, bodies of practice, and organizing social conventions. Of particular interest is the question of the extent to which religious beliefs can be changed by cognitive theory. Our discussion of Eccles, Edwards, and Freud suggests that they can be accommodated to almost any such theory. It may thus come as no surprise, then, that in the last two chapters we present both a Christian viewpoint and a secular viewpoint that construct different realities yet both accord with the principles of reality construction provided by the schema theory developed in this volume.

Summary

With the insights provided by the first three chapters of this volume, we can now summarize some main points of the perspective offered by our schema theory and philosophy of science and foreshadow the arguments and questions addressed in the chapters that lie ahead:

1. There is an everyday reality of persons and things. If you cut a person, that person bleeds. If you drop a cup of coffee, the coffee will spill, and the cup may break. Love can turn to jealousy.
2. Epistemology asks how we come to know these and other realities.
3. Schema theory answers that our minds comprise a richly interconnected network of schemas. An assemblage of some of these schemas represents our current situation; planning then yields a coordinated control program of motor schemas that guide our actions. As we act, we perceive; as we perceive, so we act. Logical deduction is an important but exceptional case of our decision making, which usually involves analogical, schema-based processes.
4. Perception is not passive, like a photograph. Rather, it is active, as our current schemas determine what we take from the environment. If we have perceived someone as a friend, we may perceive that person's remark as a pleasing joke; yet the same words uttered by someone we dislike, even if that person also intended a joke, may be perceived as an insult calling for a vicious response.
5. A schema, as a unit of interaction with, or representation of, the world, is partial and approximate. It provides us not only with abilities for recognition, and guides to action, but also with expectations about what will happen. These expectations may be wrong. We learn from our mistakes. Our schemas, and their connections within the schema network, change. Piaget gives us insight into these processes of schema change with his theory of assimilation and accommodation.

6. Even young children have distinct personalities. Each of us has different life experiences. Our schemas are thus different.

7. If we use conversation and communication, rather than grammar, as the starting point of our study of language, we see language as mediation between schema assemblages that differ. If I say, "There's a bird outside the window," our schemas are in sufficient accord that we can agree or disagree that this is the case. But, in general, a sentence in a conversation is not to be judged true or false. Rather, it opens up a different network of schema activity for each party to this conversation and is inherently metaphorical. Literal meaning is to be seen as a limiting case of language, not the norm.

8. In physics, we have seen continual progress according to the pragmatic criterion of successful prediction and control. This is despite the fact that, for example, quantum theory and relativity have changed our view of physical reality from an inherent determinism of cause and effect in absolute space and time to an inherently probabilistic causality in a dynamically curving space–time manifold. But the pragmatic success of Newtonian physics is preserved: apples continue to fall, the planets continue in their paths, and we can now put satellites in orbit and send spaceships to the moon and planets. Thus, even though we know that our scientific theories, like our individual schemas, are open to change, most of us would agree that there is an external spatiotemporal reality independent of human constructions and providing the touchstone for our attempts to build physical theories.

9. On the other hand, we can see many of the patterns of our daily lives, whether our own idiosyncracies, or the conventions of a language community or a social group, as being purely human constructs. In Mexico, we must drive on the right-hand side of the road; in Scotland, on the left. But these are purely social conventions – life is easier if the members of a single driving community observe the same basic rules. We do not hold that there is a greater Reality, the one true Road Reality, which the framers of human road rules try to approximate.

10. What, then, of religion? Is there a God reality that transcends the spatiotemporal reality? Did God create space and time? Is it true that only in God will we find salvation? Does human life lose all meaning if person reality exists solely within spatiotemporal reality? Or, can we see religions, and even the God of the Judeo–Christian tradition, as psychological or social constructs, as postulated by Freud and Durkheim? If we come to see God as a social construct, can we still choose to believe? And if we cannot accept the Great Schema of the Bible as representing the God reality that gives meaning to our lives, can we construct secular schemas that do justice to our humanity?

4 Relating mind and brain

4.1 From reductionism to schema theory

The language of mental phenomena often sets the stage for our study of the brain, and many neural phenomena can best be described in terms of their role within mental acts or the behaviors of organisms. Yet, we do not see neural levels of description as superseded by the mental. Rather, our aim is to develop a schema theory that makes contact with the phenomena of everyday experience but that can, where appropriate, be supplemented at the neural level of description.

All of the many kinds of mind/brain reductionism have in common a naturalistic basis: there are no mental events not explicable by brain science. It follows from this statement that the terms of mental language are all in principle describable in terms of brain language. As we shall see, however, it is possible that mind and brain science are not yet complete enough for the descriptions to be carried out in practice. Dualism, on the other hand (as exemplified by Eccles, Section 4.2), holds that mind involves some entity or substance not identifiable with anything in the material brain. Within reductionism, however, are weaker and stronger varieties, of which we may distinguish the following three:

1. One-way reductionism holds, first of all, that there are laws of the mental, rather than accidental regularities arising from the similar biological and social pressures on all human beings. Is it a law, for example, that emotional deprivation of children either always or with ascertainable probability leads to adult mental disturbance? We consider later (Chapter 9) how far the human sciences can be said to discover "laws" analogous to those of the natural sciences. Second, one-way reduction implies that every mental property or group of properties is in a one-to-one relation with a specific physical property or group of properties. (See the discussion in Davidson 1984 and the concepts of "token-" and "type-physicialism" in J. A. Fodor 1976, pp. 12 f.) But this does not seem to be the case. Taking the same example, it is reasonable to assume that any particular instance of "emotional deprivation"

or "mental disturbance" has a description in terms of the physical brain system, but it is not reasonable to suppose that these physical correlations are specifically the same in all instances we call "emotional deprivation" and so on. In other words, it is unlikely that the way we classify mental concepts in ordinary language corresponds exactly to any particular "natural kinds" now identified in physical theory.

A more important objection for our purposes, however, is that one-way reductionism takes no account of the dynamic character of the sciences of both mind and brain. It implies that we already know what the essential physical laws and properties are; that is, that physical brain science is already complete and uncontroversial. But this is not the case even in the parallel example from physics, often considered the most successful case of reduction: namely, statistical mechanics, which offers a means of reducing the phenomena of thermodynamics to the laws of mechanics. Many properties of bulk matter have been described in terms of the properties of their molecules in this way. But the reduction is only obtained by supplementing the laws of mechanics with statistical averaging techniques that yield a number of paradoxes (e.g., Newtonian systems are reversible, but "averaged" systems are irreversible).

2. Two-way reductionism is a more realistic view of the relation between two sciences, such as those of mind and brain. According to this view, at any given time the higher-level mental description is likely to contain laws and descriptions that cannot be identified with or deduced from lower-level brain science at that time but that provide suggestions as to how brain science should be extended to include new concepts and new laws. This is what happened with statistical mechanics. Here, phenomenal thermodynamics, largely expressed in concepts observable at the macroscopic level, has been modified to become consistent with the implications of statistical mechanics, and statistical mechanics has been extended (by averaging techniques and consideration of the initial conditions of closed systems) to become adequate to explain thermodynamic phenomena. In a successful two-way reduction, the two sciences ultimately become one science that is not identical with either of its prereductive components.

We argue for this view of reduction in this chapter. We use "top-down" and "bottom up" analysis to refer to the two-way process of modifying and extending, respectively, the lower-level science to explain the higher level, and the higher level in the light of implications of the lower level. In this sense, mind–brain systems may be regarded as "holistic"; that is, wholes are explained in terms of parts, and parts in terms of wholes. Both methods of analysis are necessary until such time as the development of both sciences ceases, which in the case of fundamental and interesting sciences is likely to be never.

It is perhaps largely a verbal matter as to whether we wish to say that at any given stage of brain science, properties of mind are emergent relative to that stage. The aim should be, as in two-way reduction, to unify the two sciences so that the former emergent properties are explained and incorporated into the new reductive science. This may be done in many ways. It is more important to notice that however it is done, there is no question of any of the properties' being shown to be unreal. For example, if we explain the hardness of tables in terms of atomic forces, we may take two extreme views of reality: (1) only the hardness of tables is real, and atoms are simply theoretical terms that allow us to give a more articulated account of this reality; or (2) only atoms are real, and the word *table* does not describe a real object but is simply a shorthand for a class of atomic configurations. We strive to avoid these two extremes because we wish to anchor our epistemology in the reality of everyday experience and yet we wish to anchor within that experience a broader reality that can extend, for example, to the mediating concepts of scientific theory or social structure.

We want a place for psychological reality and, possibly, a religious reality. Though we say cognitive science is reductionist, we in fact advocate a permissiveness with respect to ontology: there are all manner of levels of reality. What real things there are can depend on human constructions imposed on some "external stuff." The schema is then the unit of these constructions – we have a vocabulary with which we describe the world and schemas that embody our perception of the real. Note that the language of schema theory is not necessarily that of everyday discourse or of neural networks. Yet in seeking to understand the everyday world, we can enrich that understanding by relating it to the laws of physics and to the social nexus. However, the everyday concepts of interest do not "announce themselves" from a study of a lower level of analysis. Thus, our reductionism does not, for example, ask for physics sentences to provide the one true description from which all others can or must be inferred. There is no absolute scientific methodology, but the language of different subject matters mediates relative ways of looking at reality.

We are realists in that we hold that there is an external reality; but even on a naturalist view, we see that our representation and understanding of that reality may change over time, and that such changes may, in turn, literally change the external reality (atom bombs, computers, industrialization). Moreover, the philosophy of science presented in Chapter 1 precludes the acceptance of any theory language as immutable, thus weakening the claims of any reduction to one fixed level of description. With this understanding, let us consider how cognitive science escapes the straitjacket of one-way reductionism.

3. Both one- and two-way reduction may be said to be "monistic" in the sense that in principle the laws and properties of mind and brain are to be unified in one science. A weaker form was put forward by Roger Sperry, who pioneered the scientific study of split-brain patients (Sperry 1966). He holds that the ontology of mind is nothing but that of brain (in other words,

he adopts the naturalist thesis formulated above), but he considers that there are emergent phenomena at the mental level whose laws are then determinative of activity in the brain, so that causal laws at the mental level "supersede" the laws of physical parts of the brain and are not deducible from them. The mental level therefore introduces new causal relations when those physical parts are related in the complex holistic system that is a "brain." Sperry therefore talks not just of "top-down analysis" but also of downward causation from the mental to the physical level.

Consider the example of "how a wheel rolling downhill carries its atoms and molecules through a course in time and space and to a fate determined by the overall system properties of the wheel as a whole and regardless of the inclination of the individual atoms and molecules" (Sperry 1980, p. 201). This example is most instructive. The word *regardless* is misleading – if we could specify the state of motion of all the individual atoms and molecules, then we might in principle be able to give a statistical proof that a specified molecule will on average be hurled along a cycloidal path. But, even if possible, this proof would be inexpedient. It is better to use the shape of the wheel itself as a frame of reference to understand the motion of individual molecules. In the same way, most neuroscientists would agree that it would be inexpedient, even if possible, to analyze the interaction of billions of neurons as separate entities. As neuroscientists, we seek to place the firing patterns of neurons within a coherent overall organization provided by an account of an animal's behavior or a human being's mental state. "The control works both ways; hence mind–brain 'interaction': The subsystem components determine collectively the properties of the whole at each level and these in turn determine the time/space course and other relational properties of the components" (Sperry 1980, pp. 201–202).

Given this interaction, it seems too sweeping to claim that "the new emergent phenomena [are] not reducible, in principle, to their parts . . . [and that] when a new entity is created the new properties of the entity, or system as a whole, thereafter overpower the causal forces of the component entities at all the successively lower levels in the multi-nested hierarchies of the new infrastructure" (Sperry 1981, p. 11). This is Sperry's notion of downward causation. Now, it is true that we cannot deduce Newtonian mechanics from quantum mechanics without using averaging assumptions, so we might think of a Newtonian description of bulk matter as "overpowering" the causal forces of the quantum world. Yet, against this, the computer revolution is based on integrated circuits, which are non-Newtonian, and "make macroscopic" the basic quantum properties of matter. We get a new macroscopic level of theory, but we get it by using our knowledge of the microworld (which may itself be modified in the process). In the same way, the rolling of the wheel is best understood by a Newtonian analysis of the wheel itself, but a micro-analysis will be required to explain the shattering of the wheel on hitting a rock. When it comes to mind and brain, our understanding of the macrolevel (the language concepts of intentionality and conscious behavior) and the microlevel (the properties of neural circuits) are both at an early stage of development, and we may expect them to change under the analysis of multiple levels we are describing here.

To explain what we understand, we use words. Yet the words we use at best approximate that understanding. We recognize a face in terms of a set of the eyes, a flare of the nostrils, and a fullness of the lips that we cannot express in words with sufficient clarity to enable someone with only those words to guide them to pick that face from the crowd. We find the right words to console a friend without being able to articulate just how those words were chosen. We learn to drive a car by supplementing verbal instructions with hours of practice that develop the necessary visuomotor coordination, or we may develop an ability through long and careful observation of a skilled performer. Our behavior depends on subtleties of glands, musculature, and nervous system we do not know and subtleties of our culture and society we have seldom examined. We are again reminded of the discussion of the essentially embodied subject, foreshadowing our insistence on a secondary role of language in schema theory, and our view of language as metaphorical, having its meaning within the open schema networks of the participants in a discourse.

In the previous chapter, we sought to represent the individual's reality – personal perception of how to behave in the world around – in terms of a network of entities called schemas. A schema is the unit of the representation of reality. In this volume, we develop schema theory from a subdiscipline of cognitive science to present a program of action that pushes beyond the current study of knowledge representation in cognitive science. These developments will be both *down* to brain theory in seeking the instantiations of schemas within neural networks and *up* to social anthropology and hermeneutics to show how schema theory might contribute to an epistemology that can analyze the interaction of individual and society in the construction of the individual's view of reality.

Internal and external schemas

Piaget states (Beth & Piaget 1966, p. 235) that "the schema of an action is neither perceptible (one perceives a particular action, but not its schema) nor directly introspectible, and we do not become conscious of its implications except by repeating the action and comparing its successive results." There is some ambiguity here and elsewhere in Piaget's writing between the use of the term *schema* for the "external" public phenomenon and its use to denote an "internal" process or structure that can (perhaps in concert with other schemas) mediate overt behavior. In contrasting a schema as an overt manifestation with a schema as a hypothetical construct, we may compare the distinction between Chomsky's body of well-formed sentences of English with the notion of a grammar. The child learning a language never "sees" the grammar (or, we might prefer to say, the processes for perception and production) in somebody else's head but rather samples the "external schema" of approximately well formed sentences of the language. Often statements apply equally well to both senses, external and internal, and so it is easier to maintain the single term *schema,* qualifying it when necessary.

As an essentially public phenomenon, a schema is the structure of interaction, the underlying form of a repeated activity pattern that can transcend the particular physical objects it acts on and become capable of generalization to other contexts. In discussing interaction, we see that the characterization of the schema requires not only characterization of actions, but also of environmental circumstances in which such actions occur. However, even the notion of a schema as publicly observable is not without problems. Describable regularity need not imply internal mechanism; for example, we do not posit a "falling-over" schema, or a "panic-in-burning-theatre schema." Moreover, a person may behave differently on different occasions even though the environment appears the same, and such a difference will be explicable only if we can appeal to some hypothesis about the internal state of the person, at least in the form of a claim that the person is "executing" different schemas on one occasion from the other.

A schema is embedded within a cycle of action and perception. We must specify the goal of the actor and the environmental situation (both immediately sensable and contextual) to be able to specify the action appropriate within a particular schema. The execution of the action brings with it certain expectations as to consequent changes in the environment; and the match or mismatch that results will determine the ensuing course of action. With this structure of anticipations in place, our description of the schema becomes much more like a schema in the internal sense – a program or process with tests and branches –than it is like a simple table of overt stimuli and responses. If our aim is to seek the neural underpinnings of these behaviors, then we seek to instantiate the various schemas in neural networks, and we may expect the computational specification of schemas to be modified as we come to reconcile their design with the wider range of data that neuroscience and clinical observation can provide – as in studies of visuomotor coordination, or in computational neurolinguistics.

We use the realization theory for automata to offer an image of how a schema might become internalized (cf. Arbib 1973, Section V). An external schema is like the publicly observable response function of a state of the automaton, whereas an internal schema is like the internal state description. Schemas are not like internal states, but (in the internal sense) systems with internal states. An automaton (internal) has a set of states connected by a dynamics that specifies how states and inputs combine to yield new states. It is not a state but a process capable of exhibiting diverse behaviors in different circumstances. We cannot observe the latter unless we actually "go inside"; but it is such an internal structure that provides the explanation of the overt, public behavior. Realization theory has solved (in a variety of cases) the problem of going from a response function to the internal state description of an automaton that yields that behavior and teaches us that overt schemas may be mediated by different internal structures but that in terms of "mutual verification" the differences in these internal structures will be irrelevant so long as they do embody the same overt schemas. To the extent that they embody different schemas, the resultant inconsistencies can provide data for learning procedures. In Chapter 7, we discuss the extent to which these will lead to internal structures that yield consonant behavior.

Can two people share the same schema? Externally, one may describe a perceptual schema in terms of, for example, visual stimuli that lead to certain recognitions, anticipations, and performances; then, at some confidence level, we may say people have the same schema in the external sense. An internal schema is more like a program or internal state description, so that different schemas in different heads may, to some extent, yield approximately the same external schema. But due to different individual experiences, there will still be some differences in the external schemas they realize.

In thinking about the different uses of the term *schema,* we may recall the different uses of the term *program* in computer science. This term may refer to an abstract text or to the state of part of the computer circuitry that controls changes of other states. It may refer to the program *in abstracto,* or to the program written in a specific language, or to the program as variously located in different computers.

Schemas can be built of other schemas. Memory of schema assemblages may be tuned to create a new schema. What you know determines what you come to know; this, in turn, calls into question what you knew before. Unlike programs, we may not have early schemas permanently available as building blocks. As we saw in our discussion of reflective abstraction in Chapter 3, early schemas are changed by the network to whose growth they have contributed.

Relating schemas to neural nets

How do we develop a theory of the brain that is not false to issues in personality and sociology? One start is to look for levels of analysis intermediate between neuron and person. Some of these intermediate units are anatomical, such as a neural column or a layer of neurons (Szentágothai and Arbib 1974; Mountcastle 1978). In this case, we take on a bottom-up approach, aggregating neurons to find meaningful units so that we can, for example, analyze visuomotor coordination in terms of interacting layers of neurons in tectum and pretectum. We may complement this bottom-up approach by a top-down analysis, trying to posit representations and processes that could underlie observed behavior. Our interest in "the style of the brain" leads us to avoid the serial computation of much computer science. Our study of interacting layers in subserving, for example, stimulus-matching processes in stereopsis is one approach to parallelism. Another approach, within the top-down framework, is developing a theory of cooperative computation among schemas.

With experience, the brain changes. Brain theory offers models of how correlated changes in input and output may modify a neuron's connectivity to provide the substrate for pattern recognition. Such learning may be "without a teacher" (without either another individual or a "conscious self" of the learner) as certain distinctive regularities in the world become crystallized in correlated patterns of neural activity. The theory of cooperative phenomena (e.g., Haken 1978) seeks to understand how a continuous system can organize itself into relatively discrete sets of well-delimited modes. It also shows that certain phenomena cannot be understood within the vocabulary of these modes alone but are affected by the dynamics of the substrate. We suggest that the complexity of our brains and the subtlety of our interactions with the physical and social world are so great that they can support an almost limitless richness of "macroscopic modes." It is a hypothesis, however, that the modes revealed by brain theory and the schemas posited by top-down analysis of human behavior can eventually be brought "into registration."

Our philosophy of science leads us to an ontology with many anchor points, each subject to change – we seek "islands of reality," not one true science to which all others may be reduced. For example, the ability of the table to support our papers may be a more reliable "island" than a physical theory we do not fully understand. There are many sorts of reality – social, scientific, everyday. We must be able to talk of all these realities and understand how we can partially reconstruct one reality in terms of inferences based on another.

In computer science, there is an underlying physical level of circuitry, with dynamics considered completely deterministic at this level, and departures from this determinism to be treated as errors. Statements about programs, data, and users do not change this description. However, to understand the computer, it helps to know that the state of one part of the computer encodes certain data, another a program, and so on, and that at this instant a certain instruction is being executed. Here, then, is a strong sense of reductionism. There is no unique map from program level to machine level; but once given an initial map (how the program and data are loaded into the computer), we have the correspondence preserved if we pursue the dynamics at either level.

Turning to human cognition, we may want to compare the mental to the level of the program, the physical to the level of the circuitry. But mental language is not the creation of a designer who has explicitly coded it into the machine. Rather, it is an approximation developed by a community over the centuries, based on inference from inner feelings and observation of other people's behavior. There is no theory of dynamics at this level, but schema theory seeks to become a theory close to mind level, yet precise enough to allow a dynamic, predictive theory, using the developing insights of cognitive science.

We return to the action/perception cycle. A good cook has a repertoire of actions, utensils, and foodstuffs, and the perception of heat and its effects is central to deploying that repertoire to produce a good meal. This is the kitchen reality, and its heat vocabulary is well defined within the network of culinary schemas. There would be no pragmatic gain in linking it to the network of physics. However, when it comes to the quantitative analysis of physical and chemical processes, we can say we did not understand the properties of heat until we understood kinetic theory, and subsequent developments in statistical mechanics have enriched our understanding of matter. We increase our understanding of higher levels not only by a phenomenological analysis at those levels but also by an attempt to understand when the "fluctuations" of the microworld do not average out but rather cohere to yield effects in the macroworld to which we might not otherwise have attended. However, it should be noted that the pragmatic criterion is not the only motive for the kind of research. Even when a microanalysis will add nothing to the predictive accuracy afforded by the high-level phenomenological description, scientists will be motivated by the desire to produce a bridging theory that can provide a coherent level of description. As the history of the statistical mechanics of magnetism shows, physicists may tolerate decades of quantitative or even qualitative inaccuracy in their models, so strong is their conviction that the two levels of description can be reconciled.

When Sperry (1981, p. 12) argues that "in the brain, controls at the physico-chemical levels are superseded by new forms of causal control that emerge at the level of conscious mental processing," we can see the truth of this as a first approximation – people have long been able to understand much of each other's behavior without recourse to "brain talk," and this understanding constitutes a person reality that is the touchstone of our knowledge. But this knowledge is not immutable; it will change both with our personal experience and with the "ripple effect" as scientific concepts enter common parlance. Certainly, cognitive scientists cannot take the level of "conscious mental processing" as a closed reality. Scientific study of the brain will need both the "high-level" language of schema theory to describe mental states and behavior (and then we study mind rather than brain; call it cognitive psychology) and "low-level" language to describe the anatomy and physiology of neurons (call it brain theory). Our cognitive psychology is materialist to the extent that we hold mental activity to be determined by the collective interactions of neurons; our neuroscience is mentalistic to the extent that we find it best to classify neuronal behavior with respect to schemas that mediate the overall behavior (or mental state) of the organism.

Our behavior as persons is typically related to events in the real world that affect us by virtue of their meaning, which, in turn, is determined, for example, not only by what is said but also by who said it and in what circumstances. When we talk about love and remorse, we are using a rich vocabulary of the person that cannot yet be embedded within a schema network, let alone be linked to the language of neural nets. But, as we discuss further in Section 4.3, much in our everyday vocabulary – such as hunger and color – is enriched by our study of neural underpinnings. The crux of our discussion of free will in Chapter 5 is the question of whether the reality of the person does, or does not, transcend the reality of brains and schemas.

4.2 An evolutionary account of consciousness

The notion of the unconscious is an ancient one, but it was Freud who taught us to see the unconscious as a locus for real mental processes. We see more of Freud's theory in Chapter 6; here, we view a situation as represented (whether this is conscious or unconscious, repressed or not) by activating a network of schemas that embody the significant aspects of the situation. These aspects then determine a course of action by a process of analogy formation, planning, and schema interaction that need have little in common with formal deduction (recall our counter to the logic model of thought in Section 2.2).

To approach the unconscious within schema theory, we turn to neurology – the phenomenon of blindsight. Neurologists had believed that a monkey (or human being) without a visual cortex was blind. Yet, in "What the Frog's Eye Tells the Frog's Brain," Lettvin, Maturana, McCulloch, and Pitts (1959) traced activity in retina and tectum that enabled the frog to snap at prey and jump away from predators. Humphrey (1970), in a sequel entitled "What the Frog's Eye Tells the Monkey's Brain," argued that the residual brain of a monkey without a visual cortex should have a midbrain visual system more powerful than that of the frog so that a monkey should be no more blind than the frog. He trained a monkey without a visual cortex for years. Although the monkey never regained pattern recognition, she was able to catch moving objects and navigate toward a bright door, for example (see Weiskrantz 1974 for a survey of related monkey studies). It was also discovered that human beings without visual cortex could also see in this sense (Weiskrantz et al. 1974) – but, remarkably, they were not conscious that they could see. Asked, "Am I moving my left or right hand," the patient replies, "I can't see"; but asked to make a "guess" and point in the direction of the moving hand, the patient can point correctly. The patient can catch a ball even though he believes he cannot see it. The midbrain visual system is thus quite powerful but is not "connected to consciousness." Note that, when catching a ball, a normal person is usually aware of seeing the ball and of reaching out to catch it but is certainly not aware of the processes that translate retinal stimulation into muscle contraction. So, we certainly know that most neural net activity is unconscious (though by no means repressed in Freud's sense). The blindsight shows that even schemas we think of as normally under conscious control can, in fact, proceed without our being conscious of their activity. It is thus clear that consciousness is only the "tip of the iceberg" of schema activation. The questions are: Why have that "tip"? and, Is that "tip" the expression of a physical process?

Where Sperry argues for consciousness as an emergent property of brain, John Eccles, the neurophysiologist, argues explicitly that consciousness resides in a psychical world that transcends the physical (Popper & Eccles 1977). He follows Popper in distinguishing three "Worlds": World 1 comprises physical objects and states (including brain and body); World 2 comprises states of consciousness (mind and soul); World 3 comprises the knowledge accumulated by society (social reality). Eccles then elevates Cartesian dualism to a Popperian trialism. Incidentally, Eccles seems to misread Popper by locating records of intellectual efforts in World 3, whereas the records themselves are clearly in World 1. Popper holds a stronger view – that theoretical systems and social norms have some kind of reality of their own apart from any embodiment. But Eccles and Popper both see the physical, the mental, and the normative as three separate substances.

Eccles addresses the question of their interaction. Where Sherrington (1940), in his Gifford Lectures in Edinburgh in 1937–8, had been a dualist – mind talks to brain, and vice versa – Eccles has to have World 2 interact with World 3 as well as World 1. Interestingly, he eschews the sort of direct communication between World 3 and World 2 that one might associate with such terms as *collective unconsciousness* and *racial memory* and has World 3 embody itself in books and artifacts that can then be sensed as is any other part of World 1 by the brain's perceptual systems, themselves part of World 1. He then posits a specialized portion of the brain, the liaison brain (which he now identifies with the supplementary motor area, [Eccles 1982]), which communicates with World 2, the mind. Note that each mind is cut off from every other mind save to the extent that they communicate through their liaison brains, and thus through World 1. A religious believer might criticize Eccles for excluding a "World 4" of God with which World 2 minds could commune directly without the intervention of physical agency.

To develop his theory, Eccles then calls on the data on split brains (e.g., Sperry 1966). It is well known that 98 percent of people have the left hemisphere as the dominant hemisphere – it has the ability to use complex speech – whereas the right hemisphere has at best limited use of concrete words. When the corpus callosum, the massive fiber tract linking the two hemispheres, is severed, each half-brain can independently guide motor behavior, but only the left hemisphere can talk about what it is doing. This fact leads to two hypotheses: either the left brain alone has consciousness and personality, with the right brain providing additional computing power when the corpus callosum is intact (so that the functions of the right brain can then enter consciousness and affect personality via its modulation of the left brain); or, both brains embody conscious personalities (which usually reach consensus via the corpus callosum when it is intact), but only the left brain can articulate this consciousness.

Eccles opts, without further argument, for the first view and then goes much further. He rejects the possibility that consciousness and personality could be functions of the left brain as physical structure. Rather, he asserts that we have consciousness and personality as a separate entity, the mind in World 2, but that only the specialized structures of the left hemisphere enable the mind to communicate with the brain. Unfortunately, this statement explains nothing. If the mind is separate from the brain, what tasks does it perform that the brain cannot? Eccles would answer that it makes the free decisions that constitute free will. We consider an argument (in Chapter 5) that our brains are, in fact, sufficiently complex in themselves to make those "free" decisions. Even if Eccles is right, how does the World 2 mind make such decisions? Brain theory offers potential mechanisms; mind theory does not – unless we postulate schemas in World 2 in communion with their neural embodiments, but somehow able to work independently of them. Eccles states:

I believe that my genetic coding is not responsible for my uniqueness as an experiencing being. . . . Nor do my postnatal experiences and education provide a satisfactory explanation of the self that I experience. It is a necessary but not sufficient condition. . . . We go through life living with this mysterious experience of ourselves as experiencing beings. I believe that we have to accept what I call a personalist philosophy – that central to our experienced existence is our personal uniqueness. (Eccles 1977, p. 227)

Thus, where we would argue that to the extent that we are more than our accumulated genetic and individual experience, it is because of the people, society, and physical world surrounding us, Eccles explicitly postulates a "something extra" – our uniqueness cannot be embodied in World 1 but requires the separate stuff of World 2. He makes this view very explicit.

I think that for my personal life as a conscious self, the brain is necessary, but it is not sufficient. In liaison with the brain events in World 1, there is the World 2 of my conscious experience, including a personal self at the core of my being. Throughout our lifetime this personal self has continuity despite the failure of liaison with the brain in states of unconsciousness such as dreamless sleep, anesthesia, coma. The brain states are then unsuitable for liaison, but the self can achieve in dreams a partial liaison. (Eccles 1977, p. 227)

But if the World 2 self "continues to be" while there is no liaison with the brain, why does it not have "things to tell us" when contact is re-established?

Certainly, we sometimes "solve a problem in our sleep," but what evidence is there that this is the work of a disembodied mind reporting directly to consciousness rather than the fruit of the subconscious dynamics of the brain? The point we are making is not that we can prove Eccles wrong, but rather that there is no "this far can the brain go, and no further" argument to prove him right. Thus, we can hardly agree with Eccles that "there is *evidence* [our italics] that the self in World 2 has an autonomous existence, bridging gaps of unconsciousness when the brain fails to be in a state of liaison." If in this sense we reject the autonomy of World 2, we have actually rendered meaningless what Eccles calls "the ultimate question"; namely:

What happens when at death the brain disintegrates and the self has permanently lost its instrument of liaison? I evade an answer by stating that there are two linked mysteries in our existence as self-conscious beings: coming to be and ceasing to be. . . . Each human being is a person with this mysterious conscious self associated with his brain. He develops his brain potentialities from his lifetime of learning various aspects of World 3, and so becomes a cultured and civilized human being. It is the World 2 ⟷ World 3 interaction in all its various intensity and richness that distinguishes a human being from other animals. . . . (Eccles 1977, pp. 227–8)

We can only agree with Eccles about the importance of society in shaping the development of each of us as an individual. The challenge for cognitive science is to come to understand such shaping in terms of schema theory and the brain, not to abandon it to the unanalyzed influence of other-world forces. We are far from evidence that such an enterprise must fail.

Where Eccles holds that we are conscious because we have a mind that is a separate substance from our brains, with the liaison between mind and brain constituting consciousness, we give a (preliminary and hypothetical) evolutionary story for how consciousness might have evolved as a facet of brain activity. We link the evolution of consciousness to the evolution of communication and the high development of consciousness to the evolution of language. We argue that language evolved from our basic abilities to perceive and to control movement. Eventually, language lets us communicate in a counterfactual way, such as, warning children, telling stories, forming hypotheses. To link an evolutionary story to neurology, let us briefly recall the work of the nineteenth century neurologist, Hughlings Jackson (see, e.g., Jackson 1874, 1878).

Evolution was a key concept of nineteenth-century thought (Young 1970, Chapters 5 and 6). Jackson viewed the brain in terms of levels of increasing evolutionary complexity. He argued that damage to a "higher" level of the brain caused the patient to use evolutionarily "older" brain regions in a way disinhibited from controls evolved later, to reveal behaviors more primitive in evolutionary terms. We can see this evolution of the brain in complementary ways.

Let us view the "job" of a neuron in the brain to be to look for "meaningful" patterns of activity – where these meaningful patterns may be patterns of activity in central neural nets as well as patterns closely related to sensory stimulation or muscle contraction. As the brain evolves, it exhibits new patterns of neural activity that can provide new "ecological niches" for the evolution of new neural circuitry to exploit those patterns. Once such new circuitry evolves, however, there is a new "information environment" for the earlier circuitry – so it may evolve, in turn, to exploit these new patterns. Thus, evolution yields not only new brain regions connected to the old but also reciprocal connections that modify those older regions. For example, a cat's superior colliculus is far richer structurally than the corresponding brain region (the tectum) of the frog, in large part because of the immense richness of descending pathways in the cat from cortex to superior colliculus.

We suggest a similar evolutionary story for consciousness. Primitive communication subserves primitive coordination of the members of a social group. As language evolves (by mechanisms we do not yet understand), the "instructions" that can be given to other members of the group increase in subtlety – from "Look out!" to "Harry: go round the other side of the mastodon and spear him." So far, there is no consciousness in this story. Just as we say that, in blindsight, a person can reach out to a moving target without being conscious of it, so can we see processes that coordinate a group member to reach out as not involving consciousness. There is a real continuity from controlling your own body, to using tools, to "using" another member of your group in order to complete some action. As far as the brain is concerned, there is no self that stops at the end of the fingers. We go from the parietal lobe patient who ignores half the body to the car driver who can "feel" the contact of the car with the roadway. Our body schema can be tailored in task-dependent ways that can come to include artifacts and other people as well as our own body. (Parenthetically, being in love is, in part, a state in which the body schema incorporates the loved one, so that one feels a sense of loss and incompleteness in absence of that person.)

We suggest, then, that linguistic ability evolves at first purely as a way of coordinating the actions of one's colleagues with one's own. Thus, the brain must be able not only to generate such signals but also to integrate signals from other members of the group into its own ongoing motor planning. Once this ability is developed, it enriches the "information environment" for the rest of the brain. We have suggested that the brain's activity, involving billions of neurons, might be viewed more economically in terms of the activation at any one time of thousands of schemas. The channel that evolves to coordinate this complexity with the actions of other group members thus comes to provide a high-level précis of salient activity within and without the organism. But this précis is now available to other schemas, which can hence adjust their activity in light of reports of what is occurring elsewhere. Thus, a new process of evolution begins, whereby the précis comes to serve not only as a basis for communication between the members of a group but also as a resource for planning and coordination within the brain itself.

We suggest that communication evolves because coordination and social behavior can enhance the survival of the group but need have little effect at first on the actual processes of schema interaction within the individual. But then, this "communication center" evolves a crucial role in schema coordination. We suggest that the activity of this co-evolved process constitutes consciousness. Note that, in many cases, lower-level schema activity can proceed successfully without this highest-level coordination – and then we have, as we observe phenomenologically, that consciousness, if active at all, is active as a monitor rather than as a director of action. In other cases, the formation of the précis of schema activity plays the crucial role in determining the future course of schema activity and thus of action.

This new region can communicate with itself, as well as helping other regions "deal with reality," and can thus bring about a shift from one reality to another reality. It opens up the possibility for people to plan in a thoughtful way – entertaining alternative models of future reality may lead in time to new perspectives on the nature of present reality. The key is the ability to represent counterfactuals, states other than those currently perceived. Language becomes not simply a coordinating mechanism or a vehicle for high-level status reports, but it allows the human being to construct and contemplate many realities beyond those of the "here-and-now."

4.3 Mind and brain in relationship

As we saw in the previous section, Eccles argued that each of us is a nonmaterial mind in liaison with our individual bodies. The brain is the organ of certain basic bookkeeping activities, such as the control of breathing, respiration, and motion, and the receipt of sensory impressions; but on this view, will and consciousness are in a world apart, interacting with the body through a complex receiver, the so-called liaison brain. That may be the case. Yet, the more we study the brain, the more we learn that basic processes of perception and the control of movement, of hunger, and of fear can be traced to the function of complex neural circuitry. However, if we are to be honest, we have to admit that what we have so far traced is somewhat rudimentary, and that when some neuroscientists claim the mind can be totally explained in terms of brain function, they make that same existential leap of faith most of us have already made when we accept the theory of evolution as providing our descent from the amoeba without the intervention of a special creation (Chapter 1). In any case, both monists and dualists agree that much brain research remains to be done, whether or not it can capture all of mental reality.

We stress how diverse are the strategies taken by neuroscientists. Neurologists study the brains of human beings clinically and look at how lesions impair or modify how people act or talk. This study leads to a view of the brain as consisting of a number of regions, each able to carry out some rather complex function (perhaps not easily made describable in the language of

action and perception), so that any particular task may require the cooperation of many of these regions, each of which contains many millions of cells.
In the same way, different tasks may still call on certain regions in common
for their successful achievement. This much we begin to understand. And
yet, first-rate neurologists may still disagree as to which areas of the brain
are implicated in Broca's aphasia.

Workers in the brain theory component of cognitive science can be seen
as engaged in an evolutionary quest. (Arbib 1982b explicitly refers to his
modelling of frog brain as the evolution of *Rana Computatrix,* the computational frog.) Where the experimentalist analyzes simple creatures akin to our
ancestors in the biological sense, the theorist designs circuits that can be
analyzed mathematically or on the computer to reveal basic principles of
perception or motor control or memory. The theorist develops stronger techniques for analyzing complex processes, hoping to evolve to a fuller understanding of the human brain. This understanding is not to be gained in
isolation from, but in strong interaction with, what can be learned from
experiments.

Much of what we know about the brain has been learned in the last thirty-
five years through the use of microelectrodes: thin wires that allow us to
monitor the electrical activity of single cells of the brain. The trouble is, of
course, that a human brain contains hundreds of billions of cells, and a selective sample of even a hundred of those cells still leaves us a long way from
understanding the complex interaction of the whole ensemble. One strategy,
then, is to look at simpler brains in which we can hope to probe some of
the basic mechanisms. For example, Eric Kandel (1978) studied habituation
of the gill withdrawal reflex in *Aplysia* (a sea slug) and has been able to show
molecular mechanisms of change within a few synapses that underlie this
simplest of learning behaviors. Some years ago, many neurophysiologists who
were concerned with brains more akin to that of the human being would
have treated the work on *Aplysia* as being irrelevant, not worthy of the serious
neuroscientist's attention. However, the success of the study of invertebrates
in exhibiting basic cellular mechanisms has been so great that this barrier
has long since eroded. However, again note the immense gap: it is one thing
to say that one can understand how a localized change in a neural circuit
in a sea slug can correspond to the habituation with which a response dimin-
ishes over time, but quite another to understand enough about memory to
explain how a human being acquires the skill to compose music or ride a
bicycle. Nonetheless, such is our faith in a certain style of understanding that
we do not view this gap as showing that Kandel's work is irrelevant but simply
have to remind ourselves both of its value and of how many problems remain unsolved. The pragmatic criterion is not the only criterion that guides
the scientist. There exists not only the pragmatic question of "Are these results
repeatable?" but also the question, answered in part by social consensus,
in part by individual determination: "Is this study worth doing?"

Neural explanation of mental states

Can one, for example, hope to emerge from narrow-sense schema theory to an understanding of aesthetic experience, such as is taken for granted when talking about literature? Reductionists might claim there is no separate category of "aesthetic experience," since it should be explicated in terms of sociology or psychology. Such reduction, however, seems too partial to do justice to the richness of individual experience – a richness that, one suggests, may be subserved by a complex network of schemas rather than by any single or simple mechanism of aesthetic evaluation.

Aristotle noted that symmetry, unity, and universality contribute to the aesthetic experience. Levi-Strauss (1968) suggests there is, in principle, a set of finite structures of the human brain to be exploited, and such formal criteria as symmetry could fit into this type of explanation. But such notions as diversity are more difficult since they are rooted differently in different cultural traditions. It does not seem to be possible to exhaust any work of literature by the structural techniques explored to date; but this limitation does not necessarily preclude progress toward a complete explanation. Reductionists will want to view the aesthetic/nonaesthetic distinction as at best a first approximation, a useful shorthand for a continuum of diverse but overlapping processes.

Consider hunger. We now have a useful account of hunger in terms of receptors in the hypothalamus and the stomach – with high blood-sugar or stomach-distension signalling satiation (cf. Kandel and Schwartz 1981, Chapter 38). Monitoring circuitry exhibits activity that, to a first approximation, accords well with subjective reports of hunger. Lesions and electrical stimulation can yield aberrant feeding behavior. In the evolved brain, there will be many pathways to the circuitry involved in motivation beyond those coming directly from the receptors. Even reading a poem about food may stimulate that circuitry! For a human being, knowing it is mealtime can make one hungry even in the absence of the usual physiological cues. Thus, we have in hunger an example of a drive that, to a good first approximation, we understand in a neural reductionist way, yet that can be modified by evolutionary refinements (recall our discussion of Hughlings Jackson in the previous section). Now, one could still specify a gap: "You have explained why the animal eats, but you haven't explained why the animal *feels* hungry. You haven't explained the quality of hunger – the color and texture of that consciousness." A dog may eat, but only a human being can dine. Even with an explicit report of each of these colorations of hunger and of neural correlates for each of these colorations, it may still be argued that this report does not explain why they feel as they do.

We suggested in the previous section that the phenomenon of consciousness may be related to the evolution of communication and then of language. Briefly, we view the brain as a network of hundreds of billions of neurons hierarchically organized into larger units, such as modules, layers, and brain regions in dynamic interaction. When we try to communicate something of what we perceive or intend or want, we are forced to provide in a serial stream of words a small sample of that immense pattern of neural activity. Having evolved an interface, as it were, between the neural complexities and the laryngeal simplicities, we have processes in the brain that can provide a current abstract of the complexities; this abstract can then be used not only for the generation of speech or for the consideration of what not to say, but also as part of clarifying our planning activity, much of which goes on subconsciously in terms of the interaction of billions of neurons. By developing such hypotheses, we may come to see what role consciousness plays in the brain's economy.

Given all this, one may reply to the reductionist that to ask for more is to ask too much – if the scientists can explain the correlates of brain states and reportable experience, they have done all that science can do. Just as, above, we traced the neural correlates of hunger, so must we acknowledge that neuroscience has given us a fairly complete account of how we perceive and discriminate the color red. However, the question, "What explains our experience of redness?" is not a scientific question; at best, it is a hoary old philosophical conundrum – and perhaps an unanswerable one at that. There are two kinds of questions here: first, can the reductionist program be carried through convincingly as a piece of science?; and second, when it has been carried through, is there necessarily something left out, something extrascientific without which the specifically human cannot be completely understood? Let us pursue these questions in the context of "experiencing red."

We understand that light of certain wavelengths is perceived as red. With increasing subtlety of our understanding of color, we have learned that what appears red against one background will not appear red against another. We have thus learned some rules whereby we can determine how figure and ground interact to determine whether we will name something as being red. We have correlated the interactions of amacrine and horizontal cells processing the activity of rods and cones in the retina with the changing naming of the color on the basis of the surround. We are thus well on the way to understanding what is involved when we perceive a color over a great range of subtle situations. And yet, we still have not shown why light of a certain wavelength gives us the conscious experience of seeing a certain color. Going even further, we have the old question of "How do you know that when you see red you don't really see what I see when I see green?" Might it not be, we ask, that in fact the subjective experience of seeing red that I derive from looking at the top traffic light is the same subjective color experience you have from the bottom light? In the future (not the near future) of neuroscience, we might be able to push even further to learn of various subtle interactions high up in the cerebral cortex whose presence is a necessary correlate of the perception of red. We might discover this as we try to trace the pathway from the retinal patterns we come to correlate with red to the patterns in the speech area (still a long way from elucidation) that could control the vocal musculature to utter the word *red*. We might perhaps discover to our fascination that the intermediate neural pattern that goes with my seeing red is similar to what goes with your seeing green. Now the internal state that represents congruent input–output behaviors is irrelevant to behavior (Section 3.2), but we might want to conclude, nonetheless, that we do have reversed subjective experience because we have this reversed pattern of neural activity. However, even having satisfied ourselves by this subtle development beyond current neuroscience that we could tell our subjective experiences apart, we still would not know why those neural patterns provide us with these subjective experiences. Of course, some people would deny that it is in principle possible. After all, "that is the color for 'stop' " may be irreversibly connected to the subjective experience of red, which thus cannot be conflated with green – and other associations would prevail in traffic-light-free cultures.

Do such considerations put an end to scientific explanation of the mind? We think not. If we actually look at the success of science in explaining many phenomena, we must see that there is always a residue of extratheoretic identification. We have a concept called mass in Newtonian mechanics, and we have ways of placing a measuring instrument about an object and coming up with a number we then choose to identify with the mass demanded by theory. In some sense, however, this link is one we must always assume rather than prove. The theory of mechanics can show us how by calling on the universal law of gravitation we can understand how the planets move in almost elliptical orbits around the sun and how the interaction among the planets, moons, and asteroids can perturb those ellipses. And yet, if someone insists on asking, "How can you prove that those planets are obeying the law of gravitation, rather than just choosing to follow elliptical paths through the heavens?" we can only respond with exasperation. Notice, by the way, the interesting language that we as scientists accept of obeying the law. It is not really that some creator or judge or king has set forth a law that the particles of the universe consciously assimilate and follow on pain of punishment, but still we find these figures of speech useful. By showing how a relatively small set of "laws" can allow us to explain a great diversity of phenomena, we feel we have provided an explanation. So we believe it will be with subjective experience.

Hume pointed out that when we observe regular correlations between external objects and events, we cannot also intuit any "necessary connections" between them. According to the Humean view, "laws of nature" are just the regular correlations of events and their connection in comprehensive theoretical networks. We adopt a similar view with regard to the kind of events we call "consciousness" of red and hunger. There is no more to say about the brute fact that "red" appears to human perceivers as it does appear, given that we can (in our projected future science) describe all the relevant correlations of neurology, physiology, physics, and behavior with respect to external objects. This conclusion parallels Hume's: there is no more to say about the mutual interactions of billiard balls, once we can describe all relevant correlations of size, shape, mass, and motion, including, if possible, all the laws of the internal constitution of billiard balls, as far as physics is able to go.

There is more difficulty, however, in accepting the Humean conclusion in regard to the "higher" mental functions. We started by asking about aesthetic experience but quickly shifted the discussion to hunger and color. We may also ask about moral and religious experiences, intentionality, and free will. It can be argued that the reductionism of cognitive science will apply not just to the acquisition of motor and perceptual schemas, but also to cognitive and linguistic development, to motivation and emotion, and to intentionality. Such a view has often been regarded as an intolerable threat to our view of the uniqueness of the human being, whether that be the possession of individual souls or minds, or of a special sort of rationality radically distinct from what could be explained by natural evolution.

This concern for human uniqueness closes the loop from brain theory back to the concerns with which we introduced our discussion of AI in Section 2.1. In particular, religious believers have supposed that reductionism is inconsistent with belief in an essence of the human being as related in a special way to God. It is ironic, however, that it is the "death of God" in post-Enlightenment thought that has put greatest pressure on philosophers to maintain some sort of nonreductionism as the last bastion against the naturalization of the human being – if a person is neither a child of God, nor the possessor of a unique "mind," what requires us to treat persons as free and responsible agents and personal relations as the arena of moral choice? Rorty (1979) charted the theories of knowledge that have resulted from belief in people's "glassy essence" – the unique ability of the mind to reflect reality – and argued that there is nothing special here for philosophers to discuss, beyond what we are told by cognitive scientists and historians of ideas. The analysis might be extended to accounts of action, intentionality, and rationality that defend discontinuity and irreducibility between what Hollis (1977) calls "plastic man" – the product of cognitive science, however sophisticated – and "autonomous man" – who has a "real self" and essential ultimate interests as a person. It could not be more obvious that this is the humanist's surrogate for the religious believer's "soul."

However, as we argue more fully in Chapter 11, religious believers are too tender minded if they reject the reductionism of cognitive science. Belief in God can be taken to provide a release from the need to defend the uniqueness of human beings as a natural fact. That uniqueness must be defended, if at all, in terms of the extranatural relation of people to God. Here we would follow, but supplement, the line taken by Putnam (1981), who regards the question "What is a person?" as a question for social decision rather than the discovery of a unique natural essence. A person is one whom we admit into our social group with the rights and duties of a responsible individual. The decision has varied from culture to culture, sometimes including and sometimes excluding such groups as slaves, criminals, lunatics, lepers, women, and even to some extent in our society dogs, cats, whales, and foxes.

In Chapter 11, then, we shall seek to offer a reading of the Christian tradition which is consistent with the contributions of our schema-theoretic epistemology yet does not accept reductionist claims concerning the person or that person's relation to God. By contrast, Chapter 12 offers a secular perspective that seeks to reconcile a multilevel reductionism with a view of human beings not as being necessarily unique but still as being "selves" who are "moral agents." It is, of course, necessary to supplement this basic reductionism by showing that it can accommodate many discontinuities between the human and the nonhuman. These natural discontinuities are the proper concern of cognitive science and are what the new theories have shown to be potentially explicable in reductionist terms. Cognitive science gives a complex account of the relation of mind and the world, which relates mind with brain states and environments and that may in principle be adequate to account for all the variety of natural human competences. We learn to cope with the world by representing or misrepresenting "reality" in terms of mental schemas or models that are tested and modified by feedback and a variety of other processes in everyday experience, in natural situations, and by social conditioning. Note, however, the uniqueness of endowment and experience that makes each person an individual who does not live wholly within a (socially constituted) reality or invariably accept its authority.

Given this highly complex set of mechanisms, the appropriate concept of "reduction" is complex also. It is possible that the complete mechanism may never be knowable in practice or even in principle. In any case, there is no immediate prospect of our being able to translate our usual talk about language, intentionality and so on at the higher levels into talk simply about hardware and software. To this extent, the "ordinary language" philosophers were right – we cannot dispense with ordinary talk about persons because this may not in practice be reducible to talk about mechanisms, even though, ontologically speaking, persons are mechanisms. In understanding the working of computers themselves, we cannot avoid talk about "learning," "perceiving," and even "understanding meanings." In other words, these ordinary concepts are appropriate theoretical concepts in giving expression to the complex interactions and levels of cognitive systems. This is what we referred to as "top-down" analysis, in which ordinary concepts are presupposed as higher-level theories for cognitive mechanisms, though the development of the lower-level theories may redefine these higher-level constructs more adequately than everyday language.

We may summarize the relation between brain theory, within the broader setting of schema theory or cognitive science, and our study of the construction of reality (be it cognitive, social, or religious) as follows:

1. A reductionist brain theory holds that "brain mechanisms embody all that we might wish to explain about the mind." This reductionism applies not only to the acquisition of motor and perceptual schemas but also to cognitive and linguistic development, to motivation and emotion, and to intentionality. Much research on neural mechanisms for these schemas remains to be done, whether or not one accepts the reductionist claims.

2. According to cognitive science and its foreseeable extensions, we, as individuals and as a species, learn to cope with the world by representing "reality" in terms of mental schemas or models. These schemas become adapted through experience by a process of active testing, reflective abstraction, monitoring, and feedback. Thus, more and more complex levels of structure have been built up in the brain, both by socialization of individuals and by genetic selection.

3. Cognitive science is strong on formal aspects of information processing but weak on symbolic, evaluative, moral, and aesthetic aspects. This situation suggests that even though our understanding of persons is enriched by schema theory, much of person reality exceeds the present reach of cognitive science. We extend the reach of schema theory in our later analysis of free will, of Freud, of language as metaphor, and of the holistic symbol systems of ideology and religion.

4. "Reality" comes in a variety of modes. We are dealing not only with the physical object ontology of things but also with persons, mental states, social constructions and, perhaps, gods. For some people, God is *the* reality; for others, God is a reality, if at all, only as a social or psychological structure people have named as if it were a transcendent reality. In its own terms, schema theory may be neutral about its applicability to "construction" in all these realms. Our task is to examine the similarities and differences between them, with the aim of discovering how far the honorific term *reality* can properly be applied to constructions of different kinds.

5   Freedom

5.1 Problems of humanism in cognitive science

In the previous chapters, the authors take a neutral stance between two
radically different perspectives – the secular and the religious. We describe
some of the evidence and arguments for each perspective from a relatively
dispassionate standpoint. We thus hope to indicate how developments in
cognitive science can be used to illuminate both secular and religious interpretations of the human being and, in turn, be illuminated by them. In
Chapters 9 and 10, we suggest that hermeneutic and symbolic approaches
coming from the social sciences can be seen as potentially continuous with
cognitive science. Just as scientific models of the mind are schemas for perception, learning, and intelligence, so hermeneutics, which studies the interpretation of texts from within different symbol systems, can be seen as expressing
schemas for the interaction of the individual and the social. Indeed, we show
how the schema theorist can use the concepts of hermeneutic circle, dialectic, and dialogue as heuristic hypotheses for extending the science from individual to social.

We have, however, touched on some issues indicating that this conciliatory
view is not sufficient to solve the problems of the secular view of the human
nor to do justice to the religious perspective. This chapter makes explicit some
irreducible controversies between the two perspectives that we broadly describe as the "secular" and the "religious." As with all ideologies, these two
perspectives are self-reflective in that they give an account of themselves within
their own internal concept systems, and also of each other within their own
systems. Much of the secular account of religion can be taken over into a
religious account of itself, and vice versa. Also, much human experience lies
within the intersection of interpretations of the two ideologies, just as, for
example, common experience of elementary mechanics lies in the intersection of Newtonian and relativistic theory. Everyone can agree on the local
application of Newton's laws, just as everyone may agree that many capacities
of human beings can be simulated by machines, or that religions have social
components and functions. But just as the total model of space, time, and
motion is radically different, and indeed inconsistent, as between Newto-

nian mechanics and relativistic theory, so there are radical and irreducible conflicts among the total perspectives on humanity, society, and religion of scientific secularism and religious faith.

The following chapters concentrate on three issues in which the radical character of the conflict can best be seen. Let us put these issues in the form of the questions:

1. What becomes of the specifically human in the light of cognitive science?
2. What are the grounds of human values in secularism and religion respectively?
3. What interpretation can be given to the problem of evil and to the human search for meaning, salvation, and destiny?

We should perhaps make some excuse initially for speaking in terms of the secularist and the religious view. There are, of course, many different versions of both views. Rather than try to make a conscientious but pedantic catalogue of them all, which would be neither complete nor illuminating, we think it better to develop and explore particular expressions of these points of view in depth. This method has the advantage of allowing us to be constructive, speculative, and somewhat novel instead of rehearsing old solutions that we regard as sterile.

Is there an "essence" of the human being?

We have given reasons for thinking that if the essence of the human being is defined in terms of "rationality" in a broad sense, then any task proposed for a "rational" being is in principle capable of being performed by a machine. "Rationality" is here taken to include construction of mental schemas of the external world (both everyday and scientific); possession and use of language; exhibition of intentionality, motivation, and purpose in human action; the following of social rules; construction of mental schemas of society, values, and the gods; and capacity for innovation and creativity, including aesthetic activity. This is a generous list. However, if it included everything about the essence of the human, then artificial intelligences would be capable in principle of sharing that essence, and hence the human would appear to be reducible without remainder to spatiotemporally bound mechanisms.

The question to be asked from a religious perspective is: Does reduction conflict with a view of human beings as children of God, having an eternal destiny of fellowship with him? In traditional theology and philosophy, it has been usual to postulate a nonspatiotemporal "soul" to carry this eternal destiny, however that may be understood. For Plato, the soul is a denizen of the world of forms, contingently united with a temporary spatiotemporal body. For doctrines of reincarnation, the soul can be embodied in a succession of natural entities but is essentially independent of any. For Aristotle, the soul is the rational form necessarily linked with a particular human body and therefore not an independent immortal substance. For Aquinas, the soul is an eternal constituent of the human, uneasily combining both Platonic and Aristotelian elements. For Descartes, the soul is the indestructible non-corporeal and rational substance of each human being.

The crucial distinction between all these philosophies (except possibly Aristotle's) and even the most liberal type of modern reductionism is that they all contemplate realities that transcend the natural space–time framework of modern science. They all do so, however, along with a similar presup-position about the eternity and nonlocalizability of *a priori* truths or other principles of reason. Insofar as human beings are reasoning animals, they escape the limits of space and time. It is this assumption that is challenged by the development of AI systems. We therefore have to ask whether there are characteristics of persons that require a nonspatiotemporal account. Let us begin by asking how far reductionist models of persons can go.

1. It is common ground that "persons" are holistic entities in the sense that the total system requires simpler subsystems in mutual interaction and that this interaction produces properties of the whole not present in the parts taken separately. This type of holism is not always true of properties of complex entities – for example, a complex chemical molecule may have properties of weight, valency, ionization, and so on, that are different in quantity from those of its parts, but not different in kind. Capacity to refract light, on the other hand, is a holistic property in the sense required here, since bodies that are complexes of molecules may have this capacity, but the molecules them-selves do not.

AI systems are holistic in the same sense. We say they are "reductions" of human intelligence, but in a different sense from the way molecular biology is a reduction of organisms. AI systems do not show how human minds and brains are built up from their material components because the hardware of the two kinds of system is materially different. They do, however, simulate human intelligence by reproducing its software, and by doing so they show that the characteristics of "rationality" can be captured within spatiotemporal mechanisms and require no transcendent realities. The reduc-tion is, therefore, spatiotemporal but not material.

2. We have argued that there are no limits in principle to this kind of AI reduction. It might still be objected, however, that, even though "mental" aspects of personality are thus capturable by AI, there are nevertheless features of the human biological makeup (for example, that human beings move around and act in the world) that are not fully shared by computers (see the discussion in Searle 1985). The more "holistic" the person-system is, the more it may be expected that such features will interact essentially with mental life. But such disanalogies may be progressively reduced by the development of active robots, and in any case they do not seem to be the sort of disanalogies that depend on a nonspatiotemporal understanding of God–person relations. In fact, religious exploitation of the biological limits

to AI reduction would be of little help in understanding the action of God in the world, since human physiology is more obviously subject to natural causal chains than is rationality. We cannot capture the essentially nonspatiotemporal character of God–person and God–world relations by exploiting the gaps in the space–time story. In trying to understand specifically religious characterizations of the human being, we may as well assume the biological as well as the mental simulation to be complete.

We assume, then, that traditional attempts to locate the "soul" wholly within space–time but independent of scientific accounts of "matter" all fail. These traditional accounts include both Cartesianism and modern "humanist" talk about such allegedly irreducible personal characteristics as intentions, motives, beliefs, and goals. For example, cognitive science rejects such assertions as "thoughts are not in space and time." They are; they are relational properties of the complex of interacting systems that make up human brains and bodies, and in the same sense they are properties of AI systems. The purposive and intentional faculties of human beings can be mirrored in the hierarchical organization of mechanical circuitry.

3. We therefore assume that all holistic, though essentially space–time, properties of persons may be simulated by sufficiently complex mechanisms that will themselves be holistic in the same sense. It follows that the differences between persons and such mechanisms lie in accidents of material hardware and mode of construction or growth. Does it follow that religious (and indeed humanist) views of the "soul" must apply similarly to persons and to mechanisms? This debate has already been joined in relation to "human rights." When we employ robots autonomously for more or less low-grade manual and mental tasks, should we accord them equality before the law, such as the right to form unions? Shall we have created (by a different method from the normal) human individuals who from the religious point of view have an eternal destiny and potential for communion with God?

To contemplate such questions, whether they be answered positively or negatively, is to recognize that systems of values are involved that are not decidable in terms of the facts alone. It is also to recognize that AI simulation does not entail "dragging the human being down to the level of the machine," with all its attendant moral overtones, but may rather "draw the machines up to the level of the human being," indeed, the more successful the machine is, the more it suggests the latter interpretation. More fundamentally still, questions about AI simulation are in the end quite irrelevant both for humanist values and for religious interpretations of the soul. In particular, if the religious questions involve the nonspatiotemporal, then such questions arise as much for intelligent machines as they do for human beings. The crucial issues are not about simulation or reduction but about values and the nonspatiotemporal. Meanwhile, we illustrate this thesis by considering the particular question of human freedom.

5.2 Decisionist versus voluntarist on human freedom

AI reduction makes claims on the concept of "person" that seem *prima facie* to contradict both religious and humanist interpretations. If successful, AI reduction would seem to entail that human action is either mechanically determined or mechanically random, since these are apparently the only modes of action open to a machine. Both alternatives contradict the view that a person acts freely from his or her own autonomous choice, neither randomly nor totally constrained by deterministic laws. A reductionist may, however, argue that action under law is quite compatible with human freedom if this is properly understood.

The reductionist issues the following challenge: to have free will is simply to act as you would without somebody physically threatening you while telling you how to act. Therefore, to act with free will is certainly consistent with a deterministic theory because it means you have built up certain ideas about society and your place in it and about the goals and predilections in terms of which you act. On that basis, one could imagine a cybernetic model, (that is, an AI goal-selection model) that would have goals and find ways of meeting them. That is what it means to act freely, and therefore there is nothing about free will that distinguishes a human being from a sophisticated machine. We call this thesis the *decisionist* theory of free will. In using this term, we neither imply nor deny that the decision must be conscious. We imply only that actions take place as a result of schema-based interactions between person and environment. Neither do we use the term "decisionist" in the sense of Habermas (1971a, Chapter 5), where it means "action according to nonrationally or arbitrarily chosen goals," for we shall argue that rational goals may also evolve by lawlike interactions between persons and environments.

Let us make two preliminary points about our expression of the decisionist view. First, what does it mean to say, "You have built up certain ideas, goals, and so on"? This statement may suggest a "little man in the head" who, if he does not direct action, at least writes the programs according to which action takes place. However, our sketch of an evolutionary theory of consciousness in Section 4.2 attempts to avoid this homunculus view. Daniel Dennett has also described how the AI programmer designs intentional systems by breaking down their task into a hierarchy of subsystems of progressively more "stupid" intentional systems to perform simpler tasks. Like the cooperative computation of our schemas, these subsystems "talk to each other, wrest control from each other, volunteer, sub-contract, supervise, and even kill" (Dennett 1978, p. 123); and by means of all these interactions, more complex intelligent tasks get done. No "self" or "homunculus" sits at the top level, monitoring all the subsystems; neither do the subsystems themselves need to contain "intelligent" homunculi, because their tasks can be reduced at the lowest level to simple computations. The whole system of systems is, in person language, the "self" who has purposes, intentions, reasons, and, in some sense, free will. Thus, by the up-and-down analysis we have described in Section 4.1, person language can constitute a higher-level account of mechanical systems.

For example, we can incorporate talk about human goals into such a theory. As human organisms, we all have biological goals that can be described in terms of evolution theory; however, an adequate theory must also account for uniquely human goals not biologically determined. Schema theory in principle responds by showing how goals, such as loyalty, develop with perceptual and motor schemas as something learned as a member of society. You may be hungry, but you've told a friend you will wait before going into the restaurant, so you override biological goals and wait out of loyalty or friendship. The Freudian story is an account of how such secondary processes come to overwhelm primary processes of basic biological gratification. The human world is both biological and social.

In terms of such a theory, we see that our behavior rests on a more complex pattern of mental activity than we are aware of in our current, consciously understood, intentions. The complex is built up from genetic inheritance, from environment and education, and back through the history of our society and ultimately of the whole human race.

The second point is that reduction to a "sophisticated machine" should be carefully distinguished from the thesis of determinism. The crucial issue is the definition of free will. The decisionist thesis defines free will in terms consistent with determination; in this sense, of course, a machine may have free will if it simulates human actions sufficiently closely, because a person is then conceived of as a machine. We consider here another understanding of free will for which determinism is inconsistent with free will. According to that understanding, it is relatively unimportant whether a machine can be said to have free will – if it is a determinist machine, it will not; and if humans are determinist machines, they will not. Only if either machines or humans are not deterministic might it be possible for them to have free will. The important issues are how this sense of free will is to be interpreted, whether it pertains to machines or human beings, and what the arguments are for adopting it. It is not, of course, sufficient for this view to argue that physical systems are indeterminist, since if that were all there were to free will, electrons would have it.

Let us therefore put up a contrary thesis. Suppose, as a matter of fact, there exist laws of nature that are deterministic in the sense that given the initial state of the universe, they determine uniquely all its subsequent states – then there is no free will. This is the *voluntarist* view. By contrast, a *decisionist* will be able to continue to believe in free will in his sense, even if the Laplacean hypothesis just stated is true, so long as he can give an account of intentional behavior determined by internal goals, rather than by social duress. Thus, for the decisionist, free will is essentially a social concept, whereas for the voluntarist it is a semiphysical concept, since it requires the person to act in a way not determined by physical law. The decisionist will continue to believe that human freedom, relative to a person's genes and upbringing, consists in nobody coming up with a gun, a threat of jail, or more subtle psychological pressures, to make him or her act one way or another. Action is free if it takes place after reflection, by drawing on experience, and from the agent's character. But this does not help the voluntarist, who visualizes the sequence of states of the world through time, including her present state as a substate of the world, and notes that if determinism is true then this is a unique sequence in which reflection on action, and decision, has its equally determined and unique place. If I have a so-called choice to travel to Alabama or California tomorrow, this "choice" cannot make a difference to what happens tomorrow, because if it is determined that I go to California, there is no physically possible world in which I go to Alabama. My "choice" now is itself part of the "determined" causal chain leading me to California, and it is not itself the crucial initiating event that determines that, barring accidents, I get there. For a determinist, there are no forks in the sequence of world states that mean "I could do one thing or another," or "I could have done differently than I did."

However, the decisionist gives a different account of free will in terms of brain states. At any time, our conscious account of our states relative to the world is a small sample of reality. In particular, this sample is not enough to let us predict how we will behave. It may take much "decision making" before embarking on a course of action. The voluntarist would reply, "If you are going to do that 'anyway,' why go through all that spurious decision-making?" However, the decision making is part of the causal chain. If a computer is loaded with a certain program to compute sines of input data, then it can do nothing else; neither can it dispense with any steps of program execution before returning its output. The decisionist holds that part of our education as responsible adults resides in our acquiring "programs" that will help us choose appropriate courses of action, rather than acting in the unreflective manner of the young child. In telling this story, a decisionist need not talk about unique determination, but about probability. Suppose I see my past history as biasing me in particular ways, so that there is a probability distribution over what I actually decide to do and what I decide not to do; then, whatever happens is going to be consistent with there being some antecedent probability of that happening. We shall see later in this chapter that the decisionist story is not affected in its essence by a weakening of determinism to include the possibility of ultimate probabilities, with no determinist hidden variables, as seems to be the case in quantum theory.

Let us pursue the notion of what it is to "act freely from one's character." We are ordinarily prepared to make predictions about people's actions based on their character and previous history. We say "His upbringing, his unfortunate home life, his broken relationships, how his personality has developed, make it overwhelmingly probable he will run away from responsibility, perhaps treat a close friend badly." We would be surprised if he "rises above himself" and shows courage and responsibility where we would not predict it. However, sometimes people do surprise us. A usually meek person may show unexpected heroism in rescuing a child from a burning building. This may be an occasion for that person to experience a glow of self-satisfaction. The decisionist, however, would claim that the satisfaction is not properly ascribed to the sterling qualities of some nonspatiotemporal will, but rather that his schemas could "rise to the occasion" in ways of which one was not hitherto aware. This change in self-consciousness can in turn feed back to change other schemas and thus future behavior. But to say this is to presuppose that there is something underlying what ordinary observation up to now has belied, which now determines the person to do the unexpected thing relative to our previous knowledge. This, of course, is to assume more than we can ever know, and it also seems to go against ordinary ways of talking about human behavior, when we say people are responsible for their actions when they could have chosen to do otherwise, and when we praise or blame them for actions and their consequences. Nonetheless, both our schema theory of Section 4.2 and our Freudian analysis of Chapter 6 suggest that we cannot rely on this "common-sense" view that sees all mental events as being immediately accessible to introspection and public accounting.

Moral codes are as old as society. They have survival value. Social groups are in great part defined by their codes of "decent" behavior and could not survive without them. Suppose, then, that someone is brought up for murder; a decisionist will (to caricature somewhat!) say something like this: "You have this defective program that causes you to act like this; therefore, as master reprogrammers we can either say, 'It is not worth the effort to reprogram you, off to the electric chair,' or we may say, 'We are going to try to reprogram you and to help other people to debug their own programs by seeing what happens to you.' " Again, we are nowadays sometimes prepared to say that a murder is committed under diminished responsibility, and law courts recognize that there are some actions not under a person's control. A Freudian might account for this behavior by saying the acts were not under the control of the ego but were still determined by accused's mental state (e.g., an unruly id). A schema-theoretic account would appeal to the distinction of the conscious self from the totality of operative schemas. In any case, we do not blame or punish the offender to the same degree as in the past when we knew less about the causes of human behavior. Note, again, that this thesis does not require strict determinism – the story would go through as well with a probabilistic model of schema interaction.

The usual view of "diminished responsibility" still presupposes a distinction between actions caused and those we are responsible for. What the decisionist thesis suggests, however, is that the area of causal determination actually extends over all human action and will be seen to do so as we learn more. In this sense, human action is no different from the behavior of billiard balls, which is determined by physical laws, even if they sometimes do things at the observable level that are unexpected to the human observer given limited knowledge of the exact force applied by the cue and the condition of the felt on the table. The voluntarist finds it unsatisfactory that important personal notions of praise, blame, guilt, and freedom should be subject in this way to the shifting edge of current scientific knowledge, but the decisionist counters that our growing knowledge may affect our views of person–reality no less dramatically than physics has shifted our views of space–time.

One might almost question, on this decisionist account, whether the notion of free will is useful at all. The decisionist would reiterate that it is, if we interpret the term *freedom* as being at the social level of analysis – we are free if others do not unduly coerce us – rather than at the physical level of a response to something transcending physical law.

We cannot understand the human individual without seeing him or her as situated within a complex society. We find that certain things hurt us by the nature of our nervous systems; but other things hurt us, or embarrass us, only because we have learned to evaluate them within a particular social setting. At any particular time, we believe that certain ways of treating people will change their behavior, and we act accordingly. We expect the university to educate; we expect jails to act as a deterrent to potential criminals and as an agent of reform for criminals or, at least, a way of keeping criminals away from the rest of society. On this basis, the decisionist would sketch a schema-theoretic account of responsibility. At any time, members of a society agree to classify certain acts as harmful. Adults try to educate the young to share these values; citizens set up a judicial system to punish (perhaps with certain socioeconomic biases) people who do not act accordingly. Individuals know they will be punished if they transgress these norms. Arguments about whether jails could reform prisoners or should punish them are based on an essentially causal view of the human mind. The notion of responsibility, then, reduces to a social contract that people who transgress will be punished or reformed. Look at these two syllables – *re-form,* form again. When we reflect on so massive a crime as the outbreak of Nazism, we do not rejoice in the Nazis' exercise of free will, but we rather seek a causal historical analysis – what can we do to make sure it will never happen again? The fact that we cannot be sanguine about limiting such horrors (only human beings can be truly inhuman) does not in the decisionist's view argue for a view of mind transcending the physical.

There is little here with which the voluntarist need disagree; she will want to describe it differently. She does not, of course, deny that human action is constrained by physical laws – we cannot fly unaided nor read each others' minds directly. But she wishes to retain the notion that human action can make a difference to the future of the world, as between states that are equally consistent with physical laws, including the laws constraining the actions themselves and the initiating brains and bodies. The question is, how is this "making a difference" to be expressed? We have briefly noted that reference to laws giving probability distributions over physically possible future states does not essentially affect the decisionist's story about free will. It is time to justify that assertion and to consider whether the voluntarist (a) requires physical indeterminacy, and (b) finds it a sufficient condition of freedom. We answer "yes" to (a) and "no" to (b).

A determinist says the world actually is uniquely determined. What is the evidence for this? When Newtonian theory was the best theory, it gave us a determinist mechanics, but there were no necessary consequences for chemistry, let alone for a science of biology or psychology. So called Laplacean determinism (Laplace 1951, p. 4, first published 1796) made a bold extrapolation in claiming there would be no irreducible emergent properties at any level of complexity of physical entities that might refute the determinism of the Newtonian particle level. We now know that this extrapolation from a billiard-ball universe to electromagnetism, to chemistry, to biology is false, and it is false even for mechanics, because we do not now believe in Newton's laws as accurately true.

Our best theory in physics is now quantum mechanics, which seems to imply ultimate indeterminism. Strenuous efforts have been made to try to show that it is, after all, consistent with a determinist theory of the world in Laplace's sense. The question becomes a complex consideration of the possibility of hidden variable theories, which would show how the uncertainty principle is a stochastic consequence of an underlying deterministic structure. All that can definitely be said is that, although quantum mechanics may be consistent with such a theory, there is no evidence for it and much against, and perhaps there can never be conclusive evidence either way. This is in spite of the fact that Einstein and others tried hard (for ideological reasons) to disprove ultimate uncertainty. Even all this extra motivation has not produced conclusive results. Apart from the consequences of quantum theory itself, we still have no good evidence that all the sciences of more complex physical systems, up to the human brain and human societies, are "one-way" reducible without remainder to quantum theory. Even if quantum theory did turn out to be deterministic, its determinism might not apply at higher levels of complexity. Because the issue of determinism is unsettled, we have spoken of a decisionist, rather than a determinist, position on free will.

But how do the probabilistic alternatives of quantum mechanics relate to the forks in the sequence of possible world states from now to the future that the voluntarist sees as essential for free will? Let us take this in two steps. The voluntarist has strong ideological reasons for pressing ultimate indeterminism. A world that is undetermined at some physical level leaves room for the occurrence of such forks because at any given time it contemplates a probability distribution over several possible futures, where the probability is not further reducible to the determinate behavior of microhidden variables. This seems a comparatively innocuous step to take since, as we have seen, we have no strong evidence for ultimate physical determinism or for the reducibility of complex physical systems to determinist microtheory. A factual question arises here as to whether quantum indeterminacy in the brain is at the right level to generate probabilities at points at which one would wish to say "choices" are made. The answer to this appears to be yes – shot noise at the membrane can make the difference as to whether a neuron goes above threshold or below it, so that a spike is generated, and the effect of that spike could be amplified by other neurons.

This argument, however, gives the voluntarist only a necessary and not a sufficient condition for free will. The next step is the most important and difficult one. Even if our best theory allows that there is basic indeterminism, it must be asked, "What has this got to do with free will?" All that physics can tell us is that there are random events that are in some sense uncaused as individuals, although in the mass they may satisfy statistical laws. But when I say I am making a decision, this process is not like going through probability computations and then tossing an indeterministic coin – such a process is still nowhere near capturing the voluntarist's intuition about free will. It is just as difficult to ascribe responsibility to quantum jumps as to a sequence of predetermined states.

It does not follow, of course, that randomness at some crucial stages in a "decision" process introduces total arbitrariness relative to the causal network in which these stages occur. Both voluntarist and decisionist can agree that the story about "reprogramming" can still apply, but with the reprogramming now seen as a method for changing the probability distributions at crucial points, rather than as a method of unique causal determination. This modification leaves room, for example, for the probabilistically exceptional individual to "resist" any brainwashing procedures. The decisionist, however, will claim that a deterministic theory also leaves room for resistance – since the victim may have schemas whose nature is unknown to the brainwasher and that can counter the attempted mental transformation. The voluntarist on the other hand, will agree that freedom is always constrained within some incompletely determined causal network, but the nature of "choice" and "resistance" remains mysterious to her in the context of mechanistic explanation since she is not satisfied with the decisionist's schema theoretic account of a conscious "you" that is but an aspect of the total causal network of the brain.

How can we express the "something more" that the voluntarist view requires? First, a negative point needs to be made about use of the term *random,* since the voluntarists' apparent need for this concept is one of the reproaches brought against her. In probability theory, a "random" event is a member of a class that as a whole exhibits a distribution of outcomes consistent with some statistical law. But there is a well-known problem about ascribing the notion of "randomness" to an individual event apart from the class that defines its randomness. Events as complex as those occurring in human decision-making are unlikely to be members of such actual classes – that is, there are unlikely to be repetitions of sufficiently similar states that will actually exhibit human decisions as satisfying statistical laws. In this respect, human decision-making is of an order of differentiation and complexity incomparable with, for example, random molecular motions. The basis for using the technical term *random* for such complex events is therefore missing. We are always dealing effectively with single events, about which statistical laws can only make assertions of a hypothetical kind with unfulfilled antecedents: "If *n* battles of Waterloo were fought, the French would win *r* times, and the Allies *n* − *r* times." It is therefore doubly misleading to use the word *random* for the voluntarists' account of free will, since it not only has no technical basis, but it also carries the more-than-technical overtones of "arbitrary, irrational, fateful," which are the opposite of what the voluntarist intends.

Of all recent writers on this tangled subject, Daniel Dennett perhaps comes nearest to a sympathetic reconstruction of the voluntarists' case in his chapter "On giving libertarians what they say they want" (Dennett 1978, p. 286). (What he calls "libertarian" is essentially what we call "voluntarist.") Dennett agrees initially that some indeterminism must appear to be built into their model and proposes to place this among the "considerations that occur" to the agent debating a decision. Considerations occur by accident and in contingent order. They are selected by the agent by what may be a deterministic process. The agent has in practice to "decide" to terminate his deliberations within some finite time, and this may also be a deterministic process. The random element in the input of considerations introduces the sense that things could have happened otherwise, and, on the other hand, the determinist processes of selection, weighting, and termination depend on character, education of the will, and so on, and retain the element of personal authorship of decisions.

Dennett suggests that this is all his libertarians can at present intelligibly have and maybe all they ought to want. But it still, of course, falls short of what they say they want. The novel feature of Dennett's still essentially mechanist model is the placing of indeterminacy early in the deliberative process rather than at the last-minute point of choice. About this he says:

The libertarian could not have wanted to place the indeterminism at the end of the agent's assessment and deliberation. It would be insane to hope that after all rational deliberations had terminated with an assessment of the best available course of action, indeterminism would then intervene to flip the coin before action. It is a familiar theme in discussions of free will that the important claim that one could have done otherwise under the circumstances is not plausibly construed as the claim that one could have done otherwise given exactly the set of convictions and desires that prevailed at the end of rational deliberation. So if there is to be a crucial undetermined nexus, it had better be prior to the final assessment of the considerations on the stage, which is right where we have located it. (Dennett 1978, p. 295)

There are at least three things wrong with this argument. First, it begs the question of whether determinism or flipping a coin are the alternatives at the point of decision or at any other point. Voluntarists are not likely to be mollified by being told that even if everything conspires to determine their decision at the end point (which may be phenomenologically acceptable), nevertheless freedom is somehow guaranteed by the flipping of a cosmic coin earlier, to "decide" which considerations occur to them. Second, from the voluntarists' point of view, the model falls into an infinite regress about how to account for early "decisions" about what considerations to allow into deliberation and how to weigh them. Voluntarists want to take credit for the weighting given to these considerations as well as for the final outcome of decision, and for them, "taking credit" implies freedom that is neither determinate nor random at some stage of the temporal process, whether now or in the past.

Third, Dennett says that the claim that one could have done otherwise is not plausibly construed to mean "given exactly the set of convictions and desires that prevailed at the end." The thought here is again that free will is not well simulated by a last-minute flip of the coin, which seems to abrogate rational deliberation. This is not abrogated, however, because the alternatives between which the coin is flipped may have been given a different probability distribution by previous deliberation. In any case, flipping the coin at some earlier point of input (to decide, for example, how to weigh rational deliberations) does not capture any better the sense of free control over what it is that is decided. Dennett's argument again begs the question of whether the total state of "convictions and desires" at the end point, or convictions, desires, and external input earlier, are the only relevant features of decision.

The inadequacy for the voluntarist of Dennett's model is further pointed up by his correct remark (Dennett 1978, p. 298) that the model can itself be simulated in a purely determinist system. There can be no practical or behavioral difference between the cases in which "considerations occur" truly indeterministically, and in which they are in fact determined but appear random at the level of phenomenological experience. This argument shows again that from the decisionist point of view there is no issue between determinism or indeterminism, whereas for the voluntarist it is crucial in respect of necessary, though not sufficient, conditions.

The voluntarist who is also a theist will want to insist that the physical states of conviction, desire, and environment at the point of decision are not the only factors to be taken into account. Traditionally, the freedom of the person has been understood in terms of God–person relations, with accompanying belief in purpose and intentionality, which is irreducible to the space–time world. In his recent book *Elbow Room* (subtitled *The Varieties of Freedom Worth Wanting*), Dennett (1984, pp. 166, 171) dismisses any "absolutist" concept such as "guilt-before-God," although acknowledging that this is one motive for traditional voluntarism. He admits that he has not considered problems about free will depending on the infinite knowledge of God, which imply "a very literal and anthropomorphic vision of God as Knower," because he does not think this is "the way to take the idea of God seriously today." (Dennett does not tell us what a better way of taking God seriously is.) However, for theologians who do want to take some idea of God seriously, the detailed arguments of such philosophers as Dennett still leave everything to play for.

5.3 Freedom in theological perspective

Voluntarism and decisionism seem to have reached an impasse if we restrict ourselves to the terms so far discussed. Can we introduce some further features of the situation to help us resolve it – a tie-break, as it were, at 6–all?

The classic response, adopted by Cartesians and recently by Eccles (discussed in Chapter 4), is to postulate a "soul" that interacts with the brain in physically inexplicable ways and changes the sequence of physical causality. Modern theories of human action, and also Sperry's theory, do not assume that physical causality is abrogated but postulate teleological properties of the human "person" – such as intentionality, purposes, and motives – that are natural properties but that "supersede" physical theory. Apart from their philosophical difficulties, these theories contradict the monistic tendency of modern cognitive theory. They must also be said to be unsatisfactory from the point of view of a humanist or religious believer who wishes to hold on to a unity of "soul" and "body." A better option for a theist is to say that no extra entity such as a "soul" need be postulated for the person. The only such nonphysical entity is God, to whom the person can bear extraspatiotemporal relations, and these relations are necessarily irreducible to naturalistic brain theories. At the physical level, such a view maintains a mind–body unity rather than a Platonist or Cartesian dualism and is more consistent with the Christian emphasis on the resurrection of the body (that is, of the whole person) than the doctrine of the immortality of the soul as a "detachable" part of the person.

The voluntarist regards the hierarchy of schemas as essentially an open system, in which some events are uncaused at some physical level and for which we need a supplementary account in terms of properties not reducible to the physical level, whether this is regarded as determinist or ultimately random. It is difficult to understand how persons, who seem necessarily tied to the physical world, can have this type of transcendence of it. In fact, such a view seems historically parasitic on the more radical religious affirmation of the transcendental reality, "God," relations with whom constitute the transcendental "personhood" of spatiotemporal human beings. We therefore consider a theistic version of voluntarism that does not depend on a soul–body dualism at the physical level.

As a first approximation to cognitive science, we take the ordinary language of our culture to be expressing the purposive and intentional properties of human beings. We know how to describe situations in which we regard ourselves as free agents, without depending on any knowledge of physics or brain science. The voluntarist view we are considering claims that the phenomenological stories people tell about their "freedom" are in essence correct – they should not be radically reinterpreted into some other scientific story that changes their meaning. Rather, the scientific story should be constrained by the phenomenological story, in a top-down analysis. The voluntarist holds that this ordinary talk about persons is a better clue to how human relations are than is talk about physically interacting mechanical systems. The voluntarist who is also a theist will hold that it is also the best clue to how God–human relations are.

What, then of the status of possible future artificial intelligences that come as close as possible to simulating human functions? Do they have freedom in the same sense? Let us assume that these machines walk as well as talk and think; that is, that they are robots. The question, "Do robots have free will?" is not factually decidable because, as we have seen, no spatiotemporal facts stand between the decisionist and the voluntarist interpretations of freedom. It is, therefore, an evaluative question, like "Are robots 'slaves'?" We can only decide the question according to whether we are prepared (or forced?) to admit robots into the human community. Some theists may wish to exclude robots from the possibility of communion with God on the grounds that they have not been "endowed with souls." But this argument belongs to the dualist interpretations of body, mind, and soul that we have rejected. On a less dualist view, God endows human beings with souls by creating them the persons they are. Why not equally with robots, though they are created by a different route?

We arrive at a doubly ironic conclusion: "Persons" with free will in the sense postulated by the voluntarist are not reducible to space–time machine language, however complex. But then, neither are machines if we accord them the full character of persons. On the other hand, at the space–time level, person language is not necessary because it is more adequately replaced by the language of interacting machines. Modern cognitive monism implies perfect symmetry between human beings and sufficiently complex machines with regard to both machine and person language. In the same way, we may evaluate God–person and God–robot relations as perfectly symmetrical; but here, person language is all we have, and it is irreducible.

This way of putting the voluntarist position leaves the transcendental work to be done where it should be done from the point of view of the religious believer. It does not attempt to find God in the gaps of science but tells a story that is consistent with any practicable science and that also goes beyond it where the decisionist stops and the voluntarist is left unsatisfied. To understand how the question can be asked about a God reality, one has to make a hermeneutic leap that takes one inside the cognitive horizons of the believer and see how far this belief can be expressed consistently with science and how far in its turn it says relevant things about natural reality that science cannot say. A naturalist cannot be argued into belief in God in this way – all that can be done is to start with a naturalist or theist perspective and see which is the more eloquent of freedom as we experience it.

How, then, does free will look from the God perspective? We should note first that not all God perspectives are voluntarist. The eighteenth-century New England divine Jonathan Edwards, for example, held an interpretation of freedom he claimed to be consistent with determinism, in a context of Calvinist belief in predestination. Edwards's doctrine was a theological response to Newtonian determinism and was also intended to rebut the contemporary Arminian view of human freedom. The Arminians held that the will is independent of and indifferent to any natural or moral necessity; it is "self-determining" but arbitrary (like Buridan's ass), a notion that Edwards found inconsistent and unacceptable.

Edwards based his epistemology on that of Locke, with his notion of a perceptual tabula rasa. But when Edwards, as a Calvinist, talks of the "guilt and misery" of natural man (Edwards 1962, p. 102), he does not seem to posit an ethical tabula rasa. In any case, he would not be satisfied with any Lockean theory of the acquisition of ethics on the basis of impressions acquired in society. Such an account could at best only be a theory of the ethics of unregenerate human nature, and since this would inevitably be imperfect, human beings would naturally sin. However, Edwards believes that the Christian elect are endowed with a new nonnatural sense. They perceive nature illuminated by the divine and supernatural light and hence love a higher beauty and a higher truth. As a result, the will of the elect is such that all they could desire to do would be good. In "The Freedom of the Will," Edwards rejected the argument that rational human beings could make a moral choice without regard to its antecedents. The Arminians held that you could save yourself through your moral choices. But what was "you"? They talked as if this "you" were outside the web of cause and effect. Edwards offered a spirited critique of the notion that the will is free in the sense that it is not determined by what goes before and argued that one can only will on the basis of what one is; one is free only in the sense that one acts according to one's own motivation, according to the way one is constituted. Only the elect are truly "free" because they are constituted by the divine light.

Such a view is certainly consonant on the physical level with a decisionist analysis of motivation and action. Where Edwards goes beyond this analysis is in holding to the notion of the divine light. The elect, whether they know it or not, have been so constituted by God that they cannot will to act in

other than a moral way. Where a sceptic might ask why, if election is uncon-
ditional, people should restrain themselves from the enjoyments of debauch-
ery, Edwards would reply that one of the elect would be so constituted that
such "enjoyments" would not seem at all desirable. Leading the moral life
would be the joy and the pleasure. In "The Nature of True Virtue," Edwards
says the will inclines to a love of perfect beauty and excellence, which he
sees the Divine Principles as being (Edwards 1765). He speaks of the "new
simple idea" of an absolute acquiescence in the harmony of the universe,
so that even caring for one's family or country are just transformations of
self-love.

Edwards's determinist theory is primarily a religious and not a naturalist
one. Two points of traditional theology are crucial to his argument. The first
is the doctrine of the necessity of God's properties, specifically, his goodness.
This permits Edwards to ascribe all moral and natural necessity to God, as
flowing from his determinate disposal of all events. God alone may be said
to be self-determining, because he is a necessary being and is the ground and
cause of all that is. Where the modern decisionist ascribes ultimate necessity
and determination to nature, Edwards ascribes it to God. According to this
view, the Arminians are inconsistent in supposing that there can be self-
determining persons and independent initiations of events other than God
himself.

The second theological point has to do with grace and good works. The
Arminians are Pelagian; that is, they believe individuals can save themselves
by good works that they are free to choose. Edwards takes the contrary
Calvinist position that natural man is wholly corrupt, and only the grace of
God, freely given to some and not to others, can save the elect. This doctrine implies that human goodness is wholly God's work of grace, and that
both its offer and its acceptance by the elect are predetermined by his necessity. In answer to the objection that in that case there is no point in ascribing
praise or blame to good or bad acts, Edwards remarks that God's own goodness is determinate and necessary, but that we properly praise God for it;
if this makes sense for God, it makes sense for good men.

Thus, predestination emphasizes the utter dependence of human beings
on divine grace for the realization of their true selves. We have argued that
voluntarism requires some extraspatiotemporal reference for its adequate expression, and we now see that decisionism in Edwards's theological perspective also does. Not surprisingly, no theist can adequately express human
freedom without reference to God. Moreover, our account of Edwards indicates that predestination is not the crude and inhumane doctrine it may
appear at first sight, any more than decisionism is inhumane because it makes
human freedom dependent on mechanical causality. A modern predestina-
tionist might use many of the persuasive arguments for decisionism that we
have discussed. A voluntarist will, however, look for a theological perspec-

tive that gives more emphasis to a relative autonomy of the human will with respect to God – using the model of a community of persons in which each is free only when each respects the freedom of others. This middle way between Calvinism and Arminianism is what the central positions in Christianity have with difficulty tried to follow. Edwards and the Arminians become impaled on the dilemma between total determinism and arbitrary randomness because they both, like modern reductionists, presuppose physical reduction to a mechanist causal network. Seen from the level of microsystems in the brain, these are the only possibilities. But if we adopt a person model of God–human relations, we may regard freedom as an essential element in these relations and, therefore, as irreducible to the spatiotemporal world.

The theist's insistence on retaining person language here is bound to seem puzzling and anachronistic from the perspective of cognitive science. We cannot do much more to commend it here, but let us try to spell it out a little in terms of the central Biblical model of freedom, which involves a framework of concepts different from those of our previous voluntarist/decisionist debate. According to the Biblical perspective, the important constraints on human feedom are neither mechanical determinism nor arbitrary randomness, nor even our animal constitution nor the finitude of created life, but rather the bonds of evil. It is significant that Biblical metaphors for evil are drawn from the prisoner and the outcast: bondage, slavery to self and to sin, alienation from God (see the discussion in Ricoeur 1969, Part I). Freedom is described in opposite metaphors, as "casting aside all weights and oppression," "running the race of the liberty of the children of God" who seeks us as a father or a lover. Freedom is not a natural property of human beings, nor something self-made. It is not a property already realized, but a telos to be achieved in the destiny of each human being to become his or her true self in communion with God and with others; a communion moreover that does not exclude individuality. These metaphors contrast with the mystical goal of assimilation of the individual into the divine, where lack of freedom is seen essentially as finitude and not as external evil. The metaphors contrast both with Edwards's freedom, which is totally given by God, and with the Arminian notion of arbitrary choice. The model is instead a personal one, involving creative and relatively autonomous response to divine initiative. In this model, the serpent's seductive "You shall be as gods" was mistaken not in its goal but in its means – the fruit of knowledge should have been received as from a father, not as from a tyrant. The destiny of human beings is to be "as gods," at least as participants in the community of what Christians speak of as "three persons in one God."

Since God is not a space–time machine, the personal model for God–human relations requires a teleology that is dynamic but not mechanical. It is, therefore, no accident that of all the ancient philosophers, it is Aristotle, even more than Plato, who has fascinated Christian writers, or that Aristotle's cosmology provided the framework for the Church's greatest poet. All things are drawn by and strive after their perfection – the material elements and the heavens in their perfect motion; the perfection of human community glimpsed by Dante first in the eyes of Beatrice, then reinforced by reason and gravitas in the figure of Virgil, until in heaven Beatrice directs Dante's gaze to the Virgin and her son, and beyond to the divine love "that moves the sun and the other stars" (*Divine Comedy*, III, Canto XXXIII, line 145).

The myth of nature and the cosmos that accompanies this model of God–person relations is not one we can accept in detail, and its specific kind of teleology is refuted by mechanical explanations of natural design and of much human intentionality. But these developments do not refute all teleology. Consider the natural selection story about the development of species: here the history of a particular species can be reconstructed in terms of random mutations reinforced or destroyed by environment. But because the process is at crucial points a chance one, no explanation can be given of why this species or this ecosystem rather than another possible one was realized in fact. It would be perfectly consistent with Darwinian explanation, though of course otiose in our present biology, to postulate a teleology "drawing" the sequence of species toward a goal in, say, eagles, or tapeworms or human beings. Choice between any such teleological interpretations, or none, is always an evaluative and not a decidable scientific matter.

Teleological postulates of this kind about evolution are not necessary for voluntarists, however. What they need is a person model of God–human relations in which teleology is of the essence, just as it is in ordinary, premechanical, secular, person talk. We cannot derive the voluntarists' concept of freedom from ordinary person talk, but we can use ordinary talk as a model for that concept when we consider the nature of God.

We describe in Chapter 11 how Aquinas used a similar analogical method when he considered metaphors for God, such as "father." God is not a father like human fathers, because human fathers are limited and imperfect. He is a father properly speaking, that is to say, a father to the limiting degree of perfection, and fatherhood is ascribed to human beings only as an imperfect shadow of that divine fatherhood. Similarly, we only understand the interhuman concept of freedom in terms of the same hermeneutic circle: God's freedom is modeled on ours, but ours is limited and mechanically describable. Its essence, however, is to be in a personal relation with God, and human relations are properly understood only in that perspective. Lest this analogical method should seem viciously circular, we should remember that much the same has to be said of models even in physics: we understand what it is to be a microparticle by imperfect analogies with macroscopic objects, and we then throw away the ladder we climbed up by reinterpreting macroobjects in terms of ideal microparticles, at which point they look quite different from the solid continuous atomic objects we started with.

In this theistic perspective, mechanical explanations of the mind are no more difficult to accommodate than are physical and biological explanations of the body. It is as easy, or as difficult, to speak of God communing with human minds as it is to think of him as actively involved in the natural creation. There is no doubt that both these kinds of intervention are ingredients of the Biblical story, and both are almost equally foreign to the modern secular perspective. The question of whether we can meaningfully speak of God's actions in the world in this way is taken up in Chapter 11.

6   Freud on psychology and religion

To some people, Freud's psychoanalysis is a word therapy that has provided invaluable new tools for psychiatry; for others, it is a failed pseudoscience. Yet for many humanists and literary scholars, clinical or scientific criteria are simply beside the point: for them, Freud has supplied a language to chart the human mind, not just its conscious rationality but also the unconscious and repressed sources of the darkness in people's souls.

Freud was trained as a neurologist and also received an excellent nineteenth-century European education and read widely in the classics. Thus, when creating the metapsychology of psychoanalysis, he built on concepts rooted in scientific materialism yet shaped them in the light of the human, yet transcendent, dramas of Greek myth. His work took him from neurology to reaches of the human mind that, at that time, resisted neurological explanation. His studies of the individual mind were complemented by studies of society and religion, in which he saw these as expressions of the individual psyches of people coming together into groups. God was the projection of human fears and wishes, not a transcendent reality constitutive of human meaning.

We thus devote this chapter to a critique of the work of Freud. To what extent do the concepts of Freud's psychoanalysis challenge our efforts to chart the future development of schema theory from its roots in cognitive science toward religious and social critique? Can schema theory offer a scientific critique of psychoanalysis? Freud's simultaneous espousal of science and embrace of mythology point us to our later analysis of language as metaphor, of hermeneutics, and of the social construction of reality in developing our schema-theoretic contribution to a modern natural theology. Our approach does not seek to infer the existence of God from the study of nature but rather strives to understand how an individual may come, or come to refuse, to hold scientific and religious concepts within an overall network of belief.

6.1 From neurology to religion

Freud had a rationalist philosophical training in Vienna, followed by a scientific training in the Helmholtz–Brücke school of psychology. This school ex-

105

cluded from reality all save the facts of observation, holding that human reality was to be understood in terms of the laws of chemistry and physics. He saw science as dealing with an objective verifiable reality (this belief was *his* "religion"). Though we may know this reality only slowly and partially at first, this knowledge will increase.

After initial studies in physiology, Freud became a neurologist (cf. Sulloway 1979). At that time, neurologists could do little for their patients – though they conducted major postmortem studies to correlate syndromes with specific patterns of brain damage. In 1891, Freud published *On Aphasia* (Freud 1953), a critique of then current ideas on localization in the brain. He was also coming to terms with the problems of mental pathology and in 1895 published *Studies in Hysteria.**

Hysterics had been posited to have a hereditary CNS degenerative disease, but postmortems revealed no lesions in such patients. Moreover, hysterical symptoms did not correlate with the neuroanatomical localizations that had been learned from the study of stroke victims. Freud concluded that the lesion was psychic and that hysterics had converted psychic symptoms into bodily symptoms. In talking of the psyche, he was no longer talking of something demonstrably physical or chemical – a difficult conclusion to reach, given Freud's physiological background. To salvage the scientific respectability of his work and maintain a biological dimension in his theory, Freud gave a central place to instincts, which he argued were the psychic representation of the physicochemical forces of the body. He thus explained psychological motivation in terms of those instincts, and he found it necessary to trace behavior back to childhood, to instinctual motivations, rather than moving through an evolving human life cycle.

From neurology to mythology

In 1895, Freud also wrote his *Project for a Scientific Psychology* which was not then published; he sent it to Wilhelm Fliess as part of their correspondence, and it was rediscovered much later and published only in 1950 (see Freud 1954 for the English translation). In the *Project,* Freud tried to provide a theory of the mind and its disorders expressed in terms of neural nets. His notion of these nets was a "hydraulic" one of neurons discharging energy; the nervous system's task, as he then envisaged it, was to get rid of energy. In his later work, however, he could not find the appropriate data

---

*The remainder of this chapter refers to a number of works of Freud by their year of initial publication. In most cases, we do not list explicit references in the bibliography since readers can usually (*On Aphasia* is an exception) find paperback editions published by Penguin or Norton or can turn to the standard edition of *The Complete Psychological Works of Sigmund Freud,* under the general editorship of James Strachey in collaboration with Anna Freud. For the reader seeking an overview of Freud's life and work, we recommend Wollheim (1971).

to render his ideas into neurological terms. By 1900, in *The Interpretation of Dreams,* there are two interesting developments. In Chapter VII, he offers a "Psychology of the Dream Processes," which (unknown to his readership at that time) was deeply rooted in the concepts of the *Project* but now stripped of neural net terminology. In Chapter V, however, a new and crucial theme is sounded with the first discussion of the Oedipus myth. In discussing sexual drives and the effect of the mother and father in the child's early experience, he suggests that the power of the Oedipus myth, a power he found lacking in the contemporary tragedies of the Viennese stage, is that it embodies the basic drama of the young boy coming to vie with his father for the affections of his mother – wanting, at least in his wishes, to kill the father and bed the mother.

In Freud, then, we see the merging of at least two horizons as he comes to address the "facts" of his self-analysis and the analysis of his patients: the neurological perspective, which became implicit after 1895, yet surely shaped the essential terms of his metapsychology; and the humanistic perspective, especially the resonance of the Greek myths. When Freud wrote the *Project,* he was still trying to reduce everything to neural net processes. However, as he came to terms with a wealth of clinical experience, the language of myth often made more sense than the language of neurology. Later writings preserve much of the neurological terminology: libido is the residue of the neural energy of the somewhat hydraulic neurons of the *Project;* Figure 1 of *The Ego and the Id* maps his metapsychologic concepts on a schematic brain, with, for example, consciousness shown as a region that includes the left hemisphere of the brain, where the language mechanisms reside. Yet these neurological concepts cannot grapple with the clinical data. Freud thus draws parallels between the Greek myths and the behavior of his patients to invent new concepts, such as Eros and the Oedipus complex.

In *Group Psychology and the Analysis of the Ego* (1921), the basic terms in which Freud addresses cultural interactions are from the ego psychology analyzed from the child's interactions with its parents – concepts more fully developed in *The Ego and the Id* (1923), which we examine in our analysis of the unconscious in the next section. Many concepts of *The Ego and the Id* are preshadowed, in neurological terms, in the *Project* of twenty-eight years earlier, though now enriched by the notions of the Oedipus complex and of the libidinal and aggressive drives of Eros and Thanatos.

Bruno Bettelheim (1982) ignores the neurological horizon when he emphasizes only Freud's humanism, with the Greek myths seen as one aspect of Freud's attempt to make his concepts engage those of the educated layperson. Bettleheim notes that the standard English translations of Freud emphasize a medical view over that meaningful to the layperson: *das Ich* becomes *the ego* instead of *the I; das Es* becomes *the id* instead of *the it;* and *Fehlleistung* becomes *parapraxis* instead of some phrase that captures the meaningfulness of Freud's neologism, which Bettelheim translates as "error and accomplishment" (though "faulty act" may be a more literal translation) to convey the sometimes fortunate effects of unconsciously generated errors. Bettelheim thus stresses that Freud was not writing for physicians but tried to make his papers accessible to laypeople both by a vocabulary that could address and refine their naïve psychology and by an appeal to a shared culture, which at that time and place included a knowledge of Greek myth. In our culture, "Eros" may only have sexual connotations; but for someone steeped in Greek myth, "Eros" brings to mind the legend of Eros and Psyche and the problems that befell Psyche for not recognizing the sensitivities of Eros. Thus, for Freud and his contemporaries, Eros was a richer term in no way reducible to sex per se but encompassing also the greater aspects of love and appreciation. However, Bettelheim misreads Freud when he so emphasizes Freud's humanism; he does not see that even though Freud does use the German terms for *I* and *it* rather than the Latinate *ego* and *id* and uses the language of myths known to his readers, he is nonetheless trying to invest them with a scientific meaning rather than their everyday sense.

This "merging of horizons" (a theme explicated in our discussion of hermeneutics in Chapter 8) brings us back to our theme of the "construction of reality." Our account of reality must start from the everyday realities that we have acquired by the time we are teenagers. This provides the platform of reality from which we go back to ask how the newborn child growing within a particular society comes to view reality in just these (somewhat culture-dependent) terms and from which we also go forward, seeking to explicate that reality in more fundamental terms, as in the case of attempting a reduction to physical processes. At this level, we can distinguish two "base realities," the reality of things – for example, how we grasp an object – and the reality of "persons" – for example, what it means to love or hate someone. The schema theory and the Piagetian theory of Chapter 3 have tended to emphasize – from the perspective of cognitive science – the "thing" reality. By contrast, Freud helps us come to grips with the reality of "persons." Where we have talked of schemas for actions and objects, Freud talked of "identification." We might see identification as the process of the child's assimilating a schema for some aspects of another's behavior, which leads the child to act as, or identify with, that other person in some range of circumstances. Irrespective of our theological concerns, we are challenged to merge the horizons of our schema theory with the horizons of a person–centered psychology.

In Freud's later writings, the Oedipus story changes from a powerful myth resonant with aspects of infant sexuality, which had been little discussed before Freud, to become, as the Oedipus complex, the key explanatory principle in the child's development. In Chapter 11, we bring the language of metaphor to bear on the reading of the Bible, suggesting how, within our epistemology, we can make the transition from a literal reading of Genesis, say, to finding it a useful myth about the creation of human meaning. This analysis also shows that myth is not to be seen as a pejorative term; a myth is not a mere fiction but conveys deep truths about the human condition. Are we to see Freud's departure from explicit neurologizing to using the language of mythology as meaning that understanding the human condition is forever beyond the reach of brain theory? Or, does Freud's use of mythology disqualify him as a scientist, so that we must reject his ideas in building our schema theory? Our analysis of different levels of reality in Section 4.1 suggests a "compromise." Where strict reductionism says all realities are reducible to basic physics (cf. statistical mechanics), we say both table and molecules are real. We perceive aspects of the world at different levels of reality. We do not so much seek a complete explanation of one level in terms of another (making the "upper" level no more than a convenient shorthand); rather, we seek to reconcile the different levels, seeing, for example, when personal interactions must be augmented by medical treatment. Even if one believes there is no mind or person separate from the activity of body and brain, there are few cases in our handling of everyday reality in which the knowledge of neural networks will affect our actions. We can read Freud with sympathy to both horizons (contrary to Bettelheim's rejection of the "medical" reading).

We are not restricted to Freud's reading of the mind. We know more about brain than was known in his time. Yet, we also know more about persons than can be expressed in neurological terms. We must give an account at the personal and social levels that supplements the brain–level account.

If a story is told often enough, it may come to be accepted as real; but we would prefer not to ascribe reality to the Oedipus complex. In fact, Freud weakens the basic account by noting that each child exhibits mixtures of the boy's love of the mother and the girl's love of the father. We can give a different, schema-theoretic, account once we assimilate Freud's notion of identification to our schema theory.

Freud sees the "positive" Oedipus complex as at best a simplification. Rather, closer study usually discloses the more complete Oedipus complex as twofold – positive and negative: for example, a boy has not merely a positive complex, an ambivalent attitude toward his father and an affectionate object relation toward his mother, but also, like a girl, a negative complex, displaying an affectionate feminine attitude toward his father and a corresponding hostility and jealousy toward his mother. However, with this formulation, we seem to have abandoned the significance of the Oedipus myth itself. Rather, we have a general formulation in terms of which our characters can be shaped by people with whom we are emotionally involved; that these emotions can be positive and negative; and that parents, being both early influences and given dominant roles by social custom, have an exceptionally large influence. Later, teachers may have a similar role, and a wholly institutionalized child may be lacking in many human qualities.

Let us express this in a way that expands our schema theory. What does

a schema represent? There are schemas for grasping, for apples, for sky –
and for people, too. The child has schemas for its mother and father. These
schemas go beyond recognition of their faces and extend to identification –
feeling as the parent feels, acting as the parent acts. Not only are there schemas
for recognizing another person from the outside, creating expectations about
their behavior; there are also schemas for internalizing, creating a schema
for acting as that person acts. This fact should not be surprising as part of
a theory of the cognitive growth of the child. Much of what the young child
does is imitation. Such acquisition of skills can then go beyond the sensorimotor to affective skills, acquiring schemas that enable the child to behave
in ways that embody aspects of the personality of others. One thus expects
schemas internalizing the behavior of mother, father (and siblings) to play
a vital role in constituting the child's behavior. What adds an immense element of tension is that certain behaviors are the prerogative of the parents,
so that identification cannot be whole-hearted without leading to overt conflict – the avoidance of which may lead to internal conflict. One can thus
view Freud's observations not in terms of a male and female Oedipus complex but rather in terms of a general theory of schema formation and interaction (a theory still quite primitive) that includes schemas for person-
centered affective skills as well as for sensorimotor and linguistic skills.

In *Totem and Taboo* (1912–13), the Oedipus myth moves from ontogeny
to phylogeny and is ascribed a historical reality – the book is subtitled *Some
Points of Agreement between the Mental Lives of Savages and Neurotics*.
In *Totem and Taboo,* Freud sees religion and moral restraint as acquired
phylogenetically out of the father complex by the actual process of mastering the Oedipus complex itself and out of the social feeling coming from
the need to overcome the rivalry that then remained between the members
of the younger generation. Primitive religion is traced to the primal horde
murdering the father, with the consequent guilt and veneration combining
into the basic element of religion. The myth becomes first a psychological
and then a historical explanation. In *Totem and Taboo,* Freud claims to show
how culture arises as a natural phenomenon and how religious ritual and
belief enable culture to control and give meaning to the forces that produced
it. Religion does not perform this service to perfection, but if aggression is
innate, nothing can. Yet religion does express symbolically the human feeling of helplessness and offers rituals that help control and give meaning to
people's innate aggression and sense of guilt. Freud's personal rationalist
analysis of religion does not detract from his understanding of the social function of religion.

Freud plays back the Oedipus complex onto a historical narrative in *Totem
and Taboo*. He has created another myth: not the Genesis myth of God
creating man, but the primal horde myth of men creating God. Freud speaks
of this as a historical reality, but this interpretation would not be accepted
by current methods of social anthropology.

In coming to grips with human complexity and the problems of himself and his patients, Freud finds his neurology inadequate and turns to the language of myth to express the anguish of lived human experience. Just as a physicist comes to ascribe reality to electrons, so Freud comes to ascribe reality to the myth-based constructs of his metapsychology. Then, as he thinks about the structure of society, he is able to analyze much of the Judeo–Christian tradition as a projection of the concept of the father: as adults look for protection that no human being can provide in the way their own father was able to protect them from childhood feelings of helplessness (cf. the role of Christ in the Christian church and of a general in the army, as discussed in *Group Psychology and the Analysis of the Ego*). He then wants not only to explain the psychology of belief in God but also to give a historical account of the origin of that belief. He thus *projects* the Oedipus myth onto a historical scale. But this is not history, it is myth making (cf. Hillers 1969 on the covenant for a more plausible historical approach to monotheism). We must read *Totem and Taboo* not as a scientific explanation of a social phenomenon but rather as a modern myth that incorporates a new scientific world view, namely, that of psychoanalysis. Ironically, the new scientific vocabulary is itself based on the reification of an earlier cycle of myth, the Greek myths.

We, too, come to understand certain phenomena and the use of our knowledge to explore new phenomena. We have to go beyond what is sure. However, this means that we often cannot make sense of the new in terms of literal use of what we already know.

Many writers on ideology or theology live within their myth and soon can no longer see beyond its horizons. They talk as if they were proving their myth to be literally true. With our epistemology, we can no longer seek to prove that we have *the* truth, but we learn to understand how to live comfortably within a horizon while still understanding the need to shift those horizons from time to time without giving in to a hopeless relativism. We live in a process, and there is no finality except death.

Critique of religion

The Future of an Illusion (1923) is Freud's critique of religion and approaches the problem from two perspectives. His nineteenth-century materialism led him to a world view that roots the human condition in psychology rather than in an external God reality. He develops this theme, however, in terms of his metapsychology, using the ideas of *Totem and Taboo* to see God as the projection of the wish for an all-protecting father figure. In *The Future of an Illusion,* Freud links the individual's helplessness before the forces of nature and the inequities of civilization with that of the infant.

We know already that the terrifying effect of infantile helplessness aroused the need for protection which the father relieved, and that the discovery that this helplessness would continue through the whole of life made it necessary to cling to the existence of a father – but this time a more powerful one. . . . [The] benevolent role of divine providence allays our anxiety in the face of life's dangers, the establishment of a moral world ensures the fulfillment of the demands of justice . . . and the prolongation of earthly existence by a future life provides in addition the local and temporal setting for these with fulfillments. (Freud 1923)

Freud thus doubts that most people will be ready to do without religion for a long time, even though he is not always sympathetic to the human need for religion.

Certainly, our grasp of reality must be mediated by constructs. Yet, we view schemas as subject to constant testing and revision for coherence. Freud would argue that the concepts of religion are illusions precisely because they are protected from this process of reality testing by a system of rituals and defenses.

Freud distinguishes an illusion from an error or delusion. An illusion may be true, but a belief is an illusion "when wish-fulfillment is a prominent factor in its motivation, while disregarding its relation to reality." He sees religious doctrines as illusions that "do not admit of proof, and no one can be compelled to consider them true or believe in them." In picturing a race of people without illusions, of education freed from the burden of religious doctrines, and of science at the center of human development and progress, Freud comes as close to a utopian vision as he ever will; but this vision does not survive the writing of *Civilization and Its Discontents* (1930), a brooding meditation on why we are always unhappy. Freud argues that we are unhappy because civilization demands of us renunciations that we do not want to make but that are (marginally?) worth making because civilization is better than a state of nature, whatever that may be. Freud's view of that "state of nature" is a Hobbesian one of constant fighting and unbridled competition. For Freud, civilization represents a trade off rather than a transcendent experience.

In "Obsessive Action and Religious Practice" (1907), Freud compared the obsessional acts of the neurotic individual with the social structure of religious rituals "in the qualms of conscience brought on by their neglect, in their complete isolation from all other actions and in the conscientiousness with which they are carried out in every detail." Freud sees the repression of an instinctual impulse in each case – the repression of a component of the sexual instinct in the obsessive neurosis; the repression of "self-seeking, socially harmful instincts" in religious ritual. He concludes that a "progressive renunciation of constitutional instincts, whose activation might afford the ego primary pleasure, appears to be one of the foundations of the development of human civilization."

But does civilization "conquer" us, or is it civilization that has made us possible? The answer is "both." Civilization shapes us. We have escaped much of the brutality of life in, say, a seventeenth-century European village. We are defined in no small part by the books and artifacts and professional opportunities that modern society affords us. But Freud's sense of the precariousness of civilization was certainly justified by his meditations on the horror of World War I ("Thoughts for the Time of War and Death" (1919)). The war showed that the barbarian was still with us, destroying the illusion of progress of the preceding century. Such pessimism can only be encouraged by our knowledge of the rise of the Nazis (Freud was under Nazi house arrest, and two of his sisters died in concentration camps), or the threat of nuclear war. These tragedies encourage a tragic vision of humanity. Progress in electricity or computers or other technology has not guaranteed corresponding progress in the elimination of human barbarism.

Freud's theory of religion involves a theory of the projection of human needs externally and then the development of various rituals to rationalize those projections. We have instincts that we must renounce if we want civilization to persist. All cultures require this daily renunciation on the part of individuals if the culture is to survive. Freud sees renunciation as the original act that created culture. The repressed instincts are not gotten rid of; they are still there, and they come back indirectly, in neurotic symptoms, in slips of the tongue, and in religious beliefs and rituals that help us manage the aggression that is still there by projecting it elsewhere or by explaining the guilt we have because of the presence of this aggression.

The relationship among experience, culture, and religion reflects more than the need to control a general feeling of helplessness. Freud sees the inclination to aggression – an "original self-subsisting instinctual disposition in men" – as the greatest threat to civilization, opposing the whole program of culture. The progressive renunciation of constitutional instincts deals with aggression by internalizing it, directing it back toward the individual ego from which it came. The resultant sense of guilt is capable of enormous aggression against the ego. Given Freud's belief that aggression and guilt cannot be eliminated from human life, and given the frustration produced by civilization's demand for sexual renunciation, he sees that civilization will always be precariously balanced and ambivalently regarded. We are a long way from the coherence of schema networks generated solely by a Piagetian process of reflective abstraction.

Freud would replace religion by science (we consider another such proposal in Section 12.2). Kung (1979) attacks this attitude, stating that "particularly after the experience of National Socialism and communism, modern atheism has lost much of its credibility" and that "the ambivalent character of progress in science and technology – which so easily evades human control and now spreads a fear of the future often amounting to apocalyptic terror – has led many people to doubt that science automatically implies progress and is thus the source of the universal happiness of humanity, which, according to Freud, is not provided by religion." But, of course, Freud did not hold that science promised universal happiness, either. He just denied that alternatives to science would be more successful. But what, then, is science? Physical science can aid technocratic solutions to the production of food or the distribution of energy. But, as we further emphasize in Chapter 8, our view of science must embrace the moral sciences as well as the natural sciences, the *Geisteswissenschaften* as well as the *Naturwissenschaften*.

In *Civilization and Its Discontents,* Freud lists what he sees as the essential problems of civilization, including the economic realities. To the degree that Marxism could develop as a scientific theory of economics, it would for Freud be an acceptable substitute for religion. For him, the only acceptable substitute for religion was science. But he would not accept the utopian part of Marxism; in *The Future of an Illusion,* he reserves judgement about the outcome of the Russian revolution. He was skeptical of utopian notions of wish fulfillment and convinced that the dilemma of being human is changeless.

6.2 Freud and the unconscious

Before Freud, the unconscious was simply seen as a receptacle for ideas that did not currently engage our attention. However, Freud rejected the notion that the "real mind" is the conscious mind, with the unconscious no more than a passive "reference library," and saw the unconscious as a domain for crucial mental processes. Even more strongly, he spoke of unconscious processes that, though vital in determining behavior, are not available for conscious inspection. Eventually, he formulated a three-part model. The *id* embodies the primary process, the mechanisms of unconstrained instinctual gratification. The *ego* ("the I," what you really think you are) is the "real you" that does not give in to the primary process yet can stand up to society. We may note (cf. the discussion of Bettelheim in the previous section) that much of this terminology seeks to give scientific expression to intuitive concepts. The notion of "conscience" is reified to give the concept of the *superego,* which incorporates the identification with the authority figure of the father (this is part of the Oedipus complex) and the structures of society. As we see in the next section, Freud's theory of society is really a theory of the superego.

On the one hand, the theory of consciousness in terms of interacting schemas (Section 4.2) serves as a bridge from person talk to brain talk. On the other hand, we have Freud's theory, which fuses the horizons of nineteenth-century neurology and of Greek myth in its attempt to probe the unconscious roots of normal and abnormal human behavior. This dichotomy returns us to a general comment about styles of thought that underlay our discussion in Section 2.2. Philosophers whose epistemology is most influenced by mathematics have a deductive model of thought: there are a few axioms and rules of inference, and a situation is addressed by arguing rigorously from the axioms to a conclusion that specifies that a certain action will yield a desired outcome in that situation. But this is only part of thought. Rather than involving long chains of formal deduction, thought more often proceeds by analogy: we look for examples or stories similar in content to the current situation and use a rather short chain of "reasoning" to adapt it to the present circumstances. Freud's notion of *identification* addresses the fact that one's decision to act is often based on a schema that internalizes how someone influential in one's life acts on similar occasions.

An idea that is once conscious may not be so a moment later; it has become *latent*. Though it is then unconscious, it may be capable of becoming conscious later. This process leads Freud to distinguish the conscious (Cs) from the preconscious (Pcs), what is latent but capable of becoming conscious. Freud discovered that powerful mental ideas and processes exist that can produce effects in consciousness without themselves becoming conscious or even preconscious; these are ideas that cannot become conscious because a certain force is opposed to them. The state in which such ideas exist is called *repression*, and the repressing force is perceived as *resistance* during analysis. Freud uses the term *the unconscious* (Ucs) to include not only the dynamically unconscious repressed but other mental processes, too, of which we are not aware.

Freud's division of conscious (Cs) versus unconscious (Ucs) cuts across the division into superego, ego and id. The ego extends across Cs and Ucs; and the Ucs part of the ego is engaged in *repression*, the process whereby the memory of, for example, traumatic episodes is actively kept out of Cs. However, this repression distorts normal behavior, for elaborate "mental detours" must be made to avoid explicit reference to the repressed material.

In brain theory, we posit many processes that cannot be made conscious yet are not repressed in Freud's sense. They play a valuable role in the computational substrata without figuring in consciousness (which, we suggested in Section 4.2, provides a précis, inevitably distorted, of the underlying "cooperative computation" of neural activity).

As we have seen, Freud postulates that in every individual is a coherent organization of mental processes, which he calls the *ego*. It includes Cs; it controls actions (with errors then to be seen as diagnostic of the unconscious non-ego); it regulates all its own constituent processes; and it goes to sleep at night, though even then it continues to exercise a censorship on dreams. (This is a centralized rather than decentralized view of the ego. As mentioned above, the ego spans from Cs to Ucs.)

The ego starts out from the perceptual system (Pcpt) and embraces the Pcs, which is adjacent to the memory residues – Freud conceives of memory residues as contained in systems directly adjacent to Pcpt–Cs, so that activity pertaining to the memory residues can readily extend outward on to the elements of the latter system. In other words, Freud gives a topographic account of why perceptions may be "charged" by associated memories.

Freud follows George Groddeck (*Das Buch vom Es*, Vienna, 1923) in using the term *Es* (meaning *it,* which in the English translations is given the Latin form *id*) to denote the unknown and uncontrollable forces that sometimes seem to dominate our behavior. The ego is not to be seen as sharply separated from the id; its lower portion merges into it. Thus, the ego is also in part unconscious. The repressed is part of the id and is only cut off sharply from the ego by the resistances of repression; it can communicate with the ego through the id. The ego includes the speech system of the left hemisphere.

Freud holds that the essence of a word is the memory trace of hearing it spoken, though this seems mistaken since this includes only phonology, not meaning or syntactic categories. He also holds that thought processes may become conscious through visual memory residues – those of *things* rather than words. Thinking in pictures makes conscious the concrete subject matter, rather than the relations among the various elements of this subject matter.

Something that is repressed can be made (pre)conscious by supplying, through the work of analysis, Pcs connecting links. Such links have much the flavor of those in semantic nets (recall Section 2.3). Consciousness remains where it is; but, on the other hand, Ucs does not rise up into the Cs. However, if Ucs can affect Cs behavior, there must be links – but, presumably, of a different kind from those just mentioned. We thus see two approaches to an algorithmic Freud – neural nets and semantic nets. In either case, cooperative computation seems essential.

Repressions proceed from the ego, attempting to cut off certain trends not only from Cs but also from other forms of manifestation. During analysis, a patient dominated by a resistance will be unaware of the fact. But the resistance emanates from the ego – parts of the ego are unconscious. Thus, Freud does not derive neuroses from a conflict between the conscious and the unconscious but rather from the antithesis between the organized ego and what is repressed and dissociated from it. This Ucs belonging to the ego is not latent like the Pcs; if it were, it could not be activated without becoming Cs, and the process of making it conscious would not encounter such great difficulties.

To relate activation in Freud's sense to schema activation, we first note that the repressed is not Cs but may affect Cs processing. Our evolutionary view is that many cooperating processes underlie mental activity and that Cs evolves to monitor those processes but cannot monitor them all. Once Cs has evolved (cf. Section 4.2), it can be monitored by Ucs and Pcs. Repression is the process of hiding Ucs processes from Cs. Clearly, knowledge of the Ucs can only be obtained by making it conscious. Think, then, of an Ucs "automaton" interacting with Cs. Cs cannot see the inner workings of Ucs but may come to model it. The art of the therapist is then to help Cs construct an observer to aid the exploration of the search space of Ucs.

Currently, schema theory ignores personality, psychopathology, and "the dark side of the soul," whereas Freud's theory gives little notion of how "it really works" – his case studies are stories rather than scientific accounts.

Schema theory certainly includes high-level processes that cannot be tagged, *a priori,* as being conscious or unconscious. We need an articulated theory of "What am I prepared to talk about?" Freud strongly links Cs to the ability to tag a memory with words, but this link seems mistaken: schemas can be activated or not, enter consciousness or not, but their verbalizability seems little related to this dichotomy. On the other hand, schema theory says nothing of repression nor does it specify, for example, how we can be conscious of a taste we cannot describe in words.

Freud does have the modern conception of the unitary self; even though he speaks of id, ego, and the superego, he sees the aim of therapy to be to bring more of behavior under the control of the conscious ego. Certainly, though, Freud's analysis does stretch our notion of the responsible agent. A network of schemas also poses challenges to the unitary self. We do see processes working to increase coherence but deny that the normal human condition is one of total coherence and consistency.

We close this section by summarizing the major challenges that Freud poses for the future development of schema theory.

1. By confronting Freud's account of the complete Oedipus complex as twofold with our own schema theory, we see that an adequate theory of schema formation and interaction must include schemas for person-centered affective skills as well as sensorimotor or linguistic skills. Our notion of schema networks then reminds us that schemas cannot be neatly classified into these distinct categories.
2. Freud has reminded us of the power of instinctual schemas, whether or not we are prepared to reduce them to the Manichaean struggle of Eros and Thanatos. He has given us the concept of repression, linking it not only to individual psychopathology but also to the foundations of civilization. Where Piaget gives us what now seems an almost utopian vision of reflective abstraction as yielding coherent networks of ever greater abstraction integrating and illuminating our more concrete schemas, Freud reminds us that consistency is not an attribute of humanity. Our schema theory places as much stress on competition as on cooperation; Freud tells us how to confront the "darkness of the human soul."

6.3 Superego and society

Freud seems to give short shrift to enculturation – giving most emphasis to drives and Oedipal urges in the child's mental development, with little analysis of the effects of a particular society or a language community. Surely, children acquire religion in all its diversity from their social milieu rather than at the urging of some innate Oedipal urgings. Freud most explicitly addresses this process of enculturation in his description of the superego, which he views as the heir to the Oedipus complex. In emphasizing the instinctual processes, Freud tended to take much of enculturation per se for granted. But since the 1920s, ego psychologists have deemphasized the instincts and paid more attention to object relations, language, and enculturation. (In *Childhood and*

Society, Erikson [1963] offers several studies that integrate ego psychology with anthropology.)

Freud's use of the term superego reifies an element of our moral vocabulary ("conscience"), but he tries to locate it within the mind, not "out there" in society. The ego is essentially the representative of the external world, of reality. The superego results from living through the traces of biological evolution and human development that comprise the id. The id belongs to the lowest depths of the mind of each one of us; this material is changed, through the formation of the superego, into what we value as the highest in the human soul.

Freud regards Pcpt–Cs (the system of perception and consciousness described in the previous section) as the nucleus of the ego and the testing of reality as the function of the ego itself. Within the ego, he differentiates the superego and views it as less closely connected with consciousness than the rest of the ego. To a rough first approximation, we may see Freud's term *objective-cathexis* as corresponding to our concept of formation or activation of an object schema. We have seen the importance Freud gives to the abandonment or repression of many schemas in the child's development and socialization. Whatever the character's capacity for resisting the influences of abandoned object-cathexes (or, we would add, for weaving and editing them into a harmonious whole), a crucial role is played by the first identifications in earliest childhood. The superego, or ego ideal, is based on the first and most important identification, with the parents (though Freud says in *The Ego and the Id* that, to simplify his presentation, he will discuss only identification with the father). This is a direct and immediate identification and takes place earlier than any object-cathexis.

Freud asserts that, insofar as the superego is a substitute for the longing for a father, it contains the germ from which all religions have evolved. The self-judgement that declares the ego falls short of its ideal produces the sense of worthlessness with which the religious believer attests a longing. The tension between the demands of conscience and the actual attainments of the ego is experienced as a sense of guilt. Social feelings rest on the foundation of identifications with others, on the basis of commonalities of superego.

An important component of religion is the idea that "good" and "evil" and ethics receive an ultimate grounding in God. For Freud, however, ethics amounted to the constraints of the superego in the ego. This statement might be put in more Durkheimian terms (Chapter 10) as the superego comprising those instinctual renunciations that society demands; on the other hand, a theist will see the superego as God-driven.

We saw in Section 6.1 that Freud views the sexual phase of the child's development governed by the Oedipus complex in both positive and negative form (we reinterpreted this in terms of schemas). He takes the outcome of this phase to be the forming of a precipitate in the ego, consisting of the two identifications with father and mother in some way combined together.

This modification of the ego retains its special position as a superego, which is not merely a deposit left by the id's earliest object choices but also represents an energetic reaction formation against these choices. It provides precepts to be like the parent in some ways, while other ways are prohibited as the prerogative of the parent. From our perspective of schema development, we must ask: How does the child come to perceive, evaluate, and interiorize these different characteristics? It may be more like components of a skill than like explicitly verbalized value judgements.

Clearly, the repression of the Oedipus complex was no easy task. The parents were perceived as the obstacle to the realization of the Oedipal wishes; the superego was formed by the ego to realize this same obstacle within itself. The more rapidly the Oedipus complex succumbed to repression (under the influence of discipline, religious teaching, schooling, and reading), the more exacting later on is the domination of the superego over the ego – in the form of conscience or perhaps of an unconscious sense of guilt. The superego has a compulsive character that manifests itself in the form of a categorical imperative.

No external vicissitudes can be experienced or undergone by the id except by way of the ego's representation of the outer world. In fact, the ego is a part of the id that has been specially modified. However, we argue that the experiences undergone by the ego are transmitted by parents to children and by members of society to each other. However, in a burst of apparent Lamarckianism somewhat reminiscent of Piaget, Freud asserts that when ego experiences have been repeated often enough and with sufficient intensity in the individuals of successive generations, they transform themselves into experiences of the id, the impress of which is preserved by inheritance. He says that when the ego forms its superego out of the id, it may perhaps only be reviving images of egos that have passed away and be securing them a resurrection.

In the classical Freudian theory, the superego is the successor to the id's object cathexes. The ego is in conflict with both. A free communication exists between the ideal and Ucs instinctual trends, and the ideal itself can be to a great extent unconscious and inaccessible to the ego.

Although it is amenable to every later influence, the superego preserves throughout life the capacity, given by its derivation from the father complex, to stand apart from the ego and rule it. As the child was once compelled to obey its parents, so the ego submits to the categorical imperative pronounced by its superego. As we have seen, Freud further views the superego as a reincarnation of former ego structures that have left their precipitates behind in the id. Thus, the superego is always in close touch with the id and can act as its representative in relation to the ego. It reaches deep down into the id and is for that reason further from consciousness than the ego. In some sense, then, the superego functions as substrate and basic control structure for the mind and thus for implicit evaluation.

The superego manifests itself essentially as a sense of guilt (or rather as criticism, for the sense of guilt is the perception in the ego that corresponds to the criticism) and develops extraordinary harshness toward the ego. The normal conscious sense of guilt (conscience) is due to tension between the ego and the ego ideal; it is the expression of a condemnation of the ego pronounced by its criticizing function. The feelings so well known in neurotics are presumably closely related to it.

Freud ascribed preconscious verbal residues much importance in the ego. Although the superego is in part unconscious, he views it (restrictively, we would think) as derived from auditory impressions, as part of the ego that remains to a great extent accessible to consciousness by way of these verbal images (concepts, abstractions). However, he sees the cathectic energy of these elements of the superego as originating not from the auditory perceptions, instruction, reading, and so on, but from sources in the id.

The id is totally nonmoral, the ego strives to be moral, and the superego can be hypermoral and then becomes as ruthless as the id. The more a people check their aggressive tendencies toward other people, the more tyrannical they become in their ego ideal. This is contrary to the usual view that the standard set up by the superego is the motive for the suppression of aggressiveness. But even ordinary morality has a harshly restraining quality; and from this quality arises the conception of an inexorable being who metes out punishment.

The ego develops from perceiving instincts to controlling them, from obeying instincts to curbing them. In this achievement, a large share is taken by the superego, which indeed is partly a reaction formation against the instinctual processes in the id. Psychoanalysis is an instrument to enable the ego to push its conquest of the id further still. On the other hand, Freud sees the ego as menaced by three dangers: from the external world, from the libido of the id, and from the severity of the superego. Three kinds of anxiety, the expression of a recoil from danger, correspond to these three dangers. The ego tries to make the id comply with the world's demands and, by action, accommodate the world to the id's desires. Like the psychoanalyst to the patient, the ego offers itself to the id as a libidinal object in view of its power of adaptation to the real world and aims at attaching the id's libido to itself. It tries to remain on good terms with the id; it draws the veil of its Pcs rationalizations over the id's Ucs demands; it throws a disguise over the id's conflicts with reality and, if possible, over its conflicts with the superego, too.

The id has no means of showing the ego either love or hate. It cannot say what it wants; it has achieved no unity of will. Eros and the death instinct struggle within it. It would be possible to picture the id as under the domination of the mute but powerful death instincts, which desire to be at peace and (as the pleasure principle demands) to put Eros, the intruder, to rest; but this would be to run the risk of valuing too cheaply the part Eros plays.

The ego's work of identification and sublimation gives the death instincts in the id assistance in mastering the libido; however, to avoid becoming the object of the death instincts and persisting, the ego must become flooded with libido itself, and thenceforward, becoming the representative of Eros, it desires to love and to be loved. The ego develops the flight reflex by withdrawing its own cathexis from the menacing perception or from the equally dreaded process in the id and discharging it as anxiety. This primitive reaction is later replaced by the introduction of protective cathexes (the mechanism of the phobias). Freud sees that behind the ego's dread of the superego is that the higher being, which later became the superego, once threatened the ego with castration; he uses this dread of castration as the kernel around which the subsequent fear of conscience has gathered.

Freud believes that the fear of death concerns an interplay between the ego and the superego. The mechanism of the fear of death can only be that the ego relinquishes its narcissistic libidinal cathexis in a large measure; that is, that it gives up itself, just as it gives up some *external* object in other cases in which it feels anxiety. The fear of death makes its appearance under two conditions – as a reaction to an external danger and as an internal process, as, for instance, in melancholia. The fear of death in melancholia only admits of one explanation: that the ego gives itself up because it feels itself hated and persecuted by the superego instead of loved. To the ego, therefore, living means the same as being loved – by the superego, which here appears again as the representative of the id. The superego fulfills the same function of protecting and saving fulfilled earlier by the father and later by providence or destiny. However, when the ego finds itself in overwhelming danger that it believes itself unable to overcome by its own strength, it sees itself deserted by all the forces of protection and lets itself die.

A conservative theologian like Niebuhr might look at the superego and suggest it was the instrument of an Old Testament God. However, theologians seem *not* to have seized on the superego as the central religious fact in Freudian psychology. For the Freudian, there is no ultimate notion of "good" and "evil," no ultimate meaning of life. There is just life, and good and evil are defined by a particular culture. Freud's focus was always functional, pragmatic, and utilitarian. Ethics and morality are necessary if we are going to have civilization; and we need civilization because without it people would kill each other in a chaotic state of nature. However, ethics is purely social and conventional and may vary from culture to culture. The superego is then the psychic cultural mechanism that for each person internalizes these cultural conventions. It does so as the outcome of the Oedipal complex, when the aggressive wish to kill the father and the incestuous wish to go to bed with the mother are repressed and replaced by a superego, which not only prohibits those "ultimate" repressed wishes but also establishes an ego ideal transmitted to the child by the parents. This ego ideal embodies the ideals of the culture in which they grew up.

6.4 Epistemology and religion

We repeatedly come to the point that our epistemology, while convincing us that our view of Reality must be an adaptive one, seems agnostic with respect to the question of the existence of God. To reinforce this point, we contrast the epistemology of Freud with that of the New England preacher and theologian Jonathan Edwards, whose views on free will we discussed in Section 5.3. Freud, trained in nineteenth-century materialist philosophy, sought to explain belief in God by analyzing human needs and showing how they are projected outward to construct religious structures that are evolved over time by societies to give people some sense of comfort and security. However, Freud insisted that there is nothing "out there" that these structures reflect: they are projections from within to give names to the answers to questions and to create rituals that can structure people's lives.

By contrast, Jonathan Edwards (1703–58) started from Calvinism, with the basic postulate that Reality is rooted in God. (For a selection of Edwards's writings, see Edwards 1962.) Jonathan Edwards was for many years a preacher at Northampton, Massachusetts (Tracy 1980) and was a leading figure in the great awakening of New England religious fervor in the early eighteenth century. As a student at Yale, he was greatly influenced by Locke's "Essay on Human Understanding" (Laurence 1980). Yet, where John Locke saw faith and appeal to the Bible as distinct from reason – to be invoked only where experience could not settle the question – Edwards combined Calvinism with a Lockean philosophy. He did not see the Bible as a story written by men to comfort themselves in the wilderness but as revealed by God to man. Even though it is an imperfect story in that it is written in the words finite humans can understand, it is nonetheless the reflection of a greater Reality.

Clearly, if, like Freud, we start reading the Bible by asking "How did people come to make up a story like this?", we are going to get a different reading than if, like Edwards, we start by asking, "How much of the transcendent Reality that God was trying to communicate to us can we finite creatures come to know?" Freud and Edwards each build an epistemology we can see as in some sense a cousin of our schema theory. Yet, they come to diametrically opposed conclusions about Christianity. Freud develops a rich epistemology to support his *denial* of religion, whereas Edwards uses a rich epistemology to support his *espousal* of religion. It does not appear that future developments in schema theory could compel Freud and Edwards to agree on a single view as to the existence of God reality.

As we saw in Section 5.3, Jonathan Edwards held the Calvinist view of predestination, the idea that people were really of two kinds – the elect, who were pre-ordained by God to find salvation and who in their lifetime could come, through religious conversion, to appreciate the true beauty of God's works, and the unregenerate, who were damned and who in their lifetime could perceive little of God's glory. Edwards sought to reconcile this view with a Lockean epistemology by positing that God does not give the elect new ideas but gives them a new sense that allows them to perceive the world in a divine and supernatural light. He insists that what the elect learn from nature is coherent with the revelations of Scripture - the elect have no new schemas, only richer schemas. Edwards thus provides a bridge from a biblical story of revelation to natural theology.

The notion of predestination might at first seem akin to biological determinism; it is not so, however, because biological determinism addresses what happens to the organism in the spatiotemporal realm, whereas predestination speaks of one's fate in eternity. The questions with biological determinism are to what extent genetic makeup determines human cultural structures and to what extent will it determine our own personal development. To what extent do our genes fate us to be the sort of person we become? It is clear that at least they provide some constraints. For example, it seems that we human beings are the only creatures whose brains are structured in such a way that we have something we call language, and if our brain is damaged in a certain way, we do not have language. But these constraints are fairly weak - we can grow up speaking French or English, we can grow up in one religious system or another or with none at all. There appears to be a diversity of cultures consistent with our genetic makeup, and our individual personalities can be different - though to what extent our personality depends on individual circumstance beyond the social milieu and the genetic makeup is not a settled issue.

In Section 5.3, we saw that Jonathan Edwards and what we call a decisionist (a certain type of secular thinker) seem to converge on a similar doctrine of free will, yet coming from completely different starting points - one based on a concept of God rooted in the notion of predestination, the other based on a schema theory of mind. There are many concepts of God, each embedded within an elaborate symbol system. One possible definition starts from the question of who created the universe. God is the Creator.

By contrast, Freud addresses a specific Judeo–Christian view of God the Father. Freud used psychoanalysis to explain belief in God the father in terms of projection of the Oedipus complex. If, in reading Freud, one starts with a tendency to see religion as a human construct, one emerges confirmed in that view, However, the tools of psychoanalysis are surprisingly neutral, because if you start as a believer, then you can see atheism as a case of the Oedipal complex and the rejection of the father. This "neutrality" is both interesting and disturbing. With Freud, we have a schemalike theory with notions of identification, ways of assimilating schemas for persons rather than things, that addresses a whole range of human traits, such as love, hate, fear, and neurosis. However, even though Freudian psychoanalysis provides tools for exploring "the darkness of the human soul," it appears that these tools cannot help us decide the question of the existence of God.

Freud's personal outlook on religion was completely negative. "Religions originate in the child's and young mankind's fears and need for help." He will not offer what he sees as false consolation. Freud shares the philosopher's revulsion from the social consequences of religion, its barbarity and ignorance, and its conception of a vengeful God, viewing all religions as the product of the childhood of humanity, when people's fear created the gods, superstitions, and rituals of popular religion. He shares their commitment to science and reason. While analyzing how religion expresses people's deepest feelings and needs, he is not prepared to take the existentialist leap of faith. However, all psychologies of religion, including Freud's, lack a basis for deciding between theism and atheism.

Ferré (1967, p. 314) notes that psychology of religion also supports a theistic view: "If belief in God can be said to reflect infantile longing for the father's protection, then disbelief in him can equally well be traced to childish hatred, resentment, and rejection of the father. Atheism fares no better at the hands of a Freudian than theism." By the same token, Peter Berger (1962, p. 71) asserts that the parental role in religion is "not based on a loving lie. On the contrary, it is a witness to the ultimate truth of man's situation in reality. What is projected is, however, itself a reflection, an imitation, of ultimate reality." Again, Erikson's *Young Man Luther* (1958) may be read as naturalistic study of the development of a religious leader, or as how a future religious leader encountered the reality of God in the concrete, historical world in which he lived.

What, then, is the outcome for our discussion of Freud and religion? Three relevant themes have emerged in this chapter.

1. We have seen that some of the Freudian concepts may be used as indications of the *data* that have to be addressed by an adequate schema theory. To use them thus would be a logical outcome of Freud's own *Project* to make psychology into a science. It would, however, go beyond anything now seriously contemplated in brain theory because it would take up the challenge drawn by Freud from the mythical wisdom of human cultures. Freud's own theory fails to provide the detailed functional mechanisms that schema theory may be able to provide, but, on the other hand, Freud's mythical "stories" may be seen as metaphorical and theory-laden *descriptions* of the human condition. Such considerations lead us to the discussion of "Language as Metaphor" in Chapter 7 and, in the context of social anthropology, to "Religions as Social Schemas" in Chapter 10. Freud's metaphorical descriptions draw out depths of the personality undreamed of in the sort of humanist account that restricts itself to "unhappiness" due to economic deprivation, the sense of failure, and ordinary fears of sickness, death, and the future. Freud restores spirituality and darkness to the description of human experience and behavior. His warring aspects of the self belong with perceptions of the human condition, such as St. Paul's "Wretched man that I am,

who will deliver me from this body of death?" not with the facile humanism that characterized nineteenth-century myths of enlightened progress. Freud's ultimate pessimism need not close the discussion; instead, it rather brings us to the threshold of the issues addressed by religion.

We thus may accept all the help Freud gives in providing data about the human condition and look to the brain sciences to exploit these, if possible, in reductionist explanations of personality. However, what of Freud's reduction of the concepts of God and religion?

2. Genetic explanations of how the concept of God comes to be developed in human culture cannot disprove the existence of God: at best, they can reinforce the "no-need-of-that-hypothesis" type of argument. However, we have seen that, as some philosophers of religion have pointed out, many genetic arguments are double-edged – they can equally be turned against disbelief in God; atheism may be a response to hatred of the father, to repression of feelings of guilt, to resentment of renunciations, and so on. For a more positive account of religion that transcends all such reductive explanations, we must transfer the argument to a different level and ask how the concepts of *particular* religions look when analyzed in a Freudian mode. Does some element of transcendence necessarily cling to them in spite of reductive explanation?

3. One way to approach this problem is through Freud's pessimistic view of civilization and its values. So far, a close parallel exists between his attempted reduction of God to a psychic projection and Durkheim's attempted reduction to society as God, to which we turn in Chapter 10. In both cases is an ultimate appeal to explanation in terms of biological evolution. Durkheim, however, recognized and tried to address an ethical problem that Freud leaves on one side, namely, "How do we reconcile our instinctive perceptions of good and evil as somehow absolute, with a theory that accounts for them only as products of a particular evolution of biology and culture?" However strongly he believes in progress, Durkheim in the end balks at the *identification* of good and evil with what is perceived as such in the society that may ultimately evolve. Freud, however, has no belief in progress (the relative dates of *Civilization and Its Discontents* after, and Durkheim's *Society and Philosophy* largely before, World War I are, of course, significant). Freud is content to identify relative values with relative cultures. The civil war of the self and hence of society will continue essentially undiminished – there is no utopia, no heaven, no hope, no ultimate basis of the choice of good or evil.

We return to two questions asked earlier. In face of Freud's description of the human condition in terms of deep tensions and contradictions, does the humanist need either a father projection or a belief in the triumph of the proletariat, or a God or a heaven? And if so, *how* do these beliefs help? One of two conditions must be satisfied. Either they must be sincerely believed, or they must act unconsciously as ritual and symbolic systems surely do. The result of Freudian analysis is that if belief in God is *only* a father projection, then the concepts of God and heaven *cannot,* after Freud, be sincerely believed to exist in such a way that they can be a "help." The case of Marxist belief is different, since it is a this-worldly prediction and has to be judged according to all our experience and our criteria of what it is plausible to expect in human history. Freud's pessimistic judgment is here more plausible than that of the nineteenth-century Marx. But what of other-worldly hope and belief? If it were true, it would undoubtedly help, since most religious stories are precisely divine comedies found beyond tragedy; they conclude, at least for the "elect," with a "happy-ever-after." Yet, notice that the Judeo–Christian faith cannot unequivocally be regarded as a "help" in this world, for it speaks of the day of wrath, of judgment, of suffering, and of death. Why, if Freud and St. Paul are right in their dark view of the human condition, should religious "wish fulfillments" take this strange form?

Even Freud allowed that even though a religion may be genetically a wish fulfillment, or a psychic projection, or an "illusion" in this sense does not exclude the possibility of its being *true.* Let us for the moment leave the positive question of why we should believe in its truth with Pascal's partial answer: The believer *wagers* that it is true and lives accordingly. If the realistic alternative is not facilely optimistic humanism, but Freud's pessimism, the wager may even be said to yield an intellectually more coherent lifestyle, for it is not clear *what* the appropriate stance is for one who despairs in face of undoubted present facts and threatening futures. Why continue to seek the good, to act kindly, to try to improve the human lot against all the odds?

To make so explicit a wager, however, is perhaps to take too intellectualist a view. Religions act powerfully on the unconscious through symbol and ritual. Moreover, denial of religion need not entail denial of a cultural heritage. Freud himself, although not religious, never denied his Jewishness. As Peter Gay (1978) puts it:

To deny it would have been senseless and, as he also said, undignified. The Jewish bond he felt was the recognition of a common fate in a hostile world. . . . A laboratory for every known species of anti-Semitism, Vienna virtually compelled Freud to see himself as one among a band of potential victims, as one among Vienna's Jews. It was a role . . . that he took upon himself with his accustomed courage.

Our general stance on the development and testing of schemas should make us sympathetic to the view that such cultural traditions are also cognitive, though not subject to the usual positivist analyses of belief, knowledge, and truth. We continue this debate in the remaining chapters.

7 Schemas: from the individual to the social

7.1 A multilevel view of schemas

In discussing scientific knowledge in Chapter 1, we saw that scientific theories are testable and mutable and that changes yielding increasing pragmatic success may be accompanied by radical changes in the ontology posited to underlie the observable phenomena. We have based our epistemology on a schema theory with a similar quality. Our schema assemblages are not the precise formal statements of scientific explanation and observation; but they do allow us to make sense of our world, to plan courses of action, and yet to change the schemas (not necessarily consciously) when the expectations they support fail to be met.

There is a paradox at the heart of this chapter – the paradox of the individual actor discovering that much personal individuality appears to be the playing out of social forces. In this chapter, we come to a transition. The last five chapters emphasize schemas as units of cognition within the head of the individual; the next four chapters turn from psychology to the sociology of knowledge. They gather insights from philosophy of language, from social anthropology, and from hermeneutics to develop an account of *social schemas* that act as a reality external to the individual members of a society. These chapters culminate in the presentation in Chapter 11 of the Biblical worldview as a "Great Schema" that locates human reality in a God reality transcending space and time.

It will be helpful to bear in mind two sources of tension in our use of the concepts of schema theory and cognitive science. First, within the science itself is a tension between the current formal *models* of limited phenomena (whether they be expressed in computer models, mathematical equations, or neural networks) and the richer *description* of human experience that will always encompass phenomena that go beyond those explicable in terms of the current theories. Thus, cognitive scientists have the twofold job of providing explicit accounts of mechanisms for cognitive phenomena and of understanding the limitations of such accounts.

Second is the tension between cognitive science *as a science,* as a formal analysis of constrained settings, and cognitive science *as a philosophy,* in which we use schema language informally to discuss our human concerns. We know what it is to understand certain aspects of animal behavior or a child's linguistic development. But in what way would cognitive science help us better understand social systems and values? In the pages that follow, we see that schema theory may enrich our vocabulary for the critique of social systems and the understanding of human, social, and religious reality; we also see that schema theory provides no all-inclusive explanation of these value systems, much less a decision method for choosing between them.

In the previous two chapters, we have begun to look at person reality with respect to free will and Freudian psychology. The present chapter continues this development by expanding our view of schema theory. Section 7.3 offers suggestions for a schema-theoretic account of language as a socially constructed reality. We show how that reality is embodied in the schemas of individual members of the language community and then present a neo-Piagetian view of language acquisition. We explore both the commonality and individuality of the schemas held by different people. In Chapter 8, we see how this account supports the view of language as metaphor, which is part of our philosophy of science and yet is also central to the study of religious language and myth that follows. The rest of this chapter first seeks to understand how social forces influence people's thinking without precluding the possibility of dissent so that social schemas shape, but do not completely determine, the schemas whereby individuals represent them.

For Karl Marx, the term *ideology* was pejorative – it was the socially imposed false consciousness whereby the ruling class exerted its power. Viewing the injustice of many social conditions of his day, he gave as his recipe for change the uncovering of this false consciousness. He believed society would change once social structures were seen in the clear light of science. He saw people's view of society as distorted by their own interests; he also believed that the socially oppressed, the proletariat, constituted a class that, because it owned nothing, had no selfish interests. He saw it as historically inevitable that the proletariat would come to power and that they would come to build a new communist society that would be just and equal. It is difficult to maintain that today's so-called communist societies are indeed communist in the sense Marx intended, and in any case most of us would agree that Marx's doctrine of historical inevitability has not withstood the test of time. Moreover, even though we might agree with Marx that selfish interests may distort an analysis of society, we would doubt that any individual, let alone class, can be free of all such interests. Mannheim suggested that it was the intellectuals who, by their skill and critique and relatively "disinterested" stance, could at least in their arguments avoid selfish interests; but even this view seems charmingly utopian.

Let us re-examine the individual's acquisition of schemas in terms of this concept of interests. From the first, the child has schemas for interaction with its mother, and its innate schemas are intimately related with basic drives for hunger, thirst, and comfort. From the beginning, our knowledge of the world is bound up with our knowledge of how to interact with it, and such knowledge of "how to" is intimately intertwined with our knowledge (not necessarily conscious) of our goals and what we wish to achieve through our actions. Thus, as we develop as members of a society, our schemas cannot be clearly separated into those representing "facts" and those representing "norms." With such a recognition, we join those who no longer view ideology as something "imposed and bad," but rather as a necessary expression of society, though we may provide a critique of the social structures underlying ideology – to the extent that we can recognize them – and discuss ways to ameliorate what we take to be their shortcomings.

An "ideology" is expressed within the whole structure of interactions among the individuals of a society, their institutions, and their artifacts; it can only be variously and imperfectly represented within the head of any individual within that society. More generally, then, we use the term *social schema* to denote any such network, whether an ideology, a language, or a religion. In other words, it is what Durkheim (1938, p. xii) called "collective representations." We need not assume at this stage that social schemas have "external reality" independent of individuals and their mental schemas, but they need not be perfectly represented in the heads of any particular individuals. Language is the paradigm case: here, the "social schema" is a normative language system, hardly represented completely in any one speaker's head, but constituted by a shifting pattern of interactions among individual schemas. The social schema may be captured as an explicit, though temporary, norm in grammar books; it may be reconstructed as an ideal type by social linguists; or it may be wholly implicit in social relations. Such schemas are not external like the physical world, but they shape the development of our individual schemas at least as powerfully as the patterns of physical reality shape the development of our sensorimotor schemas. We give further examples of these social realities when we discuss Durkheim's philosophy of religion in Chapter 10.

We initiate our study of ideologies in Section 7.2 and then turn in Section 7.3 to an analysis of language to reconcile further the individual and the social. The study of a schema model of language acquisition gives us some sense of how an individual becomes a member of a social community.

The externalities of the schemas shared by the individuals of a community may cohere into a behavior pattern that defines a reality external to each individual. We refer to that pattern as a social schema and stress that it may not be internalized in its entirety within the head of any one individual. The coherence between the overt behaviors of all other individuals in a community, including the playing out of different social roles, shapes the development of the schemas of that individual; and to the extent that this individual comes to assimilate those communal patterns, to that extent will he or she in turn provide part of the coherent context for the development of others. In this sense, social schemas can be said to constitute a reality external to the individual.

Having said all this, we must still ask what makes a schema shared. In Chapter 4, we emphasized the distinction between a schema as an externally observable regularity of behavior of an individual and a schema as an internal structure "in the head" that could generate such patterns. In the context of social schemas, we must go further, distinguishing general patterns that may be discerned in the collective overt behaviors of many individuals from the regularities discernible in the behavior of a single individual. These populationwide patterns constitute the social schemas and have a reality even though they may not be traceable to a schema embodied in any one head. Nonetheless, these observable regularities may suffice to bring the overt behavior of many individuals into congruence. Of course, whether we talk in terms of social classes or of roles, we are reminded that the attainment of congruence of these schemas does not necessarily entail identical patterns of behavior of different individuals within the society; rather, it entails that different people will share certain common understandings of social relationships and that their own behavior may be conditioned by their appreciation of which social roles are open to them. Moreover, we reiterate that an individual's schemas are not determinants of stereotyped behavior. They are responsive to an appreciation of current circumstances to guide behavior in more or less flexible ways. Thus, the accommodation to a perceived social role may constrain but will not completely determine an individual's behavior.

In the transition from the individual to the social, note that social schemas are not presented only in terms of patterns observed in random behavior of a large population of individuals. The behavior of the members of a society can be patterned by shared rituals, shared texts, and shared artifacts – crystallizations of the social schemas into forms that increase their repeatability from individual to individual. Nonetheless, each such codification, just like any finite set of written laws, always remains in tension with the greater richness expressed by the full spectrum of behavior of the members of a given society. As our discussion of Freud emphasized, schemas do not develop just by the steady progress of reflective abstraction in a Piagetian process of knowledge acquisition. There is more than coherence to the development of schemas. Tensions will always remain between our perception of what is socially sanctioned and our understanding of what is required for the expression of our own individual schemas.

The essential point in our argument is that schemas *are in heads* and in the social relations between heads. The question of their criteria and "reality" in a different sense from the spatiotemporal is the difficult one tackled in Chapters 9, 10 and 11.

7.2 Societal schemas and individual reality

At one level of description, we may see language as a social reality external to the individual members of a community. Yet, the analysis in the next section shows how an "idiolect" of the language becomes internalized in the schemas of each individual. We may then come to see the language as constituted by the schemas of many individuals. In this section, we contrast a similar dichotomy of approaches to society and ideology – a top–down or structuralist view versus a bottom–up or interpretive view. For structuralists such as Althusser, the relations of production determine the places and functions occupied and adopted by the agents of production. This view may be regarded as a social generalization of Sperry's downward causation from persons to neurons discussed in Section 4.1. Here agents are not to be viewed as autonomous individuals but rather as supports or "bearers" for these functions, so that the relations among members of society are determined by the roles they occupy and the forces impinging on such roles at the level of social structures. By contrast, in an interpretive approach we want to understand what schemas an individual has constructed in interiorizing a social role, what is the *intersubjective* dimension acquired through growing up with others in a particular society, and how – despite the assimilation of role models or acceptance of the power structure – the individual can shape schemas that not only enable the playing of various roles but also provide a critique of them, e.g., in terms of a perception of being underpaid or exploited, a critique that may or may not emerge in overt and effective action. Just as no scientific observation language is theory-free, so will the vocabulary in which the individual expresses critique be shaped by the ideology of his or her society. (Recall George Orwell's creation, in the novel *1984*, of Newspeak, a language designed to blur meaningful distinctions in order to cripple the expression of dissent.) Again, we see the merits of twoway reductionism.

A structuralist account can look at the role of the worker in a capitalist society and clarify many features of, for example, the effects of mechanization initiated by the Industrial Revolution. But, on the interpretive view, we must also ask what capacities the individual worker must have that enables him or her to enter into such relations as working, negotiating a contract, and consuming, and what other possibilities follow from such capacities. The worker, unlike a child, must be able to entertain certain notions of responsibility and of exchange among labor, money, and goods. As Connolly (1981) observes, to understand a contract is to understand what it would mean to change the contract. To understand a role is to have the capacity to imagine different roles. Socially imposed ideologies succeed to the extent that they exclude conflicting schemas from consideration, making their reality appear untenable. As we soon discuss, the dynamics of individual change can be greatly constrained by the inertia of a whole population. (Conversely, the mass hysteria of a crowd can sweep up individuals into patterns of change they would reject totally if given the same possibilities in a framework of individual consideration. This phenomenon has been discussed from different perspectives by Freud in *Group Psychology and the Analysis of the Ego* and by Canetti [1980] in *Crowds and Power*.) An overarching schema can constitute a reality so strongly that it can reduce the credibility of certain other schemas unless some massive event or crisis serves to bring the credibility of this view of social reality into serious question. Yet, no such "reality," whether constituted by a religious or a secular system, can necessarily remain impervious to critique.

Why is it, then, that once a social system is "in place," it is difficult for people to act outside its societal schema or ideology, even if they conclude that a system of exploitation is unjust or question the efficacy of certain rituals or suspect that certain contradictions render the system illegitimate? Part of the answer inheres in relations of power, including the extent to which state power, quite apart from control of labor, serves to penalize those who overtly question ideology. If the chance of punishment outweighs the expectation of reform, individuals may come to repress (in the Freudian sense) their dissident thoughts. Such talk of power, of course, reminds us that schema theory needs the structural level of analysis to see how individual schemas become "crystallized" in institutions with rules that become in no small part constitutive of personal reality.

So, too, the vocabulary of *roles* is indispensable. We cannot analyze social issues without using such terms as *student* and *worker*. With a close friend or family member or colleague, our knowledge of the individual can overshadow general knowledge about societal roles. But making sense of a world of four billion people requires many different types of classification if we are to construct a world of manageable complexity for ourselves. Our schemas range from the general to the specific – providing our ability to react with some chance of success in novel situations while bringing more intimate knowledge to bear when applicable. Too coarse a classification (too simple, rigid, and formulaic an ideology) and our judgments will not take us beyond the well structured and routine. Too subtle an attention to the nuances of individuals and we are paralyzed from effective decision-making beyond a small circle of friends. In either case, however, we must be open to change, change based on more solid criteria than the simple flutters of fashion.

A change in society must depart from, yet build on, the way society is; and to discuss such changes, one must use a vocabulary in part shaped by the society one is in. The relation between theory and evidence is close in social life, and this proximity makes the testing of evidence complex. The participants' awareness of a theory enters into their interpretation and so may reshape the social reality. A theory might bring out a set of tacit beliefs of a group of people and show them to contradict the explicit beliefs held by the group. But once the people become aware of the theory, they can ask if they endorse these hitherto tacit beliefs. A loop thus exists between theory and practice, as tacit beliefs are brought to self-consciousness and thus become subject to modification. For example, a patient's partial understanding of Freudian theory helps constitute the therapeutic relationship. A change in theory thus helps to change practice.

Schema theory must not only look at the dynamics of schema use and change in practice (the action-perception cycle) but must also understand the new dimensions of change introduced by language, with the dynamics of discourse, of rhetoric, and of argument. Just as we distinguished the implicit effects of schema change (cf. Polanyi's [1966] *The Tacit Dimension*) from the more highly evolved effects of the conscious use of language, so Connolly has distinguished two dimensions of believing: the empiricist (the evidence of behavior) and the rationalist (the support of argument). X's belief may be evidenced by his conduct and so might be analyzed as a disposition to action. We might even show X that he holds a belief contrary to what he has said or admits to believing. X may say he believes in the importance of politics, yet you may point out to him that he never votes and always avoids political discussions. The belief is thus tacit, or implicit, in his conduct, even though he has not acknowledged he holds the belief. If X finally admits to the evidence of his behavior, his belief that politics is not important becomes explicit, but it is still incomplete. A tacit belief becomes an explicit hypothesis. This is the second dimension of believing. X must not only see that the belief is embodied in his behavior, he must also endorse it – or reject it, and reshape his behavior accordingly. To hold a belief is not only to act on it but also to be able to give reasons to support it and to understand circumstances in which it might be revised. Note that "tacit" does not equal "repressed"; I cannot be explicitly aware of all the skills involved in riding a bicycle while giving my attention to navigating the bicycle, but these skills are not repressed in any Freudian sense.

Our thinking is thus a blend of our own nuances and the overall ideology we espouse. Do we hold to a liberal view of civil rights, or do we accept certain race-related roles as immutable? Do we see poverty as the moral stain of the poor, or do we see the amelioration of poverty as the moral responsibility of the not-so-poor? These high-level ideological judgments color whatever individual analyses we may care to make out of our own being and experience. We say more of this in the book's final chapter.

The inertia of ideology

Why do agents internalize an ideology if, in fact, it is contrary to what they might themselves come up with in their own unconstrained critiques? Our Piagetian perspective provides perhaps the most compelling answer. We do not come to our own society "from outside," armed with a gift for rational critique free of all social preconceptions. Instead, as children, we grow up in a society, accommodating our schemas to assimilate its social norms and its standards of language and logic in a richly interconnected network that has no prespecified boundaries. Few decisions are reached by purely deductive analysis from well-founded axioms (Section 2.2). Rather, we act from a feeling of conviction that may be based on tacit knowledge (activation of schemas embodying related experiences) more than verbal analysis; or, we may entertain an inchoate set of possibilities and be forced to "leap" before we have had time for thoughtful reflection on them. Thus, even to the extent that, as adults, we come explicitly to develop a set of skills in logical analysis, too much of our argument is rooted in our tacit network of schemas for our critique of society to be entirely free of the ideology that constitutes it.

Moreover, thoughtful critique requires an element of freedom from everyday cares and responsibilities – an element given more to people who find the society to their liking than to the oppressed. Even scientists or philosophers, professionally committed to critical analysis, may find that the pressures of their careers leave little time to apply their skills beyond a narrow specialization. More generally, most adults have vital underlying interests in obtaining food, clothing, and shelter for themselves and their families. Once a society has a certain structure, then a certain mode of life gets locked into place. People see that their interests can be met only by accepting certain roles. Certainly, wars, geographic expansion, pestilence, technological innovation, social innovation (the abolition of slavery, votes for women, prohibition), and revolution can all open up new roles. However, few people devote much time to a full-scale critique of society or to risking life and limb in revolt against the established order.

We may speak again, as in Section 4.1, of cooperative phenomena, the stability of some global form of organization in a large system – as in the overall pattern of magnetization in a system comprising a multitude of atomic magnets. Where statistical mechanics must analyze transitions between relatively few phases of matter, social theory must understand how, with the richness of language and the diversity of artifacts, people can create a dazzlingly rich variety of new yet relatively stable social structures. Just as it is hard to reverse the magnetization of a large magnet through local changes of the magnetic field, so it is hard for the individual in society to maintain a marked discrepancy between role aspiration and role actuality. In most cases, a social critique elaborated by a small group of individuals becomes repressed or remains restricted to discussions within that small group. Nonetheless, in exceptional cases – depending both on the determination of that nucleus and on the extent to which other members of society are receptive to that critique – the critique can, in fact, spread, perhaps even to the point of effecting an enduring restructuring of society. There are also innovations that meet little resistance because they move into a vacuum – as in the discovery of the New World or the development of microcomputers.

Our histories of ideas celebrate the people who questioned the folk consciousness of their day and won through, by bringing the new into the domain of everyday reality – the pineapples and Indians brought back by Columbus, the new sights revealed by Galileo's telescope, the death of the last Czar. But for each person who reshaped the world, there are thousands – many of whom may have had visions that were equally "realistic" – who never rose from obscurity.

Do all social changes start with the acts of a determined individual? Or, are there truly social forces at work? The answer cannot be a simple either/or. One may say it was Columbus who discovered the New World. Or, one may say it was the compass that opened up a method of maritime navigation that made the European discovery of the New World inevitable. One can trace the rise of Nazism to the personality of Hitler, to the terms of the Peace Treaty of Versailles, to the hyperinflation of the 1930s, or to the flaws in the Weimar Republic. Without Hitler, Germany might still have gone to war, but the myth of the Third Reich and the genocide of the Jews might not have been part of history. The individual cannot be effective without a certain social stage, but the stage is bare without the actors.

We now add the psychological observation that most people want some congruence between their hopes and aspirations and their actual life situation. Some few people can build their lives around striving for a goal that appears important to them even if its attainment appears unlikely. But for most people, such dreams are soon discarded as the stuff of adolescence. A goal is to be strived for only if it appears likely of attainment; otherwise, one's goals and aspirations should themselves be adjusted into congruence with "reality." One can relate this secular observation to Moltmann's Theology of Hope, with its ambiguity between the socialist Utopia and a salvation beyond the reality of space and time.

But consider someone who, through personal experience or any other means, has come to a belief discordant with the "surrounding" ideology (be it political, or that of the workplace, or the peer group). If this belief challenges something central to that ideology, then holding it overtly must, by definition, have real consequences – political or religious persecution, trouble holding a job, ostracism, or just exposure to ridicule and troubled social relationships. For a few people, the conviction of the rightness of their belief makes it worth fighting for. But for most people, the price is too high and the view is increasingly held privately. The resultant lack of social reinforcement may then lead to a downplaying of the belief – the less it can be acted on, or even discussed out loud, the less important it becomes.

It is one thing to call for social reforms; it may be another to mobilize the forces to bring about these changes. Such changes depend on political reality at least as much as on the beauty of the schemas that the reforms would embody. An orthodox Christian might see the history of the Church as a triumph of God's truth over heresy, but to the outsider the fate of doctrine seems often to be settled on secular terms – either through the strength of an army or through the strength of revolt unleashed by a harsh oppression that could be interpreted as the occasion of martyrdom. Just as we may abandon a plan to plunge a knife through our heart, so may a group abandon plans for reform if they come to believe, for example, that their plans would lead to widespread disruption of industry with intolerable economic repercussions. The group may come to accept the status quo, settling back into the routines of work and family. For other people, the ends may seem so glorious as to justify any means, no matter what disruptions ensue. Others may abandon the quest and come to resent those who wish to revolt – if the others were to succeed, one's own abandonment would be seen as wrong, as a sign of indecision or weakness. The dynamic of failure can reinforce the status quo.

Here is a question for a Freudian analysis: Why is it that some repressed beliefs can simply "decay" in the fashion presented here, while others continue to fester? Much depends on how the belief arose. If it links with everyday experience (as in a worker's experience of low wages and burdensome working conditions), then this experience must either be assimilated into other beliefs (as in Marx's view of religion as "the opium of the people") or the "aberrant" belief will be continually strengthened. If it cannot be translated into overt action, it will make itself felt as a generalized and unchanneled feeling of frustration and resentment. If the belief arose from special circumstances, such as reading a book or having a conversation, which may have been compelling at the time but which are not continually reactivated by further experience, the belief gradually approaches the status of a dream. Yet in some cases – for example, the religious heretic, the confirmed revolutionary – the entrenchment of these "socially aberrant" schemas is so great, whether because of a beatific conviction or an analysis of the secular goals of the just society, that it constitutes the believer's reality. Feedback signals a discrepancy, but it does not say what – belief or society – must be changed to reduce that discrepancy.

A schema can be strengthened by activity or by public statements that share it with a larger group, enmeshing it in the discourse cycle. Not all activity requires group interaction – consider the writer polishing a manifesto in a lonely garret. But for most people, the development of ideas is a group process and rests on a large measure of intersubjectivity. (Recall our discussion of the two senses of schema: overt and internal. The overt dimension can provide the intersubjectivity; but the further it develops in isolation, the more difficult it may be to communicate about it and the less likely it will ever play a socially effective role, even though it may come to dominate the thinking of the lone person who nurtured it.) Connolly (1981, p. 55) asserts that:

Facing *social* pressure to identify himself as others do, *epistemic* pressure to adopt clear beliefs subject to public tests, and internal *moral* pressure to achieve congruence between inner beliefs and outer conduct he can respond affirmatively by adopting gradually the beliefs appropriate to his role. The others can simply be allowed to fade away.

By the time the worker reaches this point he need no longer see himself (at least consciously) as either a coward or a victim . . . and [will believe] that young dissidents who challenge these views have had little experience in the *real* world.

The suggestion is that when individuals' overt conduct and conscious beliefs are integrated, they will each see themselves as free agents. Note that this is a view of freedom compatible with the decisionist view of free will (Section 5.2) but perhaps seems to require too conscious and explicit a status for beliefs/schemas. The conditions of society are seen as desirable in certain aspects and inevitable in others. Pain is an example of the inevitable – once it has given us our warning signal, we should be able to turn it off, but, alas, we did not evolve that way. Part of what we each learned is that certain things are inevitable, even though it seems that any well-qualified Creator would have programmed them differently. Our attempt to "debug" God's plan is severely restricted (Freud's reality principle!). The same is true of ideology. If we, as individuals, see no way open *to us* to change certain features of society, it is easier to decide that these features in and of their nature *cannot* be changed. Here, we confront the construction of reality. At one level, we see society as a human construction we can shape and change. Since there are many societies, we can (if we can get the necessary visas) decide which of the available realities will be ours. But we often are attached to many aspects of a people and countryside, not to speak of our home and family and friends, and do not wish to give them up – yet we cannot abide the social system. We may then seek to reconstruct social reality, working for social change. But our experience tells us that reality has this measure of externality – we can only shape it so far. What can we hope to change? What convinces us to stop trying?

7.3 From schemas to language

To return to questions that place our analysis of social schemas more squarely within the realm of cognitive science, what does it mean to claim that two people share a language – or an ideology, or a religion? More specifically, let us focus on the English language. Is English the language spoken in England? in London? at Buckingham Palace? by the Queen? Or, should we define it as the totality of all English sentences ever uttered, or the set of sentences defined by an ideal grammar, or some other Platonic ideal of English? We suggest that to be competent in English is not to have internalized such an ideal grammar or to have in some sense mastered the competence of some ideal speaker. Rather, it rests on the ability to communicate with other people who speak English; not simply to place words in grammatical order but also to use sentences as building blocks of a conversation or for reading or writing.

But who are these "others who speak English"? We see here the notion of family resemblance – where the resemblance is measured by the ability to support communication. We each speak an "idiolect" – our own idiosyncratic dialect, marked by particularities of vocabulary, stock phrases, and turns of expression. We learned this idiolect through our interaction with other persons and their artifacts, such as books, radio, and television. Through our partial sample of the overt behavior generated by the English-schemas of others, we create our own. But because we come to these interactions with our own personality and prior stock of schemas, and because our sample of the language behavior of others is necessarily incomplete, our English-schemas remain idiosyncratic – even though they will serve adequately as a means of communication on most occasions.

Semantic naturalism posits for each word fixed, immutable meanings that can be fed through a compositional semantics machine to yield a fixed, unequivocal meaning for each sentence. We reject this view and claim instead that most sentences do not have a single, abstract meaning but rather initiate a process in each listener's head that creates a meaning structure, in the form of a dynamic schema assemblage, which depends on the listener's history and understanding of the context. There can be a continuing process of investing a sentence with meaning, with no prescribed stopping point, just as a conversation can continue to broaden the implications of the opening utterances of the dialogue. Our theory of meaning is based on the mutability of schemas, on how schemas are embedded in a network of schemas linked to experience in the world, and on appreciation of how the child develops as knower and actor, speaker and hearer. We now need to make this schema-theoretic analysis more explicit.

What is the relationship between words and schemas? Locke thought the meaning of a word is the *idea* in the mind to which the word refers and that the idea is causally related to the world; the structure of the world would thus causally determine the structure of the mind. We would hold that words can help evoke an internal schema-assemblage but would not hold that single words refer to single schemas in the brain. Moreover, we would not hold that the relationship is a directly causal one. The distinction we have in mind is this: the burn marks on a tree would causally represent the passage of a fire, whereas a symbolic representation involves no such immediate relationship in terms of physics and chemistry. Of course, there may be a sense in which any representation is causal, in that light must affect the pigments in the rods and cones of the retina and so on in terms of the structure of the neural network until one finally emits a word that describes something one is looking at. But this level of description misses the point, just as an attempt to reduce the semantics of a programming language to the operation of transistors would miss the essence of what is involved in computation. We must seek the meaning of words in terms of the hierarchical structuring of schemas; and we must seek the activation of these schemas in terms of the input/output interactions, expectations, and planning that constitute the action/perception cycle (cf. Sections 2.3 and 3.2). A word or symbol stands for an object to the extent that it can stand in for it when some total process of physical operations is replaced by some total process of symbolic operations.

An account of perception stresses the construction of schema assemblages as representing the environment, but schemas may also be activated by internal processes, as in hunger leading to activation of the "refrigerator schema" as part of a plan to go to the refrigerator to get food. We postulate that language evolves as yet another mechanism for activating schema assemblages (not necessarily with all the richness of detail that goes with, for example, visual perception). We see *a* meaning as a schema assemblage whose schemas were developed both in a sensorimotor context and thus have meanings out in the world and also in a linguistic context, gaining meaning from other schemas invoked by sentences that also invoked the given schema. Just as it is sometimes useful to speak of literal meaning, so it will sometimes be convenient to speak of *the* meaning of a sentence. In general, however, the sentence will underdetermine the schema assemblage evoked by hearing it so that the meaning on that occasion will be idiosyncratic to the extent that it depends on context and on the hearer's current mental state and stock of schemas.

Our discussion of the action/perception cycle in Chapter 3 suggests that the animal's internal model of its visually defined environment is an assemblage of schemas updated during continuing activity (both mental and physical) rather than being put together simply in response to current stimuli. We offer the same model for the human being's internal model of the state of a discourse (Arbib 1982a). The generation of movement requires the development of a plan on the basis of the internal model of goals and environment to yield a temporally ordered, feedback-modulated pattern of overlapping activation of a variety of effectors. Hence, we argue that the word-by-word generation of speech may be seen as a natural specialization of the general problem of motor control. We thus view sentence production as a process of selection and translation from an often ill-defined goal structure to a (relatively) well-formed sentence of the language (embedded within an ongoing action–perception cycle). This process invokes a great deal of knowledge, only a small amount of which is well formalized within current cognitive science.

One can view the deployment and decoding of the linguistic signal as responsive to a series of constraints. The first type of constraint is inherent in the structure of the linguistic code, which is itself a social production. The characterization of this structure is the goal of theories of linguistic competence and sociolinguistics. The second type of constraint arises from psychological limitations of the human language-processing systems, suggesting interactions between the nature of human processing routines and the nature of language structures. A third type of constraint results from the social and pragmatic facts of conversational situations. Other levels can be suggested.

Verification and language

Within the action/perception cycle, schemas assembled on the basis of perceptual processes enter into the planning of action and create expectations about the outcome of that action. We saw in Chapter 3 that when the outcome differs from such expectation, the subject may either adjust the perceptions, creating a new schema assemblage (assimilation) or begin to change the schemas themselves (accommodation). The process involves both the refinement of the internal representation of the environment and the refinement of actions, together with the development of ever more sophisticated ways of matching action to circumstance, needs, and goals. We may refer to this process as *self-verification* in that it does not involve the assistance of, or interaction with, another person's attempts to interact with the environment. Now, the early stages of language learning do, of course, involve interaction with other members of the language community. The child learns that certain words can achieve certain results, whether it be a smile or the provision of milk or the removal of a source of discomfort. A process much like self-verification may enable the child better to appreciate what is being said around it and generate utterances to achieve some desired effect. We thus analyze how the child may become a member of a language community as he or she engages in discourse with other members of the community, changing both linguistic and nonlinguistic schemas through a process of assimilation and accommodation. Only because the participants in discourse can relate a lack of correspondence to specific schemas can they hope to become more adept players of the language game. Language is seen as providing the format for the operation of coordination that regulates standards of appropriate usage. The coordinating operations are essentially public affairs and are observables by which two (or more) actors may regulate their behavior one to the other.

Piaget states that:

Owing to language . . . the general coordination of actions ceases to be uniquely intrapersonal as it may be in the animal or the very young child, to become interpersonal and contribute to an objectivity of which the individual is himself doubtless incapable, at least at a certain level. . . . The very coordination of interpersonal actions, that is, cooperation as opposed to the constraints of opinion, in fact constitutes a system of operations carried out in common all by cooperation. . . . But these operations in common require a *mutual verification* [our emphasis] of a higher level than self-verification, so that the laws of coordination become normative laws regulating intellectual intercourse between people. . . .

We suggest that Piaget's term *mutual verification* refers to a later and more important aspect of language than self-verification: namely, the achievement of a regenerative stage at which the child has acquired sufficient mastery of language to be able to engage in conversations that improve the mastery of language itself. Clearly, deixis – the ability to point at things – provides one key to the acquisition of language in that it restricts the ambiguity of a situation to which a word or phrase applies. But far more effective communication becomes possible when the hearer is able to query whether what was uttered really reflects the speaker's intentions, or the speaker may ask the hearer to clarify his or her understanding when his or her actions seem to differ from those the speaker had hoped to elicit. Different languages have different ways of expressing concepts, commands, injunctions, and queries. Just which particular scheme is embodied in a particular language may be inexplicable except by close historical analysis. For the child acquiring a language, however, the language is an external, albeit socially constructed, reality to be mastered. The rules to be mastered include the laws of coordination mentioned by Piaget, which we take to be not only those laws embodied in the use of language to describe and refer and to command and to ask but also the laws of interaction that constitute discourse. In many ways, these laws are conventional yet reflect underlying processes of coordination that cognitive science may hope to explicate. (Arbib, to appear, notes that Piaget pays little attention to the notion of mutual verification when he traces the construction of logic and language and stresses processes of reflective abstraction over social convention when he traces the dynamics of mental development.)

We now turn to a sketch of an answer to the question, "How does a new participant join the language game?" The answer is based on the attribution to children of the capacity to distinguish different patterns of interaction with their world, by grace of innate schemas and those they have already developed before their use of language to describe those situations properly. However, once its language has reached a certain richness, the child is able to assimilate and generate sentences that describe states beyond those for which he or she is cognitively competent – the language then can come to drive the development of cognition. Here, again, we see the essentially cyclic processes we spoke of in the action/perception cycle: cognition provides the basis for the enrichment of the child's mastery of language; language provides the means to express distinctions in the state of the world that can enrich cognitive capacity.

We learn the meaning of new words by inference from how they appear in a sentence; and we must then use contextual or nonlinguistic cues to provide an approximate meaning for the sentence-as-a-whole to infer back to a schema for the new word that can interact with other schemas to interpret the sentences appropriately. In a meaningful conversation, each speaker constructs a structure of expectations, and conversation continues while alternating speakers sufficiently meet the expectations of each other. But language is not purely linguistic. We may also emphasize procedure-oriented meanings. We teach children by "a hole is to dig," and so on; students are given homework; aspiring scientists conduct laboratory exercises; and the learning of the tradition is reinforced by the performance of rituals.

The processes of reflective abstraction (Section 3.1) underlie the development of symbolization and language. We see the ability to comprehend and utter words as forming perceptual and motor schemas that arise, in the first place, from abstraction from the sensorimotor schemas that represent the objects and actions to which those words refer. But this success at the level of deixis permits the reflective abstraction of the concepts of *word* and *sentence* as bearers of meaning.

We share with animals the ability to recognize an animal by the sight of it, the smell of it, or the sound it makes; and we learn that a variety of behaviors are appropriate following on that recognition, with the choice of behavior often being the result of subtle (though not necessarily conscious) planning taking into account not only context but also needs and desires. It is a small step to go from being able to pair the "meow" with the sight of a cat and the "bark" with the sight of a dog to being able to pair a sound that does not emanate from the object itself with the object, namely the spoken word *dog* with the sight or sound of the dog, and the word *cat* with the sight or sound of the cat. Humankind's evolutionary innovation seems to be the ability to become consciously aware that one may use arbitrary sound patterns to activate a schema within the mind of a hearer without having to imitate the sound whose schema is to be evoked. Once that discovery has been made, the perceptual capacities are already present to allow such assimilations to be made again and again. Let us, then, posit this ability to the young child, though with a definite upper bound, increasing with age, on the complexity of the structure that can be assimilated at any one time. Let us also posit that in a particular situation, the child is able to represent this (subconsciously, admittedly) by a number of schema assemblages, and let us further posit that such schema assemblages are still available for processing for some time after an event occurs.

Chomsky has argued that the rules of syntax are, at least to a great extent, innate. Piaget, from the viewpoint of his constructivism, would suggest that the coordination between speakers and their worlds and each other has enough richness to supply the rules over time. We note that Chomsky's account of innate syntax assumes that the constraints on this syntax, already present at least incipiently in the very young child, uses such grammatical categories as noun and verb. We would suspect, however, that such concepts are sophisticated, play no role in the child's early acquisition of language, and, in fact, are normally only learned as the result of explicit instruction in grammar. The child learns words with connections to other words to express certain ideas and situations; and as time goes by, these words may be aggregated into classes that may play interchangeable roles in sentence frames. However, there is no particular reason to expect that these words would be aggregated into the familiar categories of syntax. In fact, Hill (1983) (see also Hill & Arbib 1984) offers an explicit computational model of language acquisition in a two-year-old child that shows how word classes could develop naturally as a part of the template generalization that develops syntactic organization in intimate interaction with cognitive development in general. Even though the child may find it natural to think of such words as *cat* or *ball* as belonging to the same class, it is not clear that a word like *water* as distinct from *a glass of water,* let alone words like *love* or *drinking,* can play the same semantic, and thus syntactic, role. Hence, we see *noun* as a theoretical category not descriptive of any part of the young child's linguistic apparatus. In any case, the child starts with one-word sentences, proceeds to two-word sentences, and then to sentences of greater length and complexity. At the one-word stage, it would probably be a mistake to ascribe the word *milk* to the category of nouns rather than to the category of sentences. Moreover, as the child progresses, something we might call protocase structure may be appropriate. The child comes to use a limited set of templates whereby certain types of nouns can be fitted to certain verbs (without the child's having any such notion as noun or verb). These templates provide semantic categories, but such categories are in no way assimilated to such abstract roles as actor or instrument as used by case grammarians. These schema hypotheses are consonant with the argument that even the child's first language may be better characterized as "metaphorical" than as "literal."

Of course, we do not claim that all (or most of) the processes of language acquisition are conscious. Moreover, our model must posit certain basic mechanisms of language learning in the young child, such as the ability to pair situations (assemblages of concept schemas) with sentences (assemblages of word schemas). What we do claim, however, is that as we come to understand structures that can mediate the interaction of cognition and language in the acquisition of both cognition and language – a sort of ascending spiral – we find a notion of innateness different from Chomsky's (e.g., 1968), which posits that the categories of adult syntax and many of the observed restrictions on transformations are already innate and present from the beginning, simply requiring a trigger or two for their expression.

If we now turn to the more social aspects of language, we must stress that even though at any particular time we can expect two members of a language community to have shared many public experiences, they may have many more experiences they do not hold in common. Thus, even if their schemas will generate coordinated behavior over a wide range of common experience, it may be that there will be other situations in which they would not agree on usage. Again, even when the two actors are in what would appear to an outsider to be the same situation, their attending to different aspects of the situation may lead them to disagree about the proper choice of words. These disagreements provide grist for the mill of assimilation and accommodation, leading both to the refinement of the network of meaning for a given word and to the acquisition of new words or phrases to express the nuances that are behaviorally meaningful. This process changes nonlinguistic schemas as well as the verbal schemas to which they are related by reflective abstraction. Schemas that embody meaning will have a wider range of applicability than those public occasions that affected their development, and we might say that "literal meanings are hackneyed metaphors" whose increasing differentiation in particular experiences of interpersonal interaction has limited, and limited again, the range of applicability of the given word. This view undergirds the theory argued in Chapter 8 that "all language is metaphorical."

Mutual verification does not produce schemas as separate entities but rather as embedded within a network of knowledge. From the point of view of a given language community, much of that knowledge may be regarded, at least temporarily, as fixed and immutable since it provides a framework within which ideas can be understood or changed or new ones assimilated. However, as these new ideas become themselves part of the framework, they provide the support structure in which other ideas can in turn change. Thus, over a long period, virtually no schemas of language competence may remain unchanged, virtually no words may retain the same meaning. There is a similar development of concepts in science, in which a network of concepts forms a *paradigm,* with relatively few concepts changing at any one time, so that certain scientific ideas may seem immutable. Over the centuries, however, virtually all the concepts may change drastically. New meanings are adapted and created by new experience, as scientific models are extended to new domains of phenomena.

Natural language should not be seen as a single system. The language in which we present a mathematical proof to a colleague and the language in which we discuss the plot of a movie may both appear to be English, but they are in fact different dialects – not only in the domain of discourse but also in the "tightness" of sentence structure and in the meanings of many words that have a technical use in one domain but not in the other. We might say that English (or any other natural language) lets us play hundreds of language games. Within a particular "frame" (as Goffman 1974 uses the word), the appropriate sentences and their meanings may be rigidly determined. In discourse, however, we may not know which game is being played, or we may combine several games, or we may wish to make a move for which we do not have an appropriate expression. Sometimes we invent a new word and somehow convey its denotation. More often, we use existing words in a way that is clear in context; this pattern of words may then become a unit of usage, whose meaning may then migrate – as the meaning of penknife migrated from "a knife for sharpening quills" to "a knife whose blade folds into the shaft." In this example, there is no class of language games. Rather, the new word attaches itself to an object on account of its function but then stays with objects of this structure even as they come to have different functions. Here, then, the driving change in usage is extralinguistic, yet it still forces a change in the linguistic definition of the "proper" meaning. We thus should not see metaphor in terms of the interaction of distinct systems or languages, in one of which usage is literal and the other metaphorical. Rather, every word or phrase has its contexts or language games in which usage is recognized as normal and in which a standard meaning can be invoked, and others in which the use is unfamiliar or novel. There is no rigid distinction between the literal and the metaphorical.

The theory must explain how schemas are put together to give meaning to whole sentences. This process, however, is not like simple composition of compact, prespecified dictionary entries for each word; it is more like forming a coherent story with small extracts from the encyclopedia entries for words depending, further, on the schemas that encapsulate the experiences of the embodied subject (Section 2.3). Certain meanings will have to be activated only to be deactivated as we move to a structure that meets some semantic coherence criterion. When we combine words into a sentence, each word may find the others to invoke a "normal" context, in which case the fitting together of meanings offered by compositional semantics is a reasonable caricature of how meaning is given to the sentence as a whole. But even here, note the tentative nature of the process – we separate figure from ground, sketch the meaning of the ground, and then test for compatibility of the figure, and so on to completion. In ambiguous sentences, as in reversible visual figures, the random choice of a starting point may determine which collection of normal meanings gives meaning to the sentence as a whole.

However, the pieces may not fit so neatly together. When we read the sentence, "The sky is crying," our "normal" semantics fails, for skies do not cry. One solution is to take part of the meaning of *crying,* namely, the falling of water, to understand that "It is raining." (Indhurkaya 1985 offers a formal theory of such metaphorical inference.) But the residue of meaning then infects the sentence, suggesting, to give just one possibility, an overall air of sadness to the rainy day of the sentence. Further sentences in the context may then enhance this association or replace it by new ones. This combination of compactness with the opening of possibilities makes the sentence say more than "It is a depressing, rainy day." The sentence is not exhausted by a fixed internal semantics but rather acts as a catalyst for a dynamic unfolding of schema activity in the head of the listener – activity that is not limited by the speaker's intentions. Again, in a different context, the understanding of what is literal and what is metaphorical in this example may be reversed. We might have used "the sky" metaphorically, struck by the bright blue (or misty grey) of the eyes that are literally "crying."

As Black (1962) first argued clearly in his "interaction theory" of metaphor, there is no possibility of making literal paraphrases of metaphoric sentences without distorting and impoverishing their sense. This conclusion is reinforced by the picture of language as a complex web of semantic interactions in which there is no rigid distinction between the literal and metaphorical. Any attempt to paraphrase will itself create new contexts of use and contribute to shifting the meaning both of the metaphorical sentence and of the "literal" sentence to which it is supposed to be reduced.

We described in Chapter 1 how the realist view of scientific theory has been discredited by recent philosophical critique; the same objections also count against literalism as a theory of language. In the next chapter, then, we consider how our schema theory of language leads us to consider all language as metaphorical and thus to create a new epistemology.

8   Language, metaphor, and a new epistemology

8.1 Language as metaphor

In the previous chapter, we made some suggestions about a schema theory of language acquisition by the child, for whom language is initially an external reality to be mastered. We also noted that the external language is itself a social construction – a "collective representation," as Durkheim called it. In this section, and more particularly in Chapter 10, we start to build some bridges between the essentially individualist approach and a more comprehensive picture of language as also embodying the constructions and classifications of a culture. In this area there are plenty of empirical studies on which to draw, deriving from literary criticism, social anthropology, and the history of ideas and of science, as well as Wittgensteinian philosophy. However, cognitive science is as yet an infant in these worlds, and we cannot claim to have more than hints for an adequate theory of such social schemas. In this section, we concentrate not on the empirical aspects of sociolinguistics but on the philosophical implications of our theory of language so far.

Our emphasis on the dynamics of meaning change and its holistic character already brings us into conflict with a long-entrenched philosophical tradition. Speaking of the suggestion that the meaning of words changes whenever our mental state changes, when, for example, we acquire more knowledge about the subject matter, Putnam (1981, p. 22n) says this "would not allow any words to *ever* have the same meaning, and would thus amount to an abandonment of the very notion of the word 'meaning'." And discussing the possibility of a holistic theory of meaning, Dummett concludes:

> But when we try to take seriously the idea that the references of all names and predicates of the language are simultaneously determined together, it becomes plain that we are thereby attributing to a speaker a task quite beyond human capacities. (Dummett 1976, p. 133)

Such remarks are common in philosophical analyses of language, but they contain at least two fallacies. First, meaning change may happen in degrees, not in kind. Just as we can isolate motions in one part of a gravitational

147

field to render their effects negligible in another part, even though there are in principle changes of field everywhere, so can we isolate the effects of meaning change in parts of the semantic network and ignore them or pull them in as necessary for sufficient understanding. No understanding is ever perfect, just as no physical measures are ever precisely accurate. Second, we have already said enough to show that cognitive science can postulate human capacities far beyond what we can explain in detail or become conscious of. Computers can now make the kinds of complex determinations required in learning a semantic network for a specific "microworld," and can associate items sufficiently fast and accurately for many linguistic purposes. The process may, of course, not always work in human communication, but these are just the cases in which we say that ambiguities or misunderstandings have occurred.

Our discussion of language acquisition implies rejection of the literalist view of language as an ideal static system with fixed meanings which are dependent upon fixed syntactic and semantic rules. We must now go beyond the level at which schema theory can suggest mechanisms for language acquisition in order to view language from the point of view of the semanticist and the philosopher, for whom the literalist view has for long implied a radical distinction between the "literal" and the "metaphoric." Searle, for example, in his book *Expression and Meaning* (Searle 1979, p. 132) distinguishes the "literal meaning" of a sentence from its "utterance meaning." Literal meaning is entirely determined by the fixed meanings of words and the syntactic rules of the language; utterance meaning is a local and variable matter, depending on speaker's intentions on particular occasions. Thus, in particular, metaphoric uses of words are part of utterance meaning: when we say, "She cut him dead at the party," our utterance meaning has to be gleaned from context and expressed by literal gloss or paraphrase, and only the paraphrases can be said to have truth value.

According to this view, the literal meaning of a descriptive sentence determines its truth value: it is true if what it describes is the case in reality. Metaphors, however, have as such no truth value and therefore no cognitive value in expressing knowledge of the world. Searle follows his definitions and distinctions by just one positive argument – that the existence of literal meaning "is tied to our notions of truth-conditions, entailment, inconsistency, understanding, and a host of other semantic and mental notions" (Searle 1979, p. 132). Not surprisingly, the literalist view of language and cognition is well entrenched, and to suggest on the contrary that metaphor after all *has* cognitive status is to question the grounds of most of applied logic and semantics. Nevertheless, if we are to make any sense of most everyday speech, let alone the language of ideology and religion, we must give some cognitive status to metaphor.

To understand the connection between scientific realism, the positivist theory of knowledge, and the literalist view of language, we need to go back to the seventeenth-century scientific revolution and beyond that to Aristotle. Much of Aristotelian philosophy was discredited and explicitly rejected by the pioneers of modern science, but his theory of language remained essentially unscathed. In the seventeenth century, the rise of science was accompanied by the conception of an "ideal language" that would enable us to read off from the "book of nature" the true science that exactly expresses reality. "Reality" is, indeed, a text written by the hand of God, awaiting "decoding" by the patient experimental investigator. The metaphor of "two books" is pervasive: Bacon tells us that we read God's revealed truth in the Scriptures and his natural truth in nature; he entitles one part of his *Natural and Experimental History* (Bacon 1858) the "Abecedarium Naturae" – the "Alphabet of Nature." Galileo (1957, p. 238) tells us that the universe is a "great book . . . written in the language of mathematics"; Leibniz (Coutourat 1901) searches for the ideal language, the "characteristica universalis," which will correspond exactly to the language in which nature itself is written. Ideal human language for purposes of science will be language that has exactly one name for each distinct essence, and its grammar will reproduce the real causal relations among essences in the world. Every correctly formed descriptive sentence will represent a law of nature. Before the Fall, Bacon tells us, Adam had this language; it was the language in which he "named the animals." At the Fall, it was lost; at Babel, a confusion of tongues took over; our task is now to recover the pristine language and hence the knowledge of nature man was meant to have in his unfallen state.

The notion of an ideal language perfectly reflecting the world has a philosophical pedigree going back at least to Aristotle. Consider, however, what the world would have to be like for an ideal language to be possible. It would have to be an "Aristotelian" world in which all objects and events fall into complexes of a finite (though perhaps very large) number of fixed species or natural kinds. This is exactly the world Aristotle adopted for his ontology: a world derived from his studies of biological species, which impressed him both with their stability and their interrelatedness. He therefore saw all nature as a treelike hierarchy of species and genera, in which all objects fall into natural kinds, defined by an essence and distinguished from other species by differentiae. To "know" an object is to know its essence and differentiae. Individual objects of a single species are, of course, all different in some respects, but these respects are "accidental" if not related to the species essence, and strictly speaking there is no scientific knowledge of them. Human beings may have fair or dark hair or skins, may have blue or brown eyes, be short or tall, cheerful or melancholy, but what they are essentially is "rational bipeds."

The theory of the ideal language and the ideal science fits this ontology like a glove. Any language contains in practice a finite number of general terms, and an ideal language contains enough of them to "mirror" the fixed number of natural kinds that are to be made isomorphic with them in the ideal science. The relations among natural kinds are expressed in laws of nature, which therefore correspond to the semantic rules of the ideal language and are guaranteed to be both true and universally applicable. This program for both language and science was the seventeenth-century dream, which still maintains its hold under the guise of the correspondence theory of truth, in spite of being undermined by general rejection of the Aristotelian realist ontology of fixed natural kinds.

The seventeenth-century myth has conspired with the nineteenth-century dream of a universal logic to direct attention away from the concrete facts of ambiguity and change in language toward the formal analysis of language in terms of precise and stable meanings. In this formal analysis, metaphoric uses of words are in some way improper or deviant. If metaphor is to be taken seriously, it implies changing meanings; in a literalist theory, however, there is no room for understanding metaphor as implying continual shifts of meaning, because literal meanings are either constant, that is univocal, or equivocal. Unfortunately, equivocation destroys deductive logic because a deductive argument is invalid unless its terms retain their sense from premises to conclusion. In Section 2.2, however, we already saw that human thought cannot be adequately represented by a deductive system; it thus follows that language cannot simply be assimilated to an ideal logic, except as a limiting case in special circumstances. Meaning changes, or tropes, of various kinds are, in fact, pervasive in language. They are required in the learning of language at its most elementary levels, and they are also inescapable in the expression of social and religious "constructions of reality." (This thesis is developed with further reference to the expanding literature on metaphor in Hesse 1984).

We are going to argue for a nonliteralist theory of meaning and metaphor compatible with an account of language as rooted in schemas. Specifically, we argue for the thesis that "all language is metaphorical." This thesis will appear shocking to those writers who have labored to provide careful distinctions between the literal and the metaphoric in traditional grammar and semantics. Even among those who give metaphor a positive role in language, it is rare to find any who concedes that it is all-pervasive. Let us first explain how this thesis is to be understood.

The *Oxford English Dictionary* defines a metaphor as "The figure of speech in which a name or descriptive term is transferred to some object different from, but analogous to, that to which it is properly applicable." For example, physical "point" is transferred to denote a quality of an argument or a joke; "direction" from a road to denote "direction" of attention; or "heaviness" of a book to "heaviness" of the prose.

Lying behind this notion of "proper" and "improper" application of terms, and behind almost all subsequent discussion of metaphor, is an Aristotelian philosophy of universals. Universals are the correlates in reality of the "proper" use of universal terms; it is therefore at this level that the significance of metaphor must be analyzed. An alternative to the Aristotelian theory of universals can be found in Wittgenstein's (1953) account of "family resemblances" (FR) (For further accounts of family resemblances, see Bambrough 1961 and Hesse 1982.) Here, objects may form a class to whose members a predicate P is correctly ascribed, without assuming that there is any universal "P-ness" realized by each object. Instead, we assume that in an FR class (for example, "the Churchill nose"), the members of enough pairs of objects in the class resemble each other in some respects relevant to P so these resemblances can form, as it were, a chainlike structure through the class in such a way that there are relatively clear cases of objects falling within the class and relatively clear cases of those that do not. There may, of course, also be borderline cases where we are uncertain.

Wittgenstein argued from ordinary usage that there are such cases of irreducible FR. He gave the well-known example of "game," a predicate that applies to chess, to the Olympics, to ring-a-ring-o'roses, and to many other activities with pair-wise similarities, but no particular similarities between all pairs that can serve as sufficient conditions to define "game" as a fixed class. Other examples of FR classes are familiar to people who classify varieties of plant species, bacterial diseases, archeological remains, psychological types, schools of painting, and other objects. When predicates are used metaphorically, exactly the same process of meaning change is at work. The "point" of a joke shares with the "point" of a pin some of its physiological effects; the "point" of an argument shares some properties with the point of a joke and some with the point of a pin, but not necessarily the same ones. The extensions of meaning that occur by means of similarities and differences in metaphor are only the more striking examples of something going on all the time in the changing and holistic semantic network that constitutes language. Contrary to Aristotle's belief, no two particular objects or events share *exactly* the same properties, whether these are called "essential" or "accidental," and indeed this distinction is a false one. Because this is the case, language must contain general terms that classify objects together that are in detail different. As Locke (1947, Bk III, Ch III, 2, 3) put it, "it is impossible that every particular thing should have a distinct peculiar name. . . . Men would in vain heap up names of particular things, that would not serve them to communicate their thoughts."

General terms are necessary, but their use entails some loss of information about the world. If we describe a set of things as "square," we cannot at the same time list *all* the other properties that discriminate them from each other, even those properties connected with their squareness. To try to do so is to fall into an infinite regress, in which every further defining property is described by a general FR term, which classifies the object with other objects to which *that* term is applicable and from which it cannot be discriminated without introducing *other* general terms – and so on. The regress can only be stopped in two ways: either the world is really Aristotelian, and objects really fall into sharply discriminated species; or in practice we allow that language works by capturing *approximate* meanings, that degrees of similarity and difference are sufficiently accessible to perception to avoid confusion in ordinary usage. Of these possibilities, the second is certainly the more realistic. It does, however, imply that we lose potential information every time we use a general descriptive term – either information that is present to perception but neglected for purposes of the description (who bothers to discriminate *every* potential shade of red by a descriptive term, even if they are artists or gardeners or house decorators?), or information present in reality but below the level of conscious perception. In the latter case, of course, the information may later become accessible by instrumental aids (microscopes, etc.) or it may be already present in the senses and later brought to conscious awareness by the subject's attention being drawn to it (as in games in which one is asked to spot the differences between apparently identical drawings).

Understood in terms of this FR analysis, metaphorical shifts of meaning depending on similarities and differences between objects are pervasive in language, not deviant, and some of the mechanisms of metaphor are essential to the meaning of any descriptive language whatever. This is what is meant here by the thesis that "all language is metaphorical."

This thesis now needs some more explanation and qualification. First is the question of what sorts of relative distinction should be made between what we call the literal and the metaphorical, since this distinction is clearly present in our language even if it does not correspond to a distinction at the deepest semantic level. The distinction is properly a pragmatic, not a semantic, one. That is, it concerns how speakers learn, use, and, if necessary, define the words of their language. Literal use enshrines the use most frequent in familiar contexts – the use that least disturbs the network of meanings. Thus, literal use is the easiest to manage, to learn, and to teach. It is often, if possible, the use that is susceptible to ostensive definition and is therefore the one with direct physical applications. It is the one least open to misunderstanding and mistake. Literal use is the one generally put first in dictionary entries, where it is followed by comparatively "dead" metaphors ("point" of a pin probably comes before "point" of an argument) and where perhaps more novel and interesting live metaphors may be omitted altogether. All these features are sufficient to explain why the analysis of metaphor apparently has to start from "literal" language already understood, but it does not imply that the semantic basis for the two sorts of expressions are radically different.

Second, "metaphorical" is used here in a general sense to denote the basic facts about language in an FR analysis – namely, that the individuality of a particular object is indispensable in reality and that classification of objects by general terms in language is secondary and necessarily poorer in information content than is the reality described. In classical grammar, on the other hand, the term "metaphor" is used more narrowly than this. In the theory of meaning tropes, "metaphor" is used to denote particular forms of literary expression that depend on *explicit* recognition of similarities and analogies, as is assumed in the OED definition. In this sense, "Richard is a lion" is a metaphor because based on an elaborate analogy between particular human and animal dispositions, in which the obvious differences between human beings and animals are consciously discarded. A metaphor in this sense is usually recognized only when it is "newly minted" – lively prose and poetry will coin new metaphors that draw attention to similarities and analogies not recognized or assumed in the language before. In fact, many semanticists want to deny that "dead metaphors" are metaphors at all. When a metaphor becomes entrenched in a language, they hold, it loses its literary point and becomes simply a new literal usage. This is the fate of dead metaphors, such as "spirits" for whiskey, or "leaves" for the pages of a book, or "fiery" for a person's temperament. In fact, almost any interesting descriptive term can be shown etymologically to be a dead metaphor – a fact that supports our FR analysis, once the orthodox distinction between "literal" and "metaphorical" is discarded and "dead metaphors" are accepted as being pervasive in language. Classical grammar, however, maintains the distinction, and therefore classifies dead metaphor with literal uses. The thesis that all language is metaphorical rejects this classical analysis to highlight the fact that explicit use of metaphor and simile are themselves based on the most fundamental linguistic fact of all – namely, that linguistic reference always depends on perceived similarities and differences.

In classical grammar, many other kinds of tropes are recognized. In Chapter 10, we discuss "metonymy." Metonymy is the literary device in which parts are taken for wholes, or effects for causes, or causes for effects, or in which accidentally associated things come to stand for each other. Consider, for example, "I have no roof over my head" (part for whole); "They were gunned down" (cause for effect); "It was a piece of Californian mathematics" (association of California with a particular sort of formal approach). Explicit classifications of meaning tropes into "metaphor," "metonymy," and other grammatical categories are, however, generally *contrasted* with literal usage, from which the trope is supposed to deviate. They must therefore not be confused with the more fundamental point we are making here about the primary conditions for language learning. In Chapters 10 and 11, we see that failure to distinguish the two sorts of problems has led to misleading accounts of symbolism in general and of religious language in particular.

We assume that "all language is metaphorical" in a fundamental sense that underlies all meaning tropes; but this is only the beginning of our problems. We now need a theory of linguistic usage that does not depend on a previously established theory of the literal or presuppose that stable and univocal meanings are fundamental for language. Our starting point is Max Black's interaction theory of metaphor as modified in the light of Wittgenstein's FR. We use the term *meaning* loosely as an inclusive term for reference, use, and the relevant set of what Black calls the "associated commonplaces" (Black 1962, p. 40) called up by metaphoric usage. To understand the meaning of a descriptive expression, then, is not only to be able to recognize its referent (in a given context, in a given reading) or even to use the words in the expression correctly, but also to call to mind the ideas, both linguistic and empirical, embodied in mental schemas and commonly held to be associated with the referent in the given language community. To "understand a meaning" is thus akin to what Wittgenstein calls "grasping a concept." A shift of meaning may result from a change in the set of associated ideas as well as in change of reference or use. For intersubjective understanding, it is necessary that most of the associated ideas be presupposed in common by all speakers of the language, though our analysis of the individual's schemas in Section 7.3 reminds us that we are again in the realm of family resemblances rather than literal identities.

It may be possible as a first approximation to describe the developed use of language by a compositional semantics in which we explain how the words fit together to provide sentences. But in the acquisition of language, and in describing language change, we must proceed in the reverse direction: we can only give meanings to novel word-uses if we can grasp the sense of the overall sentences in which they are used and have enough information about other portions of that sentence and its context and associations to make some reasonable hypothesis about their new roles. Metaphor must be intersubjectively understood (and is capable of being misunderstood); therefore, its use must be constrained by internalized schemas in ways that cannot be captured in compositional semantics.

In the previous chapter, we saw how cognitive science is beginning to provide the kind of theory required. Meanwhile, however, the atomistic theory of language and the correspondence theory of truth have been so closely bound up since the seventeenth century with ontology and scientific method that rejection of compositional semantics has a more than technical significance. It implies, indeed, nothing less than a new theory of knowledge. We start to consider this new theory in a modest and manageable way by showing how our theory of language as metaphor affects our theory of truth, particularly in the first place the truth of scientific theories.

8.2 Metaphor, models, and truth

Can metaphoric utterances be true or false? Can they convey truth about the world? We saw that if "truth" is understood in the sense of ideal correspondence and if it has the meaning it has in propositional logic, then metaphorical utterances are effectively equivocal in meaning, have no truth value, and do not permit deductive inference. But we have abandoned strict correspondence and deduction, except as special limiting cases; it thus remains to find a new sense of "truth" more adequate to the new view of meaning and language.

We argued that the use of general terms is always metaphorical in the sense of relying on perceived similarities and differences between various individuals of which a term has been acceptably used in the past. Therefore, some such metaphorical utterances *must* have truth value if we are not to evacuate "truth" of any application to language at all. But what does it mean on this theory to ascribe truth to, for example, the assertion that "cats hunt mice?" It does not mean that there is a universal law relating the natural kinds of "cat," "hunts," and "mice." It means, rather, that we have perceived sufficiently stable similarities among certain individuals conventionally named "cats" in English to form for all practical purposes a family resemblance class, no doubt with ill-defined edges; and similarily for "hunts" and "mice." It further means we have observed a regular association between the individuals of these classes so that a statement of regularity expresses our experience sufficiently well and sufficiently often to be useful.

A more sophisticated scientific analysis of observation enables us to specify the classes more usefully for scientific purposes. As more is learned about the properties and relations of objects, so classifications based on relatively direct perception are modified and sometimes radically shaken up. Whales become mammals and not fish because the property of suckling their young comes to be a more salient property than the fact that they live in the sea. A small animal looking very like a mouse comes to be seen in developed animal taxonomy as akin to a kangaroo. More radically, the classification of the natural elements has undergone kaleidoscopic change from the Greek earth, water, air, and fire, through Dalton's atoms, to the currently shifting classification of fundamental physical particles.

Black (1962) and Ricoeur (1978) have emphasized that the use of metaphor in language has the functions not only of extending meanings and defining new meanings but also of the interaction and redescription of domains already seen through one metaphoric frame in terms of another. Such redescription can have disruptive effects on previously complacent ways of looking at the world. For example, Lakoff and Johnson examined many examples of extended metaphors in such language as "Argument is war" revealed by such phrases as "Your claims are *indefensible*"; "He *attacked every weak point* in my argument"; "His criticisms were *right on target*" (Lakoff and Johnson 1980, p. 4). Suppose this extended metaphor comes to be replaced in philosophical contexts by "Argument is logic." We then find such metaphors as "Your conclusion does not follow"; "You must make your premises explicit"; "That assumption is obviously true." To philosophers, this may seem the only natural and "correct" way of talking about argument, but it depends on metaphor just as the first example did and is equally revealing of a certain set of value judgments about what argument *is*. Contrast another metaphor, equally familiar in modern contexts: "Argument is negotiation," with its accompanying "Can we meet each other on common ground?"; "What compromises are possible?"; "I cannot sacrifice my most basic assumptions." To make explicit the ramifications of metaphor is to engage in critique, evaluation, and perhaps replacement. Metaphor is potentially revolutionary.

In such cases, the question "Which metaphor is true?" cannot expect a single or simple answer. There is no "fact" to which "argument" corresponds that has the natural character of "war" or "logic" or "negotiation." The extended metaphors are not in that sense true or false but are appropriate or inappropriate, more or less revealing, more or less useful, depending on the context of application and their coherence with evaluative judgments made about particular situations. That is why mixed metaphors are disturbing – they do not convey clear and consistent associations of meanings.

It may be thought that these considerations apply only to "literary" uses of metaphor and that scientific use of language must necessarily abstract from vague meaning associations and evaluations. But if we look at the implications of recent discussions of the theory ladenness of observation, of realism and the use of scientific models, we find that use of language in scientific theory conforms closely to the metaphoric model. Scientific revolutions are, in fact, metaphoric revolutions, and theoretical explanation should be seen as metaphoric redescription of the domain of phenomena. (For models and metaphors in science, see Hesse 1963.)

Scientific data are initially described either in an "observation" language or in the language of a familiar theory and are then redescribed in terms of a theoretical model that allows two apparently disparate situations to *interact* in a novel way. For example, sounds and waves on water are both parts of our everyday observation; what is novel is the suggestion that there is something about sound akin to waves – not the wetness or the sight of whitecaps but an underlying regularity of motion. We recognize some positive analogy between the two systems, and the negative analogy creates a tension that can invest the phenomena with new meaning. Metaphor causes us to "see" the phenomena differently and causes the meanings of terms that are relatively observational and literal in the original system to shift toward the metaphoric meaning. Terms such as "harmony," "resonance," and "pitch" come to be used with precise meanings derived from the wave model. Meaning is constituted by a network, and metaphor forces us to look at the intersections and interaction of different parts of the network. In terms of the metaphor, we can find and express deeper analogies between diverse phenomena; or, of course, in the case of bad metaphors we may find we are misled by them.

This interaction view of theoretical models is compatible with the thesis that observations are theory laden. It entails the abandonment of a two-tiered account of language in which some observational uses are irreducibly literal and invariant with respect to all changes of the language and content of explanatory theory. The interaction view sees all language, including the scientific, as dynamic. What is at one time theoretical may become observational (for example, "the earth is round"); and what is observational may become theoretical (for example, Francis Bacon's *observations* that "heat is a mode of motion"). There are only relative and shifting distinctions between literal and metaphorical in general and between observational and theoretical in the particular case of science. Of course, the potential mutability of observations does not deny their grounding in some highly stable "literal" readings such as the everyday statements "that is a table" or "the display on the digital clock reads 12:07." The latter example is intentionally perverse, since "digital clock" has a well-defined literal meaning, yet the meaning did not exist until recently and may shift again with changes in technology.

In the metaphorical view, logical consistency is no longer at the heart of language. Rather, as we saw in our discussion of Piaget (Section 3.1), the reconciliation of logical discrepancies assumes a driving role for change of meaning; similarly in science, we reconfigure both theory and observation language to allow us to describe and explain a wider range of phenomena. This does not mean, however, that the metaphoric view entails abandonment of logic and deduction in science. Indeed, we may see this as a chief distinction between use of metaphor in science and in poetry. Good poetic metaphors are initially striking, unexpected, and perhaps shocking. They extend and ramify by association and analogy not by logic. They may immediately give place to other metaphors that are formally contradictory and in which the contradictions are an essential part of the total metaphoric impact. Scientific metaphors, on the other hand, may be initially unexpected; once established as useful, however, they are extended and developed by logic as well as by analogy. They are meant to be internally tightly knit by logical and causal interrelations. If two models of the same system are found to be mutually inconsistent, this inconsistency is usually taken as a challenge to reconcile them by mutual modification or to refute one of them. For example, in the early days of quantum theory, inconsistent wave and particle models seemed to be required; but the radical metaphoric transfers from deterministic to inherently probabilistic accounts occurred half a century ago, and since then much of the energy of physicists has centered on mathematical deduction of the far-reaching consequences of the new theory. To use Kuhnian terminology, in the development of science a tension always exists between normal and revolutionary science: normal science seeks to reduce instability of meaning and inconsistency and to evolve logically connected theories; revolutionary science makes metaphoric leaps that are creative of new meanings and applications and that may constitute genuine theoretical progress.

Scientific models are, in the end, intended to satisfy what we have called the pragmatic criterion; this satisfaction will generally require that their local applications can be expressed in locally stable and consistent language and, if necessary, in the form of deductive arguments. This is one limiting case of the view that "all language is metaphorical." However, it does not entail a return to the view that science is distinguished by a special literal use of language in which meanings are given exclusively by empirical states of affairs ("truth conditions") and for which truth is explicated by a simple correspondence theory. It follows that we cannot assume, with some present-day realists, that the relative success of scientific models in satisfying the pragmatic criterion shows that they are ideally intended to be true descriptions of the real, underlying structure of the world. The strong realist view seems, like Bacon's alphabet of nature, to require an ideal universal language exactly matching the world in its essential features. This view neglects the facts that scientific theory has to be based in some natural language or other and that the historical sequence of fundamental theories do not exhibit convergence toward universal truth in any ideal language. Perhaps there is no such language, in which case there are no strictly universal laws of nature, only discoverable regularities in our local (though large) regions of space and time. Or, perhaps, there is such a language, but known to God only, in which case there will be universal laws of nature; but it is a strong assumption to suppose we can attain them. We have no sufficient reasons from the local success of science for making the assumption, and moreover we do not need it for the ordinary business of theorizing in the scientific languages we actually use. We could express our view here, in terms of the current debate on realism, as siding with Dummett (1978) rather than Davidson (1984). (For more on "laws of nature" as finite local regularities see Cartwright 1983; and Hesse 1974; for a moderate realism compatible with this finitary view, see Jardine, 1986.) Theories in history remain underdetermined by data, and they remain linguistic constructions, albeit constrained by the pragmatic criterion.

We are left with the problem of explaining how models and theories are, after all, significant in some sense in indicating the real, even though they are not literally true of it. We may express the point by saying that the reliability of models for prediction depends on analogical relations between diverse natural systems that they *exhibit* rather than *state, show* rather than *say*. What can be stated depends on the classificatory resources already present in the language, and any observation language is theory laden with that implicit classification. Some philosophers would contend that the notion of something in principle unsayable is a mystical notion that should have no place in the analysis of science. Such an objection would miss the point of the argument against scientific realism. To suppose that the classificatory and analogical assumptions present in language can be stated in neutral fashion and compared for correctness with the world is to suppose either that we have a non-theory-laden observation language in which to make these neutral statements, or that we have an ideal scientific theory that explicitly states the true classification of the world.

We found reason to reject both assumptions. Implied classifications and analogies can only be stated in a language containing some *other* implied classifications and analogies. Reality is never exactly captured in explicit speech. This is not, however, a nonempirical idealism because it does not deny that there is a real structure in the world, of which science progressively exhibits more as it learns more about the natural environment by the feedback method of the pragmatic criterion. Nor does it ascribe a strong realism to scientific theory because science does not capture this structure in a detailed isomorphism of true categories and true statements with the world.

Scientific theory provides constructed models of scientific reality that are distinguished from other types of social and poetic construction by being constrained by feedback loops involving experimentation in the natural world. In a philosophical tradition deriving from Kant and Hegel, this reality has been expressed in terms of the "separation of subject and object" and the consequent "objectification" of the natural world. (See, for example, Habermas (1971b, p. 33, and translator's note 23, p. 323).) Several different but related theses about science are implied by this terminology.

First, in the positivist theory of science, the knowing subject is set against an assumed independent natural reality, and the subject is supposed to "reflect" the world in knowledge, either by means of images in the mind or by propositions in language that are in one-to-one correspondence with the facts. However, this relation of neutral reflection is now recognized to be an illusion (See for example the critique in Rorty 1980). There is essential interaction between the knowing subject and the world, both in terms of the linguistic categories brought to the world in describing it, and in the activity of the subject in physical relations with the world, as emphasized by Piaget's account of children's learning through movement and manipulation as well as through language. If this is how the subject is in the world, then the attempt to represent the world in knowledge as a neutral independent object is not like a mirror image; rather, it is a projection on the world of a mental model whose framework is given by the schemas of kinesthetic activity and by the categories of language. This projection of a constructed model is not, of course, arbitrary, nor does it mean that *objectified* nature is unconnected with *objective* reality. There is an external world, which is what it is before, after, and independent of human beings and their knowledge. No one doubts that there is a pragmatic use of descriptive language in which we give true descriptions of an external world for the ordinary purposes of life and in terms of which science extends pragmatic knowledge in an instrumentally progressive way. It becomes much easier to express what is intended by the Kantian expression "objectification of the world" since the collapse from the inside of naïve scientific realism. "Objectification" can now be interpreted as the universal projection on the world of the classificatory presuppositions of scientific theories, carrying not only these classifications but also theoretical ontologies of fundamental entities and their properties: such imaginative or constructed concepts as atoms, electrons, forces, and spatial and temporal relations. Kant thought the categories of pure reason were unique and necessary; hence, his analysis of science could exist alongside realism for nearly two centuries without revealing to the casual eye their incompatibility. But now we must accept that the categories are neither unique nor necessary, but contingent on human interaction with the world, and that some of them are culturally relative and historically changeable. In this sense, scientific reality is "constituted" in the activity of seeking instrumental knowledge.

Second, the scientific construction of the world pictures it in terms of shifting spatiotemporal configurations of atoms, cells, stars, – which are, in themselves, meaningless, valueless, disenchanted. Naturalistic conclusions are drawn in positivism – namely, that this construction exhausts "reality," and that any meanings or values ascribed to it must be human creations and ultimately illusory. As Whitehead put it:

> The course of nature is conceived as being merely the fortunes of matter in its adventure through space. . . . The poets are entirely mistaken. They should address their lyrics to themselves and should turn them into odes of self-congratulation on the excellency of the human mind. Nature is a dull affair, soundless, scentless, colourless; merely the hurrying of material, endlessly, meaninglessly. . . . And yet – it is quite unbelievable. (Whitehead 1945, p. 68)

This naturalistic conclusion is a fallacy. Human beings themselves are both a natural part of this world and the creators of the very sciences that define the world in this way. They have a schizophrenic role because human activity, of which the pursuit of science is a part, must be regarded as full of subjective meaning and value; and in pursuing the Baconian dream of mastery over nature, it is human beings who define themselves as distinct from nature and even become alienated from it. The Cartesian split between the mental and physical life of individuals has become a split in Western culture between scientific "objectification" of a meaningless external world and a subjective and largely individualized world of meaning, sensibility, value, and action, to which the concepts of reality and truth have become almost inapplicable. To "objectify" the world means to describe and manipulate it within scientific classifications and ontologies, presupposing it to be a world that carries no meaningful or evaluative order of its own and presupposing it to be fundamentally indifferent to human beings. In this sense, science had ensured the absence of God from the infinite spaces centuries before the Soviet cosmonaut is alleged to have said that he had been there and found no God.

The recognition that scientific models are comparatively detached from the observable world suggests that we can make a distinction between, on the one hand, the *construction* of a world by a model and, on the other hand, the *objectification* of the model when it is proposed as an acceptable scientific theory. That is to say, we should distinguish the construction of an imaginative ontology with its internal system of meaning relations from the claim that successful empirical test justifies pragmatic acceptance of the model. This distinction enables us to perceive a continuity between scientific model-making and other forms of constructing metaphoric worlds (for example, in myth, symbol, poetry, metaphysics, or theology) as well as in forms of pure fiction: stories, novels, drama. Scientific models are a prototype, philosophically speaking, for imaginative creations or schemas based on natural language and experience, but they go beyond it by metaphorical extension to construct symbolic worlds that may or may not adequately represent certain aspects of the empirical world. These symbolic worlds all share with scientific models the function of describing and redescribing the world; and for all of them it is inappropriate to ask for literal truth as direct correspondence with the world. Symbolic worlds differ from scientific models, however, in that it is not their function to represent the state of the natural environment for purposes of prediction and control. As their functions differ, so their means of validation will also be expected to be different. If we say roughly that science is "pragmatic criterion" plus "ideology," what we have to pursue in the following chapters is the sense in which "ideology" can also be said to express the real.

Meanwhile, the interest of the religious believer should be declared. Naturalism is by definition atheistic since it excludes the existence of non-space–time reality. Any reformulation of our theory of knowledge is therefore of interest to theists because it changes the terms of debate between theists and atheists. Atheists will no longer be able to rely on precisely the arguments used by naturalists about what is real and what we can know and how. Thus, the implications and suggestions of cognitive science may help to change our views about the possibility of theism as a result of an even more radical change in standard views of reality and knowledge. We need to reinterpret questions about objectivity and truth to apply to all points of the cognitive spectrum alike. We do not suddenly put on a different hat with regard to "truth" when we speak of the good or of God from that we wear for natural science and for speech about everyday facts.

8.3 The language of symbols

It is a commonplace that the language of religion is the language of metaphor and symbol. Religion, like science, is largely concerned with describing the unobservable and, therefore, must call on all possible mechanisms for extending the everyday meaning of language. The remark is, however, often intended to imply two things not so obviously true. First, it seeks to distinguish modes of expression in religion sharply from those of science, which are assumed literal and purely descriptive. Second, it does so to the detriment of the claims of religion to be concerned with objective knowledge and truth. In the light of our claim that metaphor is pervasive in language, even in scientific language, it is clear that we must resist these implications. We therefore close this chapter with a consideration of the consequences of our theory of metaphor for the general nature of symbolism. In Chapter 10, we apply this to the concept of religions as holistic symbol systems.

Theories of symbolism have generally modeled themselves on theories of language; in particular, most such theories have presupposed the traditional literalist theory of language and the correspondence theory of truth. We therefore have the task of reinterpreting the concept of *symbol* in line with our reinterpretation of language and epistemology; we do this by extending our analysis of metaphor to symbols in general. This task is made easier by noting first that most objections to traditional theories of metaphor apply also to the classic theory of symbols.

The classic definition of "symbol" is as an object or property or action or event that has an interpretation as "standing for" something else, such as the lion for courage, the serpent for evil (but also, confusingly, for healing), red for danger or passion, washing for spiritual cleansing, the rainbow for promise of benevolence. In the classic theory, symbols are regarded as special types of signs; signs in general include also signals and linguistic expressions, all of which are definable by the relation of "standing for" something else that is their message, its reference, interpretation, or meaning. This relation is conceived as an atomistic dyad of (symbol, meaning) that clearly derives from the interpretation of linguistic signs (sentences or words) either as atomistically related to their empirical reference in facts or things or to another linguistic sign that gives their definition (e.g., Tarski's classic " 'snow is white' if and only if snow is white") or a purely linguistic definition (e.g., " 'semiology' means 'the science of signs' "). This linguistic view of symbols naturally issues in the question of how to fill the second term of the dyad; that is, "*What* do symbols mean?" or "*How* are they to be interpreted?" as if symbolisms were extended codes needing decipherment. Such questions are parallel to those asked in reductive theories of metaphor – "What does the metaphor mean?" – when the answer is expected to be in terms of a literal paraphrase. We rejected this question in our network theory of metaphor, and we shall challenge the "coding" metaphor it implies for symbolism.

We call this theory of symbolism the *semiological* view. It clearly derives from classical semantics and therefore presupposes what we called the literalist view of language, according to which literal meanings are primary and proper and the general phenomena of "meaning tropes," including metaphor, are parasitic and deviant. Most of the classic theories of symbolism we consider agree in making this presupposition. Like classic theories of metaphor, they assume that the phenomena of symbolism are extraneous to the normal working of communication systems and are to be explained typically in terms of translation or paraphrase, just as metaphor was taken to be meaningless until explicitly paraphrased into its "literal meaning." Many suggestions have been made about how to classify different kinds of signs, and there is little agreement about either terminology or substance. We look at two different types of classification of signs within the semiological theory in order to contrast them with our holistic approach.

First, we take classifications, based on Charles Peirce's semiology, that classify signs into "indices" and "symbols" (Peirce 1931, p. 372). By an index, Peirce intends various kinds of natural signs related to their referents by physical contiguity. For example, an index may be a cause or effect of its referent (smoke for fire), or a conventional indicator, like a pointing finger (the "index" finger). For some of Peirce's successors, indexes have also come to include signs associated with the referent by part–whole relations (white coat for scientific research), by functional association (the key for captivity or exclusion), or by some historical association well known in the social group (e.g., Churchill's cigar or the paving stones of the Latin Quarter). Conventional signaling systems and codes are also included among indexes. Symbols, on the other hand, are taken to be signs that relate to their meanings by some sort of resemblance or analogy. For example, the flame is taken as the sign for the heat of passion, or water for purification; or there may be analogy of form, as when Nathan's story of the rich man who coveted his neighbor's lamb is a symbol for David, who coveted his neighbor's wife.

This distinction between "index" and "symbol" repeats almost word for word the distinction we noted between "metonymy" and "metaphor" in classical grammar. As explained in Section 8.1, "metaphor" is used in the specific sense of a linguistic trope based on explicit similarities and analogies; it is contrasted with "metonymy," in which causes are taken for effects, and vice versa, or parts for wholes, or accidentally associated things stand for each other. Here, again, the theory of signs and symbols mirrors classical semantics. In terms of our network theory that "all language is metaphorical," however, we want to look more closely at this distinction between indexes and symbols.

Consider first the status of the signs of language itself. Are they indexes or symbols? On the one hand, it may be said that words are conventional signs and therefore indexes. But if we consider larger units of descriptive language – phrases, sentences, semantic networks – it then appears that the structure of these units must bear some analogy or morphism to the world that is their referent (or that, in our terms, they "construct"). In the network theory of language, this is not the one-to-one relation of correspondence truth, but a relation between general linguistic terms and perceived family resemblance classes of objects, which constitute the essentially metaphorical component of all language. There is, of course, a parallel metonymic component of language that is equally fundamental. Word tokens are conventionally associated with their "meanings," and the syntax of a language has conven-

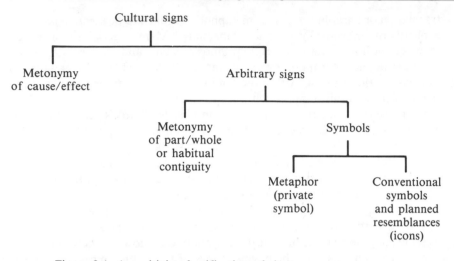

Figure 8.1. A positivist classification of signs

tional forms not dictated directly by the structure of the world. In this sense, we may say not only that "all language is metaphorical," but also that "all language is metonymic," because all language depends on conventions as well as on family resemblances.

Similarly, there are signs that are purely indexical and signs that are purely symbolic, although most signs are probably complex mixtures of the two types. This symmetry may be lost, however, if privilege is given to the naturally causal or the explicitly conventional character of indexes over recognition of similarities and analogies that is the hallmark of the metaphoric and symbolic. One interpretation that takes this asymmetrical position is due to Edmund Leach, who uses it to express unduly positivist views about the meaning of symbolic systems in prescientific thought. Leach's classification of signs can be represented in a simplified and modified form by the diagram in Figure 8.1 suggested by his book *Culture and Communication* (Leach 1976, p. 12).

Figure 8.1 represents how Leach distinguishes between cultural signs that are "arbitrary" and those based on natural cause–effect associations. The arbitrary or conventional signs are again distinguished according to whether or not there is any ground for their choice in an association between sign and signified, such as a part/whole relation or habitual contiguity (Leach includes linguistic signs in this last). If there is no such "metonymic" ground, Leach regards the sign as either purely subjective or purely conventional; in either case, he calls it a "symbol." Symbols include "private metaphors," such as are exemplified in dreams, or "obscure poetry"; they also include what he regards as arbitrary symbols, such as "the serpent is a symbol of evil"; and icons, which include such things as models, maps, and portraits (Leach 1976, p. 12).

These distinctions are by no means a merely verbal matter. They presuppose an important philosophy of communication that Leach proceeds to develop. For him, metaphor and symbol include all that is peripheral or deviant in our culture. Metaphor and symbol are characterized by arbitrariness and artificiality and also by privacy and thus subjectivity, as opposed to the objectivity of socially accepted sign systems. Leach adopts the view of similarity relations standard in our culture and our philosophy – namely, that they lie in the eye of the beholder; objectively speaking, anything can be seen as similar to anything else in some degree and in some respect. What counts as significantly similar is then a conventional cultural decision, and the relation is an explicit and external one, as when a crown stands for a brand of beer or a logo is invented for a new company.

For Leach, metaphysics belongs with metaphor as "in the mind," in contrast with metonymy, which concerns objective concepts. Metaphor is concerned with pseudo-logic and magic; metonymy with logic and causality. Typical mistakes of magic, he argues, are to confuse symbols with causality and metaphor with metonymy. Metaphor, metaphysics, magic – all are reminders for modern people of an irrational and superstitious past. They are indeed metonyms for it, metonyms for deviance. Leach admits that ordinary communication contains both metaphor and metonymy, and that they become mixed in complex relationships and paraphrases. If we say "policemen are pigs," "the association is plainly arbitrary and therefore symbolic (metaphoric); to suppose that it is intrinsic and therefore in the nature of a metonymic sign would be an error" (Leach 1976, p. 21). On the other hand, Leach says that such associations are not wholly arbitrary, presumably because there are real examples of piglike behavior among policemen. Basically, however, Leach's view is that the metaphoric element is nonsensical, and only the literal paraphrase, which is metonymic, makes sense:

In our ordinary processes of communication we make some show of keeping them apart. . . . But the latent ambiguity is always there and there are many special but important situations – as in poetic and religious utterance for example – when we go to the opposite extreme. By code switching between symbols and signs we are able to persuade one another that metaphoric non-sense is really metonymic sense. (Leach 1976, p. 22)

It is no accident that the view of resemblance as an arbitrary cultural device goes along with a rejection of metaphysics and religion as respectable cognitive systems. It is important to notice why Leach's view is mistaken. We have argued that objective relations of similarity are required both for theoretical inference in science and for the working of any natural language, and that the "nonlogicality" of metaphoric expression is necessary for it to work as it does. According to our network view, then, symbolism as an extension of metaphor should be seen as normal rather than deviant in ordinary descriptive language as well as in scientific, metaphysical, and religious cognitive systems.

Before leaving Leach's scheme, it is worth remarking that he explicitly borrowed some of it from the classic work of Jakobson and Halle (1956), *Fundamentals of Language*. Some features of this work suggest, however, that it is not the most helpful basis for the asymmetrical application of the terms "metaphor" and "metonymy" Leach takes from it. Jakobson and Halle describe the two necessary characteristics of language as the combination of contiguous signs governed by syntax and metonymy and the selection of language elements governed by semantics and metaphoric resemblance. They ask why it is that metaphor, and its accompanying modes of poetry and romanticism, are so much more thoroughly studied in our culture than metonymy, with its associations with prose and natural realism. Their reply points to an asymmetry in our culture. In the context of their primary concern with clinical disorders of speech, they conclude that this asymmetry is a pathological one. Analytic study is itself carried out in *metonymic* terms (in terms of logic or cause and effect), and so metonymy is used as the metalanguage for studying metaphor, but there is no corresponding way in which metonymy can be studied without presupposing itself. Metaphor therefore appears deviant in our culture and in need of explanation, whereas metonymy does not. Jakobson and Halle conclude that this demonstrates a "contiguity aphasia" in our culture – an excessive concentration on the problematic character of metaphor at the expense of any critique of the deeper buried, "logical," presuppositions of metonymy. In other words, our use of metonymic language, like our presupposition of "objectified" knowledge, is not self-reflexive.

Jakobson and Halle's conclusion reinforces our view of metaphor rather than Leach's. We tried to turn the analytic microscope in a self-reflexive way on the "normal," the "logical," and the "literal," to show that these concepts are at least as problematic as the metaphorical, and that metaphor and metonymy are equally primary and mutually dependent.

Not all exponents of the semiological theory of symbols adopt Leach's dismissive view. For example, Evans-Pritchard (1956, p. 134) and John Beattie (1964) use a different classification of signs. They take "symbol" to mean something whose relation with its interpretation has a natural ground, whether this ground be metaphoric or metonymic. The resulting classification of signs may be represented by the diagram in Figure 8.2. Here the primary distinction is not, as in Leach's view, between natural causes and contiguities (metonyms) and "arbitrarily imposed" similarities (metaphors), but rather between signs with some ground in the world, whether metonymic or metaphoric, and purely arbitrary and conventional codes. Beattie makes this distinction explicit in four points that summarize his views of the character and functions of symbolism, particularly in the context of prescientific thought:

1. Symbols are not purely conventional: "There is usually some reason why a particular symbol should be appropriate in a particular case" (Beattie 1964,

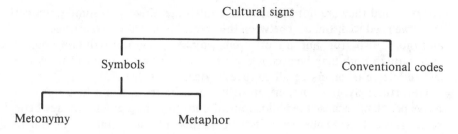

Figure 8.2. Classification of signs derived from Evans-Pritchard (1956) and Beattie (1964)

p. 69), whether this is similarity, cause–effect, or historical association, though the appropriateness may not always be obvious, or even, as in the case of dreams, capable of being made fully conscious.

2. What symbols stand for are not concrete events, but abstract actions, such as "kingship," "courage," "defilement," "atonement."
3. Symbols represent abstract ideas because these ideas are difficult to represent literally and the primitive capacity for abstract thought and expression is limited.
4. Symbols express something that is an object of value. This is indicated by the fact that peoples' feelings about symbols are often highly charged and exhibit resistance to change: for example, flags, totems, songs, the Sikh turban, spells, baptisms, sacrifices, initiation rites.

If Beattie's list were the whole truth, however, it would be easy for a positivist to solve the problem of symbolism. Since we have a developed language of abstract ideas, it might be said that we can simply decode symbols into that language, using their appropriate characters to give us the clue to the correct abstract translation. As far as its meaning is concerned, symbolism would be seen as a primitive device; when decoded, its translation would either come out false ("sticking pins in a wax image causes harm to the original"), or as a piece of platitudinous functional psychology ("eating a common meal means experiencing group solidarity"), or doubtfully meaningful and in need of further interpretation ("getting on one's knees means abasing oneself before God"). What would be left of symbolic expression and symbolic acts would be their emotive or morally strengthening quality and social effectiveness. As we see in Chapter 9, these symbolisms are what Durkheim regards as the residue of religion when its claims are superseded by science.

Beattie goes further, however, and begins to move away from a strictly semiological view. He suggests that in religion and other forms of symbolism "reality is misrepresented if the symbol, and not the often indefinable thing that it symbolizes, is taken to be the ultimate truth" (Beattie 1964, p. 239). The possibility of explicit translation is now dropped; the referent is "indefinable." Beattie suggests instead an aesthetic model. As in the Western understanding of art, there is no point in trying to "disprove" symbolic systems, and they are not intended to contribute directly to some practical end: "we need to distinguish between the 'truths' of practical experience . . . , and those, also 'true' but in a different way, of religion, myth and poetry, even though both may be accepted on the same ground of 'custom' by the less reflective members of all cultures" (Beattie 1970, p. 258).

Unfortunately, this comparison with works of art does not help our cognitive problem because the philosophical understanding of truth in aesthetic contexts is at least as obscure as in the case of symbolism. But Beattie is here moving to a more holistic view. We now look at another theory that explicitly abandons the semiological theory and replaces it by an account of symbolism more consistent with our cognitive theory of metaphor.

In his *Rethinking Symbolism*, Daniel Sperber (1975) objects to the notion of symbols as "codes" needing translation by means of simple (symbol, meaning) dyads. He points out that those who have presupposed this theory have deceived themselves into thinking that the empirical evidence about symbolism fits such atomistic dyads. But closer attention to the evidence shows that this is not the case. First, it is generally agreed that we cannot produce immediate interpretations of symbols with standard linguistic meanings, since although symbols usually have such meanings, they do not explain the symbolism but rather form part of the problem of symbolism itself. Material water used in ritual, or the word "water," do not just mean or refer to water but symbolically mean something else – purification, initiation, evil, the river of death. Thus arises the "double-meaning" theory of symbolism. The second meaning cannot just be elicited from literal language since it is itself usually metaphoric or symbolic.

Second, these arguments suggest what Sperber calls the "cryptological" view. Symbolic meanings are hidden and have to be discovered by close questioning either of ordinary speakers or of special people who are initiates of an esoteric meaning not available to ordinary speakers. Either group may be reluctant informants. Alternatively, the hidden meanings may have to be elicited by psychoanalysis, as in Freudian theory. The interpretations thus elicited from actors are often either banal ("water means cleansing"; but then why the disproportionate ritual fuss?); or contradictory (water means life, but also death); or themselves symbolic and in need of further clarification ("water means cleansing from sin"). In the most interesting cases, such as the last of these examples, the proferred exegesis itself needs exegesis. Moreover, if such interpretations are known only to an elite group or to the visiting anthropologist or psychoanalyst, how can symbolism function as a communicative system within society in general?

Sperber goes on to argue that the "grounds," such as similarity, for using symbolism in particular ways are not themselves grounds of meaning. He concludes that the question "What do symbols mean?" is a cultural artifact of Western and other cultures that foster rationalistic exegesis and is inappropriate to the elucidation of symbolism. Unfortunately, however, he does not succeed in freeing himself from another cultural artifact – namely, the literalist theory of language and the associated empiricist theory of reference. He presupposes that language is propositional, in the sense of requiring univocity, verbal substitutability, and the rule of noncontradiction, and he accepts the analytic/synthetic distinction. Thus, in his *analysis* of symbolism, he uses the standard view of language in purporting to show that symbolism is not a language and that metaphors such as "meaning" are inappropriate for it. Symbols for him are not "words" with "syntax" and "semantics." Rather, they are concerned with the organization and classification of language and hence of the world and with ensuring shared orientations in the social group. Symbols are more like an "encyclopedia" for organizing concepts and have no meaning or truth value in themselves. They may be called "cognitive," but like regulative principles or conceptual frameworks they are neither empirically nor analytically true.

Sperber too easily accepts the analytic–synthetic–conventional distinctions and thus fails to see that a new theory of meaning and new senses of the "cognitive" may be required. He does, however, provide arguments for a holistic theory of symbol systems. Instead of regarding his theory as a rejection of the whole idea of symbolism as a language, we can regard it as a cogent argument against a particular theory of what a language is – namely, the literalist theory of meaning and the empiricist theory of reference. In fact, it is noticeable how many of Sperber's arguments about symbolism echo similar arguments against the cognitive character of metaphor within the same literalist tradition. Conversely, the restoration of cognitive significance to metaphor can be made to carry symbolism along with it. Sperber rejects the question "What do symbols mean?" and replaces it by the question "How do symbols work?" The network theory has made the same replacement, in the sense that it no longer regards "meaning" as a second term in a relation between words or sentences and *some other* domain, whether this is a "world" or a metalanguage. Rather, it takes meaning to be the set of meaning *relations* within and among words, sentences, and larger holistic units of language. Meaning relations are typically neither empirical reference nor dictionary translation, but synonymy, resemblance, analogy, homology, opposition, inversion.

In our network model of language, we have the resources for a more adequate understanding of symbolism as a generalization of metaphor. We summarize this modified linguistic theory of symbolism in the following six points:

1. There are more or less complex entities that may be words, sentences, propositions, utterances, prayers, liturgies, sacred objects and locations, myths, dramatic performances, ritual acts, social roles and hierarchies, all of which may act as "symbols."
2. These complex entities become symbols in contexts of meaning, where they are related in symbolic discourses and symbolic acts. They are highly con-

text dependent and are constrained by rules of correct utterance or ritual performance that may be likened to the syntactic and semantic rules of a language.

3. Symbols may be primarily metaphoric or metonymic, but both metaphor and metonymy are necessary ingredients of a symbolic system, just as they are necessary ingredients of a natural language.

4. The "meaning" of a symbolic system resides in the fact that it constitutes a possible social or individual world, just as scientific models constitute potentially empirical worlds and as all natural descriptive languages constitute ontological classifications of things and properties.

5. Symbolic systems share with metaphorical language the property of not being constrained by the logic of propositions. Single metaphoric sentences or single symbolic acts cannot be given direct meaning exclusively in terms of something outside the network, but must be interpreted, paraphrased, and so on, in terms of the network's own internal relationships. It follows that there is no direct answer to questions of the form "Is this metaphoric sentence or symbolic act 'true,' 'correct,' or 'appropriate'?" Such judgments must be made relative to the adequacy of the whole network or constructed world, for whatever purpose this is constructed. Symbolisms therefore do not have truth value in the sense of propositional logic but require a more general theory of what it is to be a cognitive system.

6. Language may be used with the purpose of developing scientific instrumentality, in which case its criteria of adequacy are those of prediction and control, or with the purpose of persuasion and manipulation in human society, in which case the criteria are those of success in such manipulation, or it may have a function in creating imaginative worlds that are reducible to neither scientific nor human instrumentality. Similarly, the criteria for symbolic systems are dependent on their purpose: whether functional for the well being of society and its members, or for the explanation of the socionatural cosmos, or for the overt purpose of prayer or worship or purely "aesthetic" playfulness, or in religion to give expression to "unobservable" worlds other than the world of space and time.

We return to more detailed examples of the particular functions of religious symbolism in Chapter 10. Meanwhile, in this chapter we elucidated the sense in which metaphor and symbol "construct worlds," and are in that sense candidates for cognitivity. Whether they are successful candidates depends on how they fulfill the criteria of success for various kinds of mental schema, whether these are the pragmatic criteria of "objectification" or some others we now consider.

9 Interpretation and reality

9.1 Objectivity and the human sciences

Philosophy of science and schema theory have provided us with two approaches to a theory of knowledge as construction. In this theory, a knowing subject bases a dialogue with external reality on schemas or theoretical languages embodying a "construction of reality." Schema theory builds on elementary processes of assimilation and accommodation whereby the individual's sensorimotor schemas come to provide anticipations of the effects of action in the world. We have seen similar processes, operating at the level of groups rather than individuals, in the network view of philosophy of science. Both schema theory and the network view of science have led to a theory of language in which metaphor is normative, with literal meaning as the limiting case.

The resulting epistemology combines coherence and correspondence criteria of truth and dissolves the barriers between "objective" science and nonscience. In this chapter, we look at the alternatives to "objectification" proposed as modes of knowledge in hermeneutic and critical philosophy and suggest that our viewpoint reveals unities in these diversities. Just as we see a continuum between literal and metaphorical meanings, so we do not posit a sharp dichotomy between the natural sciences on the one hand and the social or literary hermeneutic sciences on the other. Special pragmatic or "objective" aims are predominant in the natural sciences, though also to some extent applicable elsewhere; on the other hand, hermeneutic considerations apply in the natural sciences, particularly in connection with theoretical interpretations and "world models." In Chapter 10, we consider modes of social and scientific knowledge as described in social anthropology and use these modes as a framework for the interpretation of religion as a cognitive enterprise. The aim of this apparent detour from cognitive science into more abstract philosophy is to demonstrate that the concept of "knowledge" as schema interactions is not peculiar to cognitive science. We find, in fact, that it is less foreign to the tradition of hermeneutics than to that of analytic philosophy.

The human sciences have always raised questions of value, interpretation, and objectivity that seem to be more intractable than questions involved in the natural sciences, so that doubt has been thrown on the applicability of naturalistic methods in human science. It is true, of course, that sociology, social psychology, social anthropology, and particularly economics have yielded significant statistical correlations and causal laws and that the standard methods of model building and hypothetical construction and test are successfully applied there. On the other hand, few people would contest the assertion that there are at present no wide-ranging systematic and successful theories in the social sciences of the same kind as and comparable to theories of the natural sciences. Social science does not exhibit long-term, cumulative success in pragmatic prediction and control.

As is further developed in Hesse (1980, Ch. 8), two extreme positions and an intermediate position may be taken about the lack of pragmatic success in the social sciences. The extreme positivist position holds that it is an indication of the immaturity of the social sciences, that it will progressively be overcome as more effort is put into systematic research, and that in any case if there is to be knowledge in this area at all, it must be acquired by the same objective and value-neutral methods that constitute the pragmatic criterion in the natural sciences. The other extreme position holds that since the subject matter of social science is human beings, there can never in principle be adequate explanations in terms of value-neutral causal theories of the natural science type. Moreover, it is argued that the pragmatic criterion is an inappropriate one to adopt, since prediction and control are not the proper goals of knowledge for human and social behavior.

The intermediate position remains agnostic about the possibility in principle of systematic social theories, but takes seriously the point that adopting the pragmatic criterion is *itself* a matter of choice. We are not bound, either in the natural or the social realm, to seek knowledge that involves the possibility of systematic prediction and control. Many societies past and present have not done this, and many voices in our society question the aim of control in the natural sciences, let alone of human society. On the other hand, some people fear that embargoes on research in socially dangerous fields, such as genetic engineering or nuclear energy, will stultify growth of theoretical knowledge; according to their understanding of "theoretical," they are right. The decision for or against particular strategic areas of research may be a decision that calls in question the ideal of knowledge as the Western world has understood it for 300 years.

The decision not to seek prediction and control in a given area may nevertheless sometimes be the right one, which makes it even more urgent to examine whether it will be a decision against the possibility of extending knowledge as such. There is no need to take sides on the two extreme positions about the possibility of causal theories of human individuals and societies because there is no sufficient evidence for either position. On the matter of principle, there have been attempts at general proofs of the non-natural character of the social subject-matter, deriving from such features as its complexity, instability, indeterminacy, and statistical character and from the fact that social research is itself a social phenomenon that may interfere unpredictably with its own subject matter. It is difficult, however, to find general proofs of this nature, if only because all these features may also be found somewhere in the natural sciences. For example, the subject matter of meteorology is complex, rapidly changing, and of statistical character; the results of experiments in quantum physics are indeterminate and exhibit irreducible interference with their subject matter, and so on. However, it is possible to see how the *degree* to which all these factors are present in the social sciences may be so great as to constitute a *practically* insurmountable barrier to the development of a causal social science of comparable generality to the natural sciences.

We may compare scientific learning to the operation of a computer that can learn to predict its environment. For any such device there will be some environments that do not permit learning to take place because they are too complex and unstable and interact too strongly with the computer. Some social environments may be like this with regard to the finite capacities of natural science as a human institution. At any rate, it seems that most social environments are now of this kind with respect to presently available resources. Moreover, the sort of comprehensive experimentation required on the social scene to push through a successful causal science is, as Apel has put it, "either absurd or dangerous in a moral or political sense":

. . . one has to concretely imagine what it would mean to establish and stabilize a subject–object relation that would be undisturbed. . . . It would be required to have the greater part of human society precluded from social knowledge in the long run, say by deprivation of higher education and by similar means of practical suppression. In other words: the society to be objectified in this way as a quasi-isolated system would have to be excluded from the proper process of history represented by the knowing subjects of (social) knowledge who are able to communicate on the proper level of the process of history. (Apel 1979, p. 12)

However, such objections are based on a static view of science. Even Newtonian mechanics has the idea of the changing state of a system, and its causal laws require the estimation of parameters of the system and its state before they can be applied in any specific situation. In particular, Newton studied how the dynamics of interacting systems affect each other. The goal of understanding in social science, then, may only be different in complexity. We seek theories that let us understand how factors can change social structures. We are not far from the concepts of schema change that guided our study of the individual.

Such considerations reinforce the view that in the study of human beings, new cognitive perspectives are required. This view first became generally apparent in connection with the explosive development of the disciplined study of history in the nineteenth century, when difficulties arose not just about discovery of "facts," but also about the validity and nature of interpretations. In German-speaking use, there was no doubt that history was a *Wissenschaft,* a species of knowledge; but the question arose as to whether it was knowledge in the same or a different sense from the natural sciences. Dilthey (1961) began his philosophy of history with this question: "How is historical knowledge possible?" This question is analogous to but distinct from Kant's question: "How is natural knowledge possible?" Both questions implicitly assume the premise that "knowledge" of the historical and the natural are possible and indeed exist in uncontroversial but distinct forms. J. S. Mill (1884, Bk. VI) made the distinction in terms of the subject matter of the natural sciences on the one hand and the "moral" sciences on the other; that is, he saw human science as essentially the science of human mores or ways of life. Mill's terminology was rendered by his German translator as the distinction between *Natur-* and *Geisteswissenschaften,* thus slightly skewing Mill's meaning toward an emphasis on the uniquely human "mind," "spirit," or "reason," rather than social value and praxis.

Three different specific concerns of the human sciences have been identified. First, the *rational* as a fundamental category; second, social *evaluations,* both as a feature of human society and as an ingredient in the interpretive task of the human sciences themselves; and third, *particularity* – it is narrative of particular cases that characterizes the human sciences rather than the discovery of general laws. In terms of methodology, the tasks of the natural sciences are to explain and predict (what we have called the pragmatic criterion), whereas the tasks of the human sciences are to describe and understand. The German term *Verstehen* has been used to indicate the type of understanding a human observer can have of human action – an understanding "from the inside," in contrast with the external objectifications of the natural sciences.

This brings us to our problem, which is to consider the relation between the subjective and the objective in different modes of knowledge and, in this context, particularly knowledge of human action and human society. There were two sources of the concepts of understanding and of reason in relation to the human sciences, one tending to objective and the other to subjective interpretations. First, there is Hegel's concept of objective rationality unfolding in history, which is at root a secularized version of Judeo–Christian doctrines of divine goodness, providence, meaning, and design, grounded in belief in the will of a Creator at work in history. In Hegel's version, rational knowledge of society and history has an objective counterpart, as does natural science – namely, the *telos* or *Geist* or absolute reason.

The second approach, more relativist in effect, was the explicit recognition that the human sciences are *hermeneutic,* that is, are sciences of *interpretation,* requiring rational methods for the translation and understanding of texts, institutions, and belief systems distant from our own in space, time, and culture. (For historical accounts of hermeneutics, see Bleicher [1980] and Palmer [1969].) The issues raised by hermeneutics extend to a wide variety of disciplines, including Biblical exegesis, social anthropology, social psychology, and history in general. These issues are raised in extreme form in Wittgenstein's (1953) philosophy, where autonomous "forms of life" are held to be conducted according to their own self-sufficient "language games."

In Schleiermacher's (1958) original philosophy of textual (particularly Biblical) interpretation, and in the more recent account of historical method given by Collingwood (1946), the prescribed method of interpretation was to "put oneself in the shoes of" the writer or historical actor under study and to "rethink his thoughts." This method of "empathy" was based on a view of the human mind as accessible in a unique way to other minds, so that connections introspectively perceived among beliefs, facts, and actions can replace the discovery of external causal connections, which is the goal of natural science. Stated in terms of mental schemas, we may say that if human beings construct their own social worlds (rules and roles, institutions, cultures, and beliefs) in terms of such schemas, then an understanding of human action is gained by reconstructing these schemas in the mind of the investigator.

Schleiermacher's hermeneutics was intended to be objective in that it posited a unique fixed meaning of the text that can be distinguished from its local significance for the interpreter. Just as Francis Bacon's theory of the natural scientist required him to come to the external "facts" with a mind purged of subjective and cultural prejudice (Bacon's "idols of the mind" [1858, IV, p. 10]), so hermeneutics was supposed to be an exercise in detachment from the local circumstances of the interpreter in order to discover the objective intentions of other texts and other minds. The significance of these meanings for the interpreter's own situation was supposed to be superseded so that all interpreters, at whatever time or place, could in principle agree about *the* meaning of the historical action, the foreign text, the symbolic belief system; this objective meaning is the meaning for the actors who produced it. It is easy to see how a fundamentalist with regard to the Bible could embrace this theory and take hermeneutics to be an exercise in uncovering God's unique meanings lying behind the newly perceived foreignness and archaism of the Biblical text.

If we consider human authorship, however, the notion of the objective "intention" is far from clear. Even before Freud, it was understood that authors can have intentions of which they are not fully conscious at the time of authorship. For example, the author may understand more of his or her intentions on rereading the text or may be persuaded by others' interpretations of what the "real meaning" was. Freud's analysis led his patients to recognize that unconscious meanings were present in previous actions. Functionalist theories may claim to see more of the game than participants, for example, in explanations of puzzling ritual behavior, or in Marxist explanations of class behavior as based on "false consciousness." Thus there is ambiguity as to what objective meaning the interpreter is looking for. Is it a meaning in the author's head (consciously or unconsciously)? Is the meaning contained in the text as such, independently of any circumstances of its writing, as recent structuralists have held? Is it the meaning as approached by a properly equipped "ideal reader"? Or, is it the meaning as reconstructed by some literary theory? Which, if any of these, is supposed to be the "objective" meaning?

Apart from such ambiguities, the theory of "empathy" may be objected to on grounds similar to those that led to rejection of Bacon's prejudice-free theory of natural science. There is no mental *tabula rasa* with which we come to the natural world; rather, as we have seen, we "construct" the natural world in a complex feedback process in which theoretical models and sensory input are assimilated and accommodated in a self-modifying sequence of prediction and test. Similarly, we cannot approach human texts and actions with a mind purged of our own local interests, preconceptions, and values. The attempt to introspect our feelings of empathy with other minds does not produce intersubjective tests of understanding – people's attempts to place themselves in the shoes of other people are notoriously dependent on their own circumstances and culture. There is no objectifying pragmatic criterion here that can enable the social sciences to achieve the "objectivity" of the natural sciences. Our task now is to build on our earlier study of philosophy of science and schema theory to develop a scientific methodology adequate to the demands of the *Wissenschaften* and yet that can be seen to be continuous with, rather than reducible to, the methodology of the natural sciences.

9.2 Hermeneutics and evaluations

We have come to reject any methodology for the human sciences restricted to the pragmatic criterion for the natural sciences, whether this be in terms of causal laws or of empathic intentions. As Max Weber put it, it is a "naturalistic prejudice that the goal of the social sciences must be the reduction of reality to '*laws*'" (Weber 1949, p. 101). Weber took what we described as the intermediate position between naturalism and the thing–person dualism of the hermeneutic philosophers. He did not deny the possibility of local causal regularities in social processes nor reject a social science that seeks to find them; he considered that such objective laws do not reveal the subjective meaning of human action and that the chief goal of human science is to understand these meanings.

Weber speaks of *Verstehen,* but we must be careful not to equate his use of this concept with the empathic understanding of the earlier hermeneutic philosophers. *Verstehen* is not subjective in that sense but is rather the categorization of social behavior by the investigator in terms of an imputation of significance and interest. To use an example of Weber's (whose datedness for us is precisely an example of the thesis illustrated) we find, says Weber, historical significance in the wars of the ancient Athenians but not in "tribal scuffles" among the Kaffirs of Southern Africa. This is not because of wealth of evidence in one case and lack of it in the other, or because of any difference of intrinsic properties of the two cases, but because the first was (from the early twentieth-century European standpoint) a meaningful part of the heritage of Western culture, whereas the second was not. History has to be rewritten in every generation, not merely because knowledge of facts changes but because the historian's interests and circumstances change. Moreover, the interests of the historian do not always coincide with those of the anthropologist or the economist even in the same society.

We note that there is little difference in principle here between the human and the natural sciences. We have argued that natural science theories are always underdetermined in the total picture they give of the world and that we may express their content in the rubric "pragmatic criterion" plus "ideology." Ideological interests are patent in such examples as Copernican astronomy and Darwinian evolution, but there are also more subtle cultural evaluations in current science where gross ideology seems to be absent. Scientists often assert that more is going on in science than pragmatic success. They may be referring to the kind of strong realism we rejected in the last chapter; more often, however, they are content with the weak pragmatic realism we described there, and yet they want to add that there are "aesthetic" qualities in theories that go beyond the pragmatic. Such qualities as simplicity and theoretical unification are part of the aim of science and provide reasons for preferring one theory to another, even when they give equally good experimental fit. We put these qualities in the ideological box here to suggest that how the "simple" and the "aesthetic" are judged is itself a cultural matter. Classic disputes between theories often turn on different judgments as to what is simple. For example, acceptance of Einstein's early relativity theory depended on greater weight being given to its undoubted mathematical and ontological simplicity, as against the complexity involved in overthrowing Newtonian concepts of space and time and his laws of motion, which were in another sense "simpler" than Einstein's radical, new world picture (Hesse 1974, Ch. 10).

Another example of cultural evaluation of theory in natural science may be taken from biology. In choosing as objects of study primarily the stable configurations of matter that form organisms and in concentrating on evolutionary sequences from "lower" to "higher" organisms (both terms are ascriptions of value), the biologist is guided by the significance of just these phenomena for understanding the place of human beings in nature. There is no temptation here to suppose that the concept of "understanding" involves "empathy" with the amoeba. On the other hand, the conditions of significant understanding in the biological domain remain more constant for human beings than do conditions of significant understanding of human history, so the element of interest-based choice of subject matter and hypothesis can attain a pragmatic factuality in biology that it cannot attain in history. In particular, the identification of the terms *lower* and *higher* to species becomes pragmatically redefined in nonevaluative terms by observations based on the fossil record and such techniques as DNA sequencing. But one only has to remember earlier classifications of animals and plants and uses of animal and plant symbolism in the interests of tribal identity, or alchemical or spiritual mythology, to realize that the evolutionary perspective is not the only possible organizing hypothesis in the biological domain.

It is useful to call on Weber again in attempting to clarify the pervasive abstractions "significance," "meaning," and "value" by using his distinction between the domains of *value relevance* and *value freedom* (Weber 1949, Ch. II). He first describes criteria of selection according to the investigator's interest in the subject matter. Subject matter and point of view are selected according to presuppositions about human meaning, intention, and interest, without any necessary evaluation in the sense of asserting the desirability or undesirability of the characteristics selected and highlighted in the study.

For example, a biologist may choose to study an ecological system from the point of view of the life cycle of the malaria parasite without any judgment about its activities good or bad; or a sociologist may study the conditions of coherence of a fascist state without, in the context of the study, either condemning or condoning the existence of such a state. Similarly, there has been a general debate within sociology as to whether conditions of functional stability or general laws of conflict are the best organizing principles around which to study advanced societies. Conservatives may favor stability and Marxists conflict, but general hypotheses resulting from such principles can be pursued by all groups alike. It is unlikely that pragmatic social science will ever be in a position to filter out one or another of such general social views in the way that, for instance, the extrascientific controversy between geo- and heliocentric theories of the solar system was filtered out. If choice between emphasizing stability or emphasizing change and conflict has to be made, it has to be made on grounds of value relevance other than the pragmatic. The naturalist might contend that the choice does not have to be made and that a unified theory of social conflict and stability is in principle achievable, yet still accept that the use to which such a theory is put will be inescapably value-laden.

Weber held this domain of value relevance to be an essential ingredient of social studies. Topics for social science are selected and structured by relevant values, but this is a matter of conceptual framework, not of fact, which remains value neutral and uncontaminated by value judgment. Knowledge, however, is for action; and Weber defines a domain of value freedom that divorces all questions of what is factual from all judgments about the desirability of goals. With respect to goals, he maintains a strict logical independence between fact and value. In his analysis of rational action, he distinguishes the rationality of means from the rationality of goals. "Means" are rational if they use factual knowledge to select the most efficient route to given ends or goals. Goals, however, are a matter of value decision; although there may be rational connections among goals, there is no ultimate rationality or objectivity of value judgements as such. Value freedom is freedom to choose ultimate value independently of facts and facts are ascertained independently of value, although their selection and presentation is influenced by value relevance.

Weber's theory is a desperate attempt to maintain the notion of autonomous facts while recognizing the subjectivity of the various standpoints from which we discern them. But the theory cannot in the end be freed from inconsistencies. In the light of his own perceptive account of value relevance, it is doubtful whether the separation of fact and value can be carried out in human science in practice or even in principle. In the first place, beliefs about facts are always theory laden and value laden, and theories are always underdetermined by the facts. It follows that if Weber's recognition of the value relevance of theory is not to conflict with his assumption of the ultimate separability of fact and value, he must assume something like the pragmatic filtering-out process found in the natural sciences; but we have argued that this assumption is inappropriate in the human sciences.

Second, it is unlikely that the presence of evaluations in theory making can be clearly recognized at the time they are made, though they may be recognized by hindsight and in the light of different implicit evaluations operating at different times. For example, the development of Weber's categories of rationality in modern theories of rational action has presupposed that "the rational" is to be equated with "most efficient means" to independent, preselected ends. But this is clearly the evaluation of the technocrat and the bureaucrat, not necessarily of the poet, the lover, the statesman, the moralist, or the religious believer. Either "rationality" has been rendered irrelevant to their distinctive actions and beliefs by mere stipulation, or we must accept that criteria for "efficiency" are themselves highly value-laden.

Third, Weber has not analyzed carefully enough the concept of the "facts," which he believes to be autonomously present from the value-permeated perspectives. He accepts the "objectivity" of these facts without considering that their recognition depends on the *choice* to adopt the pragmatic criteria of prediction and test that define the natural scientific "interest." This choice is itself a value judgment, and the resulting "world of facts" is, as we have argued, in that sense a construction.

A deeper analysis of precisely this point is given by Gadamer, who follows Heidegger in offering a radical reformulation of traditional hermeneutic philosophy of the human sciences. The title of Gadamer's definitive work, *Truth and Method* (1975), summarizes two important aspects of his view: first, he rejects all attempts to recover the "objectivity" of the human sciences by emulating the positivist method of natural science; and second, he insists that the positivist notion of autonomous "truth" of "facts" must itself be brought under scrutiny. Both "truth" and "method" as understood by earlier hermeneutics, and also by Weber, require reconstruction.

Gadamer goes behind the individualism presupposed in all accounts of the subject–object relation to the situation of all individual subjects (persons) as embedded essentially in social and cultural life. Society and culture are largely mediated to the individual by language, and it is possession of language that primarily distinguishes a social being from nonhuman nature. Therefore, Gadamer argues, tradition and prejudice (prejudgment or preunderstanding) cannot be eliminated from the individual's perspective on the world – there is no possibility of purging the social and cultural "idols," as Bacon required for the attainment of knowledge. Hermeneutics is therefore not just an optional method of investigation of the human sciences; it is the very stuff of our commerce with each other and underlies even our objectification of the natural world. Hermeneutics is the practice of communication and understanding of all kinds of expressions of mind, in language and symbol, institutions and beliefs, and as such it has the same kind of "objectivity" (or, we might prefer to say, "intersubjectivity") as any understanding of natural language. Foreign texts, cultures, forms of life are our data; our "theories" consist of interpretations of their meaning. There is a "hermeneutic circle" of understanding of part in terms of whole and whole in terms of part that is typical, for example, of the translation of any significant piece of prose in a foreign language. A similar circular process occurs in understanding the "other" in terms of our culture, and in understanding our own culture, which sometimes gets reinterpreted and revised in the light of the other.

Thus, a model of dialogue emerges; in this model, the investigators and the actors who are their subject matter engage in mutual attempts at understanding, breaking with the traditional separation of observer and object assumed in natural science. There is, in Gadamer's phrase, a "fusion of horizons" (Gadamer 1975, p. 273) in which the presuppositions and modes of understanding of both partners in dialogue are shifted. The model of dialogue applies literally to such studies as social psychology and social anthropology, and also in an extended, one-way sense to historical study, because the study of historical texts and artifacts may also result in challenge to the historian's own standpoint, which gets shifted by attempts to understand the historical data, just as if dialogue with the historical authors and actors is actually experienced.

In this account, the aim of "true reconstructions" of meaning is abandoned. There is no Archimedean point outside language and tradition for which interpretations become "objective" or in any other way absolutely authoritative. Gadamer's hermeneutics is relativist in the sense that all meanings are understood in some perspective or other. But the upshot is not purely subjective because dialogue is in principle open to all horizons, encompassing all beings in possession of language. Moreover, Gadamer develops Heidegger's

(1962) view that "reality" and "truth" are not primarily concerned with the objectification or construction of the natural world and of human persons as natural objects within it, but with understanding persons as "beings-in-the-world" – that is, as essentially experiencing and communicating social beings. For both Heidegger and Gadamer, this "reality" is disclosed in the understanding of and reflection on the total human situation; it is mediated by art, poetry, and symbolism rather than by literal "truth-functional" language.

Gadamer's hermeneutics relates to many threads in our discussion. First, our view of the history of science rejects the objectivist interpretation of an underlying natural ontology to which successive physical theories increasingly correspond. Rather, we have argued that radical discontinuities exist from one theoretical paradigm to another, although science increases in power by the pragmatic criterion of prediction and control. Thus, even natural science, in its attempt to objectify nature by using the pragmatic criterion, is involved in "hermeneutics" – scientific theory is a "reading" of the "book of nature," requiring circular reinterpretations between theory and observation and also theory and theory, and also requiring "dialogue" about the meaning of theoretical language within the scientific community.

Second, we have seen how all understanding of language requires assimilation of a dynamic network of meanings that operates by metaphoric associations and metaphoric shifts. We have argued that this is the case for the most mundane kind of linguistic communication; it is, of course, most strikingly exemplified in interpretation of poetry. In poetry, each interpretation opens up a whole network of associations that may correct and take over from the original starting point. There is no necessary consensus in the end about "best interpretation" – no pragmatic criterion. Nevertheless, interpretations are not arbitrary. Control depends on the techniques of literary theory, whether they be the attempt to "understand" the author or to discover the "archeology" of the text as in structuralism – the attempt to place the text in a structured network of other texts, irrespective of "authors' intentions." Science and poetry are at two extremes of a continuum with regard to types of controlled interpretation of their various linguistic and symbolic resources. The criteria that control "good talk" in science, in poetry, and in any other interpretive system depend on its point and purpose.

Third, and more generally, we have seen how schema theory interprets human perception, action, and communication in terms of cognitive schemas embodied in the brain, and how these schemas change with experience. They do not reflect the "full" meaning of external reality but are always (at least potentially) in a state of flux, subject to change through our "dialogue" with the world. Schema theory therefore provides a model for all controlled interpretation of texts, and schemas themselves constitute the perspectives (or, in Gadamer's terms, the preunderstanding) within which such interpretation takes place.

Schema theory shares with language an important property: structures can be put together to form an endless range of new structures. Words can be combined to form sentences that express novel ideas, and these sentences can be interpreted and put to test. Schemas share the generative property of sentences, enabling us to perceive things we have never perceived and to act appropriately in new situations. But schemas are not just texts; rather, they are texts in the way that a program is a text – it is a dynamic entity embedded in an appropriate framework. Schemas are not just representations but processes. Schema theory must not only analyze patterns of dynamic representation but also how those representations reorganize themselves over time and are not only dependent on sensorimotor interactions but also involve reflective abstraction. In particular, schemas can act on schemas and even change themselves. A new set of schemas can allow us to see things in a new light, and this understanding can reshape our schemas yet again, changing not only the structure of our sensorimotor anticipations but also the high-level organization of schemas themselves. In addition to the process of physical abstraction that better adapts our schemas to guide our interactions with the physical world, cognitive reflection can abstract from a whole population of social schemas, finding regularities that can be embedded in high-level schemas that reorganize the lower levels – just as a mathematician may reflect on many examples to come up with the notion of a group, which may then clarify and reorganize those motivating examples.

Schema theory provides a language and a program for the development of a unified epistemology, potentially encompassing the whole range of cognitive systems that depend on interpretation, construction, and controlling experience. Moreover, cognitive science is itself a human interpretative science (that is, a hermeneutic science) so what we have said about hermeneutics should apply to it also. Schema theory is itself falsifiable, underdetermined by data, controlled by its own criteria of acceptability, and claims to provide understanding of human beings. By means of it, we create a perspective on epistemology from which we can analyze and compare other perspectives; but we do not have to claim that its perspective is absolute. There is no doubt that the perspective owes its appeal to the relative success of cognitive science in explaining human thinking and to the general suspicion in our culture of such nonnatural entities as "souls" in defining persons. To admit to such perspectivism is not self-defeating since it both recognizes the need for prejudgments and allows for criteria in terms of which perspectives can be compared. We have seen what some of these criteria are in the scientific development of schema theory, and as we go on we see how criteria and goals and acceptable theories interact in other modes of knowledge, particularly the religious.

Meanwhile, we can push the comparison of schema theory and hermeneutics a bit further. Hermeneutic approaches have generally assumed a radical distinction between things and persons. We might ask whether this emphasis is consistent with the kind of mind/brain reductionism we have hitherto been arguing. It might be concluded from reductionism that if there is nothing to the mind, or to persons, other than their physical and biological structure and environment, then hermeneutics as a distinct model of knowledge is undermined. If we consider our earlier discussion, however, we can see that this is not so. In our account of reduction and free will, we saw that we might choose to evaluate even artificial intelligences as persons – that is, among other things, we might choose to treat them as "partners in dialogue." Thus, highly complex machines can themselves raise questions for hermeneutics if we seek cognitive understanding of them. It follows that interpretive understanding may be a necessary mode of knowledge of persons, whether they are regarded as just bodies plus environment, or as "souls," or in terms of any other theory of the mind/brain relation, reductionist or nonreductionist.

On the other hand, philosophers of human action often take the hermeneutic approach to imply that our ordinary language of "intentionality," "persons," and so on, is somehow unchanging and analytically necessary to rational understanding of human beings. They maintain a radical dualism between persons and things that *is* undermined by reductionism. However, the hermeneutic approach does not require such dualism. Consistently with our account of "up–down" and "down–up" reduction, we would argue for a continuity between natural and hermeneutic science based on the fact that they both have the same domain of objects (namely, bodies, including persons' bodies) carrying their properties around in space and time. At each stage of the continuum, appropriate interpretive conditions enter the process of theorizing – formal and material regulative principles at all stages from physics onward, then interpretations in terms of norms and deviances, stabilities and instabilities in biology, and finally evaluations incorporated in world views in the sciences of human beings and in history. The choice of persons and participatory meanings as fundamental concepts in the hermeneutic sciences is not a necessary one. For example, Habermas (1975, p. 2) expressed the fear that scientistic "systems theories" may, after all, prove technically successful in organizing a stable but quite impersonal society, amounting to a historic realization of *1984*.

The choice of the concept *person* becomes "transcendentally necessary" only *after* an option is taken for the categories of personal intentionality and rationality. These personal categories can then be regarded as "theoretical concepts" used to structure our knowledge of human beings in the most appropriate way given the facts, which are laden, as they must be, with our overall evaluations. Whether there are viable alternative frameworks is a further question; there certainly have been in the past, when the list of those human beings to whom personal rights and characteristics were assigned was not co-extensive with the list accepted in twentieth-century Western liberalism. At a more detailed level, we ask what is the proper vocabulary with which to analyze persons and their intentionality. We already suggested in Chapter

2 that developments in cognitive science will lead to major changes in this vocabulary.

The process of hermeneutic understanding cannot pretend to be value-free, since it explicitly adopts the criteria of significance and the standpoints of both participants in dialogue and seeks understanding partly in terms of conflict and partly in terms of negotiation and reconciliation of meanings. Language games no longer appear, as in Winch's (1970) account, as isolated atoms to be understood in their own terms without comparison with or judgment from other language games. In other words, language games have to become hermeneutic circles. On the other hand, the dialogue model still raises the question of the relativity of value systems, since judgments now become relative to the interaction of two or more participants; even if this dialogue were imagined to embrace in principle all human societies past, present, and future, the upshot would still be no more than a vast set of intersubjective understandings based on the vast variety of forms of life and achievement. However, such a network of intersubjective knowledge does not add up to transhuman criteria of value. As with the notion of an "ideal," true scientific theory, it is still open to the "moral realist" to complain that even if the universal dialogue did succeed in obtaining consensus (an assumption by no means obviously true), the "good" might *really* be distinct from that consensus. That view is certainly held by most participants in the dialogue, who generally claim some truth for their value standpoint, which is other than the attaining of consensus, however widespread.

Why should we seek further grounds for evaluative judgment? Taking seriously the parallel with scientific realism, why should we not conclude that moral realism is a mistake, just as we have argued that it is a mistake to postulate an ideal, true theory of nature? Intersubjective negotiation to find viable sets of values in particular historic circumstances might be as satisfactory a solution here as it seems in relation to scientific theories, even though most people are both natural and moral realists. Perhaps "ultimate" values just "emerge" in history by chance, and this emergence is relative to the natural and cultural possibilities of a given time and place.

We should notice that schema theory *by itself* is not able to resolve this question; its accounts of feedback learning and the development of various kinds of skills always presuppose criteria of learning and goals of the skills. These criteria and goals can be described by schema theory, and their emergence can sometimes be explained in terms of their antecedents, but they cannot be judged to be ultimate without circularity or infinite regress. However far the explanation of consensus and critique in society may go, the creation and interaction of schemas will be a chancy matter, like the origin of biological species. Indeed, the model for schemas as a theory of social development is like that of mutation and natural selection in that mutations are produced by chance diversities of genotype. As new species evolve, they change the available ecological niches through the web of their relationships with extant species; and only with respect to the resultant relationships can we speak of their "adaptation" to their dynamic environments. *Just as there is no single solution to the problem of "adaptation" in evolution, so there is no single "correspondence" of value schemas to the world.* The constructed world (specifically, of course, the social world) is altered in the interaction of schemas with itself and with the schemas of other individuals.

What is missing from the social model, however, is an analogue for the conditions of selection. What are the criteria of success of modified and newly created social schemas? Are they culturally relative, or are there constraints of value or of rationality that are in some way under freely exercised human control? Like hermeneutics, schema theory inevitably *tends* to support an ultimate relativism because it cannot itself claim to provide grounds of value. The final chapter of this book suggests that such a relativist conclusion is not necessarily insupportable or inhumane. The issue between realism and relativism about values is probably the deepest that currently divides naturalists and nonnaturalists, and even religious believers are not all in the nonnaturalist camp in regard to it. In the next chapter, we consider the pressures that come from social anthropology toward relativism in religion. In Section 9.3, we look at a more absolutist theory developed by Habermas from Marxism and the so-called Critical Theory of the Frankfurt School.

9.3 Critical theory, relativity, and realism

Marxist tradition in regard to realism and relativism has split into two opposing tendencies that are not unlike the "liberal" distinction between empirical and hermeneutic modes of knowledge. In Engels's interpretation of Marx, in the "hard" Marxism of the Soviet Union, and in the Althusserian school of French Marxists, there is an emphasis on the natural science tradition and its extension into the social sciences (Althusser 1970). This is the Marxism that claims that it is a "scientific" theory of the world and that its laws of contradiction and dialectic have a status similar to that of the causal laws of natural science. This "scientistic" Marxism is realist about sciences and values and implies that values are determined by the historical process it has claimed to discover – that is, the inevitable collapse of capitalism under its own internal contradictions and the victory of the proletariat. It is in the hitherto oppressed proletariat that ultimate success and virtue necessarily reside. Marx's own expression of this theory owed much to the fervor of a prophet grounded in the Hebrew and Christian scriptures, with their divine prescriptions of justice, mercy, and love. But within nineteenth-century secularism, the overt arguments are based on a putative science of history.

By the mid-twentieth century, the predictions of the historic dialectic did not seem to be coming to pass. Capitalism had changed its form but had not collapsed, and the practice of Communism where it was in power was not realizing the hopes of a free, equal, and classless society. Like Christianity in the first century, when the end of the world no longer appeared imminent, there had to be reinterpretations of the founding texts. The works of the "young Marx" were published, and the Marxism of the New Left arose at a theoretical level, particularly in the early Frankfurt School. (For the history of the Frankfurt School, see Jay 1973 and Held 1980). In this form of Marxism, natural science has itself been made the subject of critique, and the notion that science is detached and value free has been rejected by arguments similar to those used against positivism in non-Marxist philosophy. There has also been a tendency to regard science, technology, and positivism as necessarily linked with the capitalist–industrial societies of the Western world and, therefore, with support of the *status quo* and of technological exploitation.

Both versions of Marxist philosophy depend on *critique of ideology*. This critique takes the form of historical analysis of "ideas" as the superstructures or epiphenomena of social and economic conditions, or at least as explicable only as closely interrelated with these conditions. The dominant beliefs of bourgeois culture, including those labeled "rational," are part of the apparatus of control – inducing in the ruling class false consciousness about the justice of their position and in the proletariat false consciousness about the inevitability of theirs. The function of critical philosophy is the unmasking of ideology to reveal the "true" state of affairs, in which scientistic Marxism defines "true" in terms of its own scientific claims for its theory of history.

There is, however, an incipient contradition in this critique, which is inescapable in the more "humane" version of Marxism. The contradiction turns on this question: "Is science itself an ideology?" Scientistic Marxism has to answer No in order to get the scientific justification for its own theory off the ground. But humane Marxism has to answer Yes, at least with regard to bourgeois science, because this is part of the ideology now subject to critique. It follows that the scientific foundations of Marxism itself are undermined, and it becomes possible to ask: "What ideological functions does Marxist theory itself serve in whatever historical circumstances surround it?" The critique of ideology becomes, as Mannheim saw, a war of all against all, escalated more recently by sociological studies of the foundations of natural science itself. In their various forms, critical science and sociology of knowledge have revealed interactions between cognitive and social institutions that remained unsuspected in the traditions of rationalism. Like hermeneutics, and even more radically, critical science threatens to engulf "knowledge" in total relativity.

Habermas accepts the threat of relativism and attempts to overcome it by grounding the critique of society in rationally determined values. But he had learned in the Frankfurt School that this quest for rationality has to be preceded by a sort of "therapy" because society left to itself cannot directly recognize "rationality," any more than it can divest itself of "prejudice" about either nature or culture. Habermas's primary objection to Gadamer's dialogue model is that it neglects the social critique of power relations. It is explicitly based on traditions of ideas and tends to obscure real conflict, which may be "unconscious" in the psychological sense or based on the "false consciousness" of class domination in Marx's sense. Though ultimately relativist, Gadamer's position according to Habermas is also essentially conservative – "interpretations of texts" are always made from the standpoint of the successful exploiting classes of the past. Habermas perceives the need to transcend tradition and social domination by again finding an Archimedean point from which there can be external critique.

In *Knowledge and Human Interests,* Habermas (1971b) distinguishes modes of knowledge according to the social interest or goal they serve: the *technical interest* of successful prediction and control (empirical science); the *practical interest* of human understanding and communication (hermeneutics); and the *emancipatory interest,* which is concerned with critique of ideology and liberation from social and individual pathologies. Freudian therapy is taken in particular as a paradigm of critical theory. The aim of psychoanalysis is to unmask psychic delusions in order to restore what the patient regards as a tolerable life. The patient may recover (by his own subjective criteria) by coming to assent to a story about his childhood even if that story is not in the historical sense "true." Therapy does not proceed by "objective" theorizing but rather by the active intervention of the therapist in the patient's situation and in their subsequent interaction in the phenomena of transference. Some therapists may make the prior assumption that there is some psychic state that is "normal," but an ideal analysis does not depend on such a state, or on any definition of a future utopia; it seeks to create an unpredictable new situation out of what comes to be seen as distortion and delusion. Psychotherapy therefore provides a model for a type of nonobjectified science that remains, as it were, open-ended. Freudian theory can here be compared with Marx's rejection of essences and utopias and his insistence that man makes himself in the course of the historical dialectic.

Freud, however, was an analyst of individuals, not of societies. His patients were usually from the middle classes, and their difficulties did not arise overtly from the oppression and exploitation Marx saw as the lot of the proletariat. Thus, to assimilate Freud's insights into the Marxist tradition, they have to be generalized to take account of the disorders of society as well as of the individual. Psychoanalysis is a model of method for Habermas's critical theory but not a model for the cure of social ills.

In his more recent work, Habermas (e.g., 1979) recognized that an open-ended critique divorced from rational grounds becomes as relativist as Mannheim's view that "all is ideology," or as therapy without a normative goal. He replaced the three-fold analysis of knowledge interests by a distinction between action and discourse. *Communicative action* or "life praxis," is the unreflective following of tacit social rules; with regard to knowledge in particular, it is the following of the rules of the intellectual discipline, whatever that may be. Calling this action "communicative" indicates that the modes of all disciplines transcend both instrumentalism and individualism and are concerned with social interaction mediated by language. Such unreflective action is always subject to distortion by social interests. There also exists a level of *communicative discourse* in which, according to Habermas, critique can operate and ideological distortions can be overcome. This discourse reflects upon and seeks to justify action. The distinction between action and discourse echoes, in a somewhat free reading, Chomsky's distinction between performance and competence in the use of language, and it points to the need for normative sciences that can reveal the rational "ideals" hidden in distorted communication. Just as the use of language in actual "performance" often distorts and conceals the rules of grammar and meaning that underlie its "competent" understanding, so distorted action conceals general norms and values and requires a new science of practical reflection and action. In hermeneutics, only the syntax and semantics of social life are considered – what is required is also a "universal pragmatics" (Habermas 1979). It is not sufficient to understand the world; we must also seek to change it, and to change it according to normative foundations.

Habermas's first account (1971b p. 314) of the "norms of practical discourse" was in terms of the "ideal speech situation." In engaging in argument, he claims, participants are aiming to detach themselves, at least momentarily, from action and interest and are committing themselves to the assumptions that they are accountable for the validity of their utterances and that the function of argument and mutual critique is to arrive at truth. Such discourse is necessarily a commitment to follow the better argument and thus to recognize the goals of argument, which may be truth in empirical science or norms of the good in practical affairs. Such ideal argument, he argues, can only occur in an ideal social situation in which all participants have symmetrical chances of engaging in discourse and putting forward justifications, refutations, explanations, and interpretations. They must also have equal chances of sincerely putting forward their own inner feelings and attitudes, and they must have equal status with regard to the power to issue permissions, commands, and so on. All this talk of equality presupposes that the "ideal speech situation" can take place only in conditions of an ideal form of life, that is, under conditions of freedom, equality, and justice.

The ideal speech situation is a generalization of Peirce's concept of the ideal scientific community for which truth is approached by consensus, subject to free experimentation and corrective feedback. We have seen, however, that not even here can we assume that consensus and unproblematic truth can be arrived at in relation to scientific *theory*. Theories are underdetermined and are likely to reflect the changing world models of the time. If the process of convergence to an ideal theory is not attainable in empirical science, it is likely to be even less attainable in the search for normative values.

Habermas requires not only that ideal speech be free of local ideologies, but also that it should supersede all natural differences between times and cultures. But surely these differences would persist however long discourse is continued. How can we agree to define and adjudicate among such virtues as freedom, equality, justice, and self-fulfillment, since these virtues are matters of conflict within most societies and particularly in societies with developed economies? Consensus on such matters cannot be guaranteed by Habermas's symmetry conditions of ideal speech; indeed, consensus about these virtues is *presupposed* by ideal speech as he describes it. Moreover, the notion of following the better argument assumes that all participants recognize and accept certain norms of rationality. This is also an absolutist position, which gives privilege to a particular understanding of what are the proper constraints on human speech. The truth *might* after all have been given to Moses on the mount, in which case it would be an offense against truth itself to offer symmetrical rights to all persons to decide it in a kind of committee meeting.

Habermas does not claim, however, that the conditions of ideal speech are realizable in history. Rather he claims that there is commitment in principle to the goals of truth and value under these conditions whenever participants engage in argumentative discourse here and now. Like the kingdom of heaven for Christian believers, the ideal is *anticipated* in sincere discourse. Such commitment and anticipation are actually found in history; moreover, in Habermas's view, they constitute one of the highest functions of evolution. He further claims that anticipations of generalizable norms and interests can take us beyond plurality to the possibility of judging the values of particular social orders in the setting of total history. The values presupposed by ideal speech have become less and less Marxist in Habermas's later work and more and more dependent on the Enlightenment tradition – what he calls "old European human dignity" (1971a, p. 143). The liberal virtues of freedom and equal rights are derived from this tradition, as are the norm of participatory democracy and the search for truth by means of rational argument. Ideal speech resting on Enlightenment values is not too far from Gadamer's grounding in tradition, with some Western ethnocentrism thrown in.

In his later work, Habermas (1979) has become more explicitly Hegelian in referring to a "developmental logic" that will be found to work itself out in the history of the human species. This approach now depends less on "transcendental" arguments for ideal speech and more on particular empirical studies, such as Chomsky's linguistics, Piaget's and Mead's developmental learning theories, and Kohlberg's developmental ethics. In his "Postscript to *Knowledge and Human Interests*," Habermas (1973) distinguishes between the critique of ideology and another kind of "reflective" science in terms of which he hopes to ground rational values. Critique of ideology studies particular examples of social belief and action as *distortions* of norms which it presupposes; it therefore depends on judgements about what the norms are, and tends to fall into a Weberian account of norms as arbitrary. But Habermas also recognizes a kind of science he calls *reconstructive,* which accepts linguistic and social norms as they are and seeks to find their underlying structure. Chomsky's linguistics is a paradigm case of a reconstructive science; it not only develops an empirical analysis of the normative structures ("syntactic competence") found in ordinary speech, but also claims that a deep enough structural analysis will reveal structures common to all human speech as such. Habermas studies this and other structural theories with the aim of finding normative principles beneath the actual development of human rationality.

Kohlberg (1971) in particular makes explicit claims to have developed a normative theory of cognitive psychology in relation to ethics. Habermas (1979) rightly interprets him as recognizing a type of empirical science different from those with a primarily technical interest. The idea of normative theory is an example of the influence of cognitive psychology in extending the limits of what is taken as empirical science in the human domain, but Habermas claims it does not share the pervasive relativism of hermeneutics. Let us see whether these claims are justified.

When Piaget described the development of higher reasoning faculties in children, he took for granted that there are normative end-points of adult rationality concerning concepts of logic and mathematics, space, time and causality, where these have a status similar to the Kantian categories. Kohlberg takes this method as his model for moral development, relying here on the categories of Western moral philosophy. In both cases, the method is subject to the initial objection that it is ethnocentric – why take Western categories as normative when we have much evidence to suggest that not all cultures agree in the basic concepts of either pure or practical reason? Kohlberg's reply is to accept that the starting point is not value- or culture-neutral, but to elaborate an admittedly value-laden theory and then attempt to show that it correlates with observable facts of moral development. He hopes to show a parallelism between two independently defined sets of categories, one factual and psychological, the other normative and philosophical, in order to justify the moral ascription of "better than" to the factual stages of child and adult morality.

As a piece of empirical research, Kohlberg claims to have shown in both western and some other cultures that the growing child goes through six stages of moral awareness, from simple avoidance of punishment and deference to power, through increasing internalization of objective "law," to an orientation to universal ethical principles answerable to conscience and including respect for individual human persons and their rights. As in Piaget's theory of stages of rational awareness, these stages are necessarily gone through in a definite order and are separated by life crises that demand restoration of equilibrium by moving to the next stage. Also, although Kohlberg claims that certain premonitions of justice are present at every stage, individuals and whole societies may become fixated at earlier stages, before these pre-monitions have reached the status of universalizable moral principles.

So far, only factual claims have been made, and all value-laden terms, such as "universal," "conscience," "rights," "justice," and "rationality," are to be taken as part of the descriptive theory of what is found in people's own accounts of their actions and beliefs and in the temporal order in which these actions and beliefs are found to occur. The descriptions are admittedly structured by theory-laden language, but in this they are no different from the descriptions of any complex natural or human subject matter. No naturalistic fallacy of the simple form "factually later is morally better" is involved. Kohlberg further claims that the criteria of "moral goodness" that provided the theoretical structure for his empirical findings are *also* in-dependently defined philosophical criteria for what philosophers recognize as morality. He makes an important distinction between form and content. It is not that every individual and every culture that reach stage 6 have iden-tical moral standpoints much less that they take similar moral decisions in similar situations. The form not the content of the principles defines the stages. Thus, at stage 6, Kantian principles of consistency and universalizabil-ity, and the differentiation of morality from other cognitive modes, are em-pirically found to be fully developed and also provide the philosophical criteria according to which particular moralities must be judged. Generally speak-ing, these formal principles will dictate moral structures of justice, reciprocity, equality, and respect for individuals within which particular moral decisions will be made.

At times, Kohlberg speaks as though the formal philosophical categories of morality are just what it is to "play the moral game" (1971, p. 217). If this were all, it would be unremarkable that the sequence of factual stages structured by these categories turns out to exhibit the same hierarchy of "values" as the categories themselves. Coincidental it might be, but certainly not morally compelling. Kohlberg's theory seems capable of a little more power than this, however. Recognizing that all interesting empirical theories must be structured by some concepts from outside the facts, he adopts the concepts of moral philosophy. There seems no reason that such a choice should not be testable like any other. If the facts fit, well and good; if not, some other moral structuring principle can be tried, for example that derived from Marxist socioeconomic history rather than Enlightenment superstructures.

One empirical weakness of Kohlberg's theory is that he does not compare the adequacy of his structure with that of others. As we have indicated in general in regard to the human sciences, however, it is unlikely that the result of such comparisons would be value free, because the constraints of the prag-matic criterion are inapplicable and inappropriate to a science of moral development. We cannot systematically and under controlled conditions sub-ject different groups of western teenagers, or of Latin American peasants, to different regimes dictated by rival ethical theories.

Habermas, however, makes stronger claims for the logic of such theories than does Kohlberg. First, Habermas accepts too uncritically the factual adequacy of the data, particularly their intercultural character. Faced with the threat of relativism, it is easy to fall back on what are claimed to be "universal" needs, desires, and interests of human beings as such and therefore to postulate and try to confirm the existence of universal norms. Even though physical and biological needs may be said to have natural grounds common to human beings, it is not easy to see why this universality should extend to human cultures. Human beings cannot survive in physical and biological conditions that deviate too far from certain norms, but it appears that individuals and societies can and do survive under wide diversities of social, cultural, and ethical regime. With regard to the particular "normative" sciences discussed by Habermas, Chomsky's theory at least exhibited predictive power, even though its assumption of common interlinguistic structure has been much criticized and partly superseded. Piaget's and Kohlberg's theories have not generated the same degree of empirical support, but they may still be regarded as ordinary scientific hypotheses, subject to empirical test and refutation in the usual way.

Second, Habermas makes claims for Kohlberg's methodology that do not seem to be borne out by Kohlberg's text. We have noted that any theory of developmental ethics is likely to be value laden, but Habermas goes further to claim for it a kind of necessity or unrevisability that makes "reconstructive" sciences radically different from empirical sciences that aim at prediction and control. This claim is a strange one. In an inversion of the old positivist view of the neutrality and stability of facts and their independence of theories explaining them, Habermas accepts the theory ladenness of observation as showing that our view of facts may itself be falsified and revised by interaction with theory. This mutual adjustment in the search for "best fitting" explanations makes radical scientific revolutions possible. However, Habermas argues that "reconstructive" science does not produce such revisions of "ordinary language" and ordinary social rules. Here, theory does not revise facts because the facts are just the conventions of human normative behavior, and it is these conventional competences that are to be described. Moreover, since the facts are assumed to be given and unrevisable, a normative theory that adequately fits the facts will itself be unrevisable, like the agreed deep grammar of competent English at a particular epoch, or like the so-called "ordinary language" of the Austinian philosophers.

Kohlberg's "facts," however, are not like the "correct" grammar of a particular historical language. Kohlberg himself asserts that knowledge of grammar is already present in a child of five and does not undergo much change thereafter, whereas in his theory, morality goes through successive and distinct stages. The elaboration of these stages must introduce more underdetermination into the theory than in what Kohlberg sees as the simpler case of a natural grammar. Again, "ordinary language" will not suffice as an unrevisable basis of a reconstructive science since it does not change uniformly throughout the lifetimes of different adults and is obviously highly culture relative. We have already seen how the categories of cognitive science itself may reflexively change ordinary usage in the process of accounting for the mechanisms of human rationality.

To obtain the "facts" for a study like Kohlberg's requires the same sort of mutual interactions and reinterpretation of theory and evidence that occurs in all theory-laden science. When Habermas argues for a radical distinction between reconstructive and ordinary empirical science, he is too much influenced by his desire to find unrevisable empirical foundations for normative judgments. He also seems to conflate an assumption drawn from some forms of hermeneutic philosophy that social facts and rules are human constructions and hence conventional, with the structuralist assumption that they form the unintended "deep archeology" of social life which can be discovered in pure form, uncontaminated by ideological bias. These two views are diametrically opposed in substance, but both have the consequence that reconstructions can be discovered once and for all, either by empathy with human rationality, or by the methods of structuralism. Both views are, however, inconsistent with our earlier emphasis on the perpetual revisability of science and on the continuity of methods and subject matter between the natural and the human sciences.

The most important question to be addressed, however, is of the logical status of the passage from facts to norms that Habermas seems to require. Kohlberg's (1971) classic paper is entitled "From Is to Ought: How to Commit the Naturalistic Fallacy and Get Away with it in the Study of Moral Development." His theory of the passage from Is to Ought depends on the correlation between the universal moral stages he claims to have found empirically and the developed structure of formal criteria found in Western philosophy. These criteria can then be interpreted as the teleological goal of moral learning, just as Piaget interprets the categories of logic and physical perception as the goals of learning in the mode of pure reason. Kohlberg, however, distinguishes the argument of his paper from two other concerns of moral philosophy and thereby avoids falling into the grosser forms of naturalistic fallacy. First, his theory is not a theory of the "good life," that is, it does not prescribe the content of ultimate moral ends. Satisfaction of the moral criteria at stage 6 would still be compatible with a variety of orderings of individual and social goals, though presumably not with all types of society (for example, not with institutions of slavery or gross material inequalities). Second, it is not a theory of virtue, that is, not a prescription for praise or blame of particular actions. Kohlberg also recognizes that knowledge of stage 6 criteria does not entail action in accordance with them, particularly because much morality involves basic personal sacrifice. St. Paul's problem of "the good that I would, that I do not" is left by Kohlberg as an issue for further research in behavioral psychology.

Kohlberg thus argues that he is not committed to any naturalistic fallacy of the kind that either *derives* judgments about the good from nonmoral phenomena or *assumes* that the biologically or socially "later" is "better." Moral judgments are *sui generis:* they are derived solely from moral criteria, which are formal and not concrete or particular. The claim in relation to facts of development is merely that the formal criteria are increasingly exhibited in later stages of individual and social behavior and belief.

The theory certainly has a cumulative appeal, particularly in Habermas's generalization of it to include homologies among a great variety of types of sequential development. These types include individual and social psychology, ego identity and group identity, the evolution of species and of social systems, and of myths, religions, and world views. All of these types, Habermas claims, show "progress" toward the goal of the formal characteristics underlying the idea of communicative competence – namely, universalizability over all persons, individualization of persons, and their increasing autonomy and self-reflective rationality. A vast variety of factual evidence from biology, anthropology, sociology, psychology, politics, and history is held to support the idea that normative structures have a common "internal history" (1979, p. 117).

Habermas's theory is breathtaking in its comprehensiveness and ambition. Indeed, *if* empirical theories exhibiting all these homologies were well confirmed by all the evidence, the resulting "empirical Hegelianism" would be powerful and impressive. This would still be the case even if we keep in mind previous caveats about the revisability of all theory and all interpetations of evidence and the possibility of viewing the whole scene from radically different points of view. Habermas's explorations into reconstructive science continue, but in the light of the factual and logical objections we have outlined, there seems to be only one viable way to take his attempt to give a comprehensive theory of cultural norms. This way is to adopt the ideal of "communicative competence," and the resulting concepts of "persons" and "rights," as a normative standpoint and to embrace the various resultant forms of circularity as arguments that both support and are supported by that standpoint. The option for ideal discourse is then grounded in a whole internal network of related beliefs and evidence, but its grounds are not logically independent or transcendentally conclusive. We cannot rule out the possibility of some other rational unification of the claims of all the sciences (for instance, some form of Marxist theory of history), or the relativist view that there is no truth apart from empirical science and logic, and that there remains a plurality of rational social viewpoints not decidable with respect to "truth" at all.

If we look for a moment at how religion fares in Habermas's comprehensive world view, it appears as a typically Marxist or Comtean reconstruction of development from the "magical–animistic representational world," through myths that take on "legitimation of structures of domination," to cosmological

world views and theologies based on argumentation, and finally to demythologized principles of the unity of reason that have "lost their character *as*
world views" (1979, pp. 104–105). As we see in the next chapter, such a sequential interpretation is far from some of the relativist interpretations of
myth in modern social anthropology.

In a more explicit discussion of the traditional functions of religion,
Habermas points to the legitimation of authority structures necessary for
social control and to the provision of a personal universe of meaning that
buttresses the individual against anarchic forces and disasters, both natural
and social, and gives the individual a place to stand against society itself.
For these functions to operate, individuals must believe in the world stories
that perform the functions. How can there be such belief in a secularized
world? To impose myths by authority as "rationalizing illusions" is contrary
to the symmetries of ideal discourse and must be rejected. Therefore, the
functions of religion cannot be detached from the question of truth. However,
Habermas thinks the quest for truth need not involve the notion of a personal God:

the idea of God is transformed into the concept of a *Logos* that determines the community of believers and the real life-context of a self-emancipating society. "God"
becomes the name for a communicative structure that forces men, on pain of a loss
of their humanity, to go beyond their accidental, empirical nature to encounter one
another *indirectly,* that is, across an objective something that they themselves are
not. (1975, p. 121)

In the context of all of Habermas's arguments, it does not seem possible to
read more into this "something that they themselves are not" than reference
again to the communicative competence wherein truth dwells and that is other
than human beings at any contingent moment of their history.

On this point, Gadamer (1976, Ch. 2; McCarthy 1978, p. 187) comments
on the metaphysical character of the idea of "unconstrained consensus." Indeed any account of the function of religions that goes beyond "necessary fic-
tions" seems bound to resort to some metaphysical theory of truth. Any such
theory must be judged in terms of its internal consistency and by its conformity with what we can observe of human life and history. Perhaps the
crucial point at which Habermas's metaphysics is vulnerable to such experience is that it shares with all Enlightenment philosophy a neglect of the
facts of evil, or, in older terminology, the presence of "original sin." The
limiting conception of consensus truth is appropriate in a world view that
also embraces a belief in historical progress toward some ideal. However,
it is impossible to regard a purely rational ideal as an adequate basis for a
coherent and comprehensive metaphysics, given the observable facts that
history does not exhibit progressive agreement about fundamental social
goals, nor a progressive decrease in actual occasions of conflict. Moreover,
history does not exhibit a merely benign and fruitful pluralism that relativists
might applaud, but rather it exhibits persistent outbreaks of irrationality and

positively evil will. An adequate view must address these things as problems for world understanding and not indulge the illusion that human beings will necessarily follow the rational and the good when it is revealed to them, whether in the form of the ideal speech situation or of the will of God. To state this in more secular terms, there seems to be a universal human experience of imperfection and alienation in the total functioning of interacting schemas that is not fully addressed in Habermas's consensus view of the true and the good.

To speak of "evil will" does, of course, presuppose a nonrelativist standpoint. From the transcendental point of view, the problem of evil, and in general the problem of the validity of values, have traditionally been located in religion and theology. We have raised three issues that have led us to the frontiers of religion – namely, human freedom, values, and the problem of evil. These issues, we have suggested, cannot be addressed in their transcendental form by cognitive science or by hermeneutics. This is where relativists and realists ultimately part company. Relativists hold that there is no transcendental form in terms of which to address the issues. Realists continue to look for transcendental grounds. We have described Habermas's search for these grounds as one of the most perceptive and comprehensive available, and we have argued that it fails.

Religions, however, will continue to offer world views in which our three problems are addressed. It is not so much that religion and theology can be brought in to fill the gaps that cognitive science and philosophy have not yet colonized, but rather that the criteria of truth and knowledge within a religion are not those of cognitive science or philosophy as presently understood. On the other hand, the investigation of what these internal criteria are in particular religions is a task cognitive science should find illuminating and congenial to its general approach. Religions are also complexes of interacting schemas of actions and beliefs. In the next chapter, we therefore consider how they may be understood as social schemas.

10 Religions as social schemas

10.1 Religion as primitive science

Our discussion of hermeneutics and critical theory has led to this question: What are the constraints and criteria for the success of social schemas? A schema theory of many-leveled interactions between the individual and the social may provide the mechanism of schema correction and development, but it cannot by itself specify the social functions that the feedback systems serve, nor the consciously adopted goals that human beings intentionally feed into these systems. Guided missiles have externally specified targets, and homeostatic biological systems have a goal of survival, ensured by natural selection mechanisms. What are the goals of social systems?

There are three possible types of answer to this question, which we call scientistic, hermeneutic, and critical. Scientism is the view that the criteria for the success of social schemas can be read off the facts without intervention of any but scientific criteria. This view recognizes that facts in themselves do not entail human judgments of good and bad, but it claims that these judgments can be elicited from deep natural structures of human biology, psychology, and social interaction. These structures can be described and explained, for instance, in the science of evolution and by natural scientific methods applied to the social sciences. The model for such a scientistic interpretation of social norms, therefore, tends to be biological science, in which the goals of feedback schemas are patent: functional coherence, stability, and survival. Examples of this approach to social systems are the extrapolations of evolutionary theory in sociobiology and various functional theories of social institutions, including religion, which we discuss in Section 10.2.

We have discussed the theory of norms in hermeneutics and critical theory. Hermeneutics asks for success in mutual social communication and understanding as a necessary condition of viable social structure. Understanding must be based on prejudgments mediating and projecting tradition. This view tends to be holistic and relativist. It admits external interaction between traditions, but in the end it does not admit external input either from the results of natural science or from perennial norms of reason or revelation. Critical theory adds to the criterion of "understanding" the need for justice and eman-

197

cipation both causing and issuing from the self-criticism and free consensus of the "ideal speech situation." It tends to be absolutist rather than relativist, since, at least in Habermas's version, perennial biological and psychological norms are recognized, as are the rational norms of Enlightenment liberalism, which are held to be the high point of human evolution.

These kinds of criteria are relevant to religions seen as social schemas, as well as to the more directly individual experiences of the "holy" and the "transcendent." Religious systems, however, generally differ from modern secular systems of social norms in two ways. First, religious systems purport to refer to what transcends space–time and therefore appear to be more highly symbolic than spatiotemporal descriptions. Weber (1948) distinguished the modern from archaic worlds in terms of disenchantment and rationalization: the angels and devils and transcendent meanings are expelled from the world and replaced by rational science, rational organization, and bureaucratized institutions. It is the archaic "enchantment" that attaches to religion that more than anything else makes it appear as an alien remnant in modern society.

Second, religions generally claim a cosmological and cognitive relevance that is not scientific. That is, they claim a form of truth different from that of natural facts and different also from whatever "truth" Enlightenment society will recognize in such accepted norms as "justice" and "freedom." Whatever biological, psychological, or social explanations of religion are discovered, religious believers will generally also want to claim that the religious system represents something transcending social consensus. As we put it in the first chapter, in his religious reality, "God is more like gravitation than embarrassment."

We look to social anthropology for the most developed theories of religion as social schemas. Social anthropologists have usually concentrated on "primitive" or "traditional" religions rather than on the historically based religion of Western and Islamic civilizations (what Levi-Strauss [1963] calls "hot," that is, dynamic, societies). There are, however, irreducible "traditional" elements in the structure of all religions; hence the anthropologists' accounts can be generalized. Social interpretations of religion have moved from the view of religion as primitive science, through a biologically based functionalism, to the recognition of religions as *sui generis* holistic symbol systems, to which has recently been added the study of their "deep structure." This last structuralist phase has circled back toward explanations based on scientistic models, primarily scientific linguistics, psychoanalysis, and Marxist theory of society. We look briefly at these four types of interpretation of religion: intellectualist, functionalist, symbolist, and structuralist.

The first theory of religion in modern social anthropology was the view, put forward in different ways by Frazer (1922) and Tylor (1929, first published 1871), that religion is primitive science; this theory has recently been called "intellectualist." In primitive societies, the most obvious thing about religious cosmology is that it provides unified explanatory categories for the natural world, for social institutions, and for the proper ordering of personal life within these. Religion and magic appear to have both the explanatory and the instrumental functions of modern science; in the sequence myth/metaphysics/scientific theory, they seem to be in direct historical continuity with modern science. The particular kinds of explanation they give are now discarded, as are many of those of early science, and their instrumental aspects (magical and religious ritual and the like) fail to perform what is promised under systematic empirical test; but nevertheless there are recognizable similarities of social function.

Frazer and Tylor offered a naturalistic social anthropology, which saw the "magic" of other tribes as akin to the science of our own "tribe." The interpretation of science in their day was, however, mainly positivistic; it was difficult to interpret in these terms the "unobservable concepts" (gods, spirits, witchcraft) that pervade all religions. Robin Horton (1967) suggested that the view of religion as science ought to be revived in the light of the more sophisticated account of science given by modern history and philosophy of science, with their emphasis on unified theoretical explanations in terms of unobservable entities. He takes an example from Victor Turner's (1967) account of Ndembu childbirth to show how the apparently mystical framework of ritual and therapy can be understood as the attempt to treat disease as psychosomatic in relation to the patient, and also as socially generated by the conflicts and tensions of the patient's surroundings. When a Ndembu woman is in labor, the medicine man, her family, and other members of the clan conduct rituals outside her hut. The rituals look like pure religious or magical symbolism, but they appear to be socially and psychologically therapeutic and may therefore have a scientifically explicable basis, although our scientific knowledge does not yet permit us to understand its causation.

In judging this example as evidence for Horton's intellectualism, we should notice that there are certain differences between the aims and methods of Ndembu and of modern medicine. The tribal ritual and beliefs are highly traditional and do not respond to falsification – if the woman dies, this fact is not taken to be a reason for changing the symbol system. Moreover, the efficacy of the system depends on the participants' acceptance of a cosmology assumed by the medical practice. For the cure to work, it is essential that the presupposed symbolic theory be internalized in the patient and her relevant social group, for only in terms of *their* belief in this theory can the required effects be expected to take place.

This internalization is not generally supposed to be required for scientific medicine – the doctor's knowledge of physiology, drug action, and so on, does not depend for its efficacy on the patient's knowledge or acceptance of the "world view of modern medicine." Robin Horton (personal communication to MBH, October 1979) responded to this objection by noting that scientific medicine is now learning that psychosomatic approaches can complement therapies that simply treat the body as an object to be manipulated back to health and that efficacy is therefore connected with the patient's state of mind and social situation. Nonetheless, we hold that this argument does not show that tribal medicine constitutes science understood as a process of explicit search for predictive theories under the guidance of the pragmatic criterion. Presumably, if scientific medicine incorporates a psychosomatic component, this is not because it blindly accepts traditional methods but because, as in scientific psychology, it seeks to develop such a component through explicit and continual testing.

Moreover, once the aims of medical practice are seen to go beyond the atomic individuals and their more or less biologically obvious state of health, the symbolic "theory" takes on another characteristic not present in medicine understood purely scientifically. This characteristic is that psychological and social norms for the individual and the group are not given by obvious indicators of bodily "health," and thus what counts as successful healing itself has to be defined by the symbolic order that is presupposed. Turner gives an example from the case of a Ndembu patient, whose "cure" from indefinite neurotic-type symptoms would, in the Ndembu doctor's eyes, have been his emancipation from his late father's sphere of influence and the literal removal of his place of residence from one under patrilineal to one under matrilineal influence. To make the definition of the goal and hence the success of medicine thus dependent on values intrinsic to the symbolic theory itself is to extend the pragmatic criterion of science. It is to make medicine more like a social (hermeneutic) than a natural science and to make religious belief into a social institution that is not to be judged by the pragmatic.

The theory of religion as primitive science has the merit of providing a unified, holistic view of cognition in place of the dualism of science and religion that has more often been dominant. But the examples from symbolic medicine suggest that this theory will not help in our attempt to situate religion on the cognitive map. Here are some specific objections.

First, the theory suggests a reduction of religious myth to false scientific theory, where theory is still regarded in a naïvely realistic way as potentially true description of the natural world. It thus interprets religion as being about the objectified world of naturalism, taken to include the postulation of "gods" as unobservable entities, and it assumes that religion is to be judged by the truth criteria appropriate to natural science. We have argued, however, that the reduction required is rather the other way around – scientific theory itself needs to be understood as metaphor, model, and myth, constrained but not determined by the pragmatic criterion, not aiming only at objectified truth, but also having other social functions comparable to those of religious cosmology. Without a further analysis of "myth," the intellectualist's comparison is not yet very illuminating.

Second, as we also argued, a distinction is still required between objectified science validated by the pragmatic criterion and other cognitive systems that serve different social interests. Continuity may exist along the cognitive spectrum from natural through social science to metaphysics and religion, but the pragmatic criterion becomes less and less relevant. The religion-as-failed-science view gives no help in elucidating the other cognitive criteria we are seeking.

Third, as is generally recognized in social anthropology, Frazer's theory fails to do justice to other differences between the way a traditional society regards its religion and the way natural science relates to our society. Traditional cosmologies and their associated instrumental rituals are generally received on authority and not subjected to empirical test. They are particular and concrete, not universalizable and abstract. They are inseparable from personalized emotion and aesthetic and rhetorical motivations and do not seek value-neutral objectivity. They make no ultimate distinctions between the natural, the social, and the supernatural worlds. They know nothing of the "dissociation of sensibility," a typical product of modern science.

Fourth, and perhaps most important, study of religions and other cognitive systems has made it clear that their "instrumentality" is not to be compared to that of the technical prediction and control of natural science, but rather to the rhetorical and persuasive characteristics of human communication systems. Both religious and scientific myth, and the ritual performances of religion, are "instrumental" in social rather than natural contexts. As Mary Douglas puts it, taboos, pollution rules, and so on are not to be reduced to the rules of social hygiene (Moses was not "an enlightened public health administrator"); rather, "the whole universe is harnessed to man's attempts to force one another into good citizenship" (Douglas 1966, p. 3).

When social anthropologists speak of the "instrumental" theory of symbolism, it is almost always this social instrumentality they refer to, not just the claimed natural efficacy of magic and sacrament. The shift is important, because it means that the study of religion as a social phenomenon is thereby placed among the hermeneutic sciences of psychology and sociology as a study of meanings and communication. There is no possibility of a positivist theory of religion such as foreseen by Comte (1974), Tylor, and Frazer. Indeed, what is striking about their theories of religion is that they are not only positivist in method but also in content, in the sense that they reduce religion to the scientific end of the cognitive spectrum, regarding this as the ideal of true knowledge instead of the merely limiting case of pure technical interest. As Horton (1967) recognizes, such attempted reduction throws more light on the inadequacies of our received idea of science than on the nature of religion itself. But in the task of understanding religion as cognition, even Horton's intellectualism leaves much philosophical work to be done.

10.2 The social functions of religion

Human beings have a preconscious and unreflective physics – objects fall if you let go of them. That feeling for the natural environment is unconscious.

Similarly, in picking up the chalk and writing, I am exercising functional schemas, but I am not appealing to an explicit theory of which I am conscious. Yet my ability to do such things constitutes part of the data about the cognitive, on a more elementary level than that of scientific explanations. In traditional cosmologies, people take the cosmos as in some sense a model of human life itself, understanding themselves as related to the cyclical processes of the seasons, of day and night, of the heavenly bodies, and relating these to the processes of birth, maturation, and death. This unity of the natural and the human is perhaps also more true of Western culture than we recognize. People already have schemas that relate prereflective natural and social experience. A complete cognitive science would have to address and incorporate these schemas, and to do this, we need to extend the notion of what a cognitive system is.

One such attempt is the functionalist theory of how societies come to have their normative and religious systems. The theory derives from the model of society as an organism with interacting functional parts, and it arises naturally out of our concept of mutually interacting social schemas. Durkheim (1915) developed this model into a strong statement about the nature of religion; namely, that it defines the "sacred" character of social norms into which every individual is socialized from birth and without which no society could function or even survive. Durkheim asked, in effect, "Whence come these external constraints, these inescapable obligations, internalized by every member of society?" There must, he thinks, be *some* referent of the near-unanimous expression of obligation, power, and authority, and the awe that induces worship. But his positivist commitment ruled out from the start any concept of supranatural divinity, for the existence of which he believed we have no independent evidence. He therefore concluded that only society itself both clearly exists and has the properties sufficient to explain the experienced objective reference of religion. In short, Society is God. Durkheim suggests that society evolves in such a way that it is functional for people to create stories about God as surrogates for stories about social authority. As in organic systems, the functioning parts of society, including its religion, collaborate in the interests of stability, solidarity, and survival. Durkheim might nowadays accept a sociobiological account of social norms. In any case, he gives an account of how God could be a socially projected reality without being a supernatural Reality that transcends space and time. He gives a reductive, naturalist explanation of religion in place of the overt religious belief that, for example, God really did create Heaven and Earth and thus is not limited by space and time. We return to the face-value significance of this belief in the next chapter; meanwhile, let us see how far functionalism takes us.

First, we should notice two senses of "function," one of which is applicable in the present context but commonplace, the other of which is more significant and controversial. In the mathematical sense, a "function" is a correlation of the respective values of two or more variables – a "mapping" from one domain into others. In this sense, there is functional interaction whenever there are natural regularities, particularly where a cognitive system consists of a mutual interaction of variables or where two or more cognitive systems, such as science, religion, or ideology, interact with each other and with their environment. So far, nothing much has been said about the specific functional properties of religion.

The second sense of "function" yields an interpretation of religion based explicitly on the model of a functioning organism or symbiotic organism-environment system. In biology, such functionally adapted systems are no longer explained by "design" (as opposed to the style of nineteenth-century natural theology), but in terms of natural selection mechanisms that depend on the variability and selective fitness of genes. In the case of societies, of course, functional adaptation may be the product of design – that is, of *human* design, where human intentionality can reasonably be adduced in what Robert Merton (1957) calls *manifest* functions. For example, the functions of a police force are intentionally to prevent and discover crime, of social workers to alleviate hardship, and so on. Similarly, in religions, there is sometimes intentional structuring of ritual and doctrine with the aim of supporting or influencing religious practice. Particularly in advanced religions, explicit reasons may be given for belief and practice; for example, the Virgin Mary is worthy of honor *because* this redresses the balance of the sexes in comparison with ancient religion; the altar is brought down among the people to signify the priesthood of all believers. Part of the rational discussion of theology depends on giving such reasons, so explanation by manifest function will always have a place. However, these reasons must be seen *within* the holistic web of faith and practice and cannot be justified apart from that. Thus, intentional explanations that try to exhaust the ground for religion by appealing to manifest social function will sometimes have to represent religion as manipulation of belief for purely social purposes – the religion of the secret priestly hierarchy, which has to conceal its real motives from believers in order to retain credibility.

The more important problems for social explanation arise where functions are *latent,* that is, not consciously present to or intended by the individuals involved. The social functions of religion as discussed in anthropology are almost always of this type because believers and worshippers usually ascribe to them the manifest functions of prayer and worship of a god, not the reinforcement of social obligation or social morale. Actors' manifest accounts of causality may be unacceptable, for example, where religious rituals are claimed to be effective in bringing rain. In such cases, social explanations for the persistence of such beliefs have to be sought beyond human design or intentionality.

If a biological model of functional explanation is to work in these cases, there must be a close enough analogy between a society and its functioning parts on the one hand, and a functional organic system on the other. Consider the ritual rain dance, or the Christian Holy Communion. In both cases, the functionalist view is that these rituals have psychological effects on the worshippers and are conducive to social stability, solidarity and thus survival. One difficulty about such an explanation is that the general social purposes relative to which institutions are supposed to be functional cannot be defined in an objective way. "Stability" and "cohesion" as social goals remain vague. Moreover the *telos* assumed is not necessarily even a desirable one – some societies both have in fact, and perhaps ought morally, to seek survival of some of their values through instability, disruption, and revolution.

The second main objection to a biological type of functionalism is related to the theory of evolution itself. To back up the analogy with natural selection, there must be some concepts of "variation," "fitness," "survival," and "selection" for societies comparable to those we have for organisms. However, great difficulties arise in providing these concepts. For example, how is "a society" to be individuated? In standard cases of organisms or species, natural selection theory is able to assume criteria of individuation; it follows that the survival or extinction of an organism or species is generally a clear, well delineated concept. But what counts as the "survival" of a society? The criteria cannot just be biological, because the progeny of a given society may survive massacre, conquest, or assimilation, even though every institution that made it the society it was is destroyed. Conversely, a culture and its institutions may survive the biological clan that first exhibited it. The criteria of survival must therefore be themselves social, and these are not the kinds of criteria subject to workable distinctions like the criteria of biological life or death. Functional explanations of this kind are only plausible when applied to relatively isolated and stable societies; that is, to societies that have survived with strongly marked identity. However, there are no clear control cases in which societies lacking certain alleged functional parts have consequently "died." In particular cases, the decline and fall of a given society may be ascribable to particular manifestations historically observed; but from the point of view of functional explanation, any such causal accounts have an air of being ad hoc: they are not predictable from general theory, nor do they clearly act as potential falsifications of functional claims. One of Durkheim's major problems about religion was the comparative decline of religious observance in modern society. Far from interpreting this decline as a falsification of his functional theory of religion, he sought to explain it by finding other characteristics of modern society – for example, the existence of science itself – that take the place of established religion.

Functionalism fails as a theory of religion if it is conceived too closely on the Darwinian model. It gives no causal explanation of religions in terms of their latent functions, because (*pace* Lumsden and Wilson 1981) no satisfactory social analogue of the gene has been defined to permit explanation of social change in terms of natural selection.

Meanwhile, the language of functions remains descriptively useful and does provide a kind of Lamarckian explanation of how adaptations are transmitted in society, whether by conscious or unconscious mechanisms. It may therefore be taken as a sort of placeholder for some more detailed type of explanation yet to be developed, just as Lamarck's theory was in relation to Darwin's.

10.3 Religions as symbol systems

The more we look at religious systems, the more we become impressed by what Durkheim called their *sui generis,* internally connected character. Indeed, functional explanations in social anthropology have been largely replaced by a theory of religion as symbolism, depending on internal holistic structure as much as on external social causation. Already in Durkheim's account, religion is not an epiphenomenon entirely determined by other social structure, as in the Marxist interpretation, nor is it to be explained solely by reduction to social utility. Durkheim came to see religion as a mutually interacting part of the social complex, having a relative autonomy of its own:

> . . . a synthesis *sui generis* of particular consciousness is required. Now this synthesis has the effect of disengaging a whole world of sentiments, ideas and images which, once born, obey laws all their own . . . The life thus brought into being even enjoys so great an independence that it sometimes indulges the mere pleasure of affirming itself. We have shown that this is often precisely the case with ritual activity and mythological thought. (Durkheim 1915, pp. 423–4)

For Durkheim, religion is just one of the types of symbol systems that develop their own autonomy out of the roots of social life. In their *Primitive Classification,* Durkheim and Mauss (1963) laid the foundation of their theory of religion in a radical sociology of knowledge. By citing examples from anthropological fieldwork, they concluded that all kinds of cognitive categories are based on primitive classifications of the natural and social worlds: there are, for example, correlations of cosmic spatial and temporal categories with the topological arrangements of the clan's living space and their organization of intervals of time. Notions of natural kinds and natural causality are, they claim, derived from social classes and social authority; magical laws and rituals involving sympathy, contiguity, and participation are symbolizations of social relations and issue ultimately in the unified systems of law that constitute science and logic. The theory is explicitly a socialization of Kantian rational categories as well as of religion. Just as Durkheim believes that only society can provide the authority and transcendence ascribed to God, so he thinks that only society carries the objectivity, impersonality, necessity, and autonomy to account for the apparent inescapability and universality of the laws of thought.

Functional explanations ascribe latent functions to religion that are other than the functions ascribed to them by believers. For example, rites have a latent function of increasing social solidarity quite distinct from their overt role of communicating with the gods. By contrast, Durkheim's symbolist followers see a religious system as more like an aesthetic *jeu d'esprit*, obeying laws all its own. This emphasis on relative autonomy ought not, however, to obscure the holistic character of *all* manifestations of social life within traditional societies. It is not that different social institutions are fragmented into the economic, the social, the individual, the religious, but that a unified system reveals itself in loosely related parts. Religion is a symbolically elaborated manifestation and expression of the social order. This means that the symbolic approach requires a study of the internal structure of the whole society, including its religions. It also means that appeal is made first to how the society sees itself, rather than being an external study by anthropologists who claim to know better than the actors "what the institutions mean." Anthropological study takes the social network as a whole, starting from any point and working out from there to explore the implications of all related concepts and practices, in order to deepen understanding. This is a hermeneutic process, such as was originally applied to the text of the Bible, of which we give some examples in the next chapter.

Such a theory of interacting but relatively autonomous symbolic systems accords well with the account we have been giving of different forms of cognition and begins to put some content into that formal framework. Indeed, the study of religions may be said to provide a heuristic for cognitive science when that science begins to move into more complex forms of human schema building. Symbolism is a theory that can accommodate the intellectualist, functional, and evolutionary aspects of religion we have already discussed, although none of these will be seen as exclusive explanations and symbolism will not be regarded as reducible to any or all of them. It is also a theory that goes deeper than they do into the structure and cognitive status of symbolic systems.

Symbol systems function as makings and remakings of the world, as we argued in Chapter 8 that global metaphors do. But to linguistic relation, symbolism adds action (recall our original stress on schemas developing in the individual within the physical and social constraints of the action–perception cycle). In his account of the philosophy of the Navaho, Kluckholm sums up their world view under the following headings:

the universe is orderly, and all events are inter-related;
knowledge is power;
the basic quest is for harmony;
the price for disorder, in human terms, is illness.
    (Morris 1979, p. 129)

B. Morris (1979), who quotes this passage, goes on to say "Given these premises the ritual cermonials of the Navaho, through which the symbolic classificatory schema is made manifest, are essentially means of restoring the universal harmony" (Morris 1979, p. 129).

In his classic work on the religion of the Dinka, Godfrey Lienhardt describes a peace-making ceremony held after a man has been killed in fighting. Hostility between the camps of the dead man and his killers is overtly recognized by a show of fighting with spears and shields, but the masters of the fishing spear sit between the camps, beat themselves on the ground, and break the spears. An ox is killed in the space between the camps and its parts thrown towards one side or the other, as if to separate them. Then the fighting stops and both camps return home, leaving the onlookers to eat the ox. Lienhardt goes on:

The symbolic action, in fact, mimes the total situation in which the parties to the feud know themselves to be. . . . . In this symbolic representation of their situation they control it, according to their will to peace, by transcending in symbolic action the only type of practical action (that is, continued hostilities) which for the Dinka follows from the situation of homicide. (Lienhardt 1961, p. 288)

Rituals such as these undoubtedly have unconscious psychological effects, but they transcend these effects in an intentional acceptance of the remade world without which even such instrumentality would not be effective.

The Dorze say, "Leopards are Christians; they fast on Fridays." This belief is inexplicable unless one probes deeply into their social system to discover concepts of totem brother, of leopard as totem, and the economic and ritual importance of leopards. The Bororo say, "I am a parrot," and the Nuer say twins are birds. Levy-Bruhl (1985) concluded from such apparent factual falsehoods and logical incoherences that primitive belief systems are pre-logical and indicate a different and arational form of human mentality. Since Levy-Bruhl, it has been accepted that the distinction is not one between different stages of culture but between different forms within every culture. So-called primitives know the law of contradiction as well as we do in appropriate circumstances – the lion being hunted is here and not there, and one should throw the spear accordingly. Similarly, so-called advanced societies use symbolisms in which the law of contradiction appears to be violated – God is three-in-one, quantum entities are both particles and waves. To make logic the differentiating characteristic here is not to comment on "primitive" versus "advanced" but on classificatory ordering. In every culture, some but not all linguistic signs form a logical proposition, and these may not be the most useful ones in a natural language. It is not so much that symbolism violates logic as that it constitutes a more general system than logic, and that nonlogicality is pervasive in language itself as well as in nonverbal symbolism. Our previous account of metaphorical language and symbolism has prepared us for this generalization.

Understanding symbol systems "from the inside" in this way does lay symbolist interpretations open to the charge of uncritical relativism. Consider Evans-Pritchard's well-known study of the Azande of the Congo, in his *Witchcraft, Oracles and Magic among the Azande* (1937). Zande belief is not centered on a transcendent God, but rather in a world of spirits not subject to spatiotemporal constraints. The Zande believe in a substance called "mangu" (witchcraft) situated in certain people who are thereby witches and who can dispatch their witchcraft across time and space. They hold that whenever a disaster occurs – a disease of crop or cattle, or a human death – it is always caused by witchcraft. There is an elaborate system of divination, based on examination of chicken entrails, to discover the witch who is responsible. We might say that the cause of a fire destroying the crop is an accidental lightning flash, but the Azande have no notion of accident and ask instead who caused the lightning to strike in just that place and time where it could do damage.

Zande also recognize that the oracle's answer may be wrong, and so they have an elaborate system to tell them when not to trust it. The chicken ritual is followed by a formal court to determine the witch responsible. Ultimately, there is an appeal right up to the king, whose objectivity is guaranteed by the fact that the royal line is never tainted by witchcraft. Again, a son never accuses his father of witchcraft, because witchcraft substance is inherited, and such an accusation would be equivalent to accusing himself. The whole belief system is well-constructed both to avoid contradicting patent facts and to relieve the tensions of social disputes without subverting family or social order.

Evans-Pritchard put this case forward as an example of the need for participant observation and acceptance of the actors' own account of their beliefs if a social system is to be properly understood. He had no doubt that Zande witchcraft beliefs are "false," in the sense that a scientific account would reject the modes of causation implied. Peter Winch (1970) reinterpreted the story to suggest there might be a holistic justification of the Zande account, and indeed that one might write a Zande account of our science exactly symmetrical with Evans-Pritchard's account of theirs. This account would purport to show that either account can be taken as "true" or "false" depending on the general network of assumptions we start with. We are reminded of the Duhemian point that any theoretical system can be made to square with the facts if sufficient adjustments are made in its empirical interpretation. We have seen in our account of the Copernican revolution that justification of belief can be given in terms of the structures of society as well as from the structure of nature.

On the other hand, it is clear that Zande witchcraft beliefs are not adjusted to the pragmatic criterion or the technical interest of western science. It would not in practice be possible to produce from their beliefs a scientific theory as unified, comprehensive, and predictive as ours. However, the dominance of the pragmatic criterion is a product of the particular history of sixteenth- and seventeenth-century Europe, and it still remains the case that we need to understand alternative and more socially oriented criteria for cognitive systems. There is no need to succumb to relativism in order to recognize that the coherence of symbols is a pervasive feature of cognition that has been neglected as a result of the dominance of technical science.

10.4 Deep structures

The fourth anthropological theory of religion we consider is that of Levi-Strauss. This is a theory of myth rather than specifically of religion, but it has important implications for our study of religion as a social construction. Like other French structuralists, Levi-Strauss takes the methodology of natural science as his model but generalizes it in ways that prove useful in our search for alternative cognitive systems.

Structuralist theories in general are premised on the concept of an "epistemological break." This break occurs when a domain of study breaks through its superficial inductive form and discovers in (or imposes on) its subject matter a "deep structure." Thus, Althusser and Balibar (1970) say that such a break took place in astronomy with Copernicus, in biology with Darwin, and in economics with Marx. Levi-Strauss himself (1955, p. 50) refers to his "three mistresses": geology, psychoanalysis, and Marxism. These depend on finding beneath overt phenomena a lawlike but hidden structure that exhibits the real nature of their respective domains. The modern science of linguistics is another example, from which the metaphor of "deep structure" comes. It should be noticed that in some of these "sciences," particularly linguistics, psychoanalysis, and Marxism, evaluative as well as "factual" elements are present. That is, their "real structure" is that imputed by investigators whose goal is often prescriptive: the normative language need not be spoken by anyone but nevertheless becomes a social ideal; the structure of the "unconscious" may be *con*structed as much as discovered; the triumph of the proletariat may be a goal of action as much as a state of affairs now present in the womb of history.

Similarly Levi-Strauss's (1966–81) theory of myth contains elements of both its functional and symbolist predecessors, but in a radically different framework. The theory constitutes what Levi-Strauss would call an "epistemological break" for anthropology. Against functionalism, he holds that explanations in anthropology are not to be found in superficial generalizations that purport to relate myths and rituals to the needs of society. Rather, explanations must be sought in hidden structures. Similarly, against symbolism, he holds that there is no external "meaning" of symbols that can be understood either atomistically or in terms of symbol systems as a whole. Rather, meaning is in the form and not the content of myths; it resides in synonymy, analogy, opposition, and inversion.

We have described Sperber's similar rejection of the atomistic model for meaning. In his comments on Levi-Strauss's theory, Sperber (1975, Ch. 1) takes its formalism to imply it has abandoned altogether the linguistic model for symbolism because it abandons dependence on (symbol, interpretation) dyads. Sperber, however, takes too narrow a view of the potentialities of a linguistic model. Levi-Strauss's formal relations are just the kinds of relations we have found to generate metaphoric meaning as pervasive in natural language, and our linguistic analogy for symbols has therefore gone beyond the atomistic semiological view. Similarly, Levi-Strauss abandons the atomistic view, but the linguistic analogy for myth is still appropriate, because he recognizes that meaning resides in holistic networks and their transformations. He picks up the terminology of linguistics and communication theory and uses it with extended meaning to express his different view of the "messages" of myth, not as surface fables but as "deep structures." Levi-Strauss is thus comparatively free of the presuppositions of the literal theory of language, and his theory of meaning is holistic.

The deep structures and the transformations also provide for Levi-Strauss a means of restoring unity to diverse symbolisms and thus of overcoming the lack of generality in their study as separate autonomous systems. Within the mythical corpora of a vast variety of peoples, Levi-Strauss perceives a complex web of parallelisms, transformations, and inversions that emerge throughout myths, cosmologies, and associated magical and ritual practices. To illustrate from familiar Biblical examples, there are not only the typologies long recognized by means of parallelisms between stories, such as those of Adam, Abraham, David, and Jesus Christ, or between the deliverances from Egypt, from Babylon, and the salvation wrought in Christ, but there also are detailed relations of contrast and inversion, for example, between the salvation of Israel *from* Egypt and the salvation *from* Herod the Jew by the flight of the holy family *into* Egypt. Levi-Strauss does not apply his theory to the Bible directly, but Leach (1969, pp. 81–2) has persuasively elicited many examples from both Old and New Testament texts. To get the flavor of a Levi-Straussian analysis, while discounting the element of caricature, consider what Leach calls the "facts" about sixteenth-century history that every English schoolchild knows:

a. Henry VIII was a very successful masculine King who married many wives and murdered several of them.
b. Edward VI was a very feeble masculine King who remained a virgin until his death.
c. Mary Queen of Scots was a very unsuccessful female King who married many husbands and murdered several of them.
d. Queen Elizabeth was a very successful female King who remained a virgin until her death.
e. Henry VIII enhanced his prestige by divorcing the King of Spain's daughter on the grounds that she had previously been married to his elder brother who had died a virgin.
f. Queen Elizabeth enhanced her prestige by going to war with Spain having previously declined to marry the King of Spain's son who had previously been married to her elder sister. (Leach 1969, pp. 81–2)

Here are the familiar oppositions of promiscuous king and virgin queen; marriage to and divorce from the king of Spain's daughter and refusal of marriage to the king of Spain's son; successful king and feeble queen, and all the changes that can be rung on these and other elements. They constitute mnemonics for school children and mythmakers alike, but it is not only their memorableness that is significant for Levi-Strauss. More important is the fact that transformations between myth and myth reveal a formal, deep structure of relationships. For instance, the "message" of myths is not carried in their surface, natural language meanings or morals, but rather in the meaning structures of synonymy, analogy, homology, opposition, and inversion between different but related myths. Thus, for example, we do not find the real meaning of a story like that of Abraham's aborted sacrifice of Isaac in the "morals" of obedience to God and disregard of natural family ties, but rather in the fact that this story is only one transform of others, including, for instance, the story of Jepthah and his actual sacrifice of his daughter. All of this bears on the deeper structural themes of the "true born Jew" versus the "half-blood" Jepthah, on the roles of endogamy and the consequences of exogamy, and ultimately on the legitimacy or illegitimacy of the kings of Israel (Leach 1969).

The content of the stories enters this analysis only in the sense that if stories are to be compared as transforms of each other, they must be found in roughly similar contexts. For example, in the case of Abraham and Jepthah, this is the context of vows, sacrifices, and the giving or withholding of descendants by God. Without such marginal similarity of content there would appear to be no control at all on Levi-Strauss's ingenuity in finding transformations between story and story, and his method would fall into the arbitrariness of which it is often accused. With that understanding, however, the vast variety and complexity of the webs of transformations to be found in Levi-Strauss's volumes of *Mythologiques* (1966–81) do carry a certain illumination: We exclaim, "so *that* is why these seemingly irrelevant details of the stories are present and persist through tellings and retellings." Just as in use of natural language, repetitions and redundancies may be necessary to get the message across in noisy channels, so the repetitions and transforms of myths have a similar function – they help overcome "noise" that according to Levi-Strauss is the overt surface "meaning" of each story separately, in order to uncover the real meaning, that is, the structure.

What, one may ask, is the point? If the "meaning" is so deep that it had to await Levi-Strauss's elucidation, how can it have functioned as "message" throughout the global and perennial phenomenon that is the human capacity for myth making? Levi-Strauss has two sorts of answer to this, which are not wholly consistent. First, he suggests a psychological reductionism: the effects of form are undoubtedly unconscious, and perhaps they resonate with deep structures of the mind that have emerged in human evolution alongside the capacity for myth making. But if this is to be any more than an ad hoc explanation, we need to know more about the selective value of such mythologies. Here, Levi-Strauss's analogies with music are suggestive. We are prepared to study the history and internal structure of music without asking what its evolutionary value is. Levi-Strauss is saying that myth making is like music. There is no linguistic "message," only the unconscious reception of form; its effectiveness and even the value of studying it do not depend on having an explicit causal theory about it.

On the other hand, Levi-Strauss also suggests a more substantive content for the message of myth. He notes that the common context of sets of mythic transforms is often some paradoxical situation in social life that is felt to need resolution. In Leach's example, the ramifications of the Jepthah story introduce the problem of "Who is a Jew and who is a foreigner?" Jepthah is an Israelite only on his father's side, and although he saves his pure-blooded Israelite relations, he loses his half-blood daughter and has no descendants.

Transformations and variations of this theme are found in many Old Testament myths: the writers of Kings support the rules against exogamy when they inveigh against Solomon's foreign wives, and yet the paradox of Solomon's own dubious parentage and legitimacy remains. How can he be the offspring of a non-Jewess, whose marriage moreover was made possible by murder, and at the same time be the legitimate heir? Levi-Strauss suggests that the repetition and "living out" of myths in social groups act to resolve otherwise intolerable states of contradiction and suffering, although the mechanism of such "mediation" is not known. In some way, however, myth imposes order on chaotic and unintelligible experience.

What, then, is the relation between myth and science that also imposes order on chaotic experience? Here, Levi-Strauss implicitly makes an extension of the concept of the cognitive, which is parallel to our own search for generalizations of "scientific method." All knowledge has the function of imposing coherence and order. Science does this with practical intent – it issues in causal regularities and aims at technical control. Myth making, on the other hand, meets different intellectual requirements – it introduces symbolic order into the universe. The "savage mind" (Levi-Strauss 1966) belongs to all of us in some aspects of our thinking, and works typically by formal analogies and algebraic transformations. Scientific thinking on the other hand works typically by metonyms – by regularity of cause–effect relations. If we ask about the "truth" of myth, this cannot be propositional truth, for myths are not factual descriptions or even "morally true" tales. But they are "true" if they exhibit structures similar to those of social and individual life and are thus capable of mediating and resolving contradictions. It is not that myths should be "true" of experience, but experience is lived in the context of myth that orders experience and gives it meaning.

Levi-Strauss's theory is methodologically self-reflective. If we ask what its status is as "science," it is clearly not intended to satisfy pragmatic or realist criteria. It is not a technical science. But it is "knowledge" in Levi-Strauss's own terms because it imposes order, coherence, and meaning on the phenomena of myth making. When a particular Colombian myth turns up that threatens to overturn the whole "philosophy of honey" that Levi-Strauss painfully developed in *Myth*. II, Leach (Leach 1970, p. 117) comments acidly that "one might have expected that Levi-Strauss would be somewhat disconcerted." But no; instead, he merely comments in a footnote in *Myth*. III, "The remarkable inversion . . . does not contradict our interpretation but enriches it by a supplementary dimension" (Leach 1970, p. 117). Leach remarks,

we need to remember that Levi-Strauss' prime training was in philosophy and law; he consistently behaves as an advocate defending a cause rather than as a scientist searching for ultimate truth. (Leach 1970, p. 117)

But Leach is unfair. The method is not intended to be that of technical science but can perhaps best be compared to confirmatory metaphysics – the theory is confirmed by the multiplicity of mythic examples that are illuminated but is not falsifiable by them. It is indeed itself the (or a) myth, not the science, of mythology.

What are the consequences of Levi-Strauss's structuralism for a theory of religion? Ricoeur (1974, p. 27) objected that Levi-Strauss only considers totemic religions and not those of the dynamic societies (Indo-European, Sumerian, and Semitic) that have become the advanced world religions of today. Yet, these religions are also defined by their myths – as is evident, for example, from the impoverishment of the content of the New Testament under Bultmannian "demythologising." It is precisely the mythological elements in world religions, along with their apparently transcendental reference, that makes them alien to the scientific world and is therefore most in need of elucidation.

What is most interesting in Levi-Strauss's theory is that it offers the chance of finding common themes in the symbolism of different cultures and thus of rescuing us from the relativism that was threatened by symbolism. Levi-Strauss is right to point out that significant common themes will not be found in the overt content of the myths of different peoples. Schemes of life–death–resurrection, sin–punishment–forgiveness, defilement and purification, may recur, but the particular stories about how these perennial human problems are resolved are different and contradictory. From a generalizing viewpoint, there can be no question of asking which story is true. Levi-Strauss's analysis warns us that the abstract themes of life, death, sin, and so on that appear to be common to all cultures do not go deep enough. There is no simple decoding of mythic symbolism into abstract moralisms: "people destroy themselves by hubris"; "all will come right in the end." The paradoxes of human life go deeper than the possibility of such propositional resolution. According to Levi-Strauss, they require the overt tension of opposites and their transformations to make the paradoxes explicit and bearable. What appears as contradiction in natural language must be mediated by symbols that are nonpropositional and nonparaphrasable. It follows that demythologized symbols will be incapable, for good or ill, of performing their specific functions.

Paradoxes are expressed not only in mythological formulation but also in the theological statements of advanced religions: God is three and he is one; Christ is both God and man; evil and death are both endemic and victorious in human life, and by suffering them, they can be overcome. Seen from the rational and scientific point of view, these are contradictions to be resolved by logical argument; seen from a structuralist point of view, their ramification into further propositions will not resolve an argument but will contribute to further myth making. The only type of understanding possible is that engendered by myth. The theory has, of course, many affinities with the concepts of dialectical logic, in which thesis transforms endlessly into antithesis and synthesis, and for which there is no final propositional resolution in history.

In advanced religions, however, myths and theologies must *also* be taken to some extent at their face value, since with the development of discursive thought, they are intentionally given both overt story-morals and content for which propositional truth is claimed. In a masterly critique of Levi-Strauss in relation to Greek myth, Kirk rejects any "universalizing theory of myth" which excludes face-value meanings, but concludes that Levi-Strauss has uncovered at least part of its explanation:

From now on it will always be necessary to consider the possibility that any myth, even in the western tradition, may turn out to provide a model for mediating a contradiction, in terms of structure as well as content – along, of course, with other possibilities, such as that it is a charter myth, or is concerned with fertility and the seasons, or with the representation of fears and beliefs about the world of the dead. . . . Sometimes myth will fulfill several of these functions at once. (Kirk 1970, p. 83)

10.5 Varieties of religious evidence

We started this chapter by asking the question, "What are the constraints and criteria for the success of social schemas?" We are now in a position to summarize the answers to this question suggested in the particular case of religious schemas by the four types of theory we have discussed.

1. *Intellectualist:* the criteria of success are modeled on natural science – explanation, prediction and control of nature, and also, perhaps, of human beings in a scientific sense.
2. *Functionalist:* the criteria are modeled on biological science – cohesion, stability, and survival of social groups.
3. *Symbolist:* the criteria are modeled on hermeneutics – social understanding and communication, the imposition of meaning and a unified world view on both nature and culture.

4. *Structuralist:* the criteria are like those of confirmatory metaphysics – the imposition of order and tolerability on paradoxical human situations, perhaps by psychological effects that mediate the contradictions involved.

In Chapter 1, we suggested that schema theory might provide a framework for understanding religion and other cognitive systems that would incorporate some insights of recent philosophy of science. We have begun to see how this framework helps unify the apparently diverse methodologies of natural science, natural evolution by selection, psychoanalysis, and hermeneutics. In the light of this chapter, we can extend the list to symbolist and structuralist theories of religion. In regard to religion as understood in our society, however, two special problems seem to set it apart from the natural and social schemas we have discussed. The first problem is its individual character, and the second is the apparent immutability of its sacred texts, doctrines, and creeds.

Whitehead (1926, p. 16) once described religion as "what the individual does with his solitariness," and William James limited his discussion in *The Varieties of Religious Experience* to the religious experience of "religious geniuses," beside which the "conventional observances of . . . country" are merely habitual and second-hand (James 1960, p. 29). Such modern individualism is far from the social emphasis we have so far given. But we must not neglect the fact that in a pluralist and rationalist age like our own, most of the direct "tests" of a religion will be the experience of individuals and their judgments about what beliefs, if any, to commit themselves to, and what, if any, religious groups to join. In fact, as we noted in Chapter 1, parallels have often been drawn between the experimental evidence for scientific theory and the evidence for religious belief as tested in people's experience. Indeed, in the protestant tradition, such lived experience is often seen to be in conflict with social religious forms.

We have seen in a general way in Chapter 7 how sets of individually embodied schemas define a person, while a set of shared schemas define a community. But what makes a schema shared? We have seen that, although individual schemas may differ as internal aspects of brain and mind, overt behavior can be brought into greater congruence by shared rituals and shared texts. Whether in science or religion, we bring certain schemas to the reading or performance; in the process, these schemas are changed and added to. A religious text may be convincing because the stories resonate with personal experience or show how people of faith dealt with problems that had seemed insoluble. To the extent that people recognize the accounts of others' experiences as similar to their own, they begin to form social networks in which people can recognize commodities that were not named before. The resultant language may then enable them to move to an ideology or a religion that makes sense of their experiences and even to recognition of experiences they have not shared before but only heard reports of. Few people have transcendent spiritual experiences, just as few of us have verified the constancy of the velocity of light, yet we accept a relativity theory that presupposes this constancy. In a similar way, ritual may enable religious believers who lack direct experiences of Jesus or Nirvana to relate beliefs about them to the meaning of everyday experience and its problems, whether social, moral, emotional, or aesthetic. Some of these problems, of course, may only be real for people who have already internalized the religion; for example, the Christian language of guilt and salvation. The religious text and rituals become and remain convincing because they help believers cope with anxiety, guilt, anger, and the reality of death. Believers will no doubt still invest the text with a wide range of individual meanings, but the role of the religious institution will be to provide a structure of ritual and interpretation that can sufficiently restrict this process of individualization to maintain a community of intersubjectivity.

In modern secular societies, however, individuals may maintain a critical distance from the institution and may even combine membership of a believing community with considerable intellectual questioning and doubt. In *The Heretical Imperative*, Peter Berger (Berger 1980) offers a useful classification of the options that now face a believer in relation to the tradition of Christianity: "they can reaffirm the authority of the tradition in defiance of the challenges to it; they can try to secularize the tradition; or they can try to uncover and retrieve the experiences embodied in the tradition" (Berger 1980, p. xi).

Berger calls his three options deductivisim, reductionism, and inductivism, recalling three methodologies of theory construction in natural science. Barth, for example, treats knowledge of God rather as a rationalist metaphysician might treat his *a priori* principles: they are accepted by "faith" that is detached from ordinary experience, and in their terms ordinary experience must be interpreted willy-nilly. Bultmann, on the other hand, attempts a reduction of the mythological elements of Christian belief to the categories of individual psychology, rather as a positivist might try to reduce scientific theory to direct observations or to sense data. Berger's third option accords better with the concept of "tracing out the symbolic network" we have adopted. He describes it thus:

The inductive option is to turn to experience as the ground of all religious affirmations – one's own experience, to whatever extent this is possible, and the experience embodied in a particular range of traditions . . . induction means here that religious traditions are understood as bodies of evidence concerning religious experience and the insights deriving from experience. Implied in this option is a deliberately empirical attitude, a weighing and assessing frame of mind – not necessarily cool and dispassionate, but unwilling to impose closure on the quest for religious truth by invoking any authority whatever. (Berger 1980, pp. 62–3)

Entry into the network of belief can be made at many points; communities and individuals will differ. But the general inductivist categories remain valid: to be a believer is to adopt and live by a network of meanings that arise from individual and social experience, permeated by the interpretations of a religious schema and internalized in terms of a certain standpoint of faith and commitment. This account harmonizes well with the Piagetian description of how the child comes to acquire its networks of schemas. There also are parallels with scientific induction in the sense that we start epistemologically with experience, but experience is not what either science or faith are in the end all about. What they are about, if successful, is Reality, the external natural world, or the transcendent nonnatural world in the case of religion.

Religious systems receive reinforcement from various types of experience, which afford external support as well as addressing the internal coherence of the system. There is even the possibility of falsification of religious or ideological beliefs. For example, failure of the Stalinist USSR to work out the ideals of Marxist development led many people to abandon their Marxism. Moreover, since no one ideology exhausts the network of belief, ideas from one schema may provide the test that leads to the rejection of another schema – as criteria of democracy and social justice led many Czechs to abandon their socialist convictions after the Soviet invasion of 1968. Similarly for religions – but the experiences that disconfirm an ideology or a religion will be highly complex and highly personal, lacking the power of scientific falsification to compel general assent in the long run. The death of a child may lead one parent to turn fervently to God for consolation, whereas another parent may come to see as empty any concept of a deity that would countenance such human tragedy.

Such examples indicate important disanalogies with scientific induction. These disanalogies derive primarily from the overriding goals of science, not shared by religion, to satisfy the rigorous pragmatic criterion and to construct the "objectivized" natural world as a means to that end. Religious systems do not make detailed testable predictions of an objectively recognizable kind, and data such as those cited by Berger and William James cannot be seen as hard data in the sense of the sciences. The data may be interpreted differently on different occasions and cannot be reproduced at will in order to test religious theory. The idea of praying for the patients in one half of a hospital and not for those in the other half does not strike the religious person as a proper test – for the believer, God is not to be controlled as the environment might be controlled in setting up an artificial experiment. Moreover, as in the case of the argument from design, many apparently religious interpretations of experience may come to be given a scientific explanation and are, therefore, not unambiguous evidence for religion.

The absence of intersubjective tests of religious belief implies that a distinction must be made between the *causes* of and the *reasons* for such belief in a more radical way than is the case for science. There is, of course, a causal relation between people's scientific observation and the results of experiments, and their coming to believe in certain scientific theories. Data impinge on senses and are processed by the brain. But just because scientific data are by definition intersubjective, they can be cited as public reasons for belief and their descriptions can be placed among the inductive premises in theoretical reasoning. The individual "data" of religious experience, however, cannot be treated like this because their subjective and theory-laden character is not controlled by public agreement and public tests. Thus, causal accounts of how individuals come to religious belief may be very varied – they may include upbringing, or persuasive reasoning, or a fervent conversion experience, or as the resolution of a long period of doubt. People may come to believe because they find it comforting to go to church on Sundays or find a congenial social group at the church.

Reasons for religious belief are, however, a much more complex matter. We have described in general terms how a variety of sorts of experience and interaction enable individual schemas to integrate with social schemas and how these schemas get stabilized relative to the whole complex of social life. In modern societies, however, there is a great deal of flexibility and looseness of fit between the social institutions of belief and individual belief schemas. If we ask from the perspective of the individual, "What is it rational for me to believe?" we have not only to address the question of what counts as "rational" for religious and other ideological beliefs, but also what sense can be given here to the concept of "belief" itself.

Let us suppose we had good explanations of how religious institutions and beliefs function in society and how in interaction with other social institutions they form the symbolic underpinning of a way of life. We might then develop sets of criteria for the "goodness" of a belief system in terms either of what are regarded as its beneficial effects within this way of life or of what creates an effective basis for its necessary moral critique. Suppose, further, that we had good psychological explanations of how individual beliefs form mature and stable personalities and enable people to live with the recurrent ups and downs of life. Such criteria will, of course, be to some extent circular, because what counts as "beneficial," or "mature," or in need of "critique," is itself part of the symbolic network. But such circularity need not necessarily invalidate judgments about a holistic system, so long as there is somewhere the opportunity for experience to impinge. Then, from an external, descriptive point of view we should have a set of criteria for the "goodness" of a symbolic belief system, and that would give a sense in which individual commitment to such a system is "rational."

In fact, of course, we do not have such complete explanations, although we have given some reasons for thinking that the total *absence* of symbolic systems is not possible for a society, and that some such systems are clearly worse than others from a standpoint that can be shared by most human beings. We have, then, at least some reasons for rejecting some belief systems and for rejecting also the positivist belief that myth and symbol are always subjective irrelevancies. We can now extend the notion of "reasons" to the individuals who find that their schemas, as dependent on and integrated with some social forms to be found in their environment, do satisfy a number of the criteria of goodness recognized by outsiders for symbolic systems in general. The individuals may then be rationally justified in asserting the beliefs and entering the relevant institutional life, even though their evidence is largely personal and they have few theoretical explanations to give of the efficacy of their commitment. From the individual's point of view, "belief" then refers to their stance of commitment to symbolic system and to institution; this commitment is exhibited in the appropriate personal and social behavior. Note that although the individual's psychological state of mind, feelings of conviction by specific religious experiences, and so on, certainly enter into these rational criteria as ways in which external experience gets a grip on the holistic system, they are by no means sufficient in themselves. They may even at times be judged illusory by the institution, as in some cases of claims to "private revelation," which have been judged heretical. In any case, such experiences have to be expressed to become publicly known, and the expression has to be in some form of language or symbol that is part of the social institution.

We have been using the word "belief" in this chapter in this essentially public sense. But it is still an outsider's concept and does not satisfy the believer's own sense of believing something as *true,* whatever the varied causes and grounds for it may be in individual cases, and whatever the consensus or lack of it within the public domain. The sense in which we have used "belief" is clearly not the sense in which we would say we have justified belief in a scientific conclusion – namely, that we have tested the evidence empirically, or accept the arguments of those who have. And yet, the sense of "belief" in which religions have been traditionally "believed" is nearer to our sense of scientific belief than it is to the social belief systems we have been describing. As we said earlier, in respect of his reality, "God is more like gravitation than embarrassment." The distinctions between different kinds of cognitive system we now find ourselves constrained to make must also imply distinctions between different kinds of "beliefs," or at least different kinds of rational grounds for believing.

We have argued that scientific belief and practice are not directly and unproblematically empirical and not wholly propositional, and that there is a continuum of kinds of cognitive system rather than sharp distinctions among the scientific, the hermeneutic, the moral, and the symbolic. The same arguments suggest a family resemblance concept of "rational belief" – empirical and propositional at one end of the spectrum and socially and psychologically based at the other. In the case of religious and some ideological beliefs, however, there is a special problem that we call the "believer's dilemma." It may be put like this:

Either
1. The import of religious systems is exhausted by social and psychological criteria exhibited by their effects;

Or
2. The import of religious systems lies in their truth, or more specifically in their successful reference to how things are in a Reality that extends beyond the spatio-temporal;

But
3. It is generally the case that the effects mentioned in (1) have as a necessary condition that (2) is actually *believed* (for example, prayer is unlikely to have the relevant psychological effects unless it is believed to be an address to God).

Premise (1), however, is a reduction that leaves no room for (2). Thus if (1) comes to be accepted, believers lose their faith. But abandoning religious belief altogether would probably be at the cost of whatever social and psychological benefits there may be, because there do not seem to be any satisfactory substitutes for the religious function in modern societies. Or, more cynically, the dilemma may be taken as a practical reason on the part of authority for preaching (2) while acting on (1) and of restricting intellectual debate among the populace while manipulating their ideology in established interests. If both these options are rejected, is it possible to accept (where appropriate) the functional explanations of (1), while maintaining the possible truth of religious belief as in (2)? Provided we can make the concept of their truth intelligible (a question we address in the next chapter), there seems to be no necessary logical contradiction in this. Just as we have described a "two-way" analysis for other cases in which one-way reductions are insufficient, there is no reason why the content of particular religious beliefs cannot be maintained as true while also having their functional effects, where these may be direct or indirect, manifest or latent.

We are left with the problem of making the character of religious truth intelligible. But before tackling this question, we must consider one more comparison with scientific theory. It often seems that the essence of a religious belief is its dogmatic, authoritarian, and inflexible character. It seems not to be responsive to criticism or new evidence or interpretation as scientific theory is supposed to be. We say "supposed to be" because recent analyses of paradigms, scientific conservatism, and even vested interests have shown that theory is not totally flexible and indeed cannot be if it is to operate as a framework for natural knowledge. But it is true that scientific explanations and cosmologies come and go, under pressure of evidence as well as other things, and that criticism and testability are built into the accepted ideal of science.

Religious systems appear to be strikingly different. The main distinctions that have been canvassed in social anthropology between so-called "traditional" and modern thought are that the former is not held to be open to falsification, and the concept of experimentation is practically absent. In this respect, modern religion looks more traditional than modern. On the other hand, when outside observers look at Christian theology, they are often surprised to discover how diverse the beliefs of theologians and laypeople can be. As Berger suggests in the passage quoted above, a religious believer can accept that, as in science, religious knowledge evolves, although the evolution will take place in interaction with traditions. A religious believer may hold to the Reality of God while allowing for the changing religious language and commitments of different periods and different cultures. Monolithic as statements of Christian belief may seem across the centuries, even the most cursory historical investigation shows how varied their interpretations have been, and changing and conflicting interpretations continue to be matters of discussion and dispute. No theology need be supposed to give the final word on religious reality.

On the other hand, it must be remembered that religious systems are more comprehensive than scientific cosmologies in their interactions with personal and social life. Just because symbolisms are internally tightly knit and externally variously effective, balances of intelligible meaning within the network cannot be entirely disrupted without risk of wider social collapse. This fact is seen most obviously in the attempts to replace traditional symbolisms by modern states and modern education in non-Western cultures. Symbolisms grow organically and cannot be put together by explicit mechanical blueprints. Moreover, the complex of evidence relevant to a religion includes its own and others' traditions; and because symbolic systems interweave content closely with causation and rational evidence, no rational approach to religion can neglect the particular myths and creedal formulations of particular traditions. To rewrite creeds or even to retranslate sacred texts and liturgies in what is intended to be "modern idiom" can have effects on tacit complexes of meaning and personal interpretation that may be quite unintended. The whole system may be rendered meaningless in a modern or any other idiom, or it may unwittingly be given confused and contradictory meanings.

A responsible religious institution should not risk such consequences without some assurance that new formulations are going to be better than the old, bearing in mind the great variety of criteria of "goodness" that are relevant. What is at stake is more like the effects of the Copernican revolution than like the replacement of particular technical scientific paradigms. We have seen that there were at that time cogent reasons of a social and moral nature for not undertaking the revolution lightly, in spite of such empirical evidence as was then available. The issue of mutability of religions cannot, however, be discussed usefully in general terms; it needs illustration and argument in particular cases. In the next chapter, we therefore take a particular tradition, the Judeo–Christian one, and consider some reasons for maintaining its symbolisms, myths, and naïve stories in conjunction with a readiness, if necessary, to reinterpret these on an abstract theological or philosophical level.

11   The Great Schema

11.1 Myth and history

In this chapter, we turn to consider explicitly the Bible as religious text, regarding this as a complex and holistic symbol system that, roughtly speaking, constructs the worlds of Judaic and Christian religion. We have two purposes in mind here. First, we want to exhibit some workings of a symbol system in this particular case. Second, we want to use the Bible to address two problems that have dogged our discussion of schemas and symbolisms throughout: the problems of relativism and transcendence. Can Biblical religion be seen as anything but another functional or chance manifestation of particular societies at particular times, or can we give some sense to its claim to universality, to be speaking truly of a transcendent God?

In considering the Bible as an internally knit symbol system, we are, of course, following the tradition of hermeneutics in social theory (of which indeed Biblical hermeneutics was the first example) and in social anthropology. This approach first became explicit in the nineteenth century; it should be noted, however, that in the mainstream of interpretation, the Bible has never been taken only as a "naïve story" or as factual history. The texts established (with more or less minor variations) in the canon by the third century A.D. were already chosen for a variety of theological, moral, and political as well as historical reasons. The concept of historical narrative in our sense was not unknown to the Biblical writers (it appears, for instance, in the Chronicles of the Kings of Israel and in the Acts of the Apostles), but it is not generally their primary concern. In particular, stories such as those in Genesis of the creation and of the patriarchs of Israel are typical of the foundational myths of all peoples: They happened "in the beginning," "once upon a time." They were not intended as factual history or science; indeed, such purposes were not recognized as separable from their mythic character and would not have been regarded as of great importance taken in isolation from myth.

The literalist or fundamentalist approach to Biblical history only became possible with the rationalization of theology that occurred with the ingression of Greek thought. Theologians from Origen onward began to distinguish levels of interpretation: historical facts, typological repetitions (the motifs of Exodus and Return, Death and Resurrection are continually repeated throughout human history), and allegory (the story of Abraham and Isaac, for instance, as a reflection of God's dealing with humanity). When historical accuracy began to be questioned in the nineteenth century, this came as a shock to believers only because the earlier sophistication of interpretation had been forgotten in the course of the rationalizations of intervening centuries. A confusion is common here between "literal inspiration" of the Biblical text by God and the question of historical truth. Literal inspiration is an ancient belief and is common to all religions based on sacred texts. However, it does not imply fundamentalist historical interpretation. God, like the writers of the texts themselves, is perfectly capable of metaphor and irony and of having interests in mythic functions other than those of historical accuracy.

We need not pause long over modern literalism and fundamentalism, which are clearly dependent for their force on the kind of literalism, empiricism, and scientism it has been a main task of this volume to combat. On the other hand, there is a sense in which the Bible *does* take history seriously, and this sense makes it different from a collection of moral fables. Because typologies imply analogies between different events in history and interpret these events as God's regular and dependable acts, it is essential that there should really be such acts in history, whether exactly as reported in the type repetitions or in some other way. Typology implies that where in history there is sin, God sends the consequences of it; where there is victory, joy, and salvation, God gives it; where there is suffering and death, God is in the midst of it. Literal historical accuracy may be abrogated by mythic interpretations; the significance of history as such is not.

Another point may be made about modern fundamentalism. We live in a culture in which myth is altogether devalued, and fashionable religion itself is in danger of losing touch with its traditional texts and rituals in the supposed interest of "social relevance." If there is any truth at all in Levi-Strauss's interpretation of the importance of repetition and transformation of mythic structures, it follows that the core myths of the Bible cannot be lost sight of without loss of identity of the religion itself. If it takes fundamentalism to carry on this tradition in a secular age, then so be it; the Lord moves in mysterious ways.

Nineteenth-century historical hermeneutics attempted to repossess the original horizons in which the Biblical texts were written and particularly to establish the dates and historical circumstances of the various Biblical books. Such historical study indicated that the story was never told as naïve historical fact. The Gospels, for example, were never intended to be a biography of Jesus but were structured to show how the events of his life fulfilled Old Testament prophecy and how they could be used to address the problems of the early Church. Thus, the order of events and the significance put on them differs from Gospel to Gospel.

Such critique had the result of exposing not only the nonhistorical character of much of the Biblical text, but also the alien character of its myth and symbolism. The effort to "understand" in participant terms has become a more and more esoteric exercise of theological schools rather than something of direct relevance to the ordinary believer, much less to the secular world. But interestingly enough, the task has recently been taken up in the secular world, in an attempt to repossess the horizons of the Bible within the study of European literature and by means of the tools of structuralism.

Northrop Frye's *The Great Code* (1982) traces out the symbolic network of meanings that constitutes the Biblical world and provides a timely holistic antidote to the atomistic tendencies of analytic Biblical criticism, with its concentration on the local time and circumstances of the Bible's many books (St. John's Gospel in 50 or 100 A.D.?) and the multiplicity of authors of each one (how many Isaiahs?). Frye's book is a recovery of the Bible as a whole in the mode of literary structuralism, rather than in the mode of analytical history. This is why we adapt Frye's title for this chapter and use the term *Great Schema* to indicate how an approach to the Bible similar to his can exemplify our program for a schema theory of religious symbolisms.

At this point we must consider how the concept of "myth" has entered Biblical hermeneutics. Our account of the sophisticated theories of myth found in social anthropology has prepared us for interpretations far removed from the most usual sense of "myth" in common parlance, where it generally means "false or fictional story." We have noted that when nineteenth-century theologians and believers understood Genesis as a "mythological" story about the creation, they did not mean that it is a "fairy tale" or merely an interesting fiction. Its writers rather sought to express in narrative form certain understandings of the meaning of the world – that it was created, that it is essentially good, that it did not exist from all eternity. The story is told in such a way that it has consequences for human action. It provides a meaningful framework for human life.

The Greek lexicon of Liddell and Scott (1849) has a long article on *mythos*. The first meaning is "anything given by word of mouth." It then goes on to other meanings: "A speech in a public assembly," "a tale, story, narrative, e.g. the Odyssey, without distinction of true or false." In this last sense, the narrative might be historical or a legend. In Plato's *Timaeus*, a myth is "a likely story," but not necessarily true. Rather, it contains certain true features of the world. Eventually, *mythos* comes to share with the Latin *fabula* the sense of a fiction, and it then becomes a legend, mostly of a religious kind. Thus, "myth" is a complex concept with a rich history to which we have to be sensitive. In our culture, we have picked up the last of these meanings and opposed myth to truth. But theologians view Genesis as a myth in a sense that recaptures some of its earlier connotations – it tells a serious significant story that conveys truths not in the sense of history or natural science but truths in that they are part of a whole system for viewing values and meaning.

Nineteenth-century Biblical scholarship noted the many parallels between the Bible and traditional mythologies, examples of which were coming to be known from all over the world. Merely to assimilate Biblical myths to those of Homer and other primitive societies would have been embarrassing, especially in a climate in which historical scholarship was striving for "scientific" status, putting a premium on empirical facts. To abandon the Bible to myth would have been to repudiate its essential historicity; on the other hand, its far-reaching structural similarity with other mythologies and increasingly rigorous historical research seemed to preclude its interpretation as literal history. The general response to this dilemma was to adopt the term *myth* with positive connotations that excluded the implication of "fiction" or "falsehood." Perhaps the best early expression of this meaning was given by Baden-Powell in 1889:

[Myth is] a doctrine expressed in a narrative form, an abstract moral or spiritual truth dramatised in action and personification; where the object is to enforce faith not in the *parable* but in the *moral*. . . . Thus, every dogma is more or less a myth, as it is necessarily conveyed in analogical language and anthropomorphic action. (Quoted in Wiles 1977, p. 153)

That this baptism of the term did not take effect in popular understanding of "myth" in English is indicated by the reception of the book *The Myth of God Incarnate*, from which the above quotation is taken. This book was widely interpreted to show that its authors had abandoned the doctrine of the incarnation as false. This was in spite of the essay by Maurice Wiles that outlined how the term *myth* has been used in theology for a century.

Popular understanding is, however, perhaps not willfully blind, for the question of whether this "theological" use of "myth" expresses a coherent concept is the same question we have been facing here, namely, whether "social constructions" can be judged by rational criteria other than those of objectified fact, both scientific or historical. Because of lurking uneasiness with the concept, theologians have frequently sought to make categorial distinctions between Biblical and other mythologies, by, for example, emphasizing the historical particularity of most of its central stories, at least in the New Testament, and thereby making a virtue out of their consequent openness to falsification by historical research. Northrop Frye's comment on this procedure is apt:

Biblical scholars . . . are well aware that the Bible will only confuse and exasperate a historian who tries to treat it as a history. One wonders why in that case their obsession with the Bible's historicity does not relax, so that other and more promising hypotheses could be examined . . . perhaps we should be looking for different categories and criteria altogether. (Frye 1982, p. 44)

It is interesting to note that Frye himself adopts a very liberal understanding of the term: "myth to me means, first of all, *mythos,* plot, narrative, or in general the sequential ordering of words" (Frye 1982, p. 31). Later, he specifies a more particular use in a way similar to that of the theologians: "Certain stories seem to have a particular significance: they are the stories that tell a society what is important for it to know, whether about its gods, its history, its laws, or its class structure. These stories may be called myths in a secondary sense" (Frye 1982, pp. 32–33). This is a sense that makes them sacred rather than profane stories.

What distinguishes a myth from a mere story is that a myth is *effective* – people who live within its perspective are given means to control social and emotional reality. In traditional belief systems, myth was also regarded as effective *in nature;* indeed, in such beliefs, "society" and "nature" were not sharply distinguished. Myth was therefore involved with natural magic and with protoscience. For example, the cabalists believed that Deuteronomy gave them access to certain formulas for controlling spiritual forces, whether for alchemy or moral perfection. Belief in the Bible as potential magic has been abandoned in secular societies. Also, its public power has largely been lost – the power that came when most people not only believed it, but also lived by it and controlled reality by means of it. The function of religious mythology has now largely been taken over by scientific mythology – the paradigm cognitive system that aims at controlling the world by the pragmatic criterion. Hence, there is a deep sense of incompatibility between science and religion. It is not so much that the two systems are logically contradictory, but simply that whatever religion says does not seem to have the slightest influence on the truth or falsity of science, or vice versa, and science has become the touchstone of serious inquiry about the nature of the world.

Perhaps the most influential attempt to overcome this apparent incompatibility within modern theology is Bultmann's program of "demythologizing" the New Testament. This program is misunderstood if it is regarded simply as an elimination of all but objective facts from the Biblical text. In his short paper "New Testament and Mythology," Bultmann defines what he means by "myth." Myth, he says, has a function "to express man's understanding of himself in the world in which he lives" (Bultmann 1953, p. 10). This use has no pejorative connotations; indeed, it is inevitable in this sense that even in a scientific society people must have myths, just as, for example, Althusser and Balibar (1970) have held that even in the liberated society a person will have ideologies. Bultmann discusses the question of how a mythical understanding of existence can be *true.* One test of the truth of the Biblical myths is that they should be consistent with the *kerygma,* that is, with the gospel proclamation of salvation in Christ and the accompanying call to repentance and new life. This is an existential matter, which may be separated from the mythical form in which it is presented in the New Testament. Gadamer (1975, p. 473) points out that Bultmann's judgments of bad myths are informed much more directly by the *kerygma* than by Enlightenment points of view that reject all that is not scientific.

Bultmann distinguishes between "mythology" and "myth." Mythology is the taking of myth at face value as objectively valid. For example, this is done when the familiar story of God who sent his son to live as a man, though still God, who suffered to effect our redemption, who died and rose again and ascended into heaven, is taken as if it were the story of an old man in the sky who . . . and so on. But might mythology in this sense also be inevitable? Perhaps we cannot speak of God except in images that get distorted in this way into mythology? To this objection, Bultmann replied that we must not imply that God acts alongside other worldly happenings, for this would be to "objectify" God:

The only way to preserve the unworldly, transcendental character of the divine activity is to regard it not as an interference in worldly happenings, but something accomplished *in* them in such a way that the closed weft of history as it presents itself to objective observation is left undisturbed. To every eye other than the eye of faith the action of God is hidden. (Bultmann 1953, p. 197)

We must speak of God in analogical myths, but not in literally interpreted mythologies. For Bultmann, the primary analogy is experience of direct encounter with God, and this encounter does not make any factual difference to the world but enables us to "understand . . . in such a way that the whole world appears in a new light," (Bultmann 1953, p. 203) as in the human experience of "being in love."

Bultmann founded his analogical approach to God via experience of the existentialist categories of Heidegger's metaphysics. Thus, his distinction between "true" analogical myths and "mythologies" becomes a distinction between what he takes to be the "true" existentialist metaphysics on the one hand and misleading figures of speech on the other. He distinguishes both of these from the proper use of scientific "facts." Our approach, on the other hand, would find more continuity between "scientific" and "mythical" thinking, since both are constructions of worlds subject to various kinds of internal and external self-correction. We should also beware of too sharp a distinction between true "metaphysical myths" on the one hand and falsely objectified "mythologies" on the other. We can agree with Bultmann that "myths" are a necessary and pervasive form of human thinking, but we would doubt whether any particular metaphysics can guarantee the truth of myths, and we would not dismiss metaphorical mythologies as merely false objectifications. All mythic systems are metaphorical and symbolic – the question of what sort of criterion should be adopted for religious myths will not be solved by looking for a single adequate metaphysics, but by recognizing holistic criteria embodied in particular times and places. The Bible can be read like that with respect to its own times and places, and its resonances can be traced in ours.

11.2 The Bible as symbol system

The structuralist writers have given us a deeper perspective on the meaning of symbolism than was present in attempts merely to "decode" or "demythologize." Frye re-emphasises the importance of the unique typological structure of the Biblical corpus, and Levi-Strauss directs attention away from context and surface meaning to purely formal deep structure. These two approaches need not be interpreted as contradictory. We have seen that even Levi-Strauss has to notice some context for his myths in order to provide some constraints on which myths are appropriately regarded as transforms of which. Moreover, if we are to take his suggestion about the "mediation of paradox" seriously, then the "face-value" meaning of the paradoxes and oppositions of social and individual life are also integral parts of the structural interpretation of culture/nature.

Levi-Strauss's transformations are not really "formal." They are based on resemblances and transformations of resemblances in homology, opposition, multiple inversion. We may see structural interpretations of symbol systems as lying on a continuum. First, there are parallelisms of face-value meaning, as exemplified by Frye in the series of stories in Judges, in which Israel "deserts its God, gets enslaved, cries to its God for deliverance, and a judge is sent to deliver it" (Frye 1982, p. 40). Second, there are the allegorical "types"; for example, the Exodus, the return from Babylon, the return of Christ from the grave, the ritual rising of the believer from the waters of baptism. Third, there are the common "morals" to be gleaned from a diversity of myths and parables: We must rise "from sin to a new life"; "as we deal with our neighbor so God will deal with us," and its converse (more prominent in the New Testament) "as God *has* dealt with us in grace, so let us deal with our neighbour." Fourth, there is what Dante called the "anagogical" meaning and Frye the "sacramental," namely, the transcendental religious facts to which the stories point: "We *have* risen to a new life and *shall* enjoy the glory of heaven"; "the last enemy that *shall* be destroyed is death." This is a sequence of increasingly "abstract" and transcendental meanings. However, we should not neglect Levi-Strauss's implicit warning: When they are put in abstract and apparently propositional terms, these interpretations always land in contradiction, unless they are so simplistic as to neglect the real tensions and paradoxes of human experience. These tensions can only be taken into full account by telling stories with *contradictory* morals and expressing paradoxical transcendental "truths": "God *is* good and all-powerful, *and yet* permits evil," "sin *is* ineradicable from human history and of deep seriousness"; *and yet* "All shall be well, and all manner of thing shall be well."

These considerations point to the need to maintain a core of "naïve stories" with face-value meanings through the subsequent rationalizing and theologizing. Just as Levi-Strauss takes "the meaning" of a mythic corpus (like the Oedipus myth) to be its original manifestations *plus* all the rewritings, analyses, and explanations subsequently given, including his own and those of his successors, so "the meaning of the Bible" is contained in the text *and* in all subsequent commentary. Consistently with his scientific and nonevaluative stance, Levi-Strauss has nothing to say about how to distinguish "good" from "bad" commentary. Is Cecil B. de Mille of equal value with Karl Barth? But this is a question that adherents of a religious corpus will be bound to ask. We have indicated how it may be answered in a variety of kinds of feedback experience, which will, of course (contra Levi-Strauss), involve some face-value interpretation of the original myths.

Certainly, the original stories cannot be abandoned without destroying the meaning of the whole network. They can be interpreted and re-interpreted, historically analyzed and contradicted, and given a variety of conflicting theological expressions. Such commentary, as Frye puts it, will be "heavily conditioned by the phases of language ascendant in their time" (Frye 1982, p. 227), and the original text is likely to persist through these historical phases longer than the commentary. But, one may object, is not the Bible itself such a set of interpretations, reinterpretations, and commentaries? Are they not equally of their own time? Why, then, should the Biblical text hold a privileged position? To this query, we may reply along the lines of our discussion of scientific realism. Just as we retain the stabilized "form" of inductive generalizations and expectations from the past local success of science, through all subsequent revolutions of concepts and theory, so a religion will retain the particular naïve stories that have adequately expressed the experience and aspiration of some human beings in its past, through subsequent changes of theological commentary. The Biblical canon may be regarded as the product of this process over a period and a breadth of experience large enough to guarantee some stability, though no doubt with fuzzy edges. Whether it continues to satisfy these criteria and therefore to define a religious tradition, or whether changing experience will cause the demise of Biblical religion, is for the future to decide. What cannot be done, consistently with our understanding of symbol systems, is to excise the core of Biblical text and claim one has an updated version of Biblical "insights" carrying the same tradition and authority. Such a proceeding is also subject to the test of future survival, and the future will undoubtedly decide and then decide again.

A symbol system can only be understood and evaluated by entering its web of internal relationships and noting how and where external criteria impinge on it. The problem is that we cannot start with the complex whole all at once; and if we start at any one point, we immediately introduce distortions. We therefore pick some limited topics in the Biblical schema to illustrate how it works; we do this by following up two of the contradictions that form a large part of Biblical concern. The first contradiction, which arises directly from our discussion of the apparent relativity of symbol systems as social constructs, is the theme of "priest and prophet." The other contradiction is the more fundamental issue of evil, salvation, and destiny, which it is the primary purpose of the Bible to address and which has arisen from our concerns with the search for grounds of human value within a secular and scientific environment.

First, then, we take the topic in the Biblical schema that goes under the rubric "priest and prophet." To see why this topic is an appropriate link with our previous discussion, consider where our description of social schemas left us. Religion, we concluded, is holistic not just in its internal meaning relations, but also in that it is primarily a social and not an individual phenomenon. Even so-called "world religions" therefore seem tied to particular social and environmental contexts, and it seems impossible to make sense of their own claims to transcendence and perennial validity.

The problem arose within the Biblical schema itself. When the pagan religions were confronted by Israel on its entry into the promised land, the crucial question arose: Is Jahweh one among the gods, a social totem to be carried in Israel's wars? Or is he God, the transcendent one, the one outside all categories, all social myths: "I am that I am," or, in another interpretation, "I will (to) be that I will (to) be"? The priests of Israel maintained the social cult but were too liable to act as though their God were just one among the gods, to worship sticks and stones rather than Him, to go astray with the kings and the false prophets and the people. Against them rose the true prophets: Moses, Amos, Hosea, Isaiah, Jeremiah, who recalled priests and people to the God of righteousness, the God beside whom there is no other, beside whom the gods of the heathen are vanity. These prophets recalled the people to righteousness from the unthinking routine of the religious cult; as later did Jesus, whom Christians regard, among other things, as the culmination of the prophetic tradition. Thus, Hosea: "I desired mercy and not sacrifice, and the knowledge of God more than burnt offerings" (6.6); and Isaiah: "Your new moons and your appointed feasts my soul hateth . . . your hands are full of blood. Wash you, make you clean, put away the evil of your doings. . . ." (1.14–16). The prophets are, perhaps, apart from the kings, the first truly historical individuals of whom we read in the Bible – their conversations with God are direct and personal: "The Lord spoke with Moses face to face, as a man speaks with his friend" (*Exodus*, 32:11).

How do we know when God is speaking? The Biblical writers are aware that there is a problem about false prophets and describe epistemological tests to tell true prophecy – the true prophet breaks in on the self-satisfied rituals of priestly culture (of the kind Durkheim says conduce to social solidarity!) to claim direct revelation from God and to give social critique and warning that social disaster will occur unless the community returns to the true way of God and moral law. They make universal claims – God is not like the local gods of the surrounding tribes with their priestly cults; he is the one God of the whole earth. Israel was in a sense his people, favored by him because he was speaking to them and had given them the Law, but nevertheless not uniquely related to him, and not favored by him in the sense that he would defeat all their enemies. In fact, the prophets said at various times that the Assyrians and Babylonians would drive the Israelites into slavery because they had broken the law. Isaiah even raised the pagan Cyrus of Persia to Messianic status by calling him the "anointed shepherd" (Isaiah 44:28–45:1) of the Lord ordained by God to remove Assyrian domination from Israel.

It might be tempting to conclude from the Biblical priest/prophet syndrome that we have been regressive in our emphasis on the social character of religion. Were not the prophets the forerunners of the Protestant and Enlightenment philosophy of the individual and the inalienable right of direct access to God and to rational thought? This suggestion would be a mistake, however, for several reasons. Prophecy was, as far as we can understand it, an ecstatic experience of communication with God; it required special people with a recognized social role. More important, it presupposed the social cult as a background of belief and practice. This was true even of Protestant "individualism" – it would have been unthinkable for Luther or Calvin to speak of the "priesthood of all believers" or the right of access of every man to God, except in terms of the communal faith of the Bible and the church's traditions.

The post-Reformation phenomenon of "individualism" has complex historical and social sources and has rightly been interpreted by sociologists as being a social manifestation to be understood within the complex of social forms. Durkheim speaks of the historical passage from "organic" to "mechanical" solidarity (Durkheim 1933, Chaps. 2, 3), in which the unthinking reflection of society's norms by individuals in so-called primitive societies gives place to a more conscious internalization of "collective representations," permitting at the same time individual initiative and dissent or even rebellion. This individual/social dialectic comes to a head for Durkheim in his discussion of morality. On the one hand, his theory of society as the ultimate source of authority and sanction forbids him to assign objective rights to individuals in themselves; on the other hand, he recognizes that individual agents typically regard themselves as having a right and duty to criticize, modify, and even violate the moral codes of their own society. He falls back on an essentially evolutionary view of moral progress: It is the fundamental ideals or tendencies of the society itself that are speaking when individuals regard themselves as morally obliged to rebel:

The principle of rebellion is the same as that of conformity. It is the *true* nature of society that is conformed to when the conditional morality is obeyed, and yet it is also the *true* nature of society which is being conformed to when the same morality is flouted." (Durkheim 1974, p. 65)

We offer a different secular perspective on morality in the next chapter. Meanwhile, a dilemma similar to that of priest and prophet arises for us in the forms of both the social/individual and the relative/absolute dichotomies.

Biblical religion resolves the social/individual dilemma by reference not to transcendent religion, but to the transcendent God. (Compare Levi-Strauss's theory of myth as mediating contradictions.) The history of Israel swings between poles from a religion of the ancestors, to the prophet Moses leading the people *out of* settled society, to near-assimilation into the surrounding nature religions with their king–priests, to the great age of the prophets of the Exile, to the return to Jerusalem and the establishment of settled priestly society again, to the prophetic protest of Jesus, and again to the necessary organization and bureaucracy of the early church. We can follow the oscillations through post-Biblical history up to Bonhoefer's call for religionless Christianity and beyond. From natural fulfillment to protest to fulfillment again is one of the rhythms of history and of life – this rhythm is an embodiment of the life–death–resurrection motif that forms the warp and woof of the Great Schema.

Can a religion claim prophetic universality over against relative cultures? This is how the question seems to arise when we contemplate our new-found sophistication about the relativity of human culture and the moral dilemmas in which it places us. However, the question is misleading. According to the Biblical schema, it is God and not religion that claims universality against cultural relativity. However, this transcendent God is not detached from social relativity; indeed, the Christian myth tells how he was embodied in a particular time and place to redeem forever all times and places. The secular mind has found two problems in Christianity as a religion: one is the "scandal" of its particularity; the other is its archaism. It may perhaps be suggested that both of these difficulties can be turned to good account when we consider the relativity of schemas. Schemas are not universals; they are particular solutions to particular natural and social problems and, on the other hand, the particularities with which the Bible is concerned have in fact had their resonances as solutions to problems in diverse times and places, from the earliest books of the Chronicles of Israel to the Judeo–Christian manifestations of our own time. Far from its being a reproach to be "archaic," we may see it as a guarantee of continued validity across cultures and history. As Bultmann puts it in the passage quoted in Section 11.1, according to the Biblical myth itself, it is not one schema among other schemas; rather, all or nothing is related to God, and that it is so related is neither directly verifiable nor falsifiable by how things are but requires a conversion of point of view. (Note that even in natural science, very little is *directly* verifiable or falsifiable). Among other things, be it noted, it is neither verifiable nor falsifiable by particular discoveries within the reductive sciences; here, also, either everything in its proper natural or social kind is related to God, or nothing is. No irreducible "essence" of the human verifies it, nor does the absence of special essence falsify it.

What, then, are the tests of true prophecy? The idea that the tests are predictive success is a minor feature of the Biblical Schema. It is, of course, true that the "fulfillment" of prophecy, for example, of Old Testament prophecies of the Messiah in the events of the New, is present throughout the Biblical narrative. However, the more we look for historical "verification" in the details of these events, the more it seems as though the events have been written up by the authors of the New Testament precisely to reflect the prophecies of the Old Testament. This theme is developed by Frye (1982) and by Frank Kermode (1979) in *The Genesis of Secrecy*. There is a circular, internal, verification: The Old Testament is judged by its outcome in the New; the character of the events described in the New is what it is because that is how it was foretold in the Old. We are clearly not within the domain of verification and falsification as understood in modern science or modern scientific history.

The more important sense of "prophecy" in the Bible is the "forth-telling" of God's word: "Thus saith the Lord." The prophets were concerned with the present rather than the future – with their interpretation of contemporary historical events and their proclamation of God's acts within them and his will for human action. The tests of true prophecy are related to the faithfulness with which they reproduce in particular circumstances the overall message of creation–evil–salvation–destiny that forms the structure of God's dealings with people as revealed in the whole Biblical corpus. As our second example of the workings of the Biblical schema, we take this fundamental set of myths, starting with the Biblical interpretation of evil.

In his philosophy of symbolism and metaphor, Ricoeur (1970) noted how the "hermeneutics of symbolism" has been interpreted by Marx, Freud, and some structuralists as an exercise in "unmasking" "decoding," or "destructuring" the evil condition of things by revealing their "real" but hidden causes in socioeconomic substructures, or in the unconscious, or in other types of "false consciousness." What is wrong is said to be the oppression of class society or culture, or a sickness of the psyche; in other words, a reduction to something less than human and therefore implicitly capable of being redeemed by knowledge of the historical dialectic or of psychotherapy. Or, in the case of Nietzsche, an anarchic will to power remains the last word to be said – there is no salvation.

Ricoeur rejects the implication that there is some underlying causal structure of the world that has only to be uncovered to make possible the elimination of evil in history. All the traditional myths of evil, on the other hand, see it as a pervasively metaphysical feature of the world. Ricoeur suggests that the more fruitful development of hermeneutics is to make it a recovery of and reflection on the "deep" meanings of the symbolism of evil – to receive these as "sacred teaching" or "revelation." This is the Anselmian method, which first adopts "by faith" one mythic tradition and then gains "understanding" by reflection on it and comparison with alternative myths.

Ricoeur chooses to start with the "Adamic" myth, which is central to Biblical and Judeo–Christian religion. In the beginning, God saw that his creation was good; evil entered the human world by the serpent's incitement, not only by Eve's fault; there is an angel (Satan) who fell from heaven and goes about the earth inciting evil. Evil is not primordial, nevertheless it is an active and external force, more like a contamination than the mere absence or lack of goodness that is the Aristotelian perspective. The Fall is a historical event; and salvation also has to take place in history, to recreate a fallen world. Particular historical events (as the Exodus and the Cross) are redemptive as types of supernatural restoration. Salvation is not a matter of psychological or social adjustment or of a detached judge setting the accused free; it involves the myth of God himself entering history as the suffering servant of humanity. The myth is developed throughout the Bible in the figures of Adam, "the Messiah-king, the Shepherd-king, the Prince of Peace, the Servant of Yahweh, the Son of Man . . . the Lord and the Logos of the Apostolic Church." (Ricoeur 1969, p. 274).

What does this mean for contemporary experience of evil? Even secular thought will often recognize the need for mythological, symbolic, and ritual interpretations of evil and salvation; for here, more obviously than with cosmologies of the natural world, we are in the realm of human volition and human action, and discursive reason and "explanation" have no sufficient power to move the will. Part of the relevance of the Adamic myth can be elucidated by comparison with some alternatives from other types of mythic interpretation.

Ricoeur recognizes three of these other types. First is the primordially dualist interpretation, in which evil is a primal chaos against which the good principle of creation struggles. Creation is regarded as the process of salvation, continued by the "King" as representative man who struggles with evil in the politics of the holy war. This was the Babylonian myth, and its modern counterpart may be roughly identified with Islam. In opposition to this schema, the dominant Biblical myth sees God as the only primordial principle. God is good, and he alone brings salvation. Thus, the myth of salvation by literal war against "evil" is rejected.

Second, there is the typical Greek myth of the tragic hero, who inevitably succumbs to *hubris* and for whom there is no salvation. The stoicism of the secular humanist may be said to be its modern counterpart. Such an attitude requires an ability, if possible, to live one's life fully while accepting that human life is ultimately tragic.

Third, there is what Ricoeur calls the "Orphic myth" – that the world is irreducibly and irremediably evil, but the individual soul is in exile here and has the potentiality (perhaps after several reincarnations) of escape to another world. Salvation is therefore ultimately to be found in withdrawal from the world. Certain tendencies in Eastern religion are in this tradition.

It is noticeable that compared to these three great alternatives, only Biblical religion both takes evil to be stronger than any human response to it and provides an ultimate hope in which this world is taken up into the world beyond. The Biblical myth undoubtedly provides some explanation for the dynamic quality of European civilization. The secular myth of historical progress retains from Biblical belief a type of concern for this world not found in any other of the world myths of evil and destiny. Inevitably, however, the tensions within the original Biblical schema, and between it and the modern world, have led to controversies and contradictions in theological commentary. Moltmann's *A Theology of Hope* (1965) is a good example of the ambiguities involved. After World War II, he confronted the view that all nineteenth-century optimism about human progress seemed to have been refuted. But he does not totally abandon such optimism. At time, he seems to be saying that socialism is the hope of the future and that socialist policies will lead to a kingdom of God on earth – even that this hope in an earthly utopia is the Christian hope. If so, we might ask why Moltmann refers to God at all, and why he speaks of such a hope as "Christian." At other times, he seems to be talking of a kingdom of God that is not the result of striving to ameliorate social conditions but comes about as God's action transcending the spatiotemporal.

Traditional Christianity would seem to put more emphasis on the second view. The cycle of exile and return will continue within history, but there is an other-worldly hope and salvation to be described in symbolic extraspatiotemporal terms. The myths and models of the Bible include the marriage feast – a celebration of great conviviality – and also the holy city – not the romantics' paradisal backlash against the scientists' natural world, but a progress across deserts to a city, to the artifacts of civilization. Man is a pilgrim: "I am a stranger and a sojourner, as all my fathers were" (Psalms 39:12); "Here we have no continuing city, but we seek one that is to come" (Hebrews 13:14). But what is accomplished here in our cities is not lost: "They shall bring the glory and the honour of the nations into it" (Revelation 21:26); "Establish thou the work of our hands upon us" (Psalms 90:17).

The Biblical attitude to historical progress is twofold. First, history is meaningful because it is the area of God's action. Biblical religion is not just worlddenying and transcendental; it contains as its central metaphor the coming of the Word, the incarnation of the Christ within this world, thus contrasting with some Eastern religions. The Promised Land, the New Jerusalem, the Kingdom of God: all these metaphors are expressed as culminations of earth's history, placed at "the end of time." But the "end of time" is itself a metaphor, it is not an event *in* time. The *telos* of earthly progress is not itself a state of the world in history, even though it is foreshadowed (or symbolized) by real events in history as types of the final realization. But the final realization of the meaning of history is elsewhere and elsewhen.

This twofold attitude to historical progress is radically different from our current secular value system. It has implications for our modes of thinking that are shocking to the secular mind and therefore not often made sufficiently explicit. Two sorts of consequences are particularly relevant to our argument here. The first consequence is that Christianity offers no reason to expect an overall and monotonic improvement of the human lot in history. We have seen how the Biblical schema includes myths and typologies that are almost cyclical in their implications. What saves them from the myth of "eternal return" is that they are embedded in an other-worldly, nonspatiotemporal domain, which is the realm of God. Here again we find an important contrast with certain mythologies of Greece and other cultures, where the cycles of good and evil are never ending. As far as the essential myth of the Bible is concerned, the world may have been in existence from an infinite time or may have begun with a big bang; it may end with a bang or a whimper or may continue for infinite future time. The inhabitable world may come to an end with a humanly induced catastrophe and all life may be destroyed, or there may continue into the indefinite future the ups and downs of human fortunes that induction from history would lead us to expect. The Schema can accommodate all these possibilities.

The second consequence of the irreducibly other-worldly perspective of the Bible is equally shocking to secular thought. The test of prophecy cannot be the performance of religious institutions or communities of believers within the social or political arena. The Bible gives no reason to expect any more faithfulness or righteousness from believers than from others. The Gospel is not addressed in the first place to the Pharisees (the orthodox maintainers of the cult and the law), nor to the Zealots (the militant liberators), but to those who know themselves to be poor and sinful, who have no power of themselves to help themselves, much less to know how to do good to other people. The Bible thus contains within itself the explanation of why "religion" as such cannot be judged primarily by performance, by success or failure in bringing about various kinds of "progress." These consequences are not to be seen as potential falsifiers. However, what the Great Schema does contain in this otherwise despairing situation is the story of God's action within it and the recipe for living with it, not in resignation but in joy, without expectations in this world. Because there are types of salvation to be found throughout history, which are interpreted as God's acts, human beings must actively work for whatever causes they from time to time discern to be his will. Human judgments, however, are always fallible, corruptible, and subject to the need for repentance, and our best efforts may always fail. Our ultimate hopes and expectations are not set on them, but on the kingdom of God foreshadowed in this world and coming in the next.

11.3 Construction and transcendence

Throughout our discussion of religious schemas, we have left several hostages to fortune now due for redemption. The most important of these concern questions of transcendence – both the question of religious Reality we introduced in the first chapter and also the metaphors of the "nonspatiotemporal" we have been obliged to use in describing how the Biblical schema expresses this Reality. We first argue that space–time metaphors for what is necessarily nonspatiotemporal do not raise any linguistic problem different in kind from those of any other metaphors. Our revised theory of language and reference ought to be able to deal with them. But second, we have to confront the more difficult question of what kinds of claim for transcendence are made in the Biblical schema, in what sense they can be regarded as more than "constructions," and whether metaphorical language is adequate to express them.

In Chapter 1, we introduced the problem of nonspatiotemporal Reality by asking whether our constructions of psychological and social "realities" refer to any Reality "out there," where such a Reality is understood as what provides feedback, as the natural world does for natural science. Our subsequent discussion has to some extent weakened the contrast between these different types of "reality," by showing that the pragmatic criterion is only one among many naturalistic ways of developing cognitive systems, let alone the whole continuum of such ways that is explored in cognitive science, in hermeneutics, in symbolism, and in structuralism. Feedback comes not only from nature but also from society in the form of function and of chance developments of largely self-justifying "play" (art, myth making, religious symbolism). We are still left, however, with the question of how to justify the claims to transcend spatiotemporal Reality made in many religions and some other ideologies. An ontology is claimed that is not the spatiotemporal world, is not just in heads in the spatiotemporal world, but is "beyond."

We first note that the Biblical schema itself has problems with this nonspatiotemporal reference, but they are not identical with our problems, and we should be clear exactly what they are. The Bible has, on the whole, no problems about the existence of God – in the Old Testament that is only too evident to its writers, often to their dismay and destruction. "The Day of the Lord is darkness and not light"; it is "the fool who says in his heart 'There is no God'" – he will soon discover differently. Neither does the Bible have much difficulty about the meaningfulness of speaking in metaphors about the nonspatiotemporal. What does cause difficulty is the possibility of describing or categorizing God himself as he is in himself, as opposed to the metaphors used to describe his action in the world and the consequent ways in which we know him. Sometimes, God appears to be the great X, who is the apparently arbitrary cause of all that happens – the world, the soul, good *and* evil – but whose intimate nature it is blasphemous to attempt to delineate. In the much discussed phrase that is sometimes taken as the foundation of philosophy of religion, God says to Moses, "I am that I am – that is my name." In traditional belief, a "name" is everywhere understood to define the essence of its bearer, and the use of a name is held to be an exercise of power over him. Neither definition nor subjection is possible in the case of God. God's face is never seen: Moses sees only his "hinder parts."

Auditory imagery rather than visual is appropriate: "Thus saith the Lord," "the Lord spoke to Moses," and, as a significant and unprecedented contrast, Job says to God, "I had heard of thee by the hearing of the ear, but now mine eye seeth thee," and the appropriate response is "Wherefore I abhor myself, and repent in dust and ashes" (Job 42:5–6).

The most profound discussion in subsequent Christian theology of the two issues of God's existence and his "names" is that of Aquinas, which we use later in this section. First, it will be helpful to clarify some problems about metaphors of the nonspatiotemporal that have frequently emerged in our discussion of freedom and destiny. The Biblical metaphors presuppose that there is a nonspatiotemporal realm in which God dwells; that God created the spatiotemporal world and continues to be active within it; that there is communication between God and human beings across this divide; and (at least in later parts of the Bible) that the destiny of both societies (nations, cultures) and individuals is to be taken up into this realm, where there is no more death. It goes without saying that almost every word in this brief statement is strongly and irreducibly metaphorical. If it is reduced to this-worldly terms, the whole point of the Biblical story is lost *as a story;* it is this metaphorical story in some form or other that defines what it is to be a Christian believer. No amount of liberal demythologizing can alter the fact that *as a story* the embarrassing nonspatiotemporal elements are essential to it.

The story is perfectly intelligible in terms of a metaphorical understanding of language. It is a metaphor that works by extrapolating from the here to the elsewhere, whether that is best expressed as above or beneath the earth's surface, beyond the outermost stars, or outside space, depending on where contemporary science has got to in exploring the universe in its own terms for its own purposes. Likewise, it is "once upon a time," or "forever after," or "outside time," depending on what temporal metaphors are least misleading in the light of current science. These phrases have never been anything other than metaphors; the question always is, "What substantial assertions and contrasts are expressed by using one set of metaphors rather than another, and developing their connections with the rest of the network of belief in one way rather than another?" In current science, we are accustomed to the metaphor of subspaces within dimensionally larger spatiotemporal manifolds; this is now a good way to express what is always present in the Biblical story, namely, that the spatiotemporal is embedded within a larger Reality: "All the host of heaven shall be dissolved, and the heavens shall be rolled together as a scroll" (Isaiah 34:4).

What the metaphors imply about human destiny in this world and the next has already been partly developed in the previous section. The Biblical schema is, however, rather reticent in working out the domestic problems of the heavenly City. Dante was naïvely astonished in hell to discover that "death had undone so many" (*Divine Comedy*, I, Canto III, line 57) – how can there be room for them all? Again, will not time hang heavy on our hands? Or rather, what sort of thing could timeless existence be? And so on. Such literal pursuance of stories can become crass and unimaginative. But this literal approach points to what the Bible would regard as a more dangerous desire – to pin down God, to categorize him as an object among other objects, which is either blasphemy or idolatory. At this point, the early theologians and mystics spoke of the *via negativa* – the negative way of speaking of what God is *not,* rather than of what he *is.* Aquinas quotes Dionysius: "Of him there is neither name, nor can one be found of him" (*Summa Theologica* Qu. 13, Art. 1); and John Damascene: "Everything said of God must not signify his substance, but rather show forth what he is not" (*Summa Theologica* Art. 2). God is not person or object; he is not bound by space or time or natural power or knowledge – how then are we to speak of him? This is how Aquinas introduces his discussion "of the names of God." We can conveniently bring out the implications of our own theory in contrast with his.

Aquinas attempted to capture the Biblical sense of the unutterable otherness of God by resort to Aristotle. We saw in Chapter 8 that Aristotle classifies things into species and genera, essences and accidents, and that he adopts a view of the literal use of language as the mirror corresponding to this classification. Thus, his theory of metaphor, like that of most of his successors, is literalist. He makes the point explicitly in the *Poetics:* Discourse cannot consist wholly of metaphor, for "a whole statement in such terms will be either a riddle or a barbarism" (1458a). Aristotle, however, distinguishes "metaphor" from "analogy." Analogy is a metaphysical rather than a poetic relation – it is required where we are concerned with metaphysical concepts that do not fit the generic classification of objects. For example, the concepts of "existence," "substance," "potentiality/actuality" and "goodness" are predicated of objects in every genus and are not themselves genera. How, then, can they be defined? Aristotle discusses the question in relation to "good," which does not retain the same meaning in relation to different sorts of things: honor, wisdom, pleasure are diverse in respect to their goodness; thus, "the good is not some common element answering to one idea. Goods are one by analogy" (*Nicomachean Ethics,* 1096b). All the terms that work by analogy are interrelated in Aristotelian metaphysics – they are the terms Aquinas calls "perfections." They depend on a theory of the normative character of existence in the sense that all things strive after the fullness of their being. Potentiality becomes actuality, just as the acorn strives to become the oak tree. What is fully in being is thereby "good." Thus, for Aristotle, the distinction between good and evil is not a relation between two positive forces, as we described the Biblical conception, but between fullness and deprivation of being.

Aquinas faced a general problem in relation to Aristotle: on the one hand, the Aristotelian corpus had swept all before it in the intellectual world, which was then centered mainly in the lands of the Arab conquests. Jewish and

Islamic scholars had appropriated Aristotle for their own purposes; at many points, however, Aristotle was in conflict with theistic religion, especially Christianity. The question of the analogy of being and the metaphysical perfections was one of these conflicts. Aquinas, however, found it convenient to borrow the Aristotelian framework here as elsewhere. The notion of perfections that are not predicated in the same sense of different objects seemed well-fitted to explain how such predicates could be applied to God, who is not one among objects and whose perfections must be such as to be incommensurable with any pale realizations of them in the creation. So he distinguishes the merely metaphorical knowledge we have of God when we call him "father," or "a rock," or say that he is "angry" or "weary," from the proper attribution to him of "existence," "goodness," and "wisdom." In the case of metaphors for God, they are properly (literally) predicated of created things and only secondarily and derivatively of God. But in the case of the analogical perfections, they are properly predicated of God, who alone realizes them fully, and only secondarily of created things, which in comparison to God can hardly be said to partake of any state of perfection at all.

There are several points to notice about Aquinas's theory in comparison and contrast to our own. First, it depends in two ways on an entrenched metaphysics. Aristotle's theory of being is assumed, and so is the existence of God. The exact status of Aquinas's "five arguments" for the existence of God is a matter of continuing controversy. Some commentators would say they are not arguments from nontheistic premises at all, but rather elucidations of the concepts involved in "what all men call God" – the phrase with which Aquinas ends each of his "arguments." However that may be, it remains true that the metaphysics of perfection is required for Aquinas's theory, and to that extent he separates the background ontology from his analysis of the language we use to speak of God. Similarly, we have argued that the question of the Reality of God can be separated from a study of schemas that postulate him. Whether we also require a background "metaphysics," and what this may be, we discuss later in this section.

Second, Aquinas, following Aristotle, devalues metaphor and hence impoverishes what we can say positively of God in metaphorical terms. It has often been remarked that Aquinas's theory falls either into anthropomorphism or agnosticism – anthropomorphism if he allows *any* human meanings to give us descriptions of God, and agnosticism if he does not. Even if analogies resting on the metaphysics of being were acceptable, so many other metaphors are necessary for the piety of the faithful that a theory allowing only "negative" value to "father," "love," "shepherd," or "judge". . . . is hardly an adequate linguistic resource. It is ironic that a believer in a divine incarnation should be so nervous of incarnating language about God in human metaphor.

We have noted that in modern linguistics and anthropology, metaphor tends to be devalued in comparison with metonymy. In an account of the language of religion, Brian Wicker (1975) explicitly draws together the two themes: He follows Thomist tradition in distinguishing theological *stories* (the God of Abraham, Isaac, and Jacob) from proper analogical description of God. The distinction is between metaphor and the metonymic relations of hierarchy and causality, which are the stock in trade of philosophers and scientists, not of poets and rhetoricians. Even Evans-Pritchard (1956, Ch. 5) makes the same distinction in his description of Nuer religion. He reads them like good Thomists – their mysterious symbolic identifications and mystical participations occur only between things of the earth. To say "the ox is a cucumber" in certain ritual contexts is "mere" metaphor. But when they speak of God directly as spirit manifested in the sky, the rain, the sun, moon, and wind, this is not metaphorical utterance. Evans-Pritchard leaves the impression that the predicates of God, whether Nuer or Christian, are relatively straightforward, literal, and accessible to rational and philosophical debate. Metaphor and symbolism, on the other hand, are irrational and deviant but fortunately not required in speaking of God.

We rejected the Aristotelian presuppositions about metaphor, and we must therefore reject this sort of distinction between metaphor and analogy. In our theory, "proper" language is not an expression of our intuition of universal essence and therefore has no literal correspondence with the world. Rather, it is an expression of our beliefs, which calls on an immense network of syntactic and semantic relations and empirical and cultural associations. The network enables us to explore the "meaning" of any part of it by means of analogies, metaphors, similes, paraphrases – indeed, by any of the exemplifying stories, histories, personal experiences, and products of art that have ever illuminated the nature of God for believers. Their cognitive significance will, of course, depend on whether God exists, but their meaning does not, any more than does the meaning of the most fantastic tale of science fiction or of myth or dream.

In particular, some specific objections to Thomist theories of analogical predication can be resolved. Since in the network view, no language has a one-to-one correspondence with Reality and does not fully capture the essence of what it is describing even with the semantic resources of the network, it follows that no attribution of properties to God will do so either. Therefore, it cannot be objected that God is blasphemed by attempting to capture his essence in words, or that his infinity and otherness are compromised by description. Nothing in our suggested analysis of metaphor entails definition or limitation, even for natural metaphors.

Language, as Chomsky has insisted, is never exhausted – the number of possible meaningful sentences must be assumed infinite. Similarly, the semantic network of language is indefinitely open – new terms may be coined and given meaning by their place in the network, and new metaphors may give old terms new meanings. The "wisdom of the serpent" and the "wisdom of a man" are open-textured metaphors, potentially inexhaustible – how much more the "wisdom of God." None is adequately reducible in finite terms other than itself, but all can be glossed and paraphrased by describing part of the context in the network so that enough of the meaning can be caught for us. God is indeed unique, but so in principle is every subject of every sentence, because every term has a distinct place in the network and is differently related to the whole. God is indeed not a substance among other substances; but He may be and is the subject of many sentences – distinct from, but understandable in relation to, other sentences and other subjects. Only when language is supposed normally to be a mirror of its subject matter can the objection from God's indescribability and ontological otherness arise. Without that presupposition, he can be infinitely other in reality while being describable in intelligible, though necessarily inadequate language.

A further traditional objection to metaphoric talk of God and, indeed, to all metaphoric talk, is that it will involve uncontrollable inconsistencies. That this is the case can be seen from the history of attempts in philosophy of religion to reconcile logically the various assertions about God that have been held necessary in the theological tradition: God is omnipotent but man is free; God is good but permits evil; Jesus is both God and man; God is three persons in one, and so on. In such attempts at logical reconciliation, it has always been presupposed that metaphor is an inadequate first approximation to true expression, and that if such assertions are to be acceptable at all they must in principle be reducible to literal, univocal and consistent meaning. However, we have seen in relation to all natural language that such univocality and logical exactness is at best an idealization to be exploited for limited purposes. These purposes are not the ultimate constraints on language about God. Where metaphors are appropriate, logical consistency is not the major type of constraint.

Finally, if we reject Aristotle's "analogy of being," what other kinds of assumption would we need if we were to move from construction to transcendence? Naturalism is the secular metaphysics that denies "reality" to any world except the objectified spatiotemporal world of natural science. We have seen even in this case that something more than "construction" and feedback is needed – namely, the pragmatic criterion motivated by interest in prediction and control in the space–time environment. It is not easy to find metaphysical systems in contemporary secular thought that provide serious rivals to the general acceptance of naturalism. Thomism is the most substantial Christian rival to atheism and scepticism that has ever appeared, and we have seen that the Aristotelian assumptions on which it rests must be rejected. In their pioneering studies of metaphor and symbolism, Black (1962), Goodman (1978), and Ricoeur (1978) all speak in different ways of the cognitive significance of the fact that metaphors "make and remake possible worlds." We tried to give more scientific, social, and religious content to this idea in terms of the different ways in which mental schemas get validated by nature and society.

"Reality" for us has become that to which schemas answer in complexes of feedback mechanisms. Our "metaphysics," like every other, rests ultimately on space–time experience extended by induction and analogy. We have given reasons for rejecting the epistemological model drawn from "rational decision theory" in which the validity of religious schemas is tested like a scientific hypothesis, by relatively independent criteria of empirical test. Choice of a constructed reality is not a "rational decision" unconstrained by the historical and social standpoint in which we find ourselves; it is the exploration of one or more symbolic systems from within, by calling on any resources of tradition and of continuing natural, social, and individual experience that are to hand. Why do even naturalists accept, or decline to accept, that there is nomological and normative order in the world? Such questions are not decided but rather lived with. Their discursive consideration requires an "extra premise," which comes from their evaluation as a way of life.

The feedback mechanism that would be required for recognition of a religious Reality has traditionally been called "revelation." This has been held to provide the "extra premise," namely, the gift of faith. Perhaps, conveniently for us, consideration of this lies beyond Lord Gifford's brief. Less flippantly, however, we cannot regard revelation as an ingredient in an argument of the kind we have been exploring here. It is, rather, a picture of what is required. We might ask, in the fashion of transcendental arguments, "What must Reality be like for a God schema to have developed in human minds?" Parallels to the classic arguments for the existence of God might be suggested. For example, an argument from the "highest schema": it might be agreed that the most valuable products of the space–time world are to be found among symbolic, aesthetic, and religious schemas in human heads. Then, if there is no God, these schemas are only socially functional, or are merely play. Is this conceivable? Must there not be a Reality answering to them, of which they are the intimations? The secularist will simply answer, yes, it is conceivable; no, there need not be such a Reality. Then, there are no deeper premises that can be appealed to.

In any case, it is unprofitable in an antimetaphysical age to seek to make the world safe for religion by metaphysics. Such a procedure is anachronistic and intellectually barren for believers and unbelievers alike. But there is no need for it. In relation to the Christian religion, at least, there are no intellectual foundations for belief except in the continuing tradition of practice, theology, and changing historical experience, which are all rooted in the Great Schema itself.

12   Secular schemas

We have presented schemas as embodying a constructed reality that is always open to further adaptation, explaining why there must be a plurality of viewpoints, yet also offering mechanisms for reflective critique and self-correction that protect us from an uncritical relativism. In the previous chapter, we considered the "Great Schema," a reading of the Bible that views the God reality of which it is the schema as immutable, whereas the hermeneutic process adapts our understanding of this fixed reality to changing human conditions.

This concluding chapter presents the case for a different view: seeing secular schemas as a reading of the human condition as lying wholly within the spatiotemporal realm, with no appeal to God or to a "voluntarist" free will. Such schemas could be in flux yet maintain their ability to embody a multilevel reality encompassing persons and society as well as things. We show how ethics and human values might evolve without being grounded in a fixed God reality but rather in the critical development of a pluralist world view. First, we stress the extent to which our schema-based epistemology provides a schema that can be adapted by religious and secularist alike and that provides a measure of agreement despite dramatic disagreements about the ultimate constitution of Reality.

12.1 A measure of agreement

The last page of the New Testament offers the following stern warning of the sacredness of its text:

> I warn every one who hears the words of the prophecy of this book: if any one adds to them, God will add to him the plagues described in this book, and if any one takes away from the words of the book of this prophecy, God will take away his share in the tree of life and in the holy city, which are described in this book. (Rev. 22:18–19)

However, having constructed an epistemology stressing the mutability of schemas, we cannot enforce any one reading of a text, even if we preserve the form of its words. The Great Schema, then, is a *particular* reading of the Bible. Hermeneutics has taught us how the reading of a text depends not only on what we attend to, but also on the horizons we fuse in our reading. The horizons brought to our reading in the previous chapter include a respect for scientific method and an acceptance of pluralism. The result was a Christian viewpoint that holds to the centrality of God in giving meaning to human existence but has an openness to alternatives. The reading of the Bible continues to be central; yet this view takes account of both the continuity of tradition and the hermeneutic process that adapts this reading to changing human conditions, as was the case in the writings of Augustine, Aquinas, and Luther.

Northrop Frye found that his Canadian classes in English literature were so ignorant of the biblical background of so much of their culture that he had to set forth explicitly in *The Great Code* (1982) Biblical themes to which English literature has persistently returned. A Christian would argue that here, the human mind requires this greater depth of spiritual insight that the Great Schema offers, insight that seems to have little place in a secular schema. To this statement, the secularist would reply that even the most secular person needs myth of some kind, while denying the reality of the God of the Great Schema. For every Northrop Frye who is moved to write a book to tell ignorant students about the Bible there will be another critic who is moved to write about the Greek myths. Yet we read the Greek myths as epics that appeal to the human spirit without postulating reality to the pantheon high on Olympus.

In our examination of secular schemas, we have no one great text to refer to. Certainly, the Marxist canon provides a possible text with many readings. However, there is an overwhelming variety of secular world views, and we do not dwell on Marxism, which might be seen as a search for Godlike certainties in a Godless world. In the next section, we examine the attempts of Sperry and Wilson to ground human meaning in the imperatives of cosmic or biological evolution. By contrast, the secular schema offered in Section 12.3 seeks to come to terms with a human existence that has no ultimate grounding but that must constitute its own meaning.

Before proceeding, we must reiterate the plurality of world views. There is no such thing as *the* religious viewpoint: There are believers in Judaism, Islam, Hinduism, Buddhism, Christianity, and many other religions; and even within Christianity is a dazzling diversity of viewpoints, from Protestant to Catholic, from fundamentalist to philosopher of science. Lacking canonical texts, we may expect secularists to be even more diverse in their beliefs. The perspective of Section 12.3, then, cannot be called typical. It is one attempt to show how, having assimilated the epistemology of this volume, one can live a life that denies that there is a God Reality without necessarily denying the values that many people have sought in religion. We use the terms *our secularist* or *our perspective* to stress ideas that constitute the secular perspective of that section and that are to be distinguished from generic statements about people who deny religious reality.

We have agreed that any view of the world must embrace many levels of description, so that even though this secular schema does not posit a God reality, it does ascribe reality to the different levels of things, persons, and societies. However, we do not claim that this secular schema is a world view implied by cognitive science or schema theory. To emphasize this, let us consider two conclusions of our schema theory and then see how each conclusion is in some sense ethically neutral.

We have stressed that different people are inherently different and even from birth have different schemas. How is the structure of an ethical system to respond to all of these differences? One response might be to call for a social system that respects individuality. One might equally respond by saying that if people are inherently different, we then need tighter social controls on individual behavior to minimize the effects of such differences.

We have also seen that schemas are fragmentary representations, and that knowledge is provisional. Does this mean that our social system should be one that respects pluralism? Or, should it be one that restricts individuality to reduce the possibility of destabilizing change?

We examine a social perspective embodying the first choices in each of these dilemmas – a secular schema based on a decentralized, pluralistic, and adaptive view of society. For example, this schema values a world with many different societies enriched by peculiarities of geography and history. It does not see each society as a successive approximation to some ideal society. For example, Mexico is now going through a difficult process of finding its soul. The country is trying to see how it can integrate its Indian and colonial past and, at the same time, become part of the modern, technological world. Our secular schema holds that Mexico will succeed to the extent that it creates a society richly different from others and yet including a critique of its own traditions. Aztec sacrifices will not be part of the new Mexico!

We can relate this general viewpoint to other secular and nonsecular schemas. We do not expect to attain certainty about the secular world, but do hope to enrich our discourse about the nature and viability of such secular schemas. In particular, we must see how some questions faced by the Great Schema, the Biblical view, would be faced from a secular point of view.

One can see religion as a means to perceiving, at least dimly, a transcendent reality, so that in perceiving it we find ways to restructure our human existence. Or, we can see a religion as an ideology that involves transcendent categories but has in fact grown out of our human needs and social perceptions. We have tried to clarify how any ideology, religious or secular, may be contingent on technological or environmental factors. We have also seen that once an ideology is established, it remains remarkably resistant to falsification (Section 7.3). An ideology resists change by making it easy for people to behave in ways that reinforce the ideology and difficult for them to oppose it. If a racist or sexist remark is going to elicit the wrath of one's social group, one is unlikely to make such a remark. In a Western intellectual framework, we do not find it strange to accept certain "facts" without question. By a leap of empathy, we can see that much of the unquestioning acceptance of folk beliefs and taboos of "primitive" societies is psychologically explicable on similar grounds. In Chapter 10, we turned to social anthropology to see how members of different societies have come to assimilate social schemas (holistic symbol systems) that lead them to live in realities dramatically different from our own.

Does such empathy commit us to an extreme cultural relativism? Our answer is to temper our view of different symbol systems with the acceptance of certain dimensions of Western culture, such as science and medicine, along which empirical testing is possible, with a well-articulated social structure to ensure that the results of such tests are relatively reliable and become accepted, even if they contravene traditional wisdom. In other words, we look to systems that include rituals for changing the rituals, as contrasted with traditional societies in which anyone who contravenes the rules, apart from personal bravery or folly, loses all chance of a hearing from society. Of course, even a so-called scientific society has many areas in which experimentation is illegal or in which people espousing views contrary to, say, established public policy may risk social obloquy. We have to steer between the Scylla of relativism and the Charybdis of claiming knowledge of final reality. At any time, we believe certain things to be true, not conditioned by the structure of our present beliefs. We are also aware that not all these "truths" will survive the next round of ideological, scientific, or religious redefinition.

A Cartesian may claim there can be doubt so radical that we can strip away all assumptions to find a kernel of certitude from which we can grow a whole system of reliable knowledge. By contrast, we hold that the use of language commits us to such assumptions as that there are people and that sequences of words can (more or less) enable them to share and explore meaning. Our study of language as metaphor has gone on to clarify how the dissonance or ambiguity of meanings can lead to the exploration of new meanings. On the basis of what seems surest, we can then provide a critique of other beliefs, and the resultant new beliefs may then enable us to question and restructure what had hitherto seemed unquestionable. At each stage, we have both some coherence in what we believe and some apparent correspondence with an "external reality" as expressed (e.g., in the ability to act in ways that usually have intended consequences). The "successes" provide the framework that enables us to recognize the "errors" in our belief system. In this way, then, our approach to reality becomes congruent with out scientific methodology. Our coherence constraint on the modifications of our current understanding tempers our approach to cultural relativism. We do not expect to abandon the view that we are individual people, talking to each other and with a world about us. We do expect to see how our views of all this are not static, but in a state of continuing development. At each time, we need a platform on which to stand. This is the reality as we have constructed it, but it evolves as we continue our hermeneutic dialogue.

It is difficult to argue that human behavior shows the type of progress we ascribe to the scientific enterprise. If there were such progress, would it be a progress that would "cure us" of God, or a progress that would let us at least truly live by God's teachings – or would it be a progress that would tolerate a pluralism in which different world views could co-exist with no system justifying its adherents in humiliating or slaughtering people with whom they disagreed? Certainly, in the history of Europe, the development of religious tolerance has seemed progressive. Even in science, there is an increasing diversity of disciplines rather than a reduction of all knowledge to a few laws of physics. In physics, we may seek underlying universals; but in engineering, we accept, for example, a diversity of modes of transportation; and in biology we see a diversity of ecological niches matched by a diversity of species. We learn to understand how to build a plane for fuel economy or speed, but we do not rule that one approach excludes all others.

Different peoples have different ideologies, which change over time. Within any society are many subcultures, each with different ideologies but usually with enough in common (e.g., the use of language or money) to allow some measure of intercourse. People rarely make individual decisions as to their optimal role in society but fall into roles as a result of accidents of their own biography and the surrounding social structure rather than through conscious, rational choice. In part, then, ideology is what (no matter how it has evolved) defines and rationalizes a restricted set of roles and relationships for people within a given society. We have come to see pluralism as itself of value, so long as the pluralism is one of dynamic critique rather than implacable conflict. Our goal in Section 7.3 was thus to understand how ideologies can change, and in doing this we sought to understand how the social level of discourse can be related to the level of schemas in which we express the individual's critique (whether conscious or implicit) of society, which can turn to acquiescence or revolt.

Actions and social practices are partially constituted by the concepts and beliefs that enter into them. Our view of language as metaphor and our rooting of experience in the schemas of the action/perception cycle led us to view the self as an essentially embodied subject or agent, coming to modify personal ideas while working within the circle of individual preconceptions. This view suggests that there may be no one world view, either religious or secular, that is superior to all other views currently available. But this view will not lead us to total cultural relativism in developing our secular schema because we hold that, even though all our schemas are provisional, we nonetheless have tools for testing and extending our knowledge. We accept that there are many different world views. We also accept that each of us has only a partial world view, which is not even internally consistent. Given that it has flaws, we seek ways to learn more. But our criteria for learning are themselves conditioned by our present schemas.

Even though they deny the reality of God, secularists must certainly accept the reality of God *schemas*. There *are* people who actually believe in God, and there are religious institutions. Is Western secular society deviant with regard to the bulk of human history and the bulk of human experience? Something really new happened during the seventeenth and eighteenth centuries, when Europe became progressively disenchanted with its Gods and spirits and demons. But was this progress, or is Western society in a sort of deviant interval in which this part of humanity has had the luxury of somehow neglecting what other peoples have found to be a large part of reality? This talk of luxury could still be interpreted in a secular way, because it could be taken to mean that there are certain beneficial fantasies that human beings and societies cannot live without, even without claiming transcendental reality for them. But how should the secular schema respond if schema theorists were able to come up with results indicating that religious schemas are somehow necessary to human development and the life of human beings in society? We have seen examples in which religions have had disastrous effects and some examples in which religions have had beneficial effects, as far as we judged them. Should secularists impose religion if they find it to be a necessary part of human functioning? Or, should they follow truth as a secularist sees it and say that even if religion is beneficial it is not true and therefore should be rooted out, or that transcendental belief should be rooted out. Do transcendental beliefs as such do harm?

Today, many Christian theologians, while stressing the sense their Christian faith made of their lives, hold that Christians must now be open to different views of the world, such as Buddhism and Hinduism, that the Age of European imperialism is over, and that therefore a Eurocentric view of Christianity as the sole repository of religious truth is no longer tenable. However, many teachings of Hinduism and Buddhism and Islam and Christianity are dramatically incompatible – there is no way of melding them into a homogeneous pablum, a new universal religion. Such Christians still hold to Christianity as a good schema with which to know the world yet accept that they can learn from a Hindu and a Muslim and would not wish to convert them unless they themselves want to be converted. But then each religion becomes more like a social myth. Each religion may hold that God is transcendent and accepts that it is impossible to describe Him fully in human terms. It is simply inevitable that different descriptions with long and different historical traditions are going to be inconsistent. People who already believe may look to other religions to refine their approach to the transcendent reality; but the secularists find the disagreements to be such that they view any successes of religions not as being transcendent but as perhaps offering suggestions for ritual and social behavior that can be incorporated into their secularist view.

12.2 Scientific ethics and sociobiology

For the religious believer, questions of human values may be explored in terms of the extranatural relation of person to God. But if we do not have recourse to such a relationship, must we treat the ethical questions of what *are* the rights of persons, what constitutes social justice, and so on, as if they were wholly relative to particular cultures? Can we say any more about the possibilities of a scientifically based universal ethic? We have suggested that the secular schema is not derivable from schema theory. Nonetheless, we want to suggest that it is constrained by the considerations of preceding chapters. To see this, we turn to a critical examination of the secular perspectives of Roger Sperry and E. O. Wilson.

Sperry and the sociobiologists ground their "faith" in evolution, as did Durkheim. Whatever natural or social evolution shows to be the fittest, *is* the good; morality therefore should go along with evolutionary trends. To the objection that our moral intuitions sometimes subjectively require us to *resist* evolutionary trends, Durkheim replied that the appearance of the "prophet" proclaiming the need for such resistance is itself part of the evolutionary process and should be received as a deeper insight into the "real," long-term trends of evolution. This reply is unsatisfying, however, since it seems to place unjustified faith in the convergence of our moral intuitions with future evolutionary facts, or else is forced to disregard our moral intuitions as even partial arbiters of the good. We need a theory that gives a place both to external evolutionary facts and to the evidence from individual moral experience.

In Chapter 4, we saw that Sperry argued that the language of thoughts and intentions is central to the reality of persons, so that a science of the human mind must reject a purely reductionist neuroscience that holds that the only real description of the human mind is in terms of the physicochemical activity of networks in the brain. Sperry went further, asserting that mind talk supersedes brain talk so that one's understanding of the human being can be restricted to the level of the conscious person – that brain talk ceases to be relevant once it has yielded the emergent properties of conscious activity.

By contrast, we argued that the level of conscious mental activity is only part of the human reality. For one thing, we are embodied and so the function of our minds is still to some extent dependent on the contingencies of our brains within our bodies. Moreover, our discussion of both schema theory per se and of Freud have shown how much in the activity of our minds, let alone our brains, is not at the level of consciousness.

Sperry is among those who argue for a scientific ethics, observing that a scientific approach would not lead to a rigid, closed scheme but rather to a scheme that would continue to unfold. He does not suggest that authority for values be turned over to scientists, but rather that values be opened to a form of public examination distinguished by the rigorous demand that beliefs double check with empirical evidence. In this approach, his thinking is consonant with our stress on the adaptive dimension of the secular schema, though the talk of science may suggest a level of explicit symbolic description and experiment hard to reconcile with the subtleties and constraints of human experience. Nonetheless, we argue that certain elements in his thinking are inconsistent with our schema-theoretic account of the human being. In so doing, we see that our secular schema is constrained, though not determined, by the considerations from cognitive science that have gone before. For example, Sperry (1983) sees the logical defense of any set of values as resting ultimately on some axiomatic concept that must be accepted on the basis of faith as self-evident. By contrast to this axiomatic view, our schema theory has shown that behavior is not based on deduction from a few simple axioms, but rather on a vast array of examples that do not, by the nature of our limited experience, constitute a completely consistent logical system.

It is worth noting that we do not subscribe to the general critique of scientific ethics that it violates the fact–value distinction and is therefore untenable. Certainly, we have argued that the fact that some particular course of action may increase the chance of survival of a particular group does not imply that this action is necessarily of human value. However, we would not argue as a general principle that the facts about the effects of different courses of action can always be neatly separated from the evaluation of the outcomes. We have repeatedly suggested that our schemas are partial and approximate; they must make contact with what we know from our person reality as well as with the more quantifiable reality of things about which we can make careful predictions. Thus, a schema that enables us to *do* something will often combine fact and value, because in knowing how to do something as distinct from something else we have implicitly made a value judgment that what we know how to do is worth doing. Hence, even the acquisition of schemas for different types of skilled behavior implicitly smuggles in many values.

Much of science starts from the data of human experience, for example, "seeing red" for optics, "tasting salt" for chemistry. A similar role for ethics may be played by "feelings of obligation," for example. These feelings have often been rejected as scientific data because they are said to be purely subjective, but it would be more accurate to say that they are intersubjective within a culture and at a given time. Given these constraints, we can as scientists begin to understand, for example, how embarrassment, motivation, emotion, and feelings of obligation are rooted both in the genetically determined makeup of our brains and in how we have been shaped by our development as members of a society with its own distinctive language and belief systems. We can better understand the constraints our brains place on our educability, our adaptability, and our passions, and we can analyze the "utility" of ethical and religious systems in psychological and sociological terms. The nature of our feelings, and thus the viability of various ethical systems, will be changed in the process – just as there is a "hermeneutic circle" in the relation of theory and observation in physics.

Sperry believes that the scientific stance he described itself rules out certain value systems. For example, he opposes Marxist "scientific materialism" because it predicates the impotence of science in regard to value judgements, which, he holds "is the reason that the more materialistic and animalistic aspects of human nature are put first in Soviet philosophy before man's more idealistic, more spiritual components" (Sperry 1981, pp. 9–10). Yet, Sperry does not see his emphasis on science as antithetical to religion but actually suggests that there might be benefits from a fusion of the two. Given this quotation, it seems that Sperry has an "implicit axiom" – that human beings have an idealism and spirituality that is to be valued. However, he provides no "scientific" analysis of the "positive function" of religion that could support an argument for the "fusion" of science and religion.

Sperry further contends that "Marxism also lacks the 'free-will' concepts we have today that free individual and social decision-making from mechanistic determinism" (Sperry 1981, p. 8). He thinks this lack results from Marxism's neglect of the principle of "downward causation" from individual mental activity to its mechanical substrate. But this argument does not refute the Marxist view of social determination of the individual. We may draw an analogy from the levels of mental/physical to those of social/individual; a theory of downward causation that "frees" mental activity from the activity of our neurons (Section 4.1) may similarly be used to justify a historical materialism in which downward causation "frees" social and historical forces from the mental activity of individuals. We argue, however, for two-way interaction in both cases: just as we saw in Section 4.1 that the emergence of the mental constrains, but does not supersede, the neural, so we argued in Section 7.3 that social organization constrains but does not supersede individual initiative. Here, schema theory expresses well the more recent insights of "humanist" Marxists, who recognize a two-way causation between society and the individual and locate some of the agency of change at the individual level. Again, we see an "implicit axiom" in Sperry's ethical thought – freedom of individual decision-making.

We also note that the issue of freedom was central in Marx's writings (see Walicki 1983 for a valuable critique). The Marxist attacks a liberal view of human freedom that held that the workers are free because they can decide whether to accept a job, and that the capitalists are free because they can choose whether to invest their money here. But, a Marxist would say, these people have an impoverished view of the possibilities of social structure. Lacking schemas for changing that social structure, they have so limited their scope of action that they have come to value things that are improperly valued as seen from a broader viewpoint.

With the hindsight of our knowledge of the Soviet system, we would now reject that part of the Marxist critique that argued that downgrading individual freedom was a proper means for changing society to yield a collective increase in freedom. However, this reservation fits in with the inherently adaptive character of our secular schema. Dramatic historical attempts to change human values have succeeded in opening up new possibilities for human understanding, but their consequences provide us with new grounds of experience on which to evaluate the outcome. We thus can carry out our new critique to try to define and defend our new values. This is not too different from Marx's secularization of Hegel's dialectic of the development of spirit (of which Singer 1980 offers a concise exposition). What is different is our distrust of absolute values as expressed in Marx's case by his view that the rise of the proletariat world mark the ultimate stage of human history.

By contrast to his implicit axioms, Sperry's writings suggest explicitly that the ultimate axioms of human ethics are to be found in coming to understand people's relations to the evolution of the cosmos and to the quality of the biosphere. The secular perspective we examine in the next section instead takes the network of personal and social experience as its basis. For example, our concern for the quality of the biosphere may rest in part on religious convictions or on a scientific sense of wonder, but it also involves a concern with maintaining a livable environment *for us*. Since people have such great power for destruction of the biosphere, it might be "shown scientifically" that our extinction would be "good for the biosphere" – hardly a happy implication for a new set of human values! But even the gap between concern with human survival and an ethics that can guide everyday life is too large. When Sperry says, "Humanity needs to see itself in terms of something greater and more important than itself to give meaning and purpose to human existence" (Sperry 1972, p. 129), our secularist may agree that ethics cannot be rooted in individual selfishness and yet doubt that any decentered cosmic design can play that role. Our secularist wants to put humanity in perspective, but it is a human perspective.

We earlier rejected a reductionist materialism that excludes conscious mental activity from scientific discussion. We have thus allowed systems of values to enter scientific explanation of human activity and shown how they may interact with the neural level in mutual modification. Our secularist adopts the decisionist position (Section 5.2) that the specifically human characteristics of self-consciousness and intentionality do not require a dualism in which the "essence of the human" is irreducibly mental. The human mind is rooted in the brain, but we have so far given no analysis of how its being so rooted might influence what it means to be human and of how this might influence the shape of our ethics. Despite his research on the brain, Sperry argues that the realm of ethics supersedes the lower levels of neuroscience, but at the same time he knows that lower levels are relevant:

Social values are necessarily built in large part around inherent traits in human nature written into the species by evolution. . . . Fortunately, the social consequences from values of this kind are subject to considerable regulation . . . through . . . higher cognitive value systems. . . . It is the man-made laws . . . enforcing values of more cognitive origin, about which one can hope to do something. . . . Thus the large 'human nature' element in the value problem . . . is taken care of, if one can properly manage the supersedent systems of ideological values. (Sperry 1972, p. 123).

Such a view contrasts strongly with that of the sociobiologists, who claim that the "lower-level" mechanisms of evolution are sufficient both to explain and to direct our search for value systems. E. O. Wilson, for example, argues that we now have sufficient evidence to ground a strictly biological explanation of culture, which would be a direct application of Darwinian theory, not merely an attempt to find analogies in society for Darwinian categories. This means that the debate between nature and culture as primary determinants of human behavior would be decisively settled in favour of nature, a conclusion still strongly contested by social anthropologists and by some biologists. This is a technical argument whose outcome must await further developments in human genetics; what should concern us here, however, is the deeper philosophical challenge implied by these claims, particularly in relation to ethics.

E. O. Wilson developed his theory of sociobiology by starting from an analysis of ant and termite colonies, showing how genetically programmed patterns of interaction among individual creatures could yield complex social behavior of the whole society. His book *The Insect Societies* (1971) was followed by *Sociobiology* (1975). Starting from a summary of some of the more salient features of his account of insect societies, he went on to look at the extent to which, even in higher animals, we can see the genetic basis of group behavior. In a somewhat controversial final chapter, he then talked about human sociobiology. He followed this up with *On Human Nature* (1978), a book that Chicago theologian James Gustafson (1981, p. 122) characterized as a secular theology. In this secular theology, Wilson tried to ground human values in the claims of sociobiology by asserting that whatever natural evolution shows to be the fittest to ensure human survival is what is good.

Wilson has been alarmed by how a decline in moral values has accompanied the rise of science and technology. He seeks a return of those values within the naturalist vision. But how do we derive values from fact? He offers a sociobiological blank check: If altruism could be shown to have survival value for the human species, then there are some grounds for altruism as a virtue in a naturalist sense. Survival of the reasoning human species becomes the ultimate value:

Can culture alter human behavior to approach altruistic perfection? Might it be possible to touch some magic talisman or design a Skinnerian technology that creates a race of saints? The answer is no. . . . The genes hold culture on a leash. The leash is very long, but inevitably values will be constrained in accordance with their effects on the human gene pool. . . . Human behavior – like the deepest capacities for emotional response which drive and guide it – is the circuitous technique by which human genetic material has been and will be kept intact. Morality has no other demonstrable ultimate function. (Wilson 1978, pp. 165, 167)

But there is a fallacy here: The fact that my genes have programmed some behavior into me does not imply that I *ought* to behave in that way, in so far as I am a reflective and self-conscious person. Both voluntarists and decisionists may still protest that human freedom in part ought to undo the "preconceptions of the genes." In any case, Wilson denies the objectivity of a *value* per se while arguing for the objectivity of the *fact* that the value is conducive to the survival of the species. He appears to think there is no alternative to survival as the ultimate goal of the human being.

However, the theory of natural selection does not imply survival of the species – the vast majority of the species that ever existed are now extinct, and there is no reason to doubt the future extinction of humanity. Thus, altruism might arise genetically and then, indeed, program the extinction of the species. There is also a humanist perspective on the concern that universal altruism could be damaging to the human species. "We couldn't all be Mother Theresas" – if *everybody* sacrificed themselves, there would be no kin left to preserve their genes. Humanists and religious believers alike may feel a discomfort with the form of this argument, and this discomfort suggests that sociobiology does not provide a secular perspective that adequately meshes with our own experience of person reality. Of course, Wilson's perspective is also one that no serious religious believer can accept, for in any religious system that refuses to limit existence to the spatiotemporal world, it cannot be obvious that the continuation of the human race or its successors within the cosmos is the highest good, no matter how high are the spiritual values that may be realized within the necessary genetic limits. Humankind has always dreamed dreams of perfection – perfect and universal altruism, the ultimate significance of sacrifice for others, the redemptive power of suffering. These features are central to the "ethic" of Judeo-Christian religion and they are far from the calculated limitations on altruism that Wilson finds desirable relative to our purely biological future. One feature of religious systems is how they deal with dreams of perfection.

In any case, a strictly biological criterion for human values seems unworkable, even though human survival is important. Would it mean we should maximize the size of population, no matter what means are required? Would this be an argument for battery farming of human beings to bring about the largest possibility of human survival? By contrast, our secular schema embodies the recognition that we have not simply evolved biologically but also socially. It calls for an appreciation of the immense richness of possible patterns of human behavior. Such richness is both constrained and made possible by the genetic factors in our brain function, but is not determined by them. Much of our ethical judgment is rooted not so much in our biology per se, but rather in our wonder at the richness of human behavior and a feeling that this richness is something to be cultivated. Our secular schema thus leads us to protest against political repression and censorship of literature because we see them as unduly limiting human diversity – not because of an appeal to a biological criterion of human survival. Perhaps a sociobiologist would point to the notion of hybrid vigor in genetics and suggest that there might be an analogous grounding for the support of pluralism in the realm of ideas. However, we think it is fair to say there is no evidence in the sociobiological literature linking human population size or survival to ethical systems. Certainly, conservation of resources and steps to preclude the use of nuclear weapons are vital to human survival and do fall on our ethical agenda. However, such global goals do not yield the more detailed ethical guidelines for the human interaction of our daily lives. By contrast, our secular schema roots our ethical decisions in a whole population of subschemas acquired through a lifetime of social experience.

In human history, the propagation of ideas seems usually of greater influence than the propagation of genes. The study of the great variety of human cultures in history must convince us that the malleability of our behavior transcends any crude biological determinism of this kind. Where Chomsky (e.g., 1975) has seen a political message in his claims for innateness of language – arguing against the views of Skinner on the grounds that, if true, they would place no limit on ideological brain washing – we would respond that it were better that there is such malleability than that we are all creatures of the genes that gave us Hitler and Stalin.

A secularist alternative to the equation of value with survival of the genes is that of Jacques Monod. He faces the dilemma of naturalism and humanism in relation to his biologically reductionist view of people and of knowledge and concludes that ethics, and even the ethical value of science itself, is an existential decision, not rationally or scientifically motivatable: even the ethic of scientific knowledge itself "does not impose itself on man, *on the contrary, it is he who imposes it on himself.*" Man "must realize that, like a gypsy, he lives on the boundary of an alien world; a world that is deaf to his music, and as indifferent to his hopes as it is to his suffering or his crimes" (Monod 1972, pp. 177, 172–3).

A secularist who follows Monod or Weber will take moral norms to be arational, existential decisions that may be socially explicable but are in the end determined by arbitrary individual choice. And yet moral choice often seems to impose itself on the individual as an objective matter. Monod seeks to restore this sense of objectivity by referring to the values of science itself – holding that the sincerity, rationality, and absence of subjective bias that are the necessary conditions of science should also be the foundations of morality in general. Such foundations are, however, not only insufficient (how does one weigh up scientifically a decision to abort or not to abort, to divorce or not to divorce?), but they also elevate science to a highly questionable status of supreme good.

Habermas's view is similar: Moral and social norms will emerge, as science is supposed to do, from a consensus of participants in ideally rational discourse. This view is subject to a similar objection to its lack of specificity; in addition, one wants to ask, since the ideal speech situation does not now obtain, and perhaps never can obtain in real history, how do we *now* respond to moral and social dilemmas?

It is worth emphasizing the problem here. We find it useful to speak of gravitation as an "external reality" of which science offers descriptions that may change yet that are increasingly successful according to the pragmatic criterion. But we have recognized that the choice of whether to drive on the right-hand or left-hand side of the road is an arbitrary but necessary, and necessarily social, convention. This arbitrariness has two interesting consequences. First, we cannot imagine an ideal speech situation in which all participants would agree that the one choice of left versus right was *correct,* though diplomats might agree to a single choice as *expedient.* (Sweden changed to the right because it was connected by land with countries with that convention; island nations such as Great Britain, Japan, Australia, Bermuda, Indonesia, and Cyprus still drive on the left.) Second, however, we can see the possibility of a social analysis that explains why it is necessary to make one choice or the other – or to restrict each road to be one-way. Simply, if people choose to drive so fast that collisions are destructive and decisions of other people cannot reliably be anticipated, then (save in a society that embraces constant risk-taking as a virtue), such a convention becomes a necessity.

In the case of gravitation, we speak of universal laws; in the case of side-of-the-road choosing, we speak of a pure convention, yet hope to give an explanation of the need for such a convention. However, this explanation does not quickly return us to a set of social axioms; rather, it leads us to consider a multitude of social choices. We are faced with a network in which we seek a measure of social coherence, rather than a delimited set of phenomena for which we can subject closed models to a well-defined pragmatic criterion. In this sense, we accept Monod's existential view of ethics, but without any narrow-sense conformity to scientific method. It is defined by a set of conventions subject to individual and social critique, rather than being the subject of universal laws (no matter how dimly perceived), like gravitation.

12.3 A secular perspective

Within the Great Schema, we could see that humanity's special relation to God constituted the specifically human. Some secular humanists might reject this view yet hold that it is a human being's possession of a transcendent free will, a transcendent personality, that constitutes the specifically human.

This section presents a secular schema, based on an appreciation of person reality and on an evolving body of scientific knowledge, which lets us recognize both commonalities and differences among people, other animals, and human-made machines, without demanding that we can characterize what is uniquely or specifically human. Rather, working from our self-understanding of what it is to be a person, and its dissonance from what is currently captured by cognitive science, we can provide a critique that will be part of the dynamic for a continually changing secular schema.

Our secular perspective builds on a decisionist (nontranscendent) view of the person yet does not reduce the person to a "mere" machine. We seek grounds for ethics and morality but accept that these grounds cannot be immutable. In the end, Monod is right: A stoic, existentialist, ethic is all we can have to guide us; and from the point of view of the universe, such an ethic may seem to be arbitrary. What we add to this stoic view is an explicit acceptance of the role of tradition; but we reject the suggestion that the social schema of such a tradition must be accepted in its entirety.

There are no workable bases for morality that could be put on a computer and used to generate guides for action. Culture is a chaos of conflicting and incompatible values, and the values that emotionally go deepest are often the least moral – such as making money. In any case, the standards by which any morally serious person tries to live are more abstract and general – though, perhaps, implicit in a widely applicable network of generalizable specifics – than the "values" presented by the culture. A private house, a color television, large research grants, a "good self-image" are all "values" without ethical weight. Honesty, loyalty, fairness, and compassion do have ethical weight. However, "social definition" is not adequate to determine what constitutes a human being or who is entitled to the rights and privileges thereof. The secular view must have a more general – not other-worldly – approach to ethics. Without this approach, we would not be able to judge any society as immoral, as we clearly must (cf. The Pol Pot regime in Cambodia, for a recent example). Wilson's sociobiology is no help because the *quality* and not the quantity of human life is at issue.

Most attempts to construct an ethical system go beyond pure selfishness to relate the ethical life of the individual to a larger collective. The need for an Other that transcends the individual, even the individual family or nation, keeps coming into it. Social consensus – "My country right or wrong" – is not enough. From the secular point of view, one finds that Other by trying to increase one's social and historical awareness so that when one finds oneself in a situation in which one's society is proceeding along a path of hysterical consensus to war or intolerance, one has "somewhere to stand" to formulate a personal resistance.

The Great Schema may ground our acceptance of certain moral norms by reference to the believed nature of God. But the secular schema offers a more contingent answer. We can examine our present society and see why basic moral norms must be expanded to a complex structure of law. My decisions about how to behave in my particular situation are at most partially conscious and rest on a mixture of general argument and particular experience. Yes, it is wrong to murder. But when are there extenuating circumstances? When is one form of murder more severe than another? These are important ethical questions. They are enshrined in the legal system, and little evidence exists that they can be defined in a totally universal and abstract way. Again, our secular schema does not offer its own form of absolute values; rather, it takes current values and then subjects them to critique. It is not altogether flippant to compare "What are the grounds of human values?" to the analogous question, "What are the grounds of kangaroos?" There is no abstract account, on universal principles, of why kangaroos should exist or what kangaroos should be. The best that the theory of evolution, which is itself evolving, can do is to build on a rich account of the context of other species, terrain, weather, available food supplies, and so on, and then seek to evaluate the differential survival value of kangaroos in that ecological niche.

Analogously, we see human values as evolving as material and social conditions evolve. An important problem for a secular schema is to avoid a total cultural relativism. We argue that it is not one that lets us condone Nazi genocide or the Soviet gulag, but is rather one that starts from certain (changing) anchor points and seeks a critical account of how these points may constrain historical change.

The Great Schema uses such words as *evil, salvation,* and *destiny.* Many religions talk of evil as if it were a natural kind, a palpable presence, an operative principle, as we see in both the story of the devil and the Manichaean view of the fight between good and evil. These stories predicate evil as something well defined in and of itself. Our secular schema cannot posit evil as a transcendent reality. Rather, our schema is based on the view that there are many actions and institutions that we may criticize as being evil in some sense that so accords with our human values that they are intolerable to us. To the extent that we accept such values, these actions and institutions cannot go unresisted.

What, then, of salvation and destiny? Sociobiologists may seek a secular grounding of human salvation and destiny in terms of the preservation of the human species, a biological concept of survival. Our secular schema does not offer such absolute criteria of our destiny – only local criteria. We each have a life to live, and in living that life we learn that we are not isolated people but members of a community, a community that may be as small as the collection of people in one room or as large as a group extending over many continents and centuries. Perhaps what characterizes us as human as much as anything else is that our actions, our desires, and our intentions become conditioned by our awareness of being members of some larger totality. The Great Schema would suggest that this totality is defined in absolute terms rooted in God. The secularist would accept our human contingency and seek an adaptive, rather than an absolute, strategy in trying to address such questions as: How do we avoid nuclear war?; How do we improve education?; How do we stop certain types of sectarian and religious violence? To think of these questions within a large context, not simply a personally selfish context, is not to believe that they can only be answered in terms of a transcendent reality that goes beyond space and time.

Religious cosmologies seek to give people a sense of meaning in a universe in which the human predicament has always been immense. Much religion is rooted in the fear of death and in the consequent appeal of the notion of a soul that survives either in or "beyond" space and time. Our secularist is not convinced that such a concept is more than a projection, a wish fulfillment. Life is, for all its joys, a stage for grief and suffering, and it seems to our secularist to be more human to look the facts in the eye rather than to grasp at comfort (and diminish our humanity) by drugging ourselves with myths that are taken too literally or that have lost their evocative power. The key to this approach is that we do *not* demand certainties.

In Chapter 1, we espoused a philosophy of science that enables scientists to progress from one pragmatic (and, often, aesthetic) success to another within the world of current research without stumbling as the foundations keep shifting. In this spirit, our secularists can have the courage of their convictions even while admitting the possibility that those convictions may one day change. After all, even the religious believers in a transcendent God Reality must live with the doubts caused by the knowledge that their finite minds must inevitably misperceive much of that Reality. A general belief that God – or evolution – will make everything work out for the best beyond time – or billions of years from now – provides no guidance for moral conduct here and now.

Czeslaw Milosz (1983) speaks of life in Warsaw under the Nazis, of the horrors and the heroism and the extent to which humanity can survive. Reading of such extremities sobers one, presenting a reality so much more stark and challenging than that of most of our lives. One cannot doubt the evil of the Nazi regime. Surely, here in such evil is the rock on which cultural relativism must founder. Belief in the evil of Nazism led many people to risk, and lose, their lives in World War II defending certain ideas about human dignity and liberty and freedom. Yet, there were Germans for whom the Nazi cause was glorious. At the Nuremberg trial, one officer was asked why the authorities had simply buried the bodies at Belsen rather than pulverizing them to remove all traces of the genocide. He replied that there was nothing to be ashamed of, and that if Germans in generations to come were worthy of the glory of the Third Reich they would be proud of those who had rid Europe of the Jews.

We recoil from such a view, decrying a society that could murder its Jews, or condone any other form of genocide. Yet we do not seem to be the proud possessors of the philosophical tools to certify such judgments to be as absolute as they may seem. We agree that slavery is evil, yet only 120 years ago, many Americans were fighting to the death for its preservation. Only in 1983 was there reunification between the Northern and Southern branches of the Presbyterian Church in the United States – split because Southerners could read Christ's teachings as condoning slavery. Of current issues, perhaps abortion most dramatically captures our moral ambiguities. Even the carnivores amongst us cannot discount the possibility of a vegetarian society in which the eating of flesh is seen as an indisputable evil. Our secular schema embodies the view that we should not seek unchanging moral absolutes any more than we seek unchanging scientific absolutes, but that we *should* strive for coherent moral discourse, even if it requires accepting a pluralism of views. However, we argue below that acceptance of pluralism does not entail that we must tolerate the intolerable. We see Nazism and slavery in this category, despite the lack of absolute arguments. These are part of the data of *our* moral experience.

The "atmosphere" in which we live is provided by the particular institutions of work, family, markets, states – each of which depends in part on the beliefs of individuals, which, as we saw in Section 7.3, combine into an interdependent totality. One cannot be changed without affecting the others. Because of these interdependencies, there can be many changes in individual beliefs without there being significant social change. Yet social structures are not just external realities; they are constituted by intersubjectively held beliefs and so can be subject to critique by individuals.

Even the most secular skeptics cannot discard all tradition. We have to accept a story, for there is a limit to how much we can test. For example, what convinces us that we have a blood pump in our chest that must be protected from knife wounds at all costs, save during tightly monitored surgery? Our knowledge rests only in part on our own experience; we have been told much that coheres (in some, but certainly not in all, cases) with what else we know, and we accept this information only because it is accepted by other people, and we have no reason to judge it to be wrong.

As we move into the social realm, there are many things we have never thought to question. If someone tells us it need not be that way, our reaction may be to brand that person a fool, dismissing the claims without analysis; or we might consider the claims to have the possibility of being true in principle yet reject them on the grounds that their acceptance would prove socially disruptive. We can get locked into seeing things as unbudgeable realities even though there may be alternative realities we could construct. But what does this phrase *we could construct* mean? It is one thing to imagine the possibility that a certain social structure could be stable; it is another to plan a path that could change a given society into this new form. Changes certainly do take place, as in the development of Christianity or Islam or the Soviet Union. It is not clear that the form that emerges closely matches that envisaged by people whose dreams initiated the changes from which these structures grew. What is clear is that the changes from one system to another are not simple (such as the choice of church on Sunday, mosque on Friday, or no church at all) but have ramified through all the rituals of the law, of life, and of death.

Kuhn's *The Copernican Revolution* (1957) does not simply provide the history of pre-Copernican astronomy; it makes the reader vividly understand how satisfyingly each theory made sense of the data available at its inception. In fact, even now one can see the Ptolemaic conception making sense of the view of the heavens afforded from Earth. Nonetheless, one also comes to see how new data supported the rejection of each theory for its successor.

What, in this light, are we to say of the Bible? Which of its concepts are enduring in the way in which space and time have survived the paradigm shifts of astronomy, and which are to be taken as concepts that, though they can be seen to have once made sense of everyday observations, are now to be rejected like Ptolemaic epicycles or crystalline spheres? In religious systems, there is a tendency to say that the book remains the standard of belief. It is true that the hermeneutic approach to texts began with the Bible, and that this book has probably been the most commented on and even the most reinterpreted of all texts, but nonetheless it remains *the* Book for Christian belief – a far cry from how a modern physicist would regard the writings of Newton, let alone Ptolemy, as historical texts.

Secular humanists might, then, wish to argue that such concepts as God, Salvation, and Resurrection are to be seen as the "crystalline spheres" of social theory and are of primarily historical interest. The secularists might then see current theory as couched in such terms as *human rights* or *the human individual*. One can trace these terms back to the Enlightenment to see them historically rooted in Christianity. Yet the secular humanists might argue that such concepts are more useful than the notion of a soul in understanding human relationships, in the same way Copernicus takes us beyond Ptolemy.

If Christians want to go further and say that such a faith must be grounded in more substantial beliefs about the nature of the cosmos, they first have to answer a question at the heart of the religious/secular debate. Why postulate entities and hypotheses for which there can be no possible direct evidence, which are at best endlessly evocative stories, but which cannot gain adherence as truth? Are these merely "beneficent lies" (sometimes not so beneficent) and if so, what possible claim have they on our allegiance?

In Section 11.2, we explored the role of the dichotomy of priest and prophet in the Great Schema of the Bible. In relating the Great Schema to the problems of living in Western society in our present secular age, we note that this priest–prophet dichotomy was felt as a tension – just as we now feel a tension between progress and the frustration of our attempts to ameliorate the lot of humanity. The secular notion of progress seemed to be something people could put their hope in. In the nineteenth century, Europeans perceived the standard of living as steadily rising, and enlightenment secularism could use progress to replace myths of supernatural guidance. This progress gave meaning to individual lives, society, and the course of history. Yet we now face a collapse of any simple belief in progress. We have seen too many recurrences of barbarism in the twentieth century. Existentialists like Sartre may respond with despair. Marxism may argue that the enlightenment view of progress was too simple minded because it neglects the basic structures of economic life and that utopian visions cannot succeed until the proletariat became self-conscious. The Marxists thus argue for a radical break in social structure before radical improvement in the human condition. In religious circles, secularism itself may be seen as the problem, calling for a return to religion. We see this reaction against secularism strongly in Islam, especially in Iran.

This collapse of too simple a faith in progress relates to the view of history as both linear and cyclical. History is cyclical in that similar events crop up again and again, and we do not expect any ultimate amelioration in history. Though some Christian writers might disagree, we presented the Christian story in Chapter 11 in such a way that if there is hope and optimism, it comes from elsewhere. We described an attitude to historical progress radically different from our current secular value system, an attitude that has two sorts of consequences particularly relevant to our argument here. First, in this interpretation, Christianity offers *no reason to expect an overall and monotonic improvement of the human lot in history*. Second, this is an other-worldly interpretation of the Bible that is equally shocking to secular thought. It entails that *the test of prophecy cannot be the performance of religious institutions or communities of believers within the social or political arena*. The Bible gives no reason to expect any more faithfulness or righteousness from believers than from other people. We then concluded that what the Biblical Schema does contain for the believer is the story of God's action in this otherwise despairing situation and the recipe for living with it, not in resignation but in joy, without expectations in this world. That joy comes from an elsewhere that has to be described in metaphor and myth.

We have noted many secular protests against the retrogressions of our time and many corresponding calls for compelling grounds of human value that seem to have been lost with the demise of communal religion. With this demise have come many examples of reversion to authoritarian and fundamentalist dogmas. Does this mean that liberal secularism is unworkable, since it fails to deliver the sort of unified image of nature, people, and society that fundamentalism seems to offer? Is secularism necessarily socially unstable?

Our secularists respond that critique of possible social instability is a critique in this world. They do not find it compelling as a call to belief in a transcendent God Reality. In this light, consider the movement of liberation theology in Latin America. Some Catholics decry it because they see it as destroying the traditional apolitical role of the clergy; others applaud it as rejecting

previous neocolonial attitudes and recapturing Christ's concern for the weak
and the poor. Our secularists welcome this change, just as they welcome the
support of the Catholic church for the solidarity movement in Poland. Yet,
their review of church history leaves them sceptical as to the power of the
Great Schema by itself to lead human beings to seek social justice. The
secularists thus seek a personal and political morality that can learn from both
religious tradition and secular history but that is rooted in a person reality
within space and time.

In Chapter 6, we noted Kung's critique of Freud. Kung said that after the
barbarism of national socialism and of atheistic communism, the credibility
of a secular scientific view as the guarantor of progress must surely now be
bankrupt. We responded by noting that Freud did not say that science could
guarantee progress. Freud was a pessimist about the human condition who
saw that the benefits of civilization were always precarious ones. All he could
say was that for him the illusion of religion could not promise as much as
a scientific approach that sought to strip away such illusions.

Many Christians dismiss the modern secular position as dogmatic,
simplistic, and naïve because they equate it with the simple denial of God's
reality or with the search for a few basic axioms – Sperry's cosmic evolution,
Wilson's sociobiology – of certain secular apologists. But just as there are
many different scientists addressing different problems, and each scientist
works within a network of books, articles, friendships, and experimental techniques, so, too, our secularists have a complex and subtle and changing set
of texts whereby they face the moral and political problems of the modern
world: the threat of nuclear war, the question of abortion, the impact of
technology, civil rights, the plight of refugees, ecological issues – as well as
the more immediate joys and challenges of family, friends, and workplace.
There is nothing dogmatic or simplistic about this. Our secularists are
secularists because they try to come to grips with the staggering complexity
of real moral and social issues in our spatiotemporal world. They seek
guidance for their own personal actions, for their opinions, and for their
own contributions (where socially possible) to the great political issues of
the day. They hope that actions can be taken to ameliorate the world's problems; they are committed to seeking opportunities to take such actions, but
they know too much history to entertain a naïve belief in an earthly utopia.
Their creed is simple: One must learn, and one must keep trying. They find
many passages in the Bible useful additions to their stock of myths, but only
when the Bible passages are removed from the network of the Great Schema
and seen as parables about life in a reality that neither includes nor is included by a transcendent other.

Chapter 11 sought to explain how one might live within the Great Schema,
coming to internalize it, and in so doing make oneself part of a transcendent
reality. The secularists, however, would want to "recycle" the Great Schema.
They must break it down into pieces, destroy some of its holistic connec-

tions, evaluate the pieces in terms of experience in the modern world, and in so doing put together a new network. In so doing, they recognize that metaphors may become harmful in their evocation if they survive too long. America is currently beset by low productivity; it is vulnerable to Middle-Eastern oil politics; its exports are challenged by Japanese technology. Much of the rhetoric with which these problems are addressed is that of America as the chosen country, or "the city on the hill," the language of Biblical typology beloved by Jonathan Edwards. A more timely economic analysis might reveal how what is needed is not that America believe itself to be the new Jerusalem and seek to solve its problems by appeal to Biblical metaphors, but rather by seeking a new rhetoric, based on a realistic understanding of global interdependence. The rhetoric of the city on the hill may have played an important part in helping the early Puritan settlers; but those metaphors never helped the Indians, and they do not offer guidance today for conducting politics in a twentieth-century superpower.

Another example is not so much of a metaphor, but rather of a schema whose time has come and gone. Why do the scientific societies of East and West go on stockpiling nuclear weapons even though the numbers are more than enough to destroy their enemies, even the whole world, many times over? It may be seen as an example of how schemas learned in certain limited domains of applicability may come to be applied in other domains in which they are not appropriate but in which the necessary feedback or social pressure is not available to recalibrate them. People are unable to understand how to live in the twentieth century because their images of battle and their images of national glory are shaped by outmoded metaphors, outmoded schemas.

Perhaps one does not even need to be a secularist to find that one cannot accept the Great Schema as a whole. The secularist would not argue that we should reject it as a whole, either. Much in terms of generosity of feeling, much in terms of the ability to go beyond selfish concern, much about the complexity of human relations in the world is illuminated by the myths and parables of the Bible. Chapter 11 emphasized the theme of exodus and return, that we cannot live in a world of continuing progress but must understand how to live in a world in which there are not only successes but also horrifying failures.

The problem for the secularist is that we have not yet learned how to be fully secular. Our Western society – happily or unhappily – is pluralist. We must learn to interact sympathetically with other people who do not share our views. Our acceptance of pluralism, however, goes with a critique of pure tolerance. We do not say that "anything goes." We do not accept that it is right to kick dogs. We have, surely, made progress in rejecting slavery. We reject genocide. Many people feel we have made progress in tolerating homosexuality. We are nowhere near consensus on the issue of abortion. We cannot organize our own lives, let alone help others, unless we can make some value judgments – not about the ultimate good, but at least about moral choices that can better balance the life of a particular individual in a particular milieu and that, moving into the political arena, can help us to decide where we should work for social, rather than personal, change.

We are in no position to offer a morality that we must all obey. Rather, what our secular perspective asks is that we find a way of educating our children so they understand the need for morality, understand why certain commitments are important and yet also understand how to change. By the time one is old enough for sophisticated rational critique, one is so embedded in a network of ideas that it is difficult to remake the system; all one can do is change it incrementally. For our secularist, the goal of education, then, must be to build a "platform for change" that provides some useful moral precepts, but without dogma. This platform can include the reading of parts of the Bible, but it is a reading that removes these stories from the Great Schema. Genesis can be read as teaching that the world has meaning and that that meaning was created. Secularists might see this in terms of how we must create the meaning in our own lives. In this, they would go even further than Bultmann on demythologizing the Bible, an attempt which, we argued in Chapter 11, already does violence to the Great Schema. Our secular viewpoint can learn from the Bible but cannot accept the truth, metaphorical or otherwise, of a God Reality.

We are in a transition period. We have thrown away many traditional forms of moral teaching. We are exploring a wide range of new styles. Certain values and prohibitions are widely held in our society; others differ radically from group to group, individual to individual. Many of the latter we find hard to articulate, but they are embedded in our network of schemas as the residues of teachings we consciously deny (cf. our discussion of tacit belief in Section 7.3), as well as particularities of our own biography. We need to develop a systematic way of being in the world that can read history and the Bible without "giving in" to superstition. We need to tolerate diversity yet still have some underlying morality that we can share and count on in other people. We need to turn this morality into a structured set of teachings that we can lead our children through and that we can then come to rely on in making personal and political decisions. But the commonality will not be a set of axioms that all people will hold in totality; rather, it will be a family resemblance that makes moral discourse possible while not necessarily determining the outcome.

We thus end our view of the secular schema on a somewhat tentative note, perhaps disappointing to the reader who has looked for a definitive set of moral precepts. But though we have not offered certainties, we still seek to understand our person reality. We have seen that science has its pragmatic– even aesthetic – successes, powerful but not all encompassing. We have learned from schema theory and cognitive science, seen that they provide new insights into mind and brain and yet seen that they, too, are not all encompassing. Each of us is a person rich in human relationships, and our reality transcends these scientific findings. Our secular schema sees each person as a contingent being. Biological evolution created the species, social evolution shaped each society. There is no ultimate meaning. Yet, not believing in an absolute good, we can value the good that we know; and not believing in an absolute evil, we can nonetheless fight what we see to be evil. Living within society, each person is still an individual. The dynamic tension between social and individual schemas provides the space in which freedom can be defined. The construction of reality is in our schemas.

References

Althusser, L. 1970. *For Marx.* Translated by B. Brewster. New York: Vintage Books.

Althusser, L., and E. Balibar. 1970. *Reading capital.* London: New Left Books.

Apel, K. O. 1979. Types of social science in the light of human cognitive interests. In *Philosophical disputes in the social sciences,* ed. S. C. Brown. Brighton, Sussex: Harvester Press.

Arbib, M. A. 1964. *Brains, machines, and mathematics.* New York: McGraw-Hill.

——— 1972. *The metaphorical brain: an introduction to cybernetics as artificial intelligence and brain theory.* New York: Wiley Interscience.

——— 1973. Automata theory in the context of theoretical neurophysiology. In *Foundations of mathematical biology.* Vol. 3. *Supercellular systems,* ed. R. Rosen, 193–282. New York: Academic Press.

——— 1975. Artificial intelligence and brain theory: unities and diversities. *Annals of Biomedical Engineering* 3:238–74.

——— 1981a. Perceptual structures and distributed motor control. In *Handbook of physiology – the nervous system II. Motor control,* ed. V. B. Brooks, 1449–80. Baltimore, Md.: American Physiological Society.

——— 1981b. Visuomotor coordination: from neural nets to schema theory. *Cognition and brain theory* 4:23–39.

——— 1982a. Perceptual motor processes and the neural basis of language. In *Neural models of language processes,* ed. M. A. Arbib, D. Caplan, and J. C. Marshall, 531–51. New York: Academic Press.

——— 1982b. Modelling neural mechanisms of visuomotor coordination in frog and toad. In *Competition and cooperation in neural nets,* ed. S. Amari and M. A. Arbib, 342–70. New York: Springer-Verlag.

——— 1985. Brain theory and cooperative computation. *Human neurobiology* 4:201–3.

——— In press. A Piagetian perspective on the construction of logic. *Synthese.*

Arbib, M. A., and D. Caplan. 1979. Neurolinguistics must be computational. *Behavioral and brain sciences* 2:449–83.

Arbib, M. A., J. Conklin, and J. C. Hill. 1986. *From schema theory to language.* Oxford: Oxford University Press.

Arbib, M. A., and R. L. Didday, 1971. The organization of action-oriented memory for a perceiving system I. The basic model. *J. Cybernetics* 1:3–18.

Arbib, M. A., and D. H. House. 1986. Depth and detours: towards neural models. In *Vision, brain and cooperative computation,* ed. M. A. Arbib and A. R. Hanson. Cambridge, Mass.: MIT Press/Bradford Books.

Arbib, M. A., T. Iberall, and D. Lyons. 1985. Coordinated control programs for movements of the hand. In *Hand function and the neocortex,* ed. A. W. Goodwin and I. Darian-Smith. *Experimental brain research supplement* 10:111–29.

Arbib, M. A., K. J. Overton, and D. T. Lawton. 1984. Perceptual systems for robots. *Interdisciplinary Science Reviews* 1:31–46.

Bacon, F. 1858. *Works.* Edited by J. Spedding, R. L. Ellis, and D. D. Heath. Vol. V, 208. London: Longmans.

Bambrough, R. 1961. Universals and family resemblances. *Proceedings of the Aristotelian Society* 62:207.

Barnes, B. 1974. *Scientific knowledge and sociological theory.* London: Routledge and Kegan Paul.

1977. *Interests and the growth of knowledge.* London: Routledge and Kegan Paul.

Barth, K. 1983. *The knowledge of God.* Translated by J. L. M. Haire and I. Henderson. London: Hodder and Stoughton.

Bartlett, F. C. 1932. *Remembering.* Cambridge: Cambridge University Press.

Beattie, J. H. M. 1964. *Other cultures.* London: Cohen and West.

1970. On understanding ritual. In *Rationality,* ed. B. R. Wilson. Oxford: Oxford University Press.

Berger, P. L. 1962. *A rumor of angels.* New York: Doubleday.

1980. *The heretical imperative: contemporary possibilities of religious affirmation.* London: Collins.

Beth, E. W., and J. Piaget. 1966. *Mathematical epistemology and psychology.* Translated from the French by W. Mays. Boston: Reidel.

Bettelheim, B. 1982. Reflections, Freud, and the soul. *New Yorker* (March 1).

Black, M. 1962. Metaphor. In *Models and metaphors,* 25–47. Ithaca, N.Y.: Cornell University Press.

Bleicher, J. 1980. *Contemporary hermeneutics.* London: Routledge and Kegan Paul.

Bloor, D. 1976. *Knowledge and social imagery.* London: Routledge and Kegan Paul.

Bobrow, D. G., and A. Collins, eds. 1975. *Representation and understanding: studies in cognitive science.* New York: Academic Press.

Bultmann, R. 1953. New Testament and mythology. In *Kerygma and myth,* ed. H. W. Bartsch. Translated by R. H. Fuller. London: S.P.C.K.

Burks, A. W. 1979. Computer science and philosophy. In *Current research in philosophy of science,* ed. P. Asquith and H. Kyburg. East Lansing, Mich.: Philosophy of Science Association.

1980. Enumerative induction vs. eliminative induction. In *Applications of inductive logic,* ed. L. J. Cohen and M. Hesse. Oxford: Oxford University Press.

Canetti, E. 1980. *Crowds and power.* New York: Continuum.

Carnap, R. 1966. *Philosophical foundations of physics.* New York: Basic Books.

Cartwright, N. 1983. *How the laws of physics lie.* Oxford: Oxford University Press.

Cervantes, F., R. Lara, and M. A. Arbib. 1985. A neural model of interactions subserving prey – predator discrimination and size preference in anurans. *Journal of Theoretical Biology* 113:117–152.

Chomsky, N. 1968. Recent contributions to the theory of innate ideas. In *Boston Studies in the Philosophy of Science* 3:81–107. Boston: Reidel.

1975. *Reflections on language.* New York: Pantheon Books.

Collingwood, R. G. 1964. *The idea of history.* Oxford: Clarendon Press.

Collins, H. M. 1985. *Changing order.* London: SAGE Publications.

Collins, H. M., and T. Pinch. 1982. *Frames of meaning: the social construction of extraordinary science.* London: Routledge and Kegan Paul.

Comte, A. 1974. The essential Comte. Edited by S. Andreski. Translated by M. Clarke. London: Croom Helm.

Conklin, E. J., K. Ehrlich, and D. McDonald. 1983. An empirical investigation of visual salience and its role in text generation. In *Cognition and Brain Theory* 6.

Connolly, W. E. 1981. *Appearance and reality in politics.* Cambridge: Cambridge University Press.

Coutourat, L. 1901. *La logique de Leibniz.* Paris: Felix Alcan.

Craik, K. J. W. 1943. *The nature of explanation.* Cambridge: Cambridge University Press.

Davidson, D. 1984. *Inquiries into truth and interpretation.* Oxford: Oxford University Press.

Dennett, D. C. 1978. *Brainstorms, philosophical essays on the mind and psychology.* Cambridge, Mass.: MIT Press.

1984. *Elbow room, the varieties of freewill worth wanting.* Oxford: Clarendon Press.

Dilthey, W. 1961. *Patterns and meaning in history: thoughts on history and society.* Edited with an introduction by H. P. Rickman. London: George Allen and Unwin.

Douglas, M. 1966. *Purity and danger.* London: Routledge and Kegan Paul.

Dreyfus, H. L. 1972. *What computers can't do: the limits of artificial intelligence.* New York: Harper and Row.

Duhem, P. 1954. *The aim and structure of physical theory.* Translated by N. Wiener. Princeton, N.J.: Princeton University Press.

Dummett, W. 1976. What is a theory of meaning? (II). In *Truth and meaning,* ed. G. Evans and J. McDowell. Oxford: Oxford University Press.

Durkheim, E. 1915. *The elementary forms of the religious life.* Translated by J. W. Swain. London: George Allen and Unwin.

1933. *The division of labor in society.* Translated by G. Simpson. London: Collier-Macmillan.

1938. *The rules of sociological method.* Translated by S. A. Solovay and J. H. Mueller. London: Collier-Macmillan.

Durkheim, E., and M. Mauss. 1963. *Primitive classification.* Translated by R. Needham. London: Cohen and West.

Eccles, J. C. 1977. *The understanding of the brain.* 2d ed. New York: McGraw-Hill.

1982. The initiation of voluntary movements by the supplementary motor area. *Archiv fur Psychiatrie und Nervenkrankheiten* 231:423–41.

Edwards, J. 1962. *Representative selections.* rev. ed. Introduction, bibliography, and notes by C. H. Fawst and T. H. Johnson. New York: Hill and Wang.

1974. The nature of true virtue. In *Works of Jonathan Edwards,* ed. E. Hickman, vol. I, 122–42. Edinburgh: The Banner of Truth Trust.

Erikson, E. H. 1958. *Young man Luther.* New York: Norton.

1963. *Childhood and society.* 2d ed. New York: Norton.

Evans-Pritchard, E. E. 1937. Witchcraft, oracles and magic among the Azande. Oxford: Oxford University Press.

1956. *Nuer religion.* Oxford: Oxford University Press.

Feigl, H. and Scriven, eds. 1956. *The foundation of science and the concepts of psychology and psychoanalysis.* Minneapolis: University of Minnesota Press.

Ferre, F. 1967. *Basic modern philosophy of religion.* New York: Scribners.

Forman, G. E., ed. 1982. *Action and thought: from sensorimotor schemes to symbolic operations.* New York: Academic Press.

Frazer, J. 1922. *The golden bough.* London: Macmillan.

Freud, S. 1953. *On aphasia.* Translated from the German. London: Image Books.

1954. *The origins of psychoanalysis, letters to Wilhelm Fliess, draft and notes: 1887–1902.* New York: Basic Books.

Frye, N. 1982. *The great code.* London: Routledge and Kegan Paul.

Gadamer, H.-G. 1975. *Truth and method.* English Translation. London: Sheed and Ward.

1976. *Philosophical hermeneutics.* Translated and edited by D. E. Linge. Berkeley: University of California Press.

Galilei, G. 1953. *Dialogue concerning the two chief world systems: Ptolemaic and Copernican.* Translated by S. Drake. Berkeley: University of California Press.

1957. *Discoveries and opinions of Galileo,* ed. S. Drake. New York: Doubleday.

Gay, P. 1978. *Freud, Jews and other Germans.* Oxford: Oxford University Press.

Gigley, H. M. 1983. HOPE – AI and the dynamic process of language behavior. *Cognition and Brain Theory.* 6:39–88.

Gödel, K. 1931. *On formally undecidable propositions of* Principia Mathematica *and Related Systems.* Translated by B. Meltzer, 1962. New York: Basic Books.

Goffman, E. 1974. *Frame analysis: an essay on the organization of experience.* New York: Harper and Row.

Goodman, N. 1978. *Ways of world-making.* Brighton, Sussex: Harvester Press.

Gustafson, J. M. 1981. *Ethics from a theocentric perspective.* Vol. I. *Theology and ethics.* Chicago: Chicago University Press.

Gutierrez, G. 1973. *A theology of liberation.* Translated by C. Inela and J. Eagleson. New York: Orbis Books.

Habermas, J. 1971a. *Towards a rational society.* Translated by J. J. Shapiro. London: Heinemann.

1971b. *Knowledge and human interests.* Translated by J. J. Shapiro. Boston: Beacon Press.

1973. A postscript to *Knowledge and human interests. Philosophy of the Social Sciences* 3:157.

1975. *Legitimation crisis.* Translated by T. McCarthy. Boston: Beacon Press.

1979. *Communication and the evolution of society.* Translated by T. McCarthy. Boston: Beacon Press.

Haken, H. 1978. *Synergetics, an introduction: nonequilibrium phase transitions* and self-organization in physics, chemistry, and biology. 2d ed. New York: Springer-Verlag.

Hanson, A. R., E. Riseman, J. S. Griffith, and T. E. Weymouth. 1985. A methodology for the development of general knowledge-based systems. *IEEE Transactions on Pattern Analysis and Machine Intelligence.*

Head, H., and G. Holmes. 1911. Sensory disturbances from cerebral lesions. *Brain* 34:102–254.

Heidegger, M. 1967. *Being and time.* Translated by J. MacQuarrie and E. Robinson. Oxford: Basil Blackwell.

Held, D. 1980. *Introduction to critical theory.* London: Hutchinson.

Hempel. C. G. 1965. *Aspects of scientific explanation.* New York: Free Press.

Hesse, M. 1963. *Models and analogies in science.* London: Sheed and Ward.

1974. *The structure of scientific inference.* London: Macmillan.

1980. *Revolutions and reconstructions in the philosophy of science.* Brighton, Sussex: Harvester Press.

1984. The cognitive claims of metaphor. In *Metaphor and religion,* ed. J. P. van Noppen, 27–45. Brussels: Free University of Brussels.

Hick, J. H. 1974. *Faith and knowledge.* London: Fontana.

Hill, J. C. 1983. A computational model of language acquisition in the two-year-old. *Cognition and Brain Theory* 6:287–317.

Hill, J. C., and M. A. Arbib. 1984. Schemas, computation and language acquisition. *Human Development* 27:282–96.

Hillers, D. B. 1969. *Covenant, the history of a Biblical idea.* Baltimore: Johns Hopkins University Press.

Hollis, M. 1977. *Models of man, philosophical thoughts on social action.* Cambridge: Cambridge University Press.

Hollis, M., and S. Lukes, eds. 1982. *Rationality and relativism.* Oxford: Basil Blackwell.

Horton, R. 1967. African traditional thought and Western science. *Africa* 37:50. Abridged in *Rationality,* ed. B. Wilson, Oxford: Oxford University Press.

Humphery, N. K. 1970. What the frog's eye tells the monkey's brain. *Brain Behavior and Evolution* 3:324–37.

Iberall, T., and D. Lyons. 1984. *Towards perceptual robotics.* Presented at the 1984 IEEE International Conference on Systems, Man and Cybernetics.

Indhurkya, B. 1985. A computational theory of metaphor comprehension and analogical reasoning. Ph.D. diss., University of Massachusetts at Amherst.

Jackson, J. H. 1874. On the nature and duality of the brain. *Medical Press and Circular.* 1:19–41.

(1878.) On affection of speech from disease of the brain. *Brain* 1:304–30.

Jakobson, R., and M. Halle. 1956. *Fundamentals of Language.* The Hague: Mouton.

James, W. 1960. *The varieties of religious experience.* London: Collins.

Jardine, N. 1986. *The fortunes of discovery.* Oxford: Oxford University Press.

Jay, M. 1973. *The dialectical imagination.* Boston: Little, Brown and Co.

Jeannerod, M., and Biguer, B. 1982. Visuomotor mechanisms in reaching within extrapersonal space. In *Advances in the Analysis of Visual Behavior,* ed. D. J. Ingle, R. J. W. Mansfield, and M. A. Goodale, 387–409. Cambridge, Mass.: MIT Press.

Kandel, E. R. 1978. *A cell-biological approach to learning.* Grass Lecture Monograph 1. Society for Neuroscience.

Kandel, E. R., and J. H. Schwartz, eds. 1981. *Principles of neural science.* New York: Elsevier/North-Holland.

Kermode, F. 1979. *The genesis of secrecy.* Cambridge: Cambridge University Press.

Kirk, G. S. 1970. *Myth: Its meaning and functions in ancient and other cultures.* Cambridge: Cambridge University Press.

Kohlberg, L. 1971. From Is to Ought: how to commit the naturalistic fallacy and get away with it in the study of moral development. In *Cognitive development and epistemology,* ed. T. Mischel. New York: Academic Press.

Kuhn, T. S. 1957. *The Copernican revolution, planetary astronomy in the development of Western thoughts.* Cambridge, Mass.: Harvard University Press.

1962. *The structure of scientific revolutions.* Chicago: University of Chicago Press.

Kung, H. 1979. *Freud and the problem of God.* Translated by E. Quinn. New Haven, Conn.: Yale University Press.

Lakoff, G., and M. Johnson. 1980. *Metaphors we live by.* Chicago: Chicago University Press.

Laplace, P. S. de. 1951. *A philosophical essay on probabilities.* Translated by F. W. Truscott and F. L. Emory. New York: Dover Publications.

Lara, R., M. Carmona, F. Daza, and A. Cruz, (1984.) A global model of the neural mechanisms responsible for visuomotor coordination in toads. *Journal of Theoretical Biology.* 110:587–618.

Lara, R., M. A. Arbib, and A. S. Cromarty. 1982. The role of the tectal column in facilitation of amphibian prey-catching behavior: a neural model. *Journal of Neuroscience* 2:521–30.

Laurence, D. 1980. Jonathan Edwards, John Locke, and the cannon of experience. *Early American Literature* 15:107–23.

Leach, E. 1969. *Genesis as myth.* London: Jonathan Cape.

1970. *Levi-Strauss.* London: Fontana/Collins.

1976. *Culture and communication.* Cambridge: Cambridge University Press.

Lettvin, J. Y., H. Maturana, W. S. McCulloch, and W. H. Pitts. 1959. What the frog's eye tells the frog brain. *Proc. IRE.* 47:1940–51.

Levi-Strauss, C. 1955. *Tristes tropiques.* Librarie Plon. Translated by J. and D. Weightman, London: Jonathan Cape.

1963. Responses a quelques questions. *Esprit* 31.

1966. *The savage mind.* English translation. London: Weidenfeld and Nicolson.

1968. *Structural anthropology.* Translated by C. Johnson. New York: Basic Books.

1966–81. *Mythologiques* I–IV. Translated by J. and D. Weightman. London: Jonathan Cape.

Levy-Bruhl, L. 1966. *How natives think.* Translated by L. A. Clare. Princeton, N.J.: Princeton University Press.

Liddell, H. D., and R. Scott. 1849. *A Greek-English Lexicon,* 6th ed. Oxford: Clarendon Press.

Lienhardt, G. 1961. *Divinity and experience: the religion of the Dinka.* Oxford: Oxford University Press.

Locke, J. 1947. *An essay concerning human understanding.* London: Dent.

Lucas, J. R. 1961. Minds, machines and Godel. *Philosophy* 36:112–27.

Lukes, S. 1973. *Emile Durkheim.* New York: Harper and Row.

Lumsden, C. J., and E. O. Wilson. 1981. *Genes, mind, and culture. The coevolutionary process.* Cambridge, Mass.: Harvard University Press.

Lyons, J. 1977. *Chomsky.* rev. ed. London: Fontana/Collins.

McCarthy, T. 1978. *The critical theory of Jurgen Habermas.* Cambridge, Mass.: MIT Press.

MacKay, D. M. 1966. Cerebral organization and the conscious control of action, In *Brain and Conscious Experience.* Edited by J. C. Eccles. Springer-Verlag. 422–40.

McLellan, D. 1977. *Karl Marx: Selected writings.* Oxford: Oxford University Press.

Matthei, E. 1979. The acquisition of prenominal modifier sequences: Stalking the second green ball. Ph.D. diss., University of Massachusetts at Amherst.

Merton, R. K. 1957. *Social theory and social structure.* Glencoe, Ill.: Free Press.

Mill, J. S. 1884. *A system of logic.* 8th ed. London: Longmans Green.

Milosz, C. 1983. Ruins and poetry. *The New York Review of Books.* (March) 17:20–4.

Minsky, M. L. 1975. A framework for representing knowledge. In *The psychology of computer vision,* ed. P. H. Winston, 211–77. New York: McGraw-Hill.

Mitchell, B. 1973. *The justification of religious belief.* London: Macmillan.

Moltmann, J. 1965. *A theology of hope.* London: SCM Press.

Monod, J. 1972. *Chance and necessity, an essay on the natural philosophy of modern biology.* Translated by A. Wainhouse. New York: Vintage Books.

Morris, B. 1979. Symbolism as ideology. In *Classifications in their social context,* ed. R. F. Ellen and D. Reason, 128. New York: Academic Press.

Mountcastle, V. B. 1978. An organizing principle for cerebral function: The unit module and the distributed system. In *The mindful brain,* by G. M. Edelman and V. B. Mountcastle. Cambridge, Mass.: MIT Press.

Nagel, E., and J. R. Newman. 1958. *Gödel's proof.* New York: New York University Press.

Neisser, U. 1976. *Cognition and reality.* New York. Freeman.

Niebuhr, R. 1941. *The nature and destiny of man.* London: Nisbet.

Palmer, R. E. 1969. *Hermeneutics: Interpretation theory in Schleiermacher, Dilthey, Heidegger and Gadamer.* Evanston, Ill.: Northwestern University Press.

Peirce, C. S. 1931. Collected papers. Vol. I. ed. C. Hartshorne and P. Weiss. Cambridge, Mass.: Harvard University Press.

Piaget, J. 1954. *The construction of reality in the child.* Translated by M. Cook. New York: Basic Books.

1971. *Biology and knowledge: An essay on the relations between organic regulations and cognitive processes.* Edinburgh: Edinburgh University Press.

Piatelli-Palmarini, M., ed. 1980. *Language and learning: The debate between Jean Piaget and Noam Chomsky.* Cambridge, Mass.: Harvard University Press.

Polanyi, K. 1966. *The tacit dimension.* New York: Doubleday.

Popper, K. 1959. *The logic of scientific discovery.* London: Hutchinson.

Popper, K., and J. C. Eccles. 1977. *The self and its brain.* New York: Springer-Verlag.

Putnam, H. 1981. *Reason, truth and history.* Cambridge: Cambridge University Press.

Ricoeur, P. 1969. *The symbolism of evil.* Translated by E. Buchanan. Boston: Beacon Press.

1970. *Freud and philosophy.* New Haven, Conn.: Yale University Press.

1974. Structure and hermeneutics. In *The conflict of interpretations: essays in hermeneutics,* ed. D. I. Ihde. Evanston, Ill.: Northwestern University Press.

1978. *The rule of metaphor.* Translated by R. Czerny. London: Routledge and Kegan Paul.

Rorty. R. 1980. *Philosophy and the mirror of nature.* Oxford: Basil Blackwell.

Samuel, A. L. 1959. Some studies in machine learning using the game of checkers. *IBM J. Res. and Dev.* 3:210–29.

Schank, R., and R. Abelson. 1977. *Scripts, plans, goals, and understanding: An inquiry into human knowledge structures.* Hillsdale, N.J.: Lawrence Erlbaum Associates.

Schleiermacher, F. 1958. *On religion, speeches to its cultured despisers.* Translated by J. Oman. New York: Harper and Row.

Searle, J. R. 1979. *Expression and meaning.* Cambridge: Cambridge University Press.

1980. Minds, brains and programs, *Behavioral and Brain Sciences* 3:417–57.

1985. *Minds, brains and science.* London: BBC Publications.

Sherrington, C. S. 1940. *Man on his nature.* Cambridge: Cambridge University Press.

Singer, P. 1980. *Marx.* Cambridge: Oxford University Press.

Sperber, D. 1975. *Rethinking symbolism.* Cambridge: Cambridge University Press.

Sperry, R. W. 1966. Brain bisection and the mechanisms of consciousness. In *Brain and conscious experience,* ed. J. C. Eccles, 298–313. New York: Springer-Verlag.

1968. Hemisphere deconnection and unity of conscious awareness. *American Psychologist* 23:723–33.

1972. Science and the problem of values. *Perspec. Biol. Med.* 16:115–30.

1980. Mind-brain interaction: mentalism, yes; dualism, no. *Neuroscience* 5:195–206.

1981. Changing priorities towards a union of science with ethics and religion. *Ann. Rev. Neurosci.* 4:1–11.

1983. *Science and moral priority: merging mind, brain and human values.* New York: Columbia University Press.

Sulloway, F. J. 1979. *Freud, biologist of the mind: beyond the psychoanalytic legend.* New York: Basic Books.

Szentágothai, J., and M. A. Arbib. 1974. Conceptual models of neural organization. *NRP Bulletin.* Vol. 2. 3:310–479.

Tinbergen, N. 1951. *The study of instinct.* Oxford: Clarendon Press.

Tracy, P. J. 1980. *Jonathan Edwards, pastor. Religion and society in eighteenth-century Northampton.* New York: Hill and Wang.

Trevarthen, C. 1982. The primary motives for cooperative understanding, In *Social cognition: Studies of the development of understanding,* ed. G. Butterworth and P. Light, 77–109. London: Harvester Press.

Turner, V. 1967. *The forest of symbols.* Ithaca, N.Y.: Cornell University Press.

Tylor, E. B. 1929. *Primitive culture.* London: Murray.

Uexkull, J. von. 1921. *Umwelt und Innenwelt der Tiere.* Berlin: Aufl. Berlin.

Van Buren, P. M. 1972. *The edges of language.* London: SCM Press.

Vesey, G. N. A. 1965. *The embodied mind.* London: George Allen and Unwin Ltd.

Walicki, A. 1983. Marx and freedom. *New York Review of Books.* (November 24):50–5.

Weber, M. 1948. Science as a vocation. In *From Max Weber,* ed. H. H. Gerth and C. W. Mills. London: Routledge and Kegan Paul.

1949. *The methodology of the social sciences.* Translated and edited by E. A. Shils and H. A. Finch. New York: Free Press.

Weiskrantz, L. 1974. The interaction between occipital and temporal cortex in vision: An overview. In *The neurosciences third study program.* Edited by F. O. Schmitt and F. G. Worden. Cambridge, Mass.: MIT Press. 189–204.

Weiskrantz, L., E. K. Warrington, M. D. Sanders, and J. Marshall. 1974. Visual capacity in the hemianopic field following a restricted occipital ablation. *Brain* 97:709–28.

Whitehead, A. M. 1926. *Religion in the making.* Cambridge: Cambridge University Press.

1945. *Science and the modern world.* Cambridge: Cambridge University Press.

Whiting, H. T. A. 1984. *Human motor actions: Bernstein reassessed.* Amsterdam: North-Holland.

Wicker, B. 1975. *The story-shaped world.* London: Athlone Press.

Wiles, M. 1977. Myth in theology. In *The myth of God incarnate,* ed. J. Hick. London: SCM Press.

Wilson, E. O. 1971. *The insect societies.* Cambridge, Mass.: Harvard University Press.

1975. *Sociobiology, the new synthesis.* Cambridge, Mass.: Harvard University Press.

1978. *On human nature.* Cambridge, Mass.: Harvard University Press.

Winch, P. 1970. Understanding a primitive society. In *Rationality.* ed. B. R. Wilson. Oxford: Oxford University Press.

Wittgenstein, L. 1958. *Philosophical investigations.* 3rd ed. Translated by G. E. M. Anscombe. London: Macmillan.

Wollheim, R. 1971. *Freud.* London: Fontana/Collins.

Young, R. M. 1970. *Mind, brain and adaptation in the nineteenth century: cerebral localization and its biological context from Gall to Ferrier.* London: Clarendon Press.

Author Index

Subject Index

Abecedarium Naturae, 149
Abraham, 211
accommodated, 176
accommodation, 14, 46, 143, 171
action perception cycle, 13, 52, 71, 139,
  141, 248
Adamic myth, 233
adaptation, 59
aesthetic experience, 79
aggression, 113
altruism, 255
analogical, 158, 241
  meaning, 228
  method, 103
  schema-based processes, 61
analogy, 20, 153, 163, 169, 212, 223, 239,
  243
  of being, 242
Anselmian, 233
anti-Semitism, 126
Aplysia, 78
a priori truths, 87
Aristotelian philosophy of universals, 150
Aristotelian world, 149
arminian, 100, 102
artificial intelligence, AI, 12, 13, 25, 88,
  89, 99, 183
  reduction, 87
  systems, 87
assignment of credit problem, 46
assimilated, 176
assimilation, 14, 46, 143, 171
autonomous man, 82
Azande, 207, 208

Babel, 149
being in the world, 41
belief, 218, 219
Bible, 9, 50, 206, 222, 262
Bible as symbol system, The, 228
Biblical, 18, 102, 104, 210
  attitude to Historical Progress, 235

canon, 229
  exegesis, 175
  religion, 222
  schema, 235, 237
billiard balls, 82
biological determinism, 123
blindsight, 72
body schema, 43
Bororo, 207
bottom up, 15, 64
brain talk, 250
brain theory, 70

Calvinism, 122
Calvinist, 100, 101
Cartesian dualism, 11
Cartesian split, 160
castration, 121
categories of pure reason, 160
childhood and society, 117
Chinese box, 26
choice, 89
Christian theology, 18
Christianity, 185
civilization, 112
Civilization and Its Discontents, 112, 114
codes, 162, 168
cognitive, 6
  development, 48
  science, 11, 12, 13, 17, 20, 83, 84, 85,
    88, 99, 102, 147, 154, 161, 171, 184,
    193, 196, 202, 206
  systems, 2, 7, 8, 10, 165, 182, 200, 209,
    219, 226, 237
coherence, 10, 14, 22, 171
coherent, 20
collective representations, 129, 147, 231
collective unconsciousness, 73
communication, 162, 165, 180, 187
communicative, 168, 188, 195
  action, 187